Fodor's EXPLORING

CHINA

FODOR'S TRAVEL PUBLICATIONS

NEW YORK • TORONTO • LONDON • SYDNEY • AUCKLAND

WWW.FODORS.COM

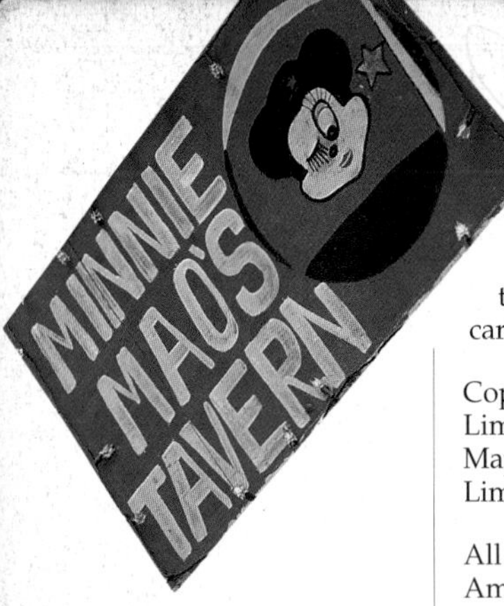

Important Note

Time inevitably brings changes, so always confirm prices, travel facts, and other perishable information when it matters. Although Fodor's cannot accept responsibility for errors, you can use this guide in the confidence that we have taken every care to ensure its accuracy.

 Published in the United States by Fodor's Travel Publications, a unit of Fodors LLC, a subsidiary of Random House, Inc., and simultaneously in Canada by Random House of Canada Limited, Toronto. Distributed by Random House, Inc., New York.

Published in the United States by Fodor's Travel Publications
Published in the United Kingdom by AA Publishing.

ISBN 0-676-90161-1
Fourth Edition

Fodor's Exploring China

Author: **Christopher Knowles**
Revision Verifier: **Christopher Knowles**
Original Photography: **Ingrid Morejohn/Bildbruket Picture Works**
Cartography: **The Automobile Association**
Copy Editor: **Susan Whimster**
Revision Copy Editor: **Sheila Hawkins**
Cover Design: **Tigist Getachew, Fabrizio La Rocca**
Front Cover Silhouette: **Catherine Karnow/Woodfin Camp**

Special Sales

Fodor's Travel Publications are available at special discounts for bulk purchases (100 copies or more) for sales promotions or premiums. Special editions, including personalized covers, excerpts of existing guides, and corporate imprints, can be created in large quantities for special needs. For more information, contact your local bookseller or write to Special Marketing, Fodor's Travel Publications, 1745 Broadway, New York, NY 10019. Inquiries from Canada should be directed to your local Canadian bookseller or sent to Random House of Canada, Ltd., Marketing Department, 2775 Matheson Blvd. East, Mississauga, Ontario L4W 4P7.

Printed and bound in Italy by Printer Trento srl
10 9 8 7 6 5 4 3 2

A01712

How to use this book

ORGANIZATION

China Is, China Was
Discusses aspects of life and culture in contemporary China and explores significant periods in its history.

A–Z
Breaks down the country into regional chapters, and covers places to visit, including walks and drives. Within this section fall the Focus On articles, which consider a variety of subjects in greater detail.

Travel Facts
Contains the strictly practical information that is vital for a successful trip.

Accommodations and Restaurants
Lists recommended establishments in China, giving a brief description of their attractions.

ADMISSION CHARGES
An indication of an establishment's admission charge is given by categorizing the standard, adult rate as:
Expensive (over 50 RMB)
Moderate (21–50 RMB)
Inexpensive (up to 20 RMB).

ABOUT THE RATINGS
Most places described in this book have been given a separate rating:

▶▶▶	**Do not miss**
▶▶	**Highly recommended**
▶	**Worth seeing**

Note on spellings
The official romanization system, *pinyin* (see page 271), has been used in this book. However, a few exceptions have been made where alternative, more familiar names have been adopted. In such cases both forms are given in the Index. The geographic legend on page 271 gives the English translations for terms used on the maps.

MAP REFERENCES
To make each particular location easier to find, every main entry in this book has a map reference to the right of its name. This comprises a number, followed by a letter, followed by another number, such as 176B3. The first number (176) refers to the page on which the map can be found, the letter (B) and the second number (3) pinpoint the square in which the main entry is located. The maps on the inside front cover and inside back cover are referred to as IFC and IBC respectively.

Contents

Christopher Knowles has 'ed dozens of tours in China since his first visit in 1981. He has also written guidebooks to Shanghai, Moscow & St Petersburg, Japan, Southeast Asia, Tuscany and The Cotswolds.

My China

No place has changed quite like China. Shanghai, which has become an almost exclusively modern city, would be practically unrecognizable to someone who visited even ten years ago. Shenzhen, until the 1980s a small frontier settlement, has become a center of international trade. Elsewhere, tangible signs of wealth, from limousines to high-rise buildings, abound.

When, in 1981, I arrived in Beijing, there was little sign that anything much had changed in the few years since the end of the Cultural Revolution. Foreign visitors were still a rarity, even in Beijing; a taxi could not be hailed on the streets, and you could not eat out after seven in the evening. The towns had been bled of color, and life in the countryside went on as it had done for centuries.

Economic miracles, however, are largely confined to the great cities. In the countryside, the problems of modernization are acute. At a time when China desperately needs enough rice to feed its massive population, its farmers are more interested in growing cash crops or leaving the farms altogether. There are other less tangible problems. China remains, appearances notwithstanding, a one-party autocracy. The Cultural Revolution produced an amoral generation which struggles to reconcile the freedom to become rich with ethical restraints. And there are the unresolved problems of the future of Tibet and indeed an indifference to the question of human rights in general.

My China is not merely a country of change, it is also a country of great beauty. Ancient villages nestle among hills whose slopes, after centuries of cultivation, have become staircases of scalloped terraces. Junks have become a rarer sight, but are still to be seen fishing on Lake Tai or struggling among the great liners and tankers in Shanghai harbor. Political upheavals have severed the Chinese from a natural sense of harmony, but they have failed to eradicate the habits of countless generations.

So, the China I love is a conundrum. Frequently comfortless, often profoundly frustrating, it is breathtaking not merely for its antiquity, or for its beauty, but, despite its years of calamity, for its self-confidence.

Christopher Knowles

China Is

Nowhere in the world is the past more woven into the present than in China, and no other country can boast the sense of continuity that has been bred into the Chinese people over at least three thousand years of continuous civilization.

PRESSURE OF HISTORY Chinese history has been a source of great strength and resilience in difficult times. Perhaps no other country could have survived such a cataclysmic event as the Cultural Revolution, only to become one of the world's fastest-growing economies a mere 20 years later. In few other countries, on the other hand, would the Cultural Revolution have occurred in the first place. The pressure to do as your forefathers have done and conform to ancient (and frequently outmoded) ideas is very great in China. Occasionally it becomes too much for some parts of society to bear. The stranglehold exerted by the past so frustrated the young people of China in the 1960s that they were easily mobilized by Mao, assisting in his radical but ultimately futile attempt to sweep away all reminders of the past and start all over again. Ironically, the communism that Mao espoused has proved to be little more than the former imperial system under a new name.

CONSERVATISM So automatic, so widespread are the age-old habits of the Chinese that they may sometimes be confused with intransigence. One example of this is always giving the answer that the listener wants to hear. For more worldly Chinese this is frustrating because these habits seem almost impossible to break.

At its best, Chinese conservatism—a determination not to change merely for change's sake, combined with a belief in the overriding power of precedent—is admirable; at other times it is tiresome, as when agreement is reached to do something in one way, only to find that ultimately the old way prevails.

OUTSIDE INFLUENCE Notwithstanding the damage wrought by time, revolution, and political upheaval, the tangible remains of China's ancient civilization are widespread; and even in the case of contemporary art and architecture the tendency is always to evoke the past. But the material residue from Chinese history is less important than the impact that the past has had on the Chinese mind. Chinese history is remarkable for the fact that outside influences have had almost no effect on the national psyche. Without an appreciation of this fundamental fact, it is impossible for the visitor to understand modern China.

> ❑ "Our nation has a great responsibility...to enrich our culture with Western culture, and to enrich Western culture with our culture, so that they may fuse into a new culture."—Liang Qichao, *Impressions From My European Journey*, 1919 ❑

Of the many issues facing the Chinese today, the most contentious is the battle between old and new: progress, in the modern Western understanding of the word, is seen in some quarters as an admission of defeat. The encroachment of Western values, for so long resisted, is considered a worrying phenomenon: for old communists, veterans of the Long March (a few of whom are still involved in the running of the country), it must sometimes seem that the values they fought for are being replaced by the free-for-all, capitalist values that they had sought so hard to suppress.

The ancient city of Beijing is now dominated by modern skyscrapers

THE TIGER AWAKES On several occasions during the 20th century, when it seemed China was about to alter course, it was in fact merely retrimming its sails. Now, change seems more certain; the challenge is to recover the best of the past and marry it to the realities of the modern world.

Opposite (top) and below: villagers in Yunnan display their effigies of local gods at Chinese New Year

The Chinese way of life is distinctive in many subtle ways. Western notions of the centrality of the self are alien to many Chinese, who see themselves in relation to family, community, and the past, rather than as entirely free agents.

FAMILY The most important element in Chinese society is the family, an institution whose strength was sorely tested by events during the 1960s and 1970s, when, under Mao, children were encouraged to report the "misdemeanors" of their parents and close relatives. But it was not long ago that most marriages were arranged by parents or by a professional matchmaker, and in more remote areas these practices have continued unchecked; even in major cities the matchmaker has recently made an unexpected comeback. Weddings are big affairs and huge sums, out of all proportion to income, are spent on the celebrations. Once married, the bride customarily moves in with her in-laws, at least until the new couple can secure their own apartment.

The idea of bachelorhood is almost unknown among the Chinese

A member of the matriarchal Naxi people sits holding his grandson

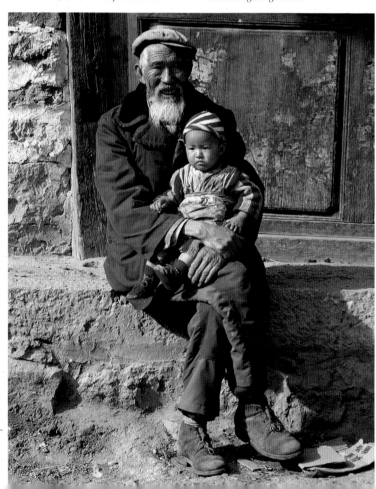

because children are considered essential to continuing the family line and for providing a means of support in old age. In this respect, the Cultural Revolution's emphasis on the enforced denunciation of relatives has only led to a subsequent resurgence of family loyalty, as well as to the pain of collective guilt.

❑ The Chinese have traditionally deferred to the elderly because, it is thought, old age brings wisdom. For this reason, the government, until recently, has consisted largely of older politicians. This is another frustration for many Chinese, for youth is admired, but only in the most patronizing way. ❑

The government's failed policy of one child per family (designed to alleviate the population problem) has led to the rise of a generation of "little emperors," to whom the absence of siblings has meant unbridled adulation. It has also brought a certain lack of confidence because a large family meant security and influence. Nothing is more important than *guanxi*, that is, obtaining favors, jobs, contracts, or gifts from your relatives—an essential feature of Chinese life that Westerners might call "nepotism."

LOSING FACE Romantic love is not a Chinese notion. Pragmatism is the order of the day, though the younger, more independent-minded Chinese are demanding the right to make their own decisions. As a result, divorce, traditionally unutterably shameful, is becoming more widespread.

Indeed, the idea of shame, usually expressed as "losing face" (*diulian*), is integral to the Chinese attitude toward life. Losing face is more than just shame, however, for shame implies a subjective feeling of guilt whereas loss of face is something more—it is a slight, a missed opportunity, family shame, regional shame, a failure to perform a duty according to the expectation and judgment of one's peers, particularly in front of foreigners. It can be just one of these things, or a little of all of them.

PRIVACY The concern with "face" creates all sorts of social tensions, especially in a highly controlled society. For this reason the Chinese tend to avoid situations where face may be lost, preferring anonymity to exposure. Contact with the outside world is making this more difficult—Western business investors in China often express frustration with Chinese lack of initiative, not recognizing that to many Chinese, being a faceless member of a crowd is the norm.

Lack of privacy also means lack of space. City apartments are generally small, and everyone has to be able to tolerate the activities of everyone else, which explains the Chinese ability to concentrate amid cacophony and to sleep at will. What seems intolerable to Westerners is in fact the essence of the Chinese way of life.

Newlyweds: today, for those who can afford it, Western dress and a videotape are common

China continues to be ruled by the Communist Party, though since the early 1980s and the beginning of the "open door" policy, the country has demonstrated a willingness to adopt foreign trade investment and new ideas.

COMMUNISM? In 1993, Ferrari made the first delivery of one of its luxury cars to a Chinese entrepreneur in China (despite the fact that there are few roads where such a car could be used). Shanghai now has a thriving stock exchange. In these, and in countless other ways, the traditional picture of Chinese life under communism is rapidly changing. Even so, all the Party maxims, slogans, shibboleths, dictums, and homilies are still trotted out by the Chinese government whenever the occasion seems to demand them. Despite a history of obstinate intolerance to democratic movements, not to mention the continuing suppression of Tibet and the detention without trial of numerous dissidents, there is reason to hope that the government has finally shed most vestiges of the Stalinist approach that once prevailed. Of course, by comparison with the years of the Cultural Revolution, life in China today is peaceful. But persecution continues (Qinghai province is known as China's gulag), and the average Chinese person has no legal means of avoiding the heavy hand of the state.

Top: Mao memorabilia
Below: McDonald's in Beijing exemplifies China's appetite for modern ideas

The Party still wields enormous influence; real freedom remains an elusive goal. If physical persecution is more of a rarity, deviation from accepted social norms still incurs the wrath of local committees who have the power to take away your job, your home, your very right to exist as a citizen. The Party also dictates where you work: for example, bright and able graduates have to work at repetitive jobs, such as sewing buttons, as "payment" for their education. Outspoken criticism of government and associating with foreigners (especially journalists) and evangelical Christianity (as opposed to passive worship), are offenses liable to lead to arrest and imprisonment.

UNDERSTANDING If one considers Chinese history, the size of the population and its accompanying social problems, and the vastness of the country with its variety of geography and peoples, then the current system of autocratic government—though still undesirable—is at least comprehensible. It is all that most Chinese have ever known; the history of intrusive government is almost as old as Chinese history itself. For many people, the years since the end of the Cultural Revolution in 1976 have been a golden era, relatively speaking. Things have improved greatly, farmers are allowed to keep and sell the surplus produce they grow, and married couples are no longer liable to be separated and sent to work in different parts of the country.

FUTURE If Chinese communism has achieved anything, it has been to instill the Chinese with a sense of nationhood and, simultaneously, to bring some sort of order to daily life. It has, arguably, done much to eradicate the chronic poverty that cursed old China, although those affected by the disasters of the Great Leap Forward and the Cultural Revolution may disagree and some areas of China, notably the arid northwest, remain as backward as ever they were. What the party has not really addressed is the issue of democracy. While political reform may not yet be a burning issue, there are indications that autocratic rule by the Communist Party might soon be challenged. Prosperity has brought confidence and in some provinces (not only the "minority" areas such as Tibet and Xinjiang), there has been talk of secession. Independence for Guangdong or Sichuan is an unrealistic proposition, but the fact that it is even considered indicates a yearning for greater autonomy and one that the central government may not be able to ignore, especially following the free elections in Taiwan, the first democratic transfer of power in Chinese history.

A Confucian ideal in communist clothing: posters asking for respect for authority are a common sight

Although China remains a communist country in formal political terms, informally ideological rectitude is the furthest thing from most people's minds. To make money has become the overriding ambition of a large number of people for whom the strictures of Marx, Lenin, and Mao are mostly irrelevant.

COMPETITION The Chinese have always enjoyed a reputation for business acumen, and it is certainly possible to become rich in modern China. A visit to any of the major cities will quickly confirm that—wealthy citizens driving Mercedes and frequenting luxury hotels, happily spend in a day what the average Chinese person could not earn in a lifetime. The competition is as fierce as in any established capitalist society, and although a lack of sophistication in business matters still shows through from time to time (in the form of overbearing salesmanship, or a disregard for the ethical implications of contracts), the Chinese have learned remarkably quickly how to package what they have to offer in an attractive and winning way.

A stretch limo at the five-star International Hotel, Beijing

IN THE BLOOD Making money, like the love of gambling, seems to be a compulsion in China. The appeal seems to be that money brings power, and it is power, more than wealth, that is seductive. Perhaps power is particularly attractive in China because it is almost the only significant way of rising above the common herd. Until recently, individuals achieved power by rising through the ranks of the Communist Party; although that remains the case to a certain extent, there is an alternative route to power and influence outside politics through money. Capitalism, albeit in diluted form, is now an accepted part of Chinese life, and although this system has its theoretical limits, the general feeling is that this strange mixture of Communist ideology and hard-faced business attitudes is here to stay.

SALARIES Only a few years ago it was impossible even to think of earning anything other than a pitiful state salary. Private enterprise was not just frowned upon, it was simply out of the question. The state would provide everything that the Chinese citizen could or, more correctly, should, desire. Everybody was on a salary scale that corresponded precisely to their social rank, and although the salary of officials tended to be higher than most, it had a defined limit—even the Chairman of the Party, the top man in China, received a salary that was in line with this. Corruption was the more or less inevitable result of this policy, as officials extracted what price they could in compensation for low salaries.

❑ The colloquial Chinese euphemism for leaping into the rising tide of private business is *xiahai* or "going down to the sea." Many Chinese are willing to try. In an interview with a Western journalist, a young entrepreneur said, "We just feel very happy when we see the company succeed." ❑

meagre state salary. This, too, has changed, and in the major cities there are few who do not have a finger in some enterprise, however humble. This period of transition is bringing immense social change, especially for the coastal Special Economic Zones, which are clones of Hong Kong, involved in low-wage mass production of low-technology products.

A newly purchased portrait of Sophia Loren is carried home on another status symbol, the motorcycle

SOCIAL CHANGE When economic reforms were first introduced in the 1980s, ambitious city-dwellers were disgruntled to see the peasants making a good living while they slogged in government bureaucracies for a

Even so, these zones have contributed to China's record-breaking economic growth, and attracted a steady stream of country people looking for work. Exploitation, low wages, and unhealthy working conditions are the result. Meanwhile, only one third of the Chinese students who are sent abroad to study actually return to China.

More than a billion people, about one-fifth of the world's population, live in China, geographically the third-largest country in the world, and the forecasts are that this figure will soon reach 2 billion. The number of cities bearing unfamiliar names, yet with populations as great as those of New York, London, or Tokyo, is astonishing.

HUMANKIND In China there are people everywhere—you are never alone, and every sidewalk is crowded. The roads between them, previously the preserve of a few trolley-buses, trucks, donkeys, and bicycles, are rapidly becoming filled with cars. Even the landscape has been shaped by man, for every patch of fertile land, no matter how small, is under cultivation. Wilderness is rare, and magnificent works of nature, such as the Stone Forest near Kunming, are not left to stand for themselves but are "enhanced" by the addition of man-made art.

SIMILARITIES Considering the size of the country, there are remarkably few regional differences north to south or east to west. A Chinese, it is true, is more likely to tell you the name of his town or province before his country, since for him the differences are great.

Top: market day, northern Sichuan
Below: a Tibetan woman and child

But for the outsider the homogeneity of Chinese culture is amazing. There is even in existence a government committee whose task is to establish that the Chinese constitute a separate species. This is largely due to China's history, for despite the presence of 56 different nationalities within its borders, 92 percent of the population is Han Chinese—that is, people with the physical characteristics of slim build, black hair and almond-shaped eyes, whose first language is Chinese, or a variant of it, and who loyally regard Beijing as the national center of power. Traditional Han China is everywhere except Xinjiang, parts of Yunnan, Tibet, Qinghai, Inner Mongolia, and parts of Manchuria, and has been so for some 2,000 years.

❑ Although most members of the minority peoples of China speak and write Chinese, there are in fact more than 30 scripts still in use throughout the country, about 20 of which, including Mongolian, Tibetan, Dai, Yi, Uyghur, Korean, Russian, and Manchurian, have been in use for many hundreds of years. Others—for example that of the Zhuang who had no script of their own—were created in the 1950s on the basis of the Latin alphabet. ❑

NATIONALITIES The other 55 nationalities, the remaining 5 percent of the population, nonetheless comprise an element of Chinese life that cannot be ignored. Three nationalities, the Tibetans, the Mongolians, and the Uyghurs, although comparatively few in number, occupy homelands that

make up a large geographical proportion of the country—Tibet and Qinghai, Inner Mongolia and Xinjiang. In at least two of the cases, Tibet and to a lesser extent Xinjiang, local opposition to Han rule has manifested itself in violently rebellious outbursts that have occasionally caught the attention of the outside world. The Chinese government, which finds it hard to conceal its disgust with "troublesome" minorities, deals with the problem by filling minority areas with Han Chinese, who are sent either under duress or through financial inducement. The result is that indigenous peoples then become minorities in their own lands.

DIVERSITY In Han China itself there is considerable cultural and linguistic diversity. There are the Hakka, for example, who were driven south during the Song dynasty and can be identified by their distinctive fringed hats. There are the dark-skinned Tujias scattered among the mountains of Hunan, Hubei, and Sichuan. Even the Cantonese, who are not a minority, differ physically from northerners and speak a dialect that is distinct from the dialects of Shanghai or Beijing.

The largest minority is the Zhuang, at over 15 million according to the 1990 Census, most of whom live peacefully in the Guangxi Zhuang Autonomous Region of southern China. Almost indistinguishable from the Han, they may be related to the Vietnamese. Most of the minorities have become absorbed into mainstream Chinese life, although the Chinese government continues to sponsor research into proving that the Chinese people constitute an individual species, distinct from homo sapiens, that had its origins in China and not in Africa as the rest of the world's scientists believe.

The Hani minority people of Yunnan hold on to their ancient ways

In China, nobody wants to be a peasant farmer, and yet that is the fate of three out of four people. City-dwellers have traditionally looked down upon their country cousins, yet recent economic reforms have radically improved the farmers' lot (at least in the fertile areas of the country), and farmers are now among the richer members of Chinese society.

RURAL CHARACTER China remains predominantly rural despite attempts since 1949 to industrialize the country. Even in the major cities, open markets—and bicycles, lorries, and beasts of burden loaded down with fresh produce to sell there—are still part of urban life. The fact that China is almost self-sufficient in food is remarkable when you consider the size of the population and that, with most of the country either mountain or desert, only a small percentage of land is suitable for cultivation.

The ingenuity and perseverance of the Chinese peasant are legendary, hence Mao Zedong's dictum, in his misguided attempts to reform China, to "learn from the peasant." This did not stop him, unfortunately, from trying to impose ideologies on these same farmers that led to the death by starvation of millions during the Great Leap Forward of 1958–1959.

Fall harvesting in northern China's loess area, in the Hengshan Mountains

LAND SCULPTURE Such is the long-standing relationship between the Chinese farmer and the land that the very landscape is often defined by human activity. The most obvious example of this is terracing, a technique developed to make the most of undulating or hilly countryside. Taking the train from Changsha to Guangzhou in midsummer, skirting the curving contours of tiers of densely planted land, or driving from Chongqing to Dazu when the rice is still under water, you cannot

> ❑ "You glorify Nature and meditate on her;
> Why not domesticate and regulate her?
> You follow Nature and sing her praise:
> Why not control her course and use it?"
> —Xunzi, philosopher, 3rd century BC ❑

Market day, Yunnan province: fast food has reached China, but out of town it's still the fresher the better

but admire the industry, creativity, and regard for nature that has gone into the working of Chinese farmland.

LAND MANAGEMENT The fact that there are so few roads in China is because every piece of land is precious. Water is precious, too, and a single canal will provide irrigation for a succession of fields, while mud from its bed will be used, along with animal dung and human waste (still collected from cities), as manure.

Fuel, too, must be managed with care. Thus in the north, houses are traditionally built facing the south and the sun, away from the harsh desert winds from the northwest. In poorer areas, a large portion of the interior of the house is given over to the *kang*, a raised brick platform heated by the stove or by straw fires from outside and which may serve as a bed. Such arrangements are becoming rarer as farmers prosper. Yet the same prosperity is bringing a new set of dilemmas, not just for farmers but for all of China—how to modernize without throwing half a billion people out of work and how to feed the population as the expansion of cash crops eats into land traditionally used for staple crops. Since the demise of the commune system in the 1980s, farmers have been responsible for providing quotas of staple crops to the government, in return for which they are theoretically allowed to rent a limited amount of land from the government for up to 30 years, and earn what they can from it. So long as farming remains largely manual, the rural population remains employed. But as entrepreneurial farmers, earning a private income from their leased plots, increasingly turn to mechanization encouraged by Western agronomists, the stability of the countryside looks unlikely to last, especially as in some areas the rural economy has stagnated, bringing social unrest, largely due to corrupt government officials who levy unrealistic taxes on local farmers.

China might be an essentially rural country, but it also has some of the largest cities in the world. In parts of those cities people still carry on their lives on the streets much as they have done for centuries.

PUBLIC FACE The reasons why the street is used as an extension to the home are not hard to fathom—poverty and a large population have meant simple and confined living space. In some parts of China, therefore, the street becomes a kitchen, a sitting-room, even a bedroom in the summer. The street is where everyone meets throughout the day so that tasks are accompanied by opportunities for constant conversation. Shelling prawns, doing the washing, pumping up a bicycle tire or playing cards may all take place simultaneously within the space of a few square yards, accompanied by exchanges of views and a general commentary on life. Although nobody appears to be taking much notice of traffic or passersby, everybody is aware of what's going on around them.

The street, the open-air office of the self-employed businessman

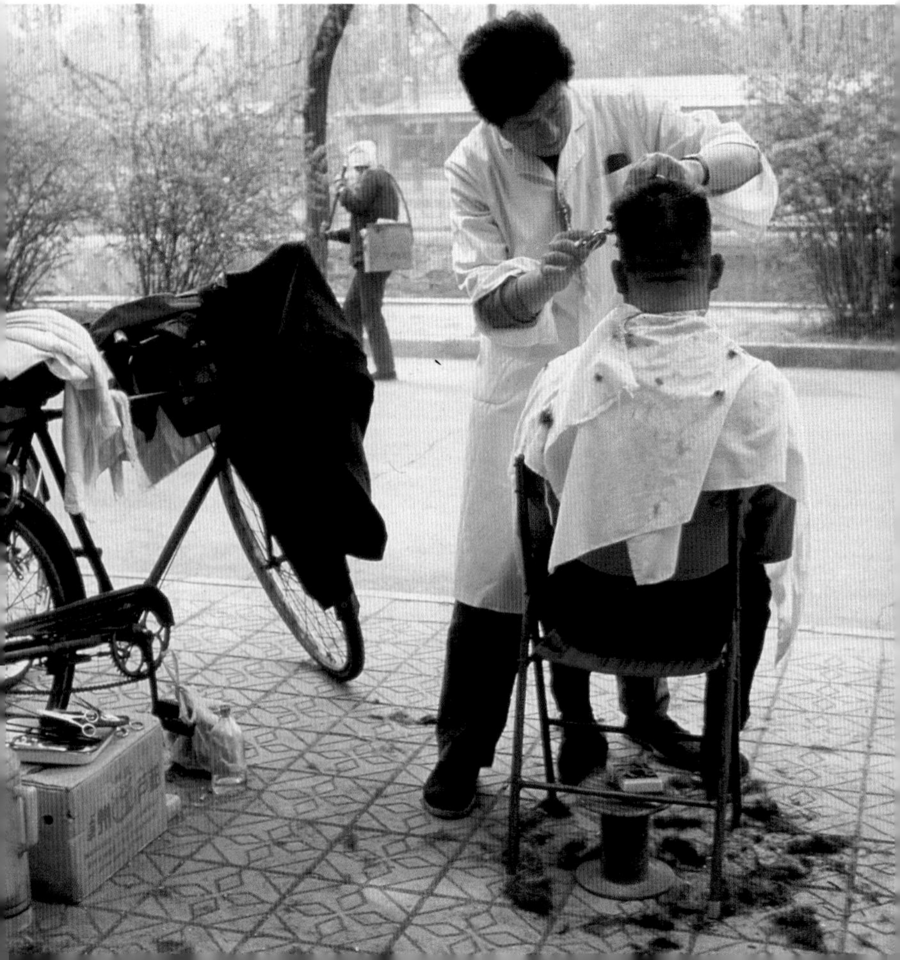

THE STREETS In the wider world (just beyond the front door) lies the

Freestyle disco dancing in the public park area of Tiantan, Beijing

commercial hub of the average small town. The open-air market is the liveliest area, but elsewhere on the streets there are barbers busy with their scissors and dentists advertising their skills with lurid paintings of a set of clackers. Noodles and bean curd are made on the spot, and dough sticks sizzle in blackened woks filled with hot oil. Tables and chairs are set up, and customers are served with simple fare; at night the tables may be illuminated with festoons of electric lights. In summer, people gather under street lamps to play cards or chess.

MOVEMENT Most striking is the restless movement that accompanies all of this. Despite the surface equanimity that appears like a glaze on Chinese daily life, there is a burning energy beneath. Watch some people eating or talking—even if the upper body is at rest, the leg pounds a beat on the floor and the eyes are constantly darting. Sometimes this latent energy can be frightening for visitors. Considering the crowded conditions, street brawls are a comparative rarity, but when they do occur it is with a ferocity blind to all plea or blandishment.

From the street it is but a short step to the public parks where, because of lack of space and privacy, local people gather to do those things impossible at home or that are preferred as group activities. The commonest of these activities is *taiji*, the slow, graceful exercise routines performed by squads of (usually elderly) people. In recent years some older residents have forsaken traditional *taiji* in favor of open-air disco dancing.

Nearby, groups of equally elderly residents are likely to be enacting favorite scenes from Chinese opera.

ENTERTAINMENT The streets of the newly prosperous cities have changed considerably and, superficially at least, are becoming similar to modern streets all over the world. However, in front of the karaoke bars and skyscrapers, and among well-dressed wielders of cellular phones, farmers from the countryside and members of ethnic minorities plod by in bewildered fascination, while peddlers and street performers are making a welcome return. Less welcome is the increasing number of beggars in the cities, but this seems to be an unavoidable part of the construction of a new China.

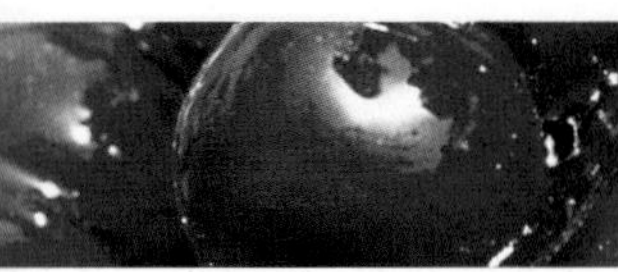

Chi fan le ma? *(Have you eaten yet?) is a form of greeting as unconscious (though not quite as flippant) as "How are you?" in English. It demonstrates where traditional Chinese priorities lie.*

VARIETY The variety of styles and ingredients involved in Chinese cooking is a marvel. There are three principal regional cuisines—hot and spicy dishes made with chili from Sichuan; northern-style cuisine using steamed bread and pancakes instead of rice, and preserved vegetables, such as salted and pickled cabbage, because of the freezing winters when nothing grows; and southern-style, involving light stir-fried dishes made from a vast array of ingredients, such as seafood, chicken, and pork.

Top: candied haw berries, a winter treat.
Below: Sichuan delicacies in traditional steamer baskets

FRESHNESS It is essential for all styles that when fresh food is used, it is as fresh as possible—and it is a testimony to Chinese genius that they have developed a style of cooking that makes refrigeration unnecessary, despite the rigors of the climate. Blessed with an abundance of good ingredients in the most fertile areas of the country, the Chinese have become expert at extracting the essence of flavor.

❑ Soy sauce, the principal accompaniment to Chinese cooking, is perhaps the oldest condiment known to man. Made from the soya bean, its origins go back to sauces made from fish and game. When soya, or meat or fish, are mixed with salt and water or rice wine, the protein is broken down into amino acids which stimulate taste. ❑

HISTORY A gourmet appreciation of food can be traced back to several centuries BC, as poetry of the period, listing dishes to tempt the departing soul back to the body, testifies. By the time of the Han dynasty a scientific approach had been formulated for cooking, and a basic rule was that the "five flavors" (sweetness, sourness, hotness, bitterness, and saltiness) should be combined in a meal to achieve balance and harmony. Mincing and the thin slicing of meat and fish were also considered essential for releasing the full flavor. Later, as China expanded its frontiers southward and westward, discovering new ingredients in the process, true Chinese cooking developed, although the basic tenets still held. The five-flavors cooking vocabulary is still used, even if it is quite inadequate to describe the full kaleidoscope of Chinese cuisine—as anyone who has experienced the true "sweet and sour" pork will readily acknowledge.

METHODS Cooking methods are vital to the craft of the Chinese master chef. The best results depend on the

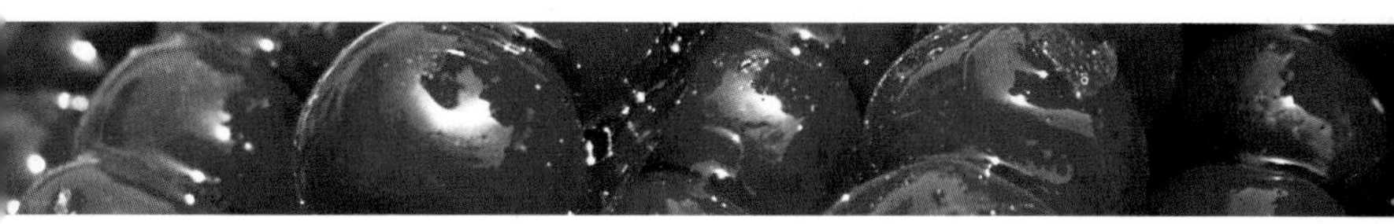

precise control of heat, and this skill is considered crucial.

Although all methods of cooking are used, from braising and baking to boiling, steaming, and roasting over a spit, there is one that is native to China: *chao*, or stir-frying, involves cutting the ingredients finely and rapidly cooking them in a small amount of oil in a preheated wok, so they are quickly and evenly cooked. Such dishes must be eaten immediately to benefit from their *huoqi* (vital essence).

As the 14th-century imperial dietitian Hu Sihui put it—"after a full meal do not wash your hair, avoid sex like an arrow, avoid wine like an enemy." If the letter of this dictum is no longer heeded, the spirit certainly is.

WESTERN TASTE Westerners are sometimes surprised to discover that Chinese food in China tastes different from the food served in restaurants back home. Chinese cooking is regional, reflecting the country's many climates and peoples, and is often more earthy than the version served in western restaurants. The stronger flavors can take some getting used to, but with a little perseverance, usually turn out to be highly satisfying to the palate.

Western-style fast food seems to have become popular among young urban Chinese. This has led to a rise in obesity among the young and a decline in the consumption of traditional snacks.

The proprietor of an outdoor restaurant hands out the food

Chinese music is unique, beautiful, and instantly recognizable. Like many things in China it is based on theories conceived at least 2,000 years ago, theories that also influenced the music of Japan, Vietnam, Mongolia, and Korea. Its distinctive qualities are dependent on two things—the instruments used and a chromatic scale that differs from that of the West.

Above: a performance in Tang costume; the instrument is the yueqin
Top: facade of a Beijing music store

HARMONY From earliest times music in China was held in the highest esteem and was an integral part of three important aspects of Chinese life: the festivals of the agricultural year, ceremonies linked to the imperial court, and religious rites. It was believed that the function of music was to enhance the harmony between heaven and earth (the earth being the fruit of the male principle of *yang* and the female principle of *yin*). The music was based on a dozen notes from which were selected the basic notes of a series of five-note scales (corresponding to the five elements of earth, water, fire, metal, and wood). The 12 notes arose from calculations based on the interval of the fourth and fifth, starting from a foundation note known as the "yellow bell" (*huang zhong*), which was thought to be imbued with a mystical power, considered one of the eternal principles of the universe and the foundation of the well-being of the state. Each dynasty, in fact, had its foundation note, arrived at after only the most careful calculations. Absolute pitch, therefore, was a vital ingredient of

❑ A man was going to play a Chinese lute in the street, and many people gathered around to listen. But when the musician began to play, the crowd thought the music too insipid and soon dispersed, except for one man who appeared to remain standing in rapt attention. The musician exclaimed: "There is still one who can appreciate fine music!" But the man replied: "If I hadn't lent you that table to use as a stand for your instrument, I'd have gone as well!" ❑

Chinese music, so vital that as early as the 1st century BC, during the Han dynasty, an imperial office had been established, and one of its duties was standardizing pitch.

MELODY Despite these potentially inhibiting rules, traditional Chinese music is far from dull. Its two principal elements are melody and timbre. Traditional Chinese orchestras are extremely large, their component parts collectively producing a sound that is euphonious and rich; some of the orchestras employed to play at imperial temples in Beijing consisted of 150 musicians.

INSTRUMENTS Traditional music is still widely played and remains quite distinctive because of the instruments, which both look and sound substantially different from their Western counterparts, even when they share some broad similarities. The most typical instrument is the *zheng*, a long, narrow stringed instrument plucked as it rests across the player's lap. This was the instrument of philosophers. Its main rival, an instrument that belongs more to the realm of traditional popular song, is the *pipa*, something like a lute, which became fashionable in the 7th century to accompany the songs of the Tang dynasty. Both these instruments simply sound solemn to Western ears. The Chinese originally classified their instruments according to the materials they were made of,

Flute player, Iron Pagoda, Kaifeng

which fell into eight categories—instruments with the qualities of stone, metal, silk, bamboo, wood, skin, gourd and clay. Music remains an ubiquitous feature of Chinese life. Although there are great differences between Chinese and European musical traditions, a little practice can allow anyone to acquire the Chinese taste.

In China, the principal spoken language is Modern Standard Chinese, based on the dialect of north China, especially Mandarin (from Portuguese "mandar," to rule). It (and all China's many other dialects) is distinctive by virtue of its tones. The Chinese script goes back to 4000 or 5000 BC, is justifiably claimed to be the world's oldest written language, and has a staggering 50,000 characters.

PICTOGRAPHS Chinese script has evolved from comparatively straightforward, miniature representations of the object in question, to highly stylized designs that need to be unravelled in order to be understood. It is thought that the original pictographs became more sophisticated as attempts were made to convey a meaning that could not be drawn. So, for example, the character for "to arrive at" (*zhi*) derives from a picture of an arrow hitting a target. The next stage was to convey abstract concepts by combining two (or more) characters: thus the characters for sun and moon placed together became the character *ming*, meaning "bright" or "brightness."

PRONUNCIATION By the time of the Han dynasty the written language had evolved to the point that a modern Chinese person would be able to read it aloud, although the meaning might be obscure. Chinese characters do not convey their pronunciation precisely, so the advantage of the script is that it is the same throughout the country and thus permits written communication between speakers of different dialects. There is almost nothing in common between spoken Cantonese, for example, thought by some to have preserved Tang dynasty pronunciation, and Mandarin. The government has promoted a simplified version of Mandarin (*putonghua*), with some success, as official Chinese, and in efforts to improve literacy introduced both a common system for writing the language with a Latin alphabet (romanization), known as *pinyin*, and a system for simplifying the most commonly used characters, now the norm in mainland China. In their traditional form the characters are too complex and numerous for the majority of people to learn.

Massive characters on a column in the Forbidden City, Beijing

China Was

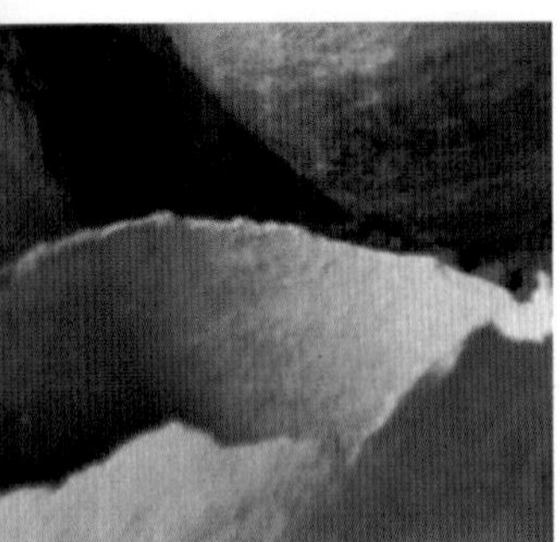

Although China has the longest continuous civilization in history, it was nevertheless a relatively late starter. Current evidence suggests that the first organized Chinese state did not appear until several dynasties had already come and gone in ancient Egypt. Once under way, however, Chinese civilization has proved durable and, although it has occasionally been bruised and battered over the centuries, its basic foundations have proved rocklike.

PREHISTORY Little is yet known of Chinese prehistory. About 40,000 years ago it seems that the area was populated by people of the Mongoloidal type, and that a recognizably Chinese type with flatter features appeared 20,000 years later, possibly in response to the freezing conditions of the era. However, it is only from 7,000 years ago that it is possible to trace the origins of the Chinese we know today.

Bronze Shang ritual wine vessel

CHINESE CIVILIZATION Although historians once thought that Chinese civilization was founded on influences from the Mediterranean, the spontaneous development of a separate culture is now accepted.

The first dynasty of which there is any concrete evidence is the Shang (there still exists considerable doubt about the legendary Xia, supposedly overthrown by the Shang in 1750 BC), who probably ruled the areas of the North China plain around the Yellow River in the modern provinces of Shandong, Henan, and Hebei, and parts of the provinces of Shanxi and Shaanxi. They were skilled and well organized—excavated remains of a Shang city at Zhengzhou show walls 33 feet in height extending around an area of some 2 miles—and used bronze, worked not with hammer and anvil, but cast in pottery molds. Crucially, Shang architecture and

❑ Traditional accounts of the origins of Chinese civilization talk of various figures from whom all Chinese claim descent. The Yellow Emperor is the father of the Chinese but others include Yu the Great, said to have created China's waterways, and Shen Nong, the Divine Husbandman. ❑

family values were to influence Chinese civilization to our own times.

There is no doubt that Shang influence spilled across its borders, but there was as yet no sense of Chinese statehood, and other states of varying degrees of power and cultural development operated around the Shang borders, sharing much of its culture but remaining politically independent. One such was the Zhou, who ruled an area not far to the west of Xi'an and who eventually overthrew the Shang in about 1050 BC and extended the area of a cultural influence that was becoming recognizably Chinese.

THE ZHOU DYNASTY

The Zhou (1050–256 BC) solved the problem of ruling what was now an extensive domain by establishing a feudal system in which relatives of the Zhou ruler were empowered to govern the various Zhou states. As for the Zhou ruler himself, he was seen as a Son of Heaven, and the supernatural influence he wielded (largely founded on the relationship to illustrious ancestors) was sufficiently powerful to linger even after the fall of the dynasty. Just how great was the extent of the Zhou realm is hard to gauge—it seems to have extended through much of Shaanxi, Shanxi, and Hebei, reaching the Gansu border in the west and Shandong in the east, and possibly the Yangtze Valley. It was sufficiently large to warrant the construction of a secondary capital at Luoyang.

In 771 BC, however, the western Zhou rulers met defeat at the hands of a mixture of barbarian invaders and disgruntled subjects, displaced by the eastern Zhou rulers. They moved east to Luoyang, but their vitality was sapped.

Top: neolithic pottery at Banpo
Left: a decorated ritual vessel, in the form of a stylized animal, dated to the Zhou dynasty

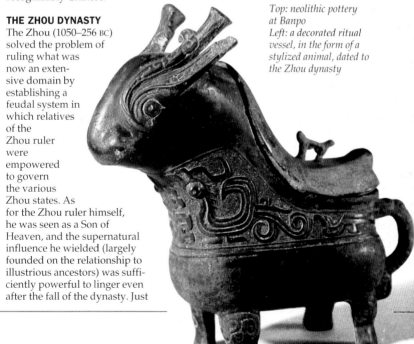

Although the Zhou lasted 800 years, its rule was largely nominal. Effective power lay with the nobles in far-flung regions of the kingdom, who frequently fought among themselves while continuing to defer to the Zhou king at Luoyang. Eventually, a newer, stronger state was to exploit this weakness.

The famous "Flying Horse of Gansu," Eastern Han dynasty

FALL OF EASTERN ZHOU Echoes of the ritualistic deference shown to the Zhou king exist even today in public life, for some of the Zhou's administrative features lasted into the 20th century. The eastern Zhou, the second period of Zhou rule, is subdivided into two, both named after the principal historical source books—the Spring and Fall period (during which Confucius lived) and the Warring States period, characterized by internecine warfare among the various states, any one of which might finally have toppled the Zhou.

But it was the Qin, occupying the area around the original western

❏ The First Emperor believed his empire would last for 10,000 generations—in fact his own dynasty outlived him by only a few years, although the imperial structure he built lasted for 2,133 years.

The emperor died in 210 BC, on a trip away from the capital. His chief advisor, Li Ssu, returned the body in a sealed carriage to preempt revolt and changed the wording of the emperor's will in favor of a younger, weaker son. The true heir committed suicide and the new emperor was murdered by Li Ssu, who was himself killed in the ensuing chaos. ❏

capital, that was to prove strongest, using its favored position on the fringes of the Chinese and uncultured worlds to expand to a point where it was able to defeat the Zhou in 256 BC and the other states in 221 BC.

THE MIGHTY QIN The Qin dynasty (221–206 BC), although one of the shortest in Chinese history, was to prove one of the most influential. Its founder—Qin Shihuangdi, "the First Emperor of China"—brought to fruition an incipient sense of Chinese statehood. Qin ideology was not very innovative, but the adoption of the authoritarian tenets of Legalist philosophy ensured that the Qin triumphed. The emperor's principal aims were centralization, standardization, and unification: China was divided into military regions and counties and governed from the center; weights and measures and the written script were regularized; and intellectual opposition was ruthlessly suppressed. By 214 BC, he had extended Chinese domains as far as Vietnam, but with his death in 210 BC the dynasty fizzled out. His three short-lived successors were unable to cool the simmering resentments that resulted from the severity of the First Emperor's rule.

THE HAN The Han (206 BC–AD 220), though founded upon opposition to the Legalist framework that had been the key to Qin success, was left with a base upon which to develop into one of the greatest of Chinese dynasties. Confucianism became the state doctrine, absolute imperial power was enshrined as "the Mandate from heaven," and a rudimentary examination system for selecting officials was introduced. It was a period of cultural, scientific, and foreign expansion and of consolidation of the Chinese identity. Many regions previously under nominal Chinese tutelage were better integrated, and the way west via the Silk Road, a conduit for Buddhism, was opened.

Although the Han fragmented into warring states, the idea of a united China never died. The demise of the Han can be attributed in part to economic factors: before, the southern states had been no match for the Qin once it had acquired the prosperous northern plains; by the end of the Han, the wealth of the Yangtze Valley and the Sichuan Basin was well developed and, when rebellions led to the fall of the Han, China split into three.

A "Fairy Mountain" incense burner, as found in a Western Han tomb, made of bronze inlaid with gold

In China philosophy has played a role not unlike that of a religion. Most of the great Chinese philosophers emerged during a period of unrelenting instability, which was perhaps the inspiration for the quest to right human ills.

CONFUCIUS If a word had to be chosen to describe Chinese society for the last 2,000 years, that word might well be "Confucian."

Confucius was born in 551 BC in the state of Lu (now Shandong province). Although his parents were probably minor nobility, he developed a concern for the poor and dispossessed, and the belief that the goal of mankind was happiness. Each individual and each government, therefore, should desire happiness for others. Anyone could be a good ruler, not just the high-born. All that was required was the right education, the will to learn, and the desire to govern well. Together with his disciples he founded the first private school in China, accepting pupils of any background, providing they demonstrated intellectual curiosity.

Education had been confined to the well-born, or for those learning to become government officials. Confucian education also aimed to train people to govern but with a crucial difference. Confucius believed that public servants should play an active role in government, taking initiatives and criticizing bad policy.

Top: Taoist monks. Below: the pagoda (here, at Tiger Hill, Suzhou) is a tribute to Chinese Buddhism

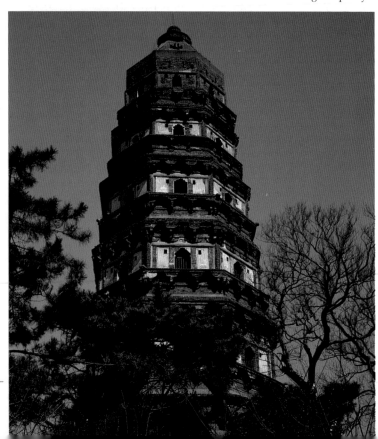

❑ "One Chuang Chou (Zhuangzi) dreamed he was a butterfly. He did not know he had ever been anything but a butterfly, and was content to hover from flower to flower. Suddenly he woke and found to his astonishment that he was Chuang Chou. But it was hard to be sure whether he really was Chou and had only dreamed that he was a butterfly, or was really a butterfly, and was only dreaming he was Chou."—Arthur Waley, *Three Ways of Thought in Ancient China*, 1939 ❑

In Confucian philosophy ritual was important but was deemed useless if it consisted of inflexible rules. It was the spirit of the ritual, not its mechanical application that was important.

While Confucius seems to have believed in a moral force called Heaven, he declined to tackle the question of life after death. One of his best-known responses to a question from one of his disciples was "You do not yet understand life; how can you understand death?" Instead, he emphasized "the Way" or the "Golden Mean." This was a way of action, which followers should be prepared to stand by, and die for if necessary. It taught that people should play an active role in society, observing conventions, yet not following the crowd. For Confucius, the concept of the well-rounded individual, rigorously intellectual yet emotionally balanced, was paramount.

Confucius's stress on universal government was too radical for most. Although he was eventually given a government post, he realized that it was a way of keeping him quiet and he soon resigned. He traveled throughout China spreading his ideas, and died in 479 BC.

TAOISM The other important Chinese philosophy was Taoism, in many ways complementing Confucianism. Its first major figure is Laozi (ca570–490 BC), a near contemporary of Confucius reputed to have written the *Daodejing*, which translates as "The Way and its powers." The nature of the *dao*, "Way," which is the great underlying principle of human and natural life, is never properly defined, but it might be said to be the bond that unites man with nature, with the concept of *wuwei* or "no action" as its ethos. The second important Taoist figure is Zhuangzi (369–286 BC) who wrote a volume of allegorical tales illustrating the tenets of Taoism. Taoism is a counter to the rigid propriety of Confucianism. It is still possible to see both points of view mirrored in the outlook of modern Chinese men and women.

Statue of Confucius, Confucian Temple, Beijing

The yin-yang *Taoist symbol*

After the fall of the Han, China divided into the three states known as the Wei, Shu, and Wu. Constantly at war with each other over the following centuries, the three states eventually fragmented into a jigsaw of small dynasties. Two of China's greatest dynasties were to emerge from the chaos.

AFTER THE HAN Paradoxically, the era of confusion that followed the disintegration of the Han dynasty was also one of cultural flowering. The Tang dynasty (AD 618–907) that followed is often considered the most accomplished of the Chinese dynasties.

THE TANG Its founder, a general, came from mixed barbarian and Chinese stock. He retained the fundamental Confucian outlook, encouraged education, and promoted contact with foreigners.

Unusually, the general abdicated in favor of his son when he felt that China was sufficiently stable.

THE GOOD LIFE Life in Tang China was cosmopolitan, vital, and stimulating. Chang'an (Xi'an), the capital, had an estimated population of two million, probably the largest city in the world at the time. One of the hallmarks of the dynasty was its organization—elaborate laws were codified throughout the empire, which extended to Korea and Vietnam. On main roads there were post stations every 10 miles with hostels and restaurants. Confucianist schools were augmented by others specializing in law, mathematics, and science. The development of the examination system, which was started in the Han, helped to create the first bureaucracy based on merit. Bills of exchange ("flying money") were introduced. The Tang was also notable for contact with the outside world, as Persians and Jews, for example, found themselves among the traders in Canton and as Chinese influence reestablished itself along the Silk Road.

Buddhism reached its apogee during this period, before its sudden decline as a result of official attacks on its influence. Painting and music flourished. For the first time central and south China vied in importance with the traditional northern heartland around the Yellow River. Confucian gentry began to earn money from the offices they held, rather than from land, heralding the burgeoning of a "middle class." Yet there were no exceptional or striking political innovations in the period and, ultimately, economic problems—such as the displacement of tax-paying peasants by land-hungry merchants, and the increasing wealth of the aristocracy—led to strife and disintegration.

Above: Song dynasty mirror box

THE SONG Five decades of bickering ensued before reunification under the Song (AD 960–1279). This was to be another of the great Chinese dynasties, despite barbarian invasions that compelled the court to move south to Hangzhou from its capital in Kaifeng. During this period increasing urbanization brought about a commercial revolution, education and literacy improved, and a cultural renaissance was underway, noted for simple but beautiful glazed porcelain, and the finest painting in Chinese history.

FIRST INVASIONS The first Song emperor decided to centralize the bureaucracy, placing as many ministries under his personal control as possible, in order to consolidate reunification. But the threat of invasion was ever-present, and by 946 the Khitans, of Mongol origin, had reached Kaifeng. Over 3,000 courtiers were captured, and the Song, driven south, were forced to coexist with the barbarians, who occupied the north for 300 years.

This was, nonetheless, a period of progress. Foreign trade prospered and Chinese cities became more sophisticated. The Chinese genius for innovation inspired a series of inventions, including the compass and inoculations against smallpox; a less notable innovation was the fashion for binding girls' feet. It was also an era of decadence and military feebleness that accentuated the Chinese tendency to introspection. As Buddhism continued to atrophy due to government suppression during the Tang dynasty, Neo-Confucianism dominated Chinese thought. Thus China remained, more or less, for a further eight centuries.

Buddhist monks at Xi'an's Big Wild Goose Pagoda (left), built AD 652

The Yuan was the first foreign dynasty to rule China, and although it was to last little more than a century it was to influence the Chinese outlook for hundreds of years to come.

THE KHANS The Mongols' success in taking China can be accredited partly to their use of the latest military technology, principally a mobile cavalry; added to this, lack of water in Central Asia finally forced the squabbling Mongol tribes to unite under a single dynamic leader, Ghengis Khan, with the aim of conquering less arid territory. In 1215, Beijing fell, but Ghengis did not live to see the full conquest of China; upon his death the Mongol Empire was divided into four "khanates" ruled by three sons and a grandson.

Ghenghis Khan's son Ogodai, who ruled from the Mongol capital of Karakorum, reinvaded China. Although he conquered the Khitan rulers of the North China plain, he met stiffer opposition from the southern Song, who resisted all attempts at conquest for half a century. Finally they were overcome by Ghengis Khan's grandson, Kublai, in 1279.

Now ruler of all China, Kublai Khan took the Chinese name Yuan ("First Beginning") for his dynasty. The Mongols also pushed into Indochina and briefly reached Java, provoking huge migrations and indirectly contributing to political changes in neighboring lands as they did so. In 1260, the Mongol capital was moved from Karakorum to Beijing, with Xanadu (now Dolon Nor, in Inner Mongolia) then retained as a summer residence for the imperial family.

Genghis Khan's mausoleum, Ejin Horo Qi, Inner Mongolia

Left: lions on the Beijing bridge mentioned by Marco Polo. Top, opposite: the Forbidden City or, in Mongol days, the "Great Within"

MONGOL CHINA Kublai Khan employed able men of all nationalities and listened to all philosophies. Dispensing with the civil service examinations, he streamlined the bureaucracy to four ministries—Justice, War, Rites, Finance—and although he hired foreign contingents for Mongol armies, the Chinese were forbidden to carry arms.

Despite the changes, Confucian ideology and bureaucratic political life were maintained. To the disgust of the Chinese, however, Mongolian customs of dress, food, traditions, and language were imposed. The Mongols did not use surnames, for example, a barbarian custom to the family-conscious Chinese. But cultural and literary activity flourished—with the abolition of the examinations, frustrated scholars had to find other uses for their literary skills. Popular drama also developed fast.

FOREIGN LINKS Furthermore, expeditions were sent to find the source of the Yellow River, while links with the Muslim world inspired the introduction of Persian design elements into Chinese art and architecture. China and Europe entered a new era of cultural exchange. Europeans began to arrive as adventurers or as representatives of European nation states, sent to export Christianity and possibly find a powerful new ally against the Muslims. There was even a Mongolian counterpart to Marco Polo, a certain Rabban Sauma, a Nestorian monk who traveled to Rome to meet the Pope. With the collapse of the Yuan, however, and the re-establishment of native rule under the Ming, the Catholic Church lost the ground it had made in China, at least for the time being.

Eventually the Mongols lost their grip on their huge and unwieldy empire. None of Kublai's successors matched his ability. Distance and cultural divide wore down the conquerors. Once the Mongols began to lose their cultural identity, the familiar symptoms of dynastic decline appeared: famines, uncontrolled floods, excessive taxation, and revolts. As is always the case, the rebellious chiefs were not able to unite, and it took a single strong Chinese general to seize control.

The Ming (which means "brilliant") was to become the archetypal Chinese dynasty—peaceful, prosperous, and stable, the image of traditional China ruled by the scholar-gentry on Neo-Confucian principles. The Qing, another foreign dynasty, was to bring more than 2,000 years of imperial rule to a close.

Spirit Way, Nanjing, leads to the tomb of the first Ming emperor
Top: detail, Qing palace, Shenyang

THE MING Zhu Yuanzhang, the founder of the Ming dynasty (AD 1368–1644), rose from a peasant background to become a general and then an emperor, driving out the Mongols and establishing the first Ming capital in Nanjing. Although Confucianism was revitalized, the emperor became increasingly autocratic. After his death, civil war broke out: his grandson and heir was usurped by his son, who had been ruling Beijing as Prince of Yan. He became the Yongle Emperor, the greatest of the Ming emperors.

GREAT WORKS Yongle relocated the capital to Beijing, creating his own power base close to the Mongol border. He oversaw the beginning of great public works, such as the reconstruction of the Great Wall, the mass movement of populations for colonization, and the reclamation of areas laid waste by war. This was an era of seaborne expeditions, led by a eunuch admiral hoping to promote Chinese prestige along new trade routes; at one stage 16 states, including Aden, were paying tribute to China and its emperor.

When these expeditions came to a sudden end—due to resentment against the eunuch leaders and fear of the Mongol menace—foreign relations went downhill. Pirate raids intensified on the coast and along the Yangtze. Chinese citizens were forbidden to travel abroad, and China turned in on itself. Despite this, Jesuit scientists were still tolerated, and cultural life flourished, albeit in a scarcely innovative way. Widespread printing allowed the dissemination of encyclopedias and treatises. Surprisingly, given the inhibiting effects of Confucianism, the novel flourished, and several classics were published at this time.

LAST YEARS After 300 years the Ming was in its death throes. The state eunuchs, in important ministerial positions at the palace, had become too powerful. Court favorites and their families built up great estates, and dispossessed peasants joined together to form rebel bands that marched on Beijing. In response, the last Ming emperor committed suicide on Coal Hill, just behind the Forbidden City, but the peasant army did not enjoy the victory for long—taking advantage of the civil strife, a Manchu army swept down from the northeast to capture Beijing in 1644.

THE LAST DYNASTY The Manchus were a confederation of Jurchen tribes from central and southern Manchuria. Their leader was Nurhaci, who founded the Manchu state in 1616. He established his capital at Shenyang, and by adopting Confucianism won the support of the three million Chinese who lived in Manchuria. His son Abahai proclaimed the new Qing dynasty in 1636, captured Beijing in 1644, and over the next several decades established control over all of China. Unlike the Mongols before them, the Manchus decided to preserve the Chinese government structure while also enforcing some of their own traditions on the Chinese.

MANCHU CHINA Internal peace was maintained by military might, but the dynasty produced two notable emperors. The Kangxi Emperor (1654–1722) completed the agricultural reforms started under the Ming, initiated attempts to tame the Yellow River, supported scholarship, and encouraged artistic endeavor. His grandson, the Qianlong Emperor (1711–1799), extended the empire's boundaries despite several unsuccessful military campaigns that were to leave the country defenseless. But by 1800 there were already signs of cyclical decline. Peasant revolts and the specter of Western influence, which was taking hold in Canton despite disapproval in Beijing, could no longer be ignored.

Ming vase, with peacock and peony patterns

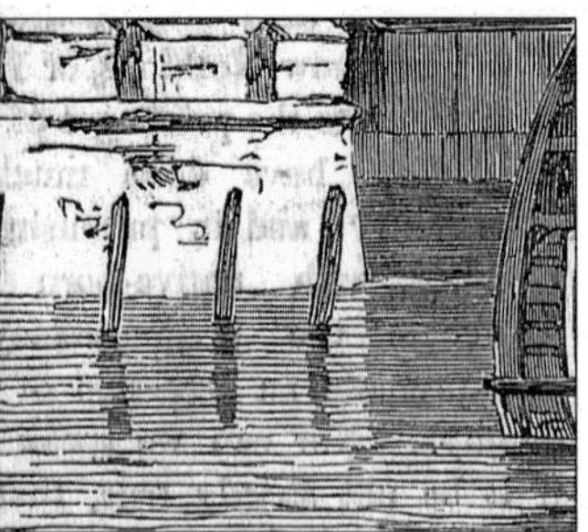

The decline and eventual fall of imperial China was a long, painful process. During the final 100 years of the Qing dynasty, influences were at work that traditional resources could not meet. One was the arrival of foreigners in unprecedented numbers, determined to force the Chinese government to enter free trade—a goal that was eventually accomplished through the Treaty of Nanjing, which opened certain treaty ports to foreign companies.

EUROPEAN BARBARIANS The reactions of Manchu rulers and Chinese intellectuals alike to the presence of foreigners on their soil were mixed: some ignored them while others expressed interest in the new ideas offered by Westerners. Those who favored Westernization could not agree on how to proceed. The official line taken by the Manchus was that the foreigners should be ignored; but they were not so easily disposed of, and there were other matters to consider. One of these was the Taiping "Heavenly Peace" Rebellion (1850–1864), the gravest of many uprisings at that time.

Sun Yatsen, Father of the Republic

MESSIAH This rebellion lasted more than 20 years and cost at least 20 million lives. It began when a Hakka peasant, who had failed the official examinations, adopted Christianity, proclaiming himself the head of a new Confucian hierarchy with Christ as the Heavenly Elder Brother. He made considerable headway, taking Nanjing and even enjoying temporary Western support. A typical manifestation of the agrarian unrest of the time, the rebellion, although unsuccessful, showed how vulnerable the Chinese government really was when faced with a challenge.

❏ The Taiping Rebellion ended in ignominious failure but some of the ideas of its leader, Hong Xiuquan, were remarkable: he believed in state ownership of land and sharing food, clothing, and money. Every 25 households were to be organized as "comradeships" (*wu*), headed by a comrade leader (*wuzhang*). ❏

NEED FOR CHANGE The British and French, in particular, frequently found excuses for acts of aggression. The weak Chinese government seemed powerless to prevent additional treaty ports being added to the list originally

Port of Shanghai in 1857 (top) and (above) The Shanghai Club—for foreign members only until 1949

agreed to in 1842, under the Nanjing Treaty, or to halt the ruinous opium trade. Some in the Chinese government saw that reforms were necessary and minor changes were made—land tax was reduced and collected more efficiently, Chinese were sent abroad to learn Western technological skills, an office was established specifically to deal with foreign affairs, and there was some railroad and telegraph construction, and industrial development. The so-called "self-strengthening" movement was undermined, however, by a determination to ignore the virtues of Western political systems.

DRAGON EMPRESS Predictably there were those who opposed any modernization. The imperial concubine Cixi (1835–1908), who acted as regent during the minority of her son, the nominated heir, became the *de facto* ruler for the rest of her life when he died in 1875, and was replaced by a four-year-old. Cixi ousted reformers but in 1898 the young emperor, attracted by foreign ideas, initiated the "Hundred Days of Reform" movement. This proposed educational change, included the foundation of a university in Peking, and the reform of the Civil Service examination system. Cixi came out of retirement and ruthlessly put an end to it, but foreigners were now permitted to reside in Beijing. All this time, China's foreign residents continued to exploit the country (though, strangely, this had an upside: maintaining trade relations with the outside world).

LAST DAYS Tensions finally culminated in the Boxer Rebellion of 1900–1901. Initially anti-Manchu, it quickly became anti-foreign. Following its suppression by a powerful international army, more humiliating demands were made on the Chinese. Western influence also encouraged the appearance of several revolutionary groups, notably those led by Sun Yatsen (see page 229), who had been exposed to democratic ideals in Japan, America, and Britain. Last-minute reforms by the government were too little too late; in 1912 Sun was elected President of the Republic of China after the abdication of the last emperor.

During the 20th century China was shaken by a series of major upheavals, caused by the struggle to modernize the country after 2,000 years of backward-looking imperial rule. Inevitably the process was accompanied by ideological battles, notably between the conservative nationalists and the communists who believed in forging a new order based on the common ownership of property and resources.

THE FIRST REPUBLIC On February 12, 1912, the last Chinese emperor, the six-year-old Puyi (1906–1967), was forced to abdicate and the first Chinese Republic was declared in Nanjing. Sun Yatsen, the leader of the reformist movement that opposed imperial rule, was duly elected Provisional President. His plans to create a more modern and democratic

Top: Chiang Kaishek, Burma 1942
Below: a statue of Mao (in Shenyang), nowadays a rare sight

state were thwarted, however, by Yuan Shikai. Yuan was the treacherous head of the imperial army who, despite his duty to protect the boy emperor, had actually orchestrated the emperor's abdication.

Yuan regarded Sun Yatsen as a challenge to his own bid for power but, in public at least, supported the republicans. In 1912, Sun Yatsen reluctantly agreed to stand aside for Yuan, who was unanimously declared President. Yuan dropped all pretense of republican sentiment in 1915 when he declared himself emperor, but his dictatorial ambitions came to nothing: he died the next year. He paved the way for a grim period in Chinese history, when the various thuggish warlords, who controlled sections of the Chinese army, battled against each other for supremacy over North China and the possession of Beijing. All Sun Yatsen and his followers could do was work for much-needed reform from the distant southern Chinese capital in Guangzhou (Canton).

CHIANG KAISHEK At Sun Yatsen's death in 1925, his place as leader of the Nationalist Party (Guomindang) was taken by Chiang Kaishek (1887–1975). The party's main goal was to overthrow the Beijing-based warlords, thus reuniting China through military conquest under its leadership. In preparation for armed rebellion, the nationalists were trained by advisers from the newly created Soviet Union who were working to influence China's political situation. At the same time Soviet revolutionaries were active in Shanghai, where the Chinese Communist Party was formed in 1921.

In 1923, the communists joined forces with the nationalists, but strong tensions existed between the two parties, not least because Chiang Kaishek knew that his goals would not be achieved without the support of foreign governments and Chinese industrialists who were implacably opposed to Marxism. When Chiang led his army north in 1927 and declared a new nationalist government in Nanjing, his first act was to ban the Communist Party and to carry out a purge of left-wingers within his own ranks.

Many were killed and many imprisoned during this period, and communists all over China were harried by means of so-called "encirclement campaigns" whereby the army tried to get rid of the forces in south central China. To escape the nationalists, the communists undertook an arduous 14,400 mile trek in 1935, heading through China's far west, an expedition that has gone down in history as the Long March (see page 111). Of the nearly 100,000 people who undertook the march, fewer than 10,000 survived. These veterans, including their leader Mao Zedong, would eventually form an elite within the Communist Party that would come to rule China and force its people into a series of equally heroic, if misguided, campaigns.

Now, however, the bitterest of enemies agreed to cease hostilities and put up a united front against the Japanese, who invaded those areas not already in their control in 1937. Until the surrender of the Japanese at the end of World War II, the communists kept up a constant guerrilla campaign from their bases in the west, while the nationalists, supported by the Western Allies, operated out of bases in the province of Sichuan.

Mao's Red Book, *symbol of Chinese communism*

Hostilities broke out again between communists and nationalists at the defeat of Japan in 1945. U.S. envoys sought to find a compromise, and Stalin himself put pressure on the communists to cast aside differences with the nationalists, but Mao showed all the stubbornness and determination that were to be his hallmarks for the next 30 years.

Mao came from Chinese peasant stock (born in Shaoshan, in Hunan province, in 1893), and his masterstroke was to win the support of the mass of Chinese peasant farmers for his revolutionary ideals—unlike the university-educated intellectuals who led the urban-based Russian Revolution.

Eight years of war against the Japanese had taught the communists how to survive and win even in the face of extreme hardship. They outclassed and outwitted the nationalists at every stage of the bloody civil war that began in 1946 and ended in October 1949, when Mao finally stood with his supporters at the gates of the Forbidden City in Beijing. Chiang Kaishek fled to Taiwan where he set up a rival government.

THE PEOPLE'S REPUBLIC One of Mao's first acts was to redistribute all land (former landlords were often beaten up or killed), and by 1956 all industries had been nationalized. The West was prepared to support Mao at first, but China was later ostracized for helping Communist North Korea invade the U.N.-supported South in the Korean War of 1950–1953.

At first, China turned to the U.S.S.R. for aid, and in cities such as Beijing and Shanghai the visible symbols of this era are the hotels and office buildings constructed for and by Russian advisers. Increasingly, however, Mao began to develop his own idiosyncratic brand of communism, launching one mass-action campaign after another and seeming to exercise an extraordinary power to control the collective will of his people. In 1956, his cry was to let "a hundred flowers blossom, a hundred schools of thought contend." The aim was to revitalize Chinese culture, but the Party drew the line at criticism of its own role, and the campaign died in 1957 with the imprisonment of many dissidents.

Next came the Great Leap Forward of 1958–1959, intended to mobilize the country into superhuman feats of agricultural and industrial productivity. Instead it resulted in mass starvation, as peasants spent more time in political debate than in physical work, a problem made worse by two years of poor harvests, floods, and typhoons. When most in need of help, Mao then quarrelled with the Soviet Union, ostensibly in the name of Chinese "self-reliance" but really out of pique because the Soviets would not share their nuclear technology with China.

Finally Mao lost all patience with his critics and turned to the young. In 1966, he launched the Cultural Revolution, encouraging armies of young Red Guards to wipe the slate of history clean and build a totally new China. This resulted in an orgy of iconoclasm, as the Red Guards smashed up historic buildings and museum displays, beat up intellectuals and teachers, and turned on their own parents. Three years of terror and anarchy and ten years of repression were unleashed.

China's travails only came to an end with Mao's death in 1976. Mao's wife, Jiang Qing, tried to seize power but she, and the other members of the so-called "Gang of Four," were arrested within a month. Deng Xiaoping, Mao's long-time opponent, then emerged as China's new leader. His pragmatic form of communism, and his economic reforms to encourage foreign investment, led to a period of calm and the gradual strengthening of

the economy. Democracy still remains a distant dream, however, as proved by army intervention in Tiananmen Square in 1989.

Since then a comparatively free market has enabled some Chinese to buy themselves material independence but without the personal freedom to enjoy it. China remains an essentially autocratic state in which dissident views are not tolerated and where the rights of minority peoples are consistently violated (most notably in Tibet, but also among the Muslims of Xinjiang). Religion has been allowed to flourish, yet worshipers are still exposed to harassment. Power is still centralized and, increasingly, riddled with corruption, leaving many Chinese frustrated and powerless.

Mao (below, as seen on the Tiananmen Gate) is depicted greeting the People's Army

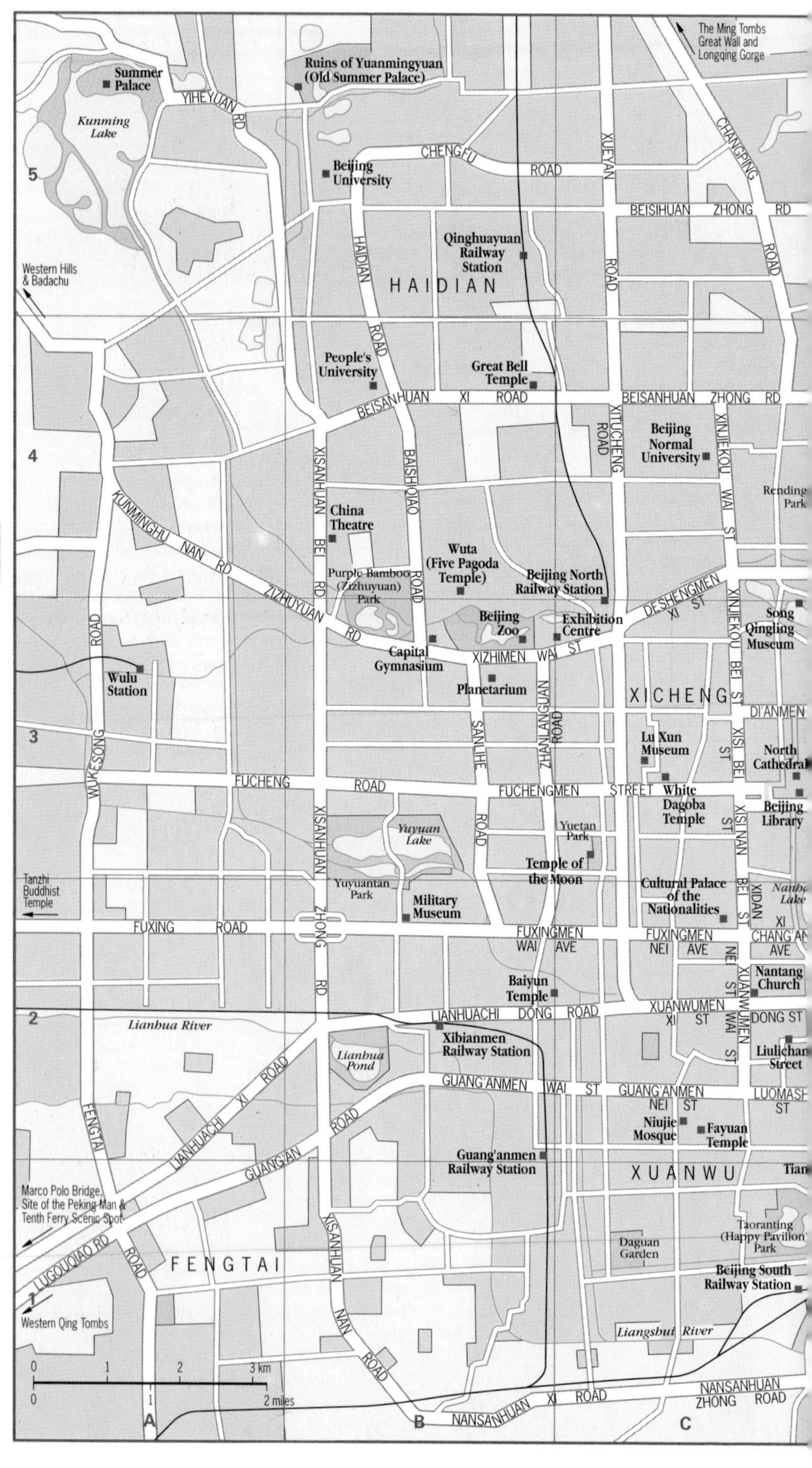

The Ming Tombs
Great Wall and
Longqing Gorge
Summer Palace
Kunming Lake
Ruins of Yuanmingyuan
(Old Summer Palace)
YIHEYUAN RD
CHENGFU ROAD
Beijing University
XUEYAN ROAD
CHANGPING ROAD
BEISIHUAN ZHONG RD
Qinghuayuan Railway Station
HAIDIAN
HAIDIAN ROAD
Western Hills
& Badachu
People's University
Great Bell Temple
BEISANHUAN XI ROAD
BEISANHUAN ZHONG RD
XITUCHENG ROAD
Beijing Normal University
XINJIEKOU WAI ST
Rending Park
XISANHUAN BEI RD
BAISHIQIAO ROAD
China Theatre
KUNMINGHU NAN RD
Wuta
(Five Pagoda Temple)
Purple Bamboo
(Zizhuyuan)
Park
Beijing North Railway Station
ZIZHUYUAN RD
DESHENGMEN XI ST
XINJIEKOU BEI ST
Beijing Zoo
Exhibition Centre
Song Qingling Museum
Capital Gymnasium
XIZHIMEN WAI ST
Planetarium
WUKESONG ROAD
Wulu Station
XICHENG
DI'ANMEN
SANLIHE ROAD
ZHANLANGUAN ROAD
Lu Xun Museum
XISI BEI ST
North Cathedral
FUCHENG ROAD
FUCHENGMEN STREET
White Dagoba Temple
Beijing Library
XISI NAN ST
Yuyuan Lake
Yuetan Park
Temple of the Moon
Tanzhi Buddhist Temple
Yuyuantan Park
XISANHUAN ZHONG RD
Military Museum
Cultural Palace of the Nationalities
XIDAN BEI ST
Nanhai Lake
FUXING ROAD
FUXINGMEN WAI AVE
FUXINGMEN NEI AVE
XI CHANG'AN AVE
NEI ST
XUANWUMEN WAI ST
Nantang Church
Baiyun Temple
LIANHUACHI DONG ROAD
XUANWUMEN XI ST
DONG ST
Lianhua River
Xibianmen Railway Station
Lianhua Pond
Liulichang Street
LIANHUACHI XI ROAD
GUANG'ANMEN WAI ST
GUANG'ANMEN NEI ST
LUOMASHI ST
FENGTAI
Niujie Mosque
Fayuan Temple
GUANG'AN ROAD
Guang'anmen Railway Station
XUANWU
Marco Polo Bridge,
Site of the Peking Man &
Tenth Ferry Scenic Spot
XISANHUAN NAN ROAD
Taoranting
(Happy Pavilion)
Park
Daguan Garden
LUGOUQIAO RD
ROAD
FENGTAI
Beijing South Railway Station
Western Qing Tombs
Liangshui River
0 1 2 3 km
0 1 2 miles
NANSANHUAN XI ROAD
NANSANHUAN ZHONG ROAD
A
B
C
1
2
3
4
5

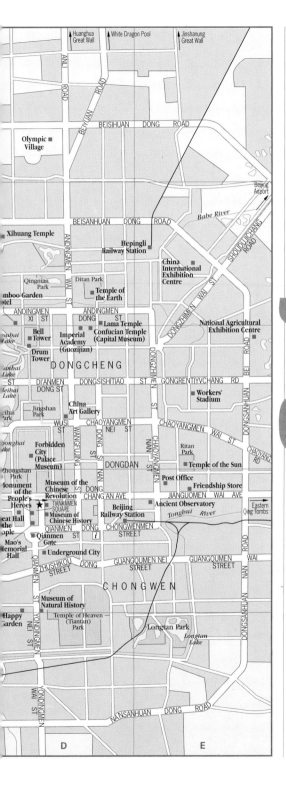

A-Z Beijing

Huanghua Great Wall
White Dragon Pool
Jinshanung Great Wall
ANLI ROAD
BEIYUAN ROAD
BEISIHUAN DONG ROAD
Olympic Village
Beijing Airport
Babe River
BEISANHUAN DONG ROAD
Xihuang Temple
Hepingli Railway Station
ANDINGMEN WAI ST
China International Exhibition Centre
SHOUDUJICHANG ROAD
Qingnian Park
Ditan Park
Temple of the Earth
Bamboo Garden Hotel
DONGZHIMEN WAI ST
ANDINGMEN XI ST
ANDINGMEN DONG ST
Lama Temple
National Agricultural Exhibition Centre
Bell Tower
Imperial Academy (Guozijian)
Confucian Temple (Capital Museum)
Houhai Lake
Drum Tower
DONGCHENG
DONGZHIMEN ST
BEI ROAD
Qianhai Lake
DI'ANMEN DONG ST
DONGSISHITIAO ST
GONGRENTIYVCHANG RD
Beihai Lake
Workers' Stadium
Jingshan Park
China Art Gallery
Beihai Park
WUSI ST
CHAOYANGMEN NEI ST
CHAOYANGMEN WAI ST
DONGSANHUAN
Zhonghai Lake
Forbidden City (Palace Museum)
WANGFUJING ST
DONG SI NAN ST
CHAOYANGMEN NAN ST
Ritan Park
CHAOYANG RD
DONGDAN
Temple of the Sun
Zhongshan Park
Post Office
Monument of the People's Heroes
Museum of the Chinese Revolution
DONG CHANG'AN AVE
Friendship Store
JIANGUOMEN WAI AVE
TIANANMEN SQUARE
Ancient Observatory
Eastern Qing Tombs
Great Hall of the People
Museum of Chinese History
Beijing Railway Station
Tonghui River
QIANMEN DONG ST
CHONGWENMEN STREET
Qianmen Gate
Mao's Memorial Hall
Underground City
ROAD
ZHUSHIKOU DONG STREET
GUANGQUMEN NEI STREET
GUANGQUMEN WAI STREET
QIANMEN ST
NAN
CHONGWEN
Museum of Natural History
Happy Garden
Temple of Heaven (Tiantan) Park
YONDINGMEN NEI ST
Longtan Park
Longtan Lake
DONGSANHUAN
YONDINGMEN WAI ST
NANSANHUAN DONG ROAD
D
E

►►► CITY HIGHLIGHTS

Beihai Park *page 53*

Forbidden City *pages 53–55*

Great Wall *pages 56–57*

Lama Temple *page 66*

Summer Palace *pages 61–63*

Temple of Heaven *page 64*

Tiananmen Square *pages 64–65*

Shopping facilities are burgeoning in Beijing, adding to an already extensive range of places to purchase both international and locally made products

THE NORTH During China's long history there have been many capital cities. Some were no more than regional capitals for dynasties that did not control all of the country. Others, like Xi'an, were state capitals for the earlier dynasties. Beijing was the last of the imperial capitals and has remained the capital since 1949. What is left of its ancient glories derives mostly from the last two dynasties, the Ming and Qing, but it has been a capital on and off for some 3,000 years.

EARLY DAYS Before the unification of China in 221 BC, Beijing was Jicheng or Yanjing, the capital of the Kingdom of Yan located a few miles east of the current site. It remained a provincial town of some significance during the Tang, but became a secondary capital in AD 947 under the Liao rulers who controlled the north. The only reminders of this period are the Tianningsi pagoda near Guang'anmen and a stele in the Western Hills. During the 12th century, the Jin rulers named the city Zhongdu and made it their main capital. The most splendid relics from that period are the Marco Polo Bridge and a group of pagodas at Changping.

Peking Opera—colorful, noisy and very Chinese

In 1215, Zhongdu was razed by the Mongols. By 1260, when all of northern China had been conquered, the Mongol leader Kublai Khan, the grandson of Genghis Khan, moved his capital from Karakorum to Zhongdu, rebuilt the city, and called it Khanbaliq (Khan's Town), or Dadu (Great Capital) in Chinese. It was centred on today's Beihai Park—before that the city's focus was the area of Guang'anmen. The principal streets ran mostly north–south and the intersecting *hutongs* (from a Chinese word meaning "barbarian"), or lanes, ran east–west. Some of these lanes still exist.

MING AND QING The Mongol Empire began to crumble after Kublai's death in 1297 and was replaced in 1368 by the Ming dynasty. The first Ming emperor chose to move the capital to Nanjing ("Southern Capital"). One of his sons was made ruler of the principality of Yan, with Dadu, now renamed Beiping, as its capital. In 1403, when the prince became the third Ming emperor, Beiping was called Beijing ("Northern Capital") and became capital of China once again. It was rebuilt mostly on the foundations of Dadu, although it was larger, and the basic dimensions of today's city center date from this period, as do its principal monuments, the Forbidden City and the Temple of Heaven.

During the Qing dynasty, which lasted from 1644 to 1911, the city's layout was altered and additional palaces were built in and around the center. In the main, however, Beijing retained its Ming flavor.

BEIJING TODAY Modern Beijing is no longer a classically beautiful city—mindless destruction, planned or politically inspired, has seen to that. But its extraordinary history has bequeathed to it a certain grandeur, and there is no doubt that it impresses. The Forbidden City, one of the most magnificent architectural structures in the world, and the other snippets of the past that linger here and there, still make a visit essential.

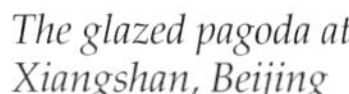

The glazed pagoda at Xiangshan, Beijing

52

Forbidden City

The description of the Forbidden City on pages 53–55 guides you on a walk, starting at the South (Meridian) Gate, along the main central axis to the exit at the Gate of Divine Prowess (Shenwumen). You will pass all the major ceremonial pavilions used by the emperors, the imperial bedrooms and, by taking a couple of diversions, the former residence of the imperial concubines, the imperial treasure exhibition rooms, the painting exhibition, and the imperial Clock Collection.

The Hall of Supreme Harmony in the Forbidden City

►►► Beihai (North Lake) Park (Beihai Gongyuan) 49D3

Open: daily 7–7. Admission: inexpensive
Xianmen Dajie. Buses 5, 13, 100

If you have time, visit this park and classical garden just northwest of the Forbidden City. The area, which was the heart of the Mongol capital, Dadu, retains from the Mongol period only the jade bowl in the **Tuancheng** (**Round City**, just inside the main entrance on Wenjin Jie). Several buildings in the Tuancheng, and the **Dragon Screen** on the north bank of the lake, date from the Ming. The **White Dagoba** was built in 1651 to honor a visit by the Dalai Lama. Most of the pavilions on the east side were the Qing dynasty pleasure gardens. On Qionghua Island is the **Fangshan Fandian**, which serves dishes favored by the Dowager Empress Cixi. The park is said to have been a favorite spot of Jiang Qing, wife of Mao and one of the "Gang of Four."

►►► Forbidden City (Zijincheng) 49D3

Open: 8:30–5 (last entry 3:30). Admission: moderate
Xichang'an Jie. Buses 1, 5, 54, 101

The center of Beijing is dominated by the imperial yellow roofs and vermilion walls of the Forbidden City, sometimes called the Imperial Museum or Palace Museum (Gugong). In Mongol times it was the "Great Within." Under the Ming and Qing, Beijing was divided into walled sections or cities—the Forbidden City was the innermost and the most important because it was the residence of the emperor, the focal point of the empire, and the middle of the "Middle Kingdom" (i.e., China). Entry was forbidden to all but those on imperial business until 1911, when the last emperor, Puyi, was overthrown. It occupies 775,000 square feet, there are (allegedly) 9,999 rooms, and it is surrounded by a moat and a 33-foot-high wall with a perimeter of 3.75 miles.

Entry to the Forbidden City is on foot only and is via the south or north gates; the south (Wumen or Meridian Gate) is preferable, because the audio-guided tour (extra charge) takes you that way.

BOXER MURDER

In Zhongshan Park is a memorial to Baron Clement August von Kettler, a 19th-century German minister to China. He was murdered by a mob on June 20, 1900, on his way to the Chinese Foreign Office to protest at the violence of the Boxers (an anti-Manchu and anti-foreign sect, see page 43).

The White Dagoba in Beihai Park

BIRTH OF AN EMPEROR
When Dowager Empress Cixi was a "virtuous imperial concubine," she became pregnant. Cixi was permitted to select six maids to help her at the birth as well as the two midwives and two doctors. As a reward for producing a son, Cixi was promoted and given 300 taels of silver and 70 bolts of top-quality fabric.

Flying cranes on a glazed panel in the Imperial Garden

HAIR-LOOM
Preserving the hair of ancestors has long been a sign of respect in China. In the Forbidden City there is a solid gold stupa built by Emperor Qianlong to store his mother's fallen hair.

Golden characters on a column in the Forbidden City

The main structure is made up of two groups of three palaces, mostly 18th century, situated one after the other on a central axis called the Meridian Line. Behind them, at the north end, is the Imperial Garden. Alongside the palaces to the northwest are the former apartments of the concubines; to the northeast are the palaces of Emperor Qianlong and Empress Cixi.

The first group of three palaces (the outer court) were for official functions; the second three (the inner court) were for private ones. Before you reach them, you pass the **Meridian Gate**, reserved for the emperor, and so-named because it was here that the new lunar calendars were distributed. Each morning the principal officials would wait atop the gate for the emperor's arrival, which was announced by the drums and bells in the pavilions on either side of the gate. Beyond is a magnificent courtyard across which runs the **Golden Water Stream** spanned by the five **Inner Golden Water Bridges**. The **Taihemen** (**Gate of Supreme Harmony**) follows, and to the right is a group of buildings devoted to Confucian studies and containing the imperial library. To the left is the **Hall of Martial Valor** where the Ming empresses received their female subjects. After Taihemen is a courtyard and the three main palaces of the "outer court."

The first of these is the **Taihedian** (**Hall of Supreme Harmony**), once the tallest building in Beijing, where the emperor ascended the throne, received high officials, and celebrated important festivals. The Taihedian is considered to have 55 rooms, a room being the space between four pillars. No commoner was permitted to build higher than this hall. Roofs were accorded rank, too, and naturally this was of the highest, built in the *wudian* (thatched hall) style with four fully hipped double roofs with curved, overhanging eaves. At each end of the ridge are giant dragon heads (the dragon was the imperial symbol); the mythological figures running down the side ridges ward off calamity, particularly fire. The marble ramp leading up to the terrace was for the emperor's sole use. On the terrace are a sundial and grain measure, testifying to the imperial concern for the harvest, four incense burners in the form of tortoises and cranes, symbols of longevity, and bronze cauldrons for water in the event of fire.

After Taihedian comes **Zhonghedian** (**Hall of Middle Harmony**), venue for rehearsals and receptions for officials from the Ministry of Rites. Then comes the **Baohedian** (**Hall of Preserving Harmony**), where the emperor gave banquets for princes from vassal states on Lunar New Year's Eve. Here during the Qing the emperor supervized the final stage of the civil service examinations (see panel, page 67).

As you leave the Baohedian, before you, protected by two gilded lions, is the **Qianqingmen** (**Gate of Heavenly Purity**), the gateway to the inner court or residential quarters, in many ways the true seat of power. Proceed through here and come to the **Qianqinggong** (**Palace of Heavenly Purity**), the emperor's bedroom and also the office of quotidian administration. Large banquets were given here on festival days. Behind it is the smaller **Jiataidian** (**Hall of Heavenly and Terrestrial Union**), which was used for lesser ceremonies. The empress raised silkworms here to demonstrate her industry, and the building was also used to house the imperial seals. You then come to the **Kunninggong** (**Palace of Terrestrial Tranquility**, symbol of the earth), the empress' bedroom and, under the Qing, the emperor's bridal chamber. Behind the palaces is the **Imperial Garden** and the north exit, the **Gate of Divine Prowess** (**Shenwumen**).

Two longer routes also bring you to the Shenwumen. Turn left before the Qianqingmen and then right, and walk along an alley to the left of the Qianqinggong, you reach a gateway on the left that leads to the concubines' quarters. Among them is the **Yangxindian** (**Hall of Mental Cultivation**), which became the residence of all the emperors from 1723. Within, to the right, is the **Dongnuange**. Here the boy emperors were told how to conduct affairs of state by the dowager empresses, who sat behind a screen.

Alternatively, turn right before Qianqingmen, pass under a portico, bear diagonally left to a doorway and emerge into a courtyard. On the left is a building housing the **Imperial Clock Collection**. This was where Emperor Qian lived long after his retirement. Return through the doorway, turn left and left again, and you come to the **Nine Dragon Screen**. Opposite is a doorway. Go as straight as you can, pass on the left the painting exhibition, and eventually reach the exhibition halls of imperial treasure. From here you can easily find your way to the exit gate.

THE COOK AND THE DRAGON

In 1803, an unemployed cook, Chen De, tried to assassinate Emperor Jiaqing. As the emperor entered the Forbidden City, a very drunk Chen De slipped through the gates and leaped at the emperor, dagger in hand. The emperor escaped by jumping off his sedan chair. At his trial Chen explained that a dream had shown him that he was destined to be emperor by using his skill in martial arts.

A Forbidden City dragon, symbol of the emperor, chasing the "flaming pearl"

GREAT WALL INFO

- In China, the Great Wall is also known as the "10,000 Li Wall," *li* being an ancient Chinese measure of distance, while the figure 10,000 simply expresses the magnitude of the project.
- It is a matter for debate whether the wall was ever truly successful as a line of defense. It is quite likely that its main functions were to provide a convenient conduit across difficult terrain and as a means of passing information.

Keeping the "barbarians" out of the Middle Kingdom: a restored section of the Great Wall at Badaling, north of Beijing

TOURS FROM BEIJING

Many hotels organize tours to the Great Wall. Otherwise tourist buses regularly depart for Badaling from Qianmen, Beijing Train Station, Dongdaqiao, and Beijing Zoo. For Mutianyu, buses leave from Dongzhimen Bus Station or by the Great Hall of the People. Tourist minibus No. 1 for the Ming Tombs leaves regularly from Qianmen.

▶▶▶ The Great Wall (Changcheng) *Off 48C5*

Open: daily 8–4. Admission: moderate

The Great Wall is a symbol of Chinese genius. Although the present wall dates mainly from the Ming dynasty, at least 20 states and dynasties were involved in its construction over a period of 2,000 years, following different routes or building extensions according to need. Stretching 3,700 miles, the wall was garrisoned by up to a million soldiers and was complemented by over 1,000 fortified passes and 10,000 beacon towers. Walls were first built as barriers between states during the Spring and Fall period—the oldest was built by the Kingdom of Qi in 500 BC and extended for 300 miles. When China was finally united in 221 BC under the Qin, the existing walls were linked together to protect the new China from invaders from the north. Different building materials were used according to the terrain—rammed earth or stone and brick (as in the Ming wall). Thousands of conscripts were involved in the project, many of whom died of exhaustion and malnutrition. The Han emperor extended the wall, but it was not until the Ming dynasty in the 14th century that an imperial regime was to have total control over its entire length again. The early Ming emperors almost entirely rebuilt the wall, extending it westward over 4,000 miles from Shanhaiguan to Jiayuguan. It was never to play such a significant role in Chinese history again—with the advent of the Manchus, who controlled the territory on both sides, the wall fell into disrepair.

Visitors head for the restored section at **Badaling**, 45 miles northwest of Beijing. You need a ticket to climb on to the wall; you will find the less crowded (although steeper) side to the left. Another access point is at **Mutianyu**, (50 miles northeast) which is less crowded but not as well preserved.

A cable car operates at Badaling to ease congestion. Other sections open to foreigners are at **Simatai** (60 miles northeast), **Huanghua** (40 miles north) and **Jinshanling** (56 miles northeast) and are much less commercialized.

▶ The Ming Tombs (Shisanling) *Off 48C5*

Open: daily 8:30–4:30. Admission: moderate

The tombs of the Ming emperors are about 15 miles from the Great Wall and 30 miles north of Beijing. Only 13 of the 16 emperors are buried here—the first Ming emperor is buried at Nanjing. The second emperor's whereabouts are unknown, and the seventh emperor is buried somewhere in Beijing. Three tombs are open: **Dingling**, tomb of the 13th emperor (died 1620), and the only excavated tomb; **Changling**, the largest, tomb of the third emperor (reigned 1403–1424); and **Zhaoling**.

The search for a burial site, based on the rules of geomancy (or *feng shui*, wind and water), was started by the third emperor in 1407. Rolling hills form a screen to the north, Dragon Hill and Tiger Hill stand to the south, and the Wenyu River provides the water element. The tomb area, once surrounded by a 25-mile wall, is approached via a sacred way. It begins at a commemorative gateway (perhaps the finest in China) erected in 1541, passes through a vermilion gatehouse and then between stone animal and human figures. After another gatehouse, the road diverges to the tombs, each marked with a yellow-roofed "visible tower." The vault at Dingling has vases, marble thrones, and doors, and reconstructed coffins. Some of the treasure is exhibited above ground. Changling, although unexcavated, is grander, and has an exhibition of some of the treasures found at Dingling in the magnificent main hall.

Changling ("Long-lasting Tomb"), one of 13 tombs of the Ming emperors occupying a burial site 34 miles north of Beijing

Guards in mock Ming period costume stand sentinel on the Great Wall at Badaling

CHINESE NURSERY RHYME

The Emperor of Qin
Shihuangdi
Built a wall
From the hills to the sea.
He built it wide,
He built it stout
To keep his subjects in
And the Tartars out,
The Emperor of Qin.

Since 1949 Beijing has experienced destruction, both deliberate (zealous town planning) and spontaneous (Cultural Revolution). But pockets of magnificence survive amid a network of anaemic boulevards.

URBAN CHINA
The old walled city was considered a perfect example of Chinese town-planning theory, which extends back to the Warring States Period (475–221 BC). It is rectangular, surrounded by a wall; its palace, close to government ministries, is at the center. It is also excellently situated according to geomantic criteria—open to the south and east, with water at the front and well screened by mountains to the north, to protect the city from evil.

The great tower gate at Dongbianmen, a reminder of the city wall's former grandeur

Imperial cities Beijing still exudes greatness, partly because the street plan devised under the Ming remains to remind the visitor of its "celestial geometry." But as recently as the 1950s Beijing would have looked like a very different place.

Under the Manchus (the Qing dynasty), Beijing was divided in four. The innermost city was the walled Forbidden City. Outside the Forbidden City lay the Imperial City, where government officials resided. This, too, lay behind a wall, the remains of which still stand (along the north side of Tiananmen Square) and behind which today's government officials continue their work. The whole area was surrounded by the 15th-century city wall, from which some of the towers survive. During the Qing this wall enclosed what foreigners called the Tartar City, the northern part of Beijing reserved for Manchus, particularly troops. The southernmost point of the Tartar City wall was the southern margin of Tiananmen Square, today marked by two ancient towers, which conversely were part of the northern wall of the Chinese City. The latter was the quarter where the Chinese were compelled to live; its walls extended originally south to beyond the Temple of Heaven. This was the business area of the city. The attempt to separate Manchu and Chinese failed—although the walls survived until the 1950s, their purpose had long been forgotten.

The streets outside the areas of the Imperial Court ran north–south and east–west, and were lined with low buildings in gray brick that surrounded family courtyards. At strategic points throughout the city were the imperial temples, visited by the emperor at certain propitious times of year (the Temple of Heaven was one, but there were also the Temples of the Earth, Sun, and Moon, which still survive).

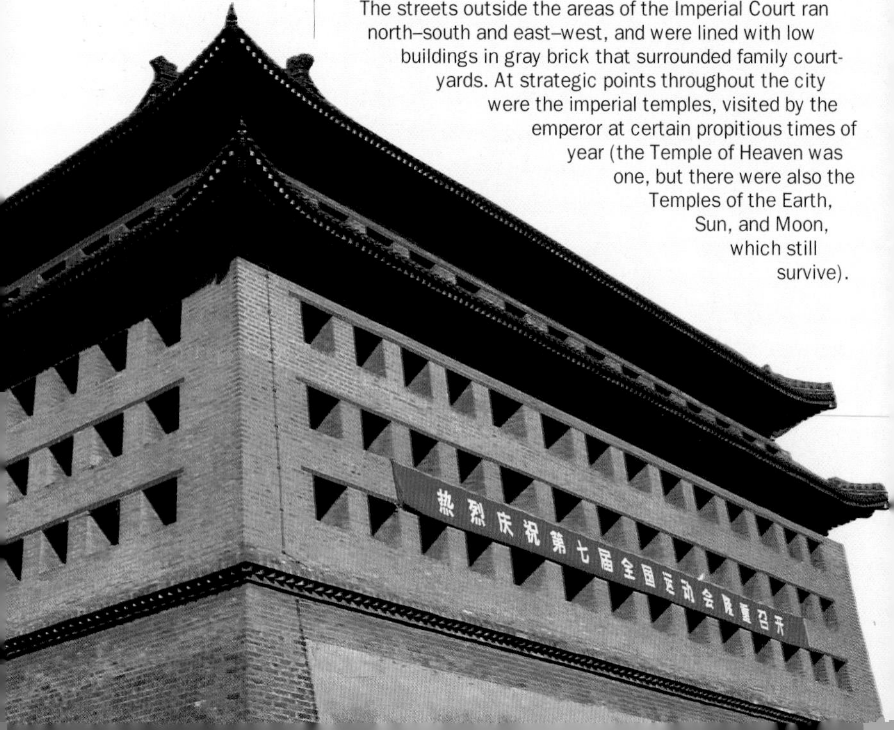

The city walls The city walls, of rammed earth with a carapace of gray brick, were thought to be the finest and grandest in the world. They were an astounding 25 miles in length and between 10 feet and 13 feet in height. There were 16 gateways, each surmounted by a tower, and the whole area was surrounded by a moat. In winter its frozen water was cut out and preserved underground to be used in the summer. The streets within the walls were a riot of color and movement—silken pennants hung outside stores and offices, and all manner of noises and smells mingled together in the bustle of activity. It is still possible to experience something of this atmosphere by walking through the old shopping district of Qianmen, to the south of Tiananmen Square, especially along Dazhalan.

PLEASURE DOMES

After the Japanese took control of Beijing in 1937, opium dens were openly allowed in parts of the city. Attendants brought smokers opium, a pipe, an oil lamp, and a pin. Addicts speared the opium on the pin and heated it before inhaling the fumes.

Beijing's Bell Tower, a little way north of the Forbidden City

The Legation Oddly enough, one of the areas of the city that retains the sort of charm that comes with continuity is not really Chinese at all, but European: many of the buildings of the old Legation area east of Tiananmen Square still stand and provide a sort of leafy graciousness absent elsewhere in the city. In the late 19th century the Legation area was less compact, but following the Boxer Rebellion of 1900 it was decided to group the legations together in a compound, with its own crenelated wall.

Beijing was also celebrated for its *hutongs*, the network of alleys and traditional courtyards, most of which have now disappeared. However, the areas between Wangfujing and the east wall of the Forbidden City, or the areas between Wangfujing and Dongdan, still give much of the flavor of old Beijing.

HIGH FLYERS

In the past kite-flying was a favorite pastime frequently to be seen all over the city and particularly at New Year, when market stalls were piled high with kites made of bamboo and paper in a variety of shapes, including birds, goldfish, and mythical characters. Nowadays kites are still flown in Tiananmen Square—an uplifting sight.

Fragrant Hills
North Palace Gate
YIHEYU
West Palace Gate
Boathouse
Back Lake
Suzhou Creek
Lake-Boundary Bridge
Arch Bridge
Pine Grove
Porcelain Pagoda
Site of Sumeru Temple
Boat House
Longevity Hill
Cloud-Entertaining Eaves
Temple of Gathering Clouds
Hall of Buddhist Tenants
Heart-Purifying Pavilion
Sea of Wisdom Temple
Pagoda of Buddhist Fragrance
Revolving Scripture Repository
Strolling in Scenery
Bronze Pavilion
Cloud Dispelling Hall
Pavilion for Listening to Orioles
Rowboat Dock
Marble Boat
Long Corridor
Ferry Dock
Pavilion of Fish and Water Plants
Jade Palace under Clouds
Ferry
Hall of Infinite Spain
South Lake Isle
Temple of the Dragon Kings
Kunming Lake
Hall of Distant View
SEVENTEEN-ARCH BRIDGE
Pavilion of Broad View
Bronze Ox
South Lake

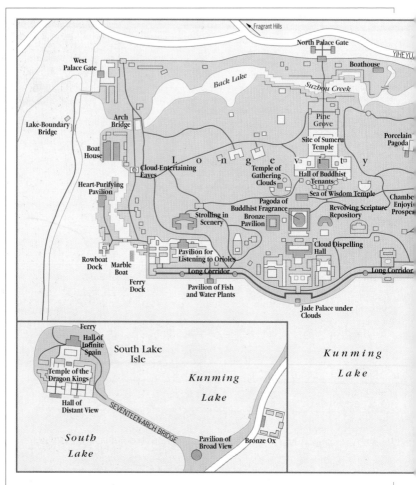

The Summer Palace

The walk through the Summer Palace, described in detail on pages 61–63, is essentially scenic. Enter through the East Palace Gate, then bear right, and carry straight on to pass near the main halls that were used by the last emperors. Walk along the Long Corridor, the covered walkway that runs beside Kunming Lake, visiting more of the pavilions to the right. A detour at the beginning will take you to the Garden of Harmonious Interest with its own miniature lake. You can return to the entrance by taking a ferry from close to the Marble Boat.

Taking a rest in the Long Corridor

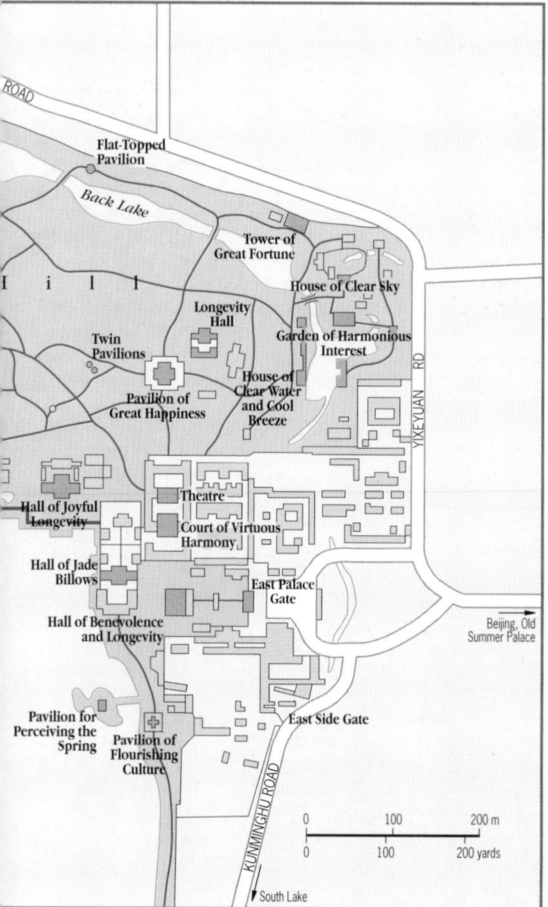

These women in Qing costume are attendants at the theater museum in the Summer Palace

▶▶▶ Summer Palace (Yiheyuan) *48A5*

Open: daily 9–7. Admission: moderate

The buildings of the Summer Palace, known as Yiheyuan, date back only to the turn of the 20th century. The site, however, goes back to the 12th century when the first Jin ruler built his Gold Mountain Traveling Palace on what is now Longevity Hill. The water from the Jade Spring was diverted to form the Gold Sea, an early Kunming Lake. During the Yuan dynasty the Gold Mountain was renamed Jug Mountain, and the lake was enlarged. Another palace was built here under the Ming, but the area was transformed during the reign of the Qianlong Emperor. Longevity Hill was named in honor of the 60th birthday of Qianlong's mother, and the Kunming Lake in honor of a lake near Xi'an that the Han emperors used for naval maneuvers.

In 1764, the area became the Park of Pure Ripples (Qingyiyuan) and was part of a grand plan to build a set of pleasure grounds in the lee of the Western Hills. Aside from Qingyiyuan there was to be Jingmingyuan at Yuquanshan, Jingyiyuan at Xiangshan, Changchunyuan,

BENEFICENT BOVINE
At the mainland end of the Seventeen-Arch Bridge in the Summer Palace is the Bronze Ox, which has been guarding Kunming Lake for over 200 years. Its presence is based on the legend that said that the Great Yu tamed lakes and rivers by throwing oxen made of iron into the water.

EXCLUSIVE PEKING
Non cuivis Homini Contingit adire Corinthium. It is the lot of few to go to Pekin.—John Barrow, Lord Macartney's Private Secretary. *Travels in China*, 1801

THE GARDEN OF PURE BRIGHTNESS
Although all that is left of the Yuanmingyuan are romantic ruins, it once included a labyrinth, an aviary, a gazebo, palaces with fountains, and representations of the countryside of Turkestan with moving scenery. Engravings of the pleasure-dome by the Jesuits are to be found in the British Museum, London, and the Bibliothèque Nationale, Paris.

A remnant of the south facade of the waterworks at Yuanmingyuan, the Old Summer Palace

and Yuanmingyuan. The last mentioned, the Park of Perfection and Brightness, was the original Qing dynasty Summer Palace, destroyed in 1860 by the British and French; by 1895 a replacement was constructed in the Park of Pure Ripples, but when the Anglo-French force reinvaded Beijing in 1900, the new Summer Palace was destroyed. Reconstruction began in 1902, and the result is what we see today. The Summer Palace became a classical Chinese garden, the south face of Longevity Hill laid out in vague imitation of Hangzhou's West Lake, the north face following the architectural style of Suzhou. After 1908, the palace was no longer used by the imperial family, and in 1924, it became a public park.

The main entrance is at **Donggongmen** (**East Palace Gate**), which leads to the **Renshoudian** (**Hall of Benevolence and Longevity**, derived from an old saying "Benevolent people live long lives"), where affairs of state were conducted by Cixi. The gray-roofed buildings between the gate and the hall were the waiting rooms for officials on duty. The bronze *qilin* (a legendary beast with dragon's head, lion's tail, deer's antlers, ox's hooves, and fish-scaled body) in front of the hall was at the original Summer Palace.

To the right of the Renshoudian is the **Deheyuan** (**Court of Virtuous Harmony**) with its theater, the largest in China, where Cixi watched performances of Peking Opera. Trapdoors in the ceilings and floors of its three stories were designed for the entrances and exits of supernatural characters. Beyond the Renshoudian, is the former residential area; here the first and principal building is the **Leshoutang** (**Hall of Joyful Longevity**), the residence of the Dowager Empress between May and November. South of the Leshoutang, at the waterfront and to the rear of the Renshoudian, is the **Yulantang** (**Hall of Jade Billows**), named after a poem by Lu Ji, a third-century poet), the former residence of the Guangxu Emperor. The interiors of the Leshoutang and Yulantang have been preserved intact. The side halls of the Yulantang were blocked off in 1898 on the instructions of Cixi, thereby confining the Guangxu Emperor to house arrest for his involvement in the 1898 "Hundred Days of Reform" movement.

Farther west along Kunming Lake is the famous **Long Corridor** (**Changlang**), a covered walkway 800 yards long, painted with views of the famous West Lake in Hangzhou and scenes from Chinese legend, history or literature. It breaks into two halves at the **Paiyundian** (**Cloud Dispelling Hall**, from a poem by

An imperial folly: the Marble Boat on Kunming Lake

the 3rd-century poet Guo Pu), where Cixi celebrated her birthdays. Built on the site of an earlier Ming temple, the tower above is called the **Foxiangge** (**Pagoda of Buddhist Fragrance**). Behind the pagoda is the **Zhihuihai** (**Sea of Wisdom Temple**), covered in religious statues, many disfigured by troops in 1860. To the east of the pagoda is the **Zhuanluncang** (**Revolving Scripture Repository**), containing a tablet inscribed with an essay on Kunming Lake in the hand of the Qianlong Emperor.

The Long Corridor continues and passes the **Pavilion for Listening to Orioles** (**Tingliguan**) on the right, the site of a restaurant and store. The corridor comes to an end at the corner of the lake. In front of you to the right is the **Marble Boat**, an ironic reminder that the funds appropriated by the Dowager Empress to reconstruct the Summer Palace had been earmarked for the Chinese navy. During the summer, pleasure cruises run from here back to the entrance. You can rent rowboats from the nearby jetty.

The way to the **West Palace Gate** lies beyond the Marble Boat. An old Japanese-built steamboat—part of the old Chinese navy—lies in dry dock near the old boathouses. Beyond is a beautiful arched bridge in the south China style.

The north and northeast areas of the palace gardens are in quiet contrast to the showy areas at the lakeside. In the northeast corner is the **Xiequyuan** (**Garden of Harmonious Interest**), a series of small pavilions around a landscaped miniature lake. Opposite its entrance is a staircase up the hill to **Jinfuge** (**Tower of Great Fortune**), which offers a fine view to South Lake Isle and the magnificent Seventeen-Arch Bridge. The area of the **North Palace Gate** was badly affected by the French and British invasion. Following the restoration work in 1998, the teahouses and stores at Suzhou Creek are now open, revitalizing a part of the Summer Palace that had fallen into decay and which was hardly ever visited. In addition, there is a **Cultural Relics' Hall**, housing the palace's collection of Qing dynasty art.

Also in the northwest suburbs (Bus 375) are the remains of the **Old Summer Palace▶**, **Yuanmingyuan**, razed by the British and French in 1860. This is mostly still in ruins, but a brick maze with a central pavilion has been restored.

LAKE OF POETICAL INSPIRATION

Kunming Lake in the Summer Palace is as famous as the West Lake in Hangzhou. The Ming poet Wen Zheng wrote: "The sun sets on blue waters of the spring lake. Sky-high pavilions are reflected down below. The *tenli* green hills are like a scroll painting. Two white birds fly high in a scene of watery land."

IMPERIAL STAFF

The Dowager Empress liked to travel with a retinue of at least 1,000. Her arrival at the rebuilt Summer Palace in 1905 was met by 458 eunuchs, and her two main meals consisted of 100 dishes.

MAO'S MEMORIAL HALL
Mao's resting place was built by 70,000 volunteers in ten months between October 1976 and August 1977. It is screened by pine trees from Yenan, recalling the 13 years Mao spent there. Within is an air-conditioned hush, a white statue of a seated Mao gazing prophetically in front of a giant landscape tapestry based on a design by the contemporary painter Huang Yongyu. Mao himself lies in state in a crystal coffin.

HEROIC WORK
The granite obelisk known as the Monument to the People's Heroes is inscribed with the calligraphy of Chairman Mao. It reads "The people's heroes are invincible."

▶▶▶ Temple of Heaven (Tiantan) Park *49D1*

Open: daily 6:30–6. Admission: inexpensive

Built in 1420, Tiantan became part of the city during the Qing, when the Manchus extended the city walls. It is China's most famous temple and stands within a 667-acre park. Entrance was originally through the west gate, but is now via the north or south gates.

The whole area is enclosed by a wall, the northern portion of which is round (heaven) and the southern half square (earth). The principal buildings are at either end of the Cinnabar Stairway Bridge. **Qiniandian** (**Hall of Prayer for Good Harvests**) is to the north and is an 1890 replica of the building destroyed by lightning the preceding year.

It was here that the emperor came to pray for a good harvest during the first lunar month each year. The day before the main ceremony was devoted to minor rituals, after which the emperor fasted in the Hall of Abstinence, west of the causeway. The sacrifice to heaven was made in the Qiniandian. Constructed without nails, this has wooden mortise and tenon joints and wooden brackets on supporting pillars. The 28 pillars (representing the constellations) are made of *nanmu* hardwood. The four large ones represent the seasons, the 12 inner pillars are the months of the lunar calendar and the outer 12 are the two-hour periods into which the day was traditionally divided. Together they become the 24 solar periods of the year.

At the end of the causeway is the **Echo Wall**, inside which is the **Huangqiongyu** (**Imperial Vault of Heaven**). This was the storehouse for the spirit tablet of the Supreme Ruler of Heaven, that, during the ceremony of the winter solstice, was moved to the vast round Altar of Heaven to the south.

▶▶▶ Tiananmen (Gate of Heavenly Peace) Square (Guangchang) *49D2*

Today's vast, grandiose space, scene of tragic student demonstrations in 1989, bears little resemblance to its imperial ancestor. During the Ming and Qing, it was narrower, and in addition to the Tiananmen Gate to the

Tiananmen Square, backed by the Gate of Heavenly Peace

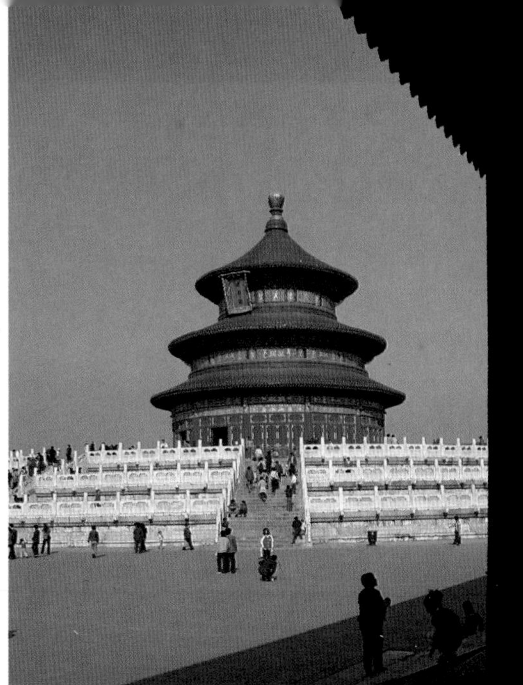

ECHO CHAMBER
The Temple of Heaven is renowned for its acoustic qualities. Most famous is the Echo Wall, where your whispered words are amplified to a listener opposite. In the same compound is the Imperial Vault of Heaven, before which are several flagstones—depending upon where you stand on them, the sound made by clapping your hands will echo once, twice, or three times. If you speak at the center of the Imperial Altar, your voice will echo back louder.

The Hall of Prayer for Good Harvests, Temple of Heaven

A watchful "lion" atop one of the ceremonial columns (huabiao) *in front of the Tiananmen Gate*

Imperial City (which still stands), there were two more gates on today's Chang'an Avenue and another, to the south, where the Qianmen now stands. It was surrounded by a vermilion wall beside which ran a covered corridor for use by officials. To the east and west were the imperial ministries. After 1949 most of this was torn down and replaced with what you see today. Each sunrise the national flag is hoisted with military precision. The square is now open to the public.

The **Tiananmen Gate** has survived since 1651. The central bridge over the Outer Golden Water Stream forms part of the Imperial Way, used on ceremonial occasions and over which only the emperor could pass. Two columns are surmounted by dishes containing a stone lion-like creature. The dishes were supposed to catch the "jade dew" imbibed by the emperor to ensure longevity; the lions were to watch over him if he were away from the palace.

Along the spine of the square, north to south, are the **Monument to the People's Heroes** (1958), **Chairman Mao's Memorial Hall**, where Mao lies in state (*Open* daily 8:30–11, 1–3:30. *Admission free*), the **Arrow Tower**, and **Qianmen**. On the west side is the **Great Hall of the People**—opposite is the revamped **Museum of the Chinese Revolution** and the **Museum of Chinese History** (*Open* Tue–Sun 8:30–3:30. *Admission: inexpensive*), one of the most important in China.

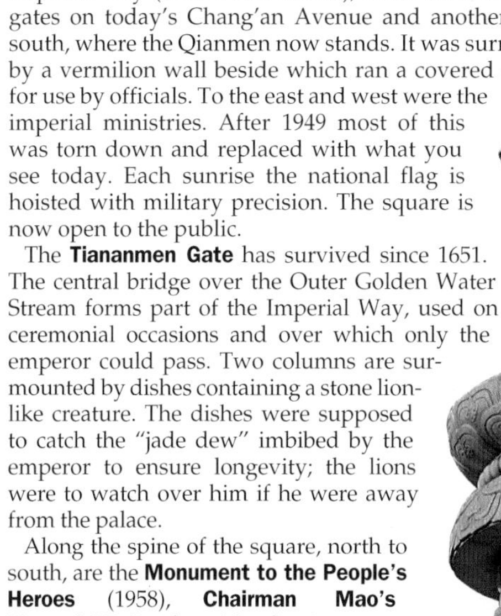

EAST IS BEST
Before the break with the U.S.S.R. in 1960, Mao was confident of a shared, bright future. In Moscow in 1957 he said: "I believe it is characteristic of the situation today that the East Wind is prevailing over the West Wind. That is to say, the forces of socialism have become overwhelmingly superior to the forces of imperialism."

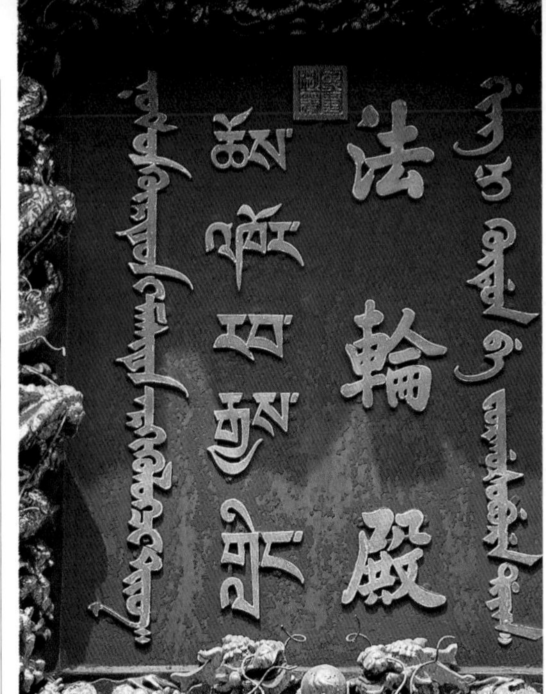

Polyglot inscriptions in Mongolian, Manchurian, Tibetan, and Chinese welcome visitors to the Lama Temple

Other sights
Lama Temple (**Yonghegong**)►► (Andingmen Dong Lu. *Open* Tue–Sun 9–4. *Admission: inexpensive*). Built in 1694 by the Kangxi Emperor as a residence for his son, Yinzhen, Yonghegong was partly turned over to the Lamaists for scripture recitation when Yinzhen became emperor. It is an extravagant building of some beauty, with remarkable examples of joinery and craftsmanship, and consists of a series of courtyards and pavilions, many with statues of the various incarnations of the Buddha. In the center of the **Hall of Infinite Happiness** (**Wanfuge**), at the rear, stands the grandest statue, an 85-foot-tall Tathagagata (Maitreya) Buddha made from a single sandalwood trunk. Tibet's China-appointed Panchen Lama was sworn in here in 1995.

An equinoctial sphere, one of the beautiful scientific instruments to be seen at the Ancient Observatory

The Western Hills (**Xi Shan**)►► This is an area of recreation and worship, excellent both for sightseeing and strolling (*Temples open* daily 8:30–5). Here you may visit the **Temple of the Reclining Buddha** (**Wofosi**), where a bronze Buddha instructs his disciples from his deathbed. Weighing 275 tons, the statue dates from the Yuan dynasty. The **Temple of Azure Clouds** (**Biyunsi**) dates back 600 years. In the **Hall of Arhats** are 500 statues of Buddha's disciples, and at the rear is the **Sun Yatsen Memorial Hall**, where Sun Yatsen, the revolutionary and former Provisional President, lay in state after his death in 1925 (see page 229).

Part of the area is known as the **Fragrant Hills Park** (**Xiangshan Gongyuan**), formerly the emperor's pleasure park. Now it is a recreation area with a cable car.

Churches► The Jesuits, who became active in China during the Ming dynasty, bequeathed several churches. The grandest (Nantang) is found at 181 Qianmen Xidajie.

A building was erected on the site in the 16th century, but the current version is from 1904. Another church is at 74 Wangfujing. The North Cathedral is on Xishiku.

The Ancient Observatory (Guanxiangtai)▶ (*Open* Wed–Sun 9–11, 1–4. *Admission: inexpensive*). Not far from the Friendship Store, mounted on a section of old wall just off Jianguomenwai Dajie, are the remnants of an observatory which can be traced back to the Yuan dynasty. It was built between 1437 and 1446 to provide astrological predictions. Within is a display of navigational equipment, reproductions of ancient Chinese maps, and other items relating to the stars. Outside, on the parapet, are instruments designed by the Jesuits, who in 1601 gained permission to work with Chinese scientists eager to learn about European firearms. The emperor, impressed by the Jesuits' scientific knowledge, later appointed them court astronomers in place of his Muslim advisers. The instruments are not all original but are of considerable beauty. There is also a small museum.

Beijing Zoo▶ (Xizhimenwei Dajie. *Open* daily 8:30–4. *Admission: moderate*). The zoo itself is not representative of enlightened animal management, but the animals look healthy, and there are several examples of China's rarities, notably pandas (giant and red), and Golden Monkeys.

Underground City▶ A network of tunnels honeycombs Beijing's subterranean depths, a result of the fear in the 1960s of a Soviet attack. Part of the system now includes stores and even a hotel, but the main interest lies in the entrances, several of which are concealed beneath sliding floors in busy stores above ground.

Other temples▶ The ruins of the former imperial temples can still be seen in Beijing—in the north is **Ditan** (**Temple of the Earth**); to the south is **Taoranting** (**Happy Pavilion Park**); to the east is **Ritan** (**Temple of the Sun**); and to the west is **Yuetan** (**Temple of the Moon**). Although these resemble parks more than temples, hints of their past abound, and they are interesting places to observe Chinese

EXAMINATION HALL
Opposite the Ming observatory, to the north, were the former imperial examination halls—8,500 brick cells where, every three years, candidates were locked in for three days and two nights to take the first stage of the civil service examinations that led to high office. In operation for over 2,000 years, these examinations ceased in 1900, and the halls were demolished in 1913.

Beitang, the North Cathedral, with its defiantly European facade, stands stiff behind curving Chinese roof profiles

Listening in at the Echo Wall, Temple of Heaven

HANDFULS OF DUST
One of the quirks of Beijing weather in the spring is the dust that arrives in clouds from the Gobi Desert.

life, especially in the early morning. The **Confucian Temple (Kongmiao)** (*Open* daily 8:30–5. *Admission: inexpensive*) is on Guozijian Jie, an interesting street spanned by commemorative arches. The **Baiyun Temple (White Cloud Temple)** (*Open* daily 8:30–4:30) on Binhe Lu near the southwest corner of the old city was once the center of Taoism, while the **Niujie Mosque** is in the Muslim area in the southwest of Beijing. The **Five Pagoda Temple (Wutasi)** is northwest of the zoo, while the **Great Bell Temple (Dazhongsi)** on Beisanhuan Xi Road has a 46.5-ton bell, cast in 1406.

About 30 miles west of Beijing (Bus 336) is the ancient **Tanzhi Buddhist Temple▶▶** (*Admission: inexpensive*), the largest in the area. It dates back to the 3rd century AD and contains decorative features not found elsewhere in Beijing.

Marco Polo Bridge (Lugouqiao)▶ This bridge 10 miles southwest of Beijing (Bus 339), mentioned by the Italian traveler, dates back to the late 12th century, although most of the present edifice is from the 17th century.

Qing Tombs▶ The tombs of the Qing imperial family are divided into two groups—Western Qing (Xiling) and Eastern Qing (Dongling). The former are 70 miles southwest of Beijing and include the excavated tomb of Emperor Guangxu at Chongling, the last to be built (between 1905 and 1915). The latter are 80 miles east of Beijing and are more impressive, having a "spirit way," or avenue lined with bridges and statues to guard the tomb. The tombs of Emperor Qianlong and Dowager Empress Cixi are open.

Other Parks▶ Beijing boasts a number of parks. The **Longtan Park (Longtanyuan)** is east of the Temple of Heaven; the **Purple Bamboo Park (Zizhuyuan)** is west of the zoo; and the **Yuyuantan Park** is in the west of the city. The area around the moat of the Forbidden City is also popular.

Other Museums and Galleries▶ The **Song Qingling Museum (Song Qingling Guju)** is the former residence of the wife of Sun Yatsen, the founder of the Republic of China. The **China Art Gallery (Zhongguo Meishuguan)** is of interest, particularly when there are temporary exhibitions. The **Lu Xun Museum (Lu Xun Bowuguan)** is dedicated to the career of the revolutionary writer.

The open space of Longtan Park provides a peaceful setting for early morning meditation

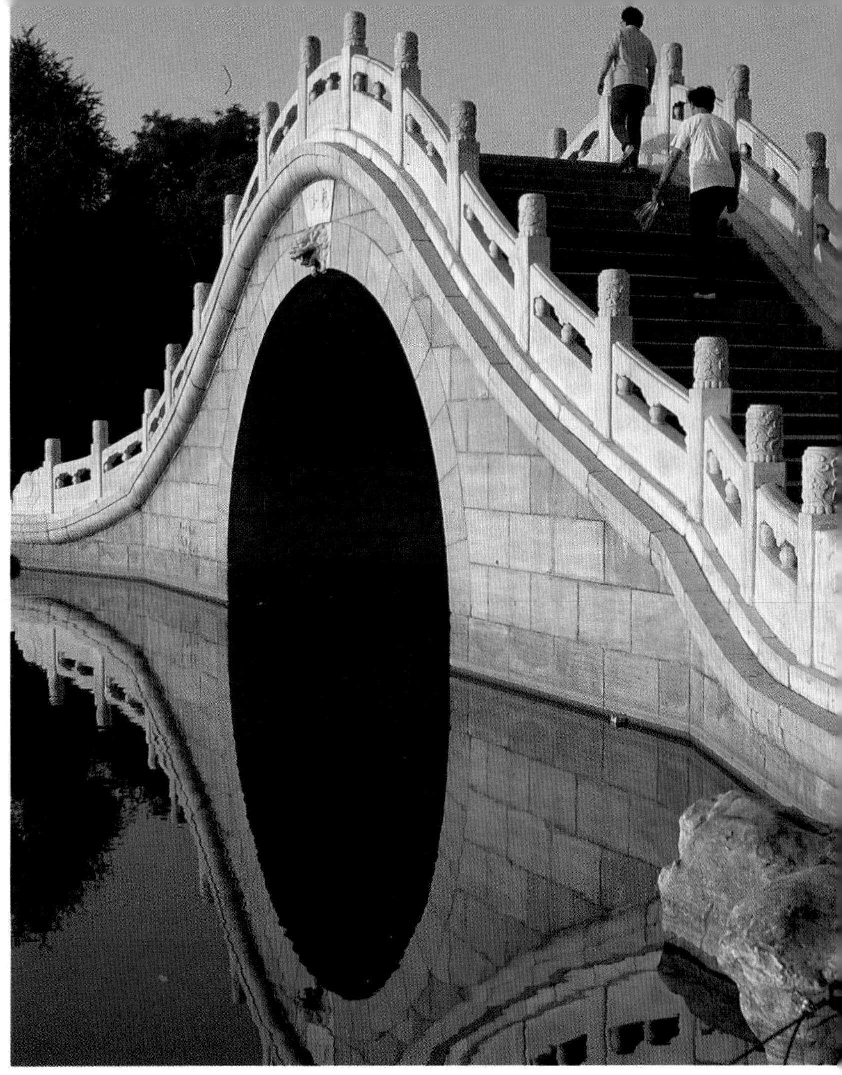

A perfectly formed marble bridge in Longtan Park, east of the Temple of Heaven

Bike ride

From Tiananmen Square

See *highlighted route*, page 49.
Bicycles can be rented from most hotels very inexpensively. Start near Tiananmen Square and go up Beiheyan Street, east of the Forbidden City. At a main junction (Wusi Street), turn left and then right, by Jingshan Park. Take the road as it goes left, then turn right along Di'anmennei, cross an intersection and continue to the old Drum Tower. Bear right, then left and then take the second lane on the left to bring you to Jiugulou, near the Bamboo Garden Hotel (Zhuyuan Binguan), former home of a Qing official. Turn south down Jiugulou, then right, then left along narrow streets to cross Qianhai Lake. Turn left, to Di'anmen Xi Street; turn right and then left and follow streets south beside Beihai Lake and Nanhai Lake to return to Tiananmen Square.

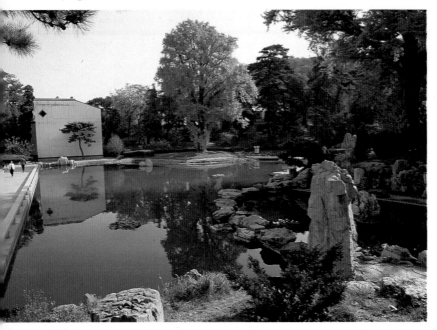

The garden of the Fragrant Hills Hotel outside Beijing, designed by Chinese-American architect I. M. Pei

The standard of accommodations is now high in Beijing—almost too high, because there is a lack of midrange or budget hotels. However, improvements have been remarkable—there are some 200 hotels receiving foreigners, of which 13 are five-star standard. The main criticism, aside from expense, is their perceived lack of character.

A central location in some respects is less important than in other major cities: many of the principal sights are outside the city altogether, and the worsening traffic can make a journey across Beijing frustratingly long. However, nobody would quibble with a hotel within easy walking distance of Tiananmen Square. There are two. The Beijing Hotel has three sections—the original Wagons-Lits hotel, built in 1901, another section added in the 1950s, and a third dating from the 1970s. A fourth wing is under construction. Although not truly luxurious, it exudes a sort of grandness and is comfortable, well equipped, and has some excellent, if expensive, restaurants. Some of the rooms have views across the roofs of the Forbidden City. Adjoining the Beijing Hotel is the Grand Hotel Beijing, of a higher grade, and a bar overlooking the Forbidden City.

There are several other luxury hotels, some grouped in the northeast corner. The Great Wall Sheraton, with its striking exterior, is efficient, expensive, comfortable, and rather soulless. Nearby are the Kunlun (the Sheraton's Chinese cousin), the Kempinski, and the Hilton. In the same area is the less glamorous Zhaolong, representing value for money. The Jianguo has a reasonably central location near the Friendship Store and, although it was the first foreign-designed hotel to appear in Beijing (in 1982), it remains one of the best. Next door is the Jinglun (Beijing-Toronto), of equal standard and with an excellent restaurant. The Guoji (International) has a central location

The five-star Guoji (International), typical of Beijing's modern hotels

Modern luxury—Jinglun (Beijing-Toronto) Hotel…

on Jianguomennei Dajie but is huge and impersonal. Nearby are the five-star Otani and the four-star Gloria Plaza. The Shangri-La, in the northwest corner of the city, has a good reputation. Besides the Beijing Hotel and Grand Hotel Beijing, the hotels with the best central locations are the Holiday Inn on Wangfujing and the nearby luxury Palace. Other central quality hotels are the Taiwan, the Peace, the Novotel, and the China World.

The Lido Holiday Inn is not in the luxury bracket but is comfortable enough and is well located for the airport, even if not so convenient for downtown. There is a Mövenpick hotel at the airport itself.

There are a number of less expensive hotels built in the 1950s, before the open-door policy. The Friendship Hotel, a sprawling building on the road to the Summer Palace, was originally constructed for Russian experts in the 1950s. Set in attractive gardens, it now houses many of the new wave of "foreign experts," as well as visitors, and is reasonably comfortable. The Qianmen (Front Gate) is another modernized hotel dating from the Russian period and has a good location on Yong'an Lu in a colorful part of downtown.

Outside the city there is the luxurious Fragrant Hills Hotel (Xiangshan Hotel) in the park of the same name—it is also convenient for the Summer Palace and the Great Wall, though somewhat less so for Beijing city.

At the budget end of the market there are a few reasonable propositions, one of which is the Haoyuan, 9A Tiantan Donglu, Chongwen (tel: 6701 4499; fax: 6701 2404). There are also some hotels with triple or dormitory-style rooms, such as the Jianghua, Nansanhuan Zhonglu (tel: 6722 2211). These hotels are inexpensive but the barrackslike rooms, although likely to be clean, provide no privacy. However, some of these rooms are being remodeled into double rooms.

There is a hotel desk at Beijing Airport beyond customs.

HOUSING SHORTAGE
When Beijing first opened to foreigners, there was a severe shortage of accommodations. As tourism expanded in the early 1980s, things got out of hand. Groups of tourists landed at Beijing airport only to be placed on the next flight out because there was nowhere to accommodate them. Or they arrived to be told that they were staying in Tianjin (several hours away) and would be driven to Beijing each day for sightseeing.

临时住宿登记表
REGISTRATION FORM OF TEMPORARY RESIDENCE

姓 Surname	名 Name
	性别 Sex / 出生年月 Date of birth
国籍 Nationality	证件号码 Document's No.
证件种类 Document's type	签证有效期 Visa's expiration
签证种类 Visa's type	
永久地址 Permanent address	何日去何处 Date of departure where to
何日何处抵 Date of arrival where from	房号 Room No.
停留事由 Purpose of stay	
接待单位 Received By	

请用正楷填写 Please Fill in block letters.

…traditional style—the Bamboo Garden

East meets West: Coca-Cola—made in China

"Do-it-yourself" dining: one of the Mongols' few tangible legacies, the Firepot

Food and drink

In Beijing it is now possible to sample most styles of Chinese and foreign cooking but it remains difficult to categorize the average restaurant for quality—most reliable restaurants are still to be found in the main hotels, although Beijing Tourism Administration is placing plaques on the doors of those restaurants it recommends. On the whole, it is fairly difficult to eat badly, even in some of the shabbier establishments. Many ordinary restaurants have two floors—a utilitarian first floor and an upper floor where the food usually will be more sophisticated, better presented, and more expensive. If you want a full meal, then upstairs is a better proposition; if a snack, then confine yourself to the first floor. The streets, meanwhile, are still filled with stalls selling tasty, inexpensive food.

Although Beijing cuisine is in the robust and rustic northern tradition, it has been subject to many influences throughout its long history and also has its own specialties, the most famous of which is "Peking Duck." Air is blown between the duck's skin and flesh, and then boiling water. The skin is covered in a malty solution after which the duck is hung and then roasted in a fruitwood oven. It is eaten wrapped in a pancake, with scallions and a bean sauce (Tianjiang). There are a number of restaurants specializing in this dish, notably the Qianmen and Hepingmen branches of the Quanjude Kaoyadian, and also the Jiuhuashan on Zhengguang Lu.

Another specialty of Beijing (in winter) is the Mongolian Firepot. Patrons cook thinly sliced mutton with vegetables and other ingredients at the table in a pot with a vertical funnel containing burning charcoal, which keeps the cooking liquid constantly boiling. The Hongbinlou and the Nengrenju restaurants are famous for this dish.

Another famous Chinese restaurant is Fangshan. It was established in 1925 by a former imperial cook on the site of an imperial dining room that once stood on the island

"Peking Duck," complete with pancakes, scallions, and Tianjiang sauce

in the lake at Beihai Park. It specializes in imperial-style banquets or Manchu-Han feasts, which include "all known or available delicacies from land and sea." For example, the Eight Marine Delicacies include shark's fin and sea cucumber, the Eight Mountain Delicacies camel's hump and deer tendons. Advance bookings are essential.

Other recommended restaurants are the Fengzeyuan at 38 Zhushikou Xidajie, famous for seafood and soups and good for Beijing-style cooking; and the Ren Ren at 18 Qianmen Dongdajie specializing in *dim sum*. The Sichuan at 51 Rongxian Hutong, popular among high-level government officials, is housed in the palatial former mansion of a Qing prince and serves the excellent spicy food of Sichuan province.

Also recommended are the Cuihualou (Shandong), the Xiangshu (chicken specialties), the Laozhengxing (Beijing and Shanghai style), the Xiheyaju Canting (Beijing style), and the Guangdong (Cantonese). The Kaorouji, which is just north of Beihai Park on the east bank of Qian Lake, specializes in Mongolian barbecued food. The Weiguncun Uighur Village, Baishiqiao Lu specializes in noodles and grilled mutton. The Bamboo Garden Hotel on Xiaoshiqiao Jiugulou Lu serves good Chinese food in a classical garden.

The standard of the best Chinese restaurants in the hotels is very high, with good service and presentation and prices to match. European and American food is of varying standard and often disappointing but all types are represented, mostly in the hotels. Otherwise most hotels have coffee shops, some of which stay open until 11PM or later. There are many branches of McDonald's, including one on Wangfujing, a K.F.C. on Tiananmen Square, and a Pizza Hut on Dongzhimenwai Dajie.

PROVERB

An enigmatic saying in China goes: "If you rattle your chopsticks against the bowl, you and your descendants will always be poor."

Left: chopsticks, both reusable and disposable, are nearly always supplied in hygienic sleeves

FEAST FOOD

Imperial hospitality, like many things in old China, was rigorously graded. Dukes were to be treated to three morning meals and three evening banquets; counts to two in the morning and two in the evening; barons to one in the morning and one in the evening. Morning banquets were usually simply a matter of protocol; but in the evening guests were expected to "remove their shoes and drink until wine-rapt."

WATCH OUT
It is worth keeping an eye out for interesting fob watches in antiques shops. Many were left by foreign residents living in China before 1949, and although a good one will not be inexpensive, the price may compare favorably with the cost at home.

Shopping

Not long ago the only place where you could buy high-quality goods was the Friendship Store on Jianguomenwai Dajie. It remains one of the best stores in China, with three floors of beautiful merchandise. Within are two excellent food areas, one a supermarket for daily needs, the other selling foreign and domestic-made foods and drinks.

There has been a shopping revolution of late. The once-gloomy traditional shopping streets have been transformed into emporiums filled with consumer goods and often staffed by people eager to sell them. Try the local stores along Wangfujing that sell well-designed clothes in cotton and silk at reasonable prices, jewelry, toys, antiques, and crafts. The Foreign Languages Bookstore is at No. 235, and No. 275 is the excellent Beijing Department

Guanyuan bird market in northwest Beijing

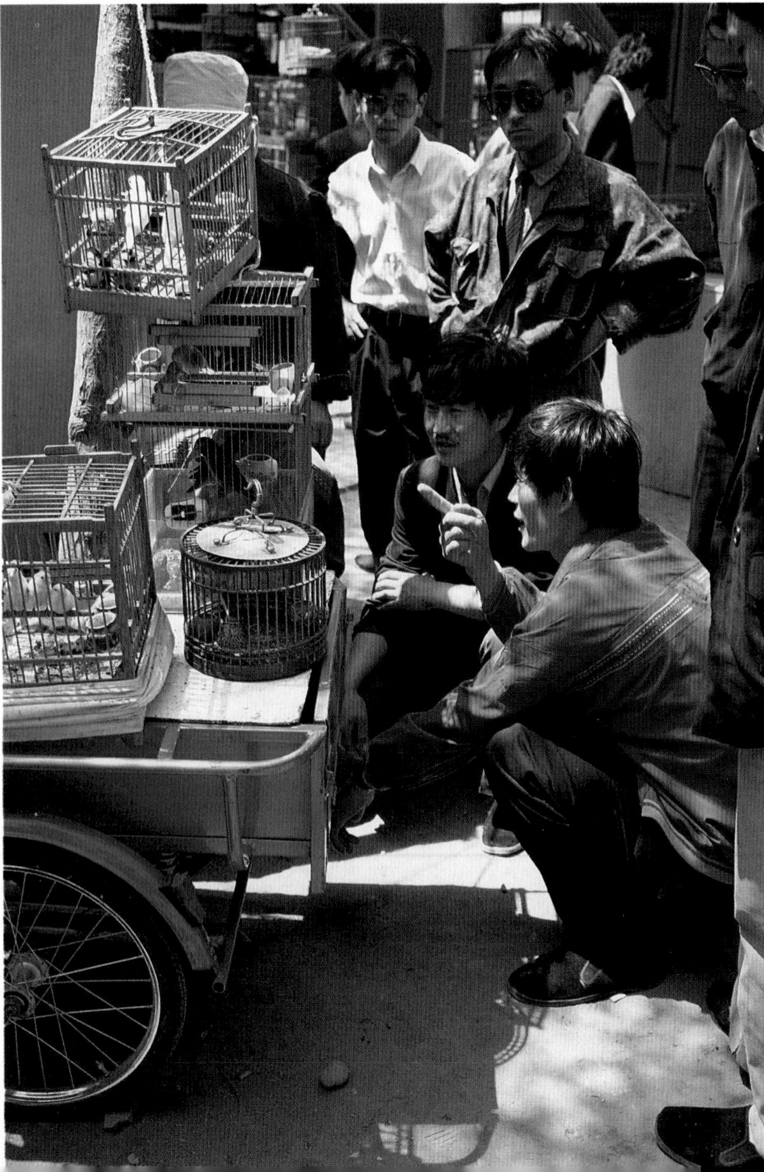

Store Toy Store. Other stores sell more pedestrian items, but you may be able to get your camera fixed here or buy film for a lower price than in the Friendship Store.

Atmospheric Liulichang Street, lined with 18th-century antiques and crafts shops, was restored in 1981, and has high-quality goods, but few bargains.

The Qianmen area, south of Tiananmen Square, is the nearest you will get to the colorful lanes of old Beijing. Many stores retain their original facades, carved or decorated with wrought iron, especially along the narrow lane of Dazhalan. Here are stores selling stationery, silks, Mongolian "hot pots," and everyday clothes, and pharmacies with selections of traditional medicines using fungus, deer antlers, and other unusual items—the best known is the Tongrentang on Dazhalan.

Specialty stores dot the city. The most famous store for silk is the Yuanlong Silk Store at 55 Tiantan Lu; another is the Beijing Silk Store at 5 Qianmen. For teas try the Beijing Tea and Honey Shop at 78 Xuanwumennei Dajie. For carpets visit the Huaxia curio shop at 12 Chongwenmennei or the Qianmen Carpet Factory at 44 Xingfu Dajie. For something different try the store at 130 Qianmen Dajie—it specializes in costumes for opera performers but also has items like embroidered shoes and black cotton boots.

Although Beijing's street markets are not the most colorful in China, they are pretty interesting, and it is worth having a look around them. The best market for antiques and curios is the Panjiayuan (Sat and Sun only). At the northeast corner of the Temple of Heaven is the Hongqiao antique market, and the Chaowai antique furniture market is to the north of Ritan Park. The bird and fish market (*niao shi*) is near the zoo on Xizhengmen, west of the Pinganli junction; while the Shichahai Market on the south of Houhai deals in flowers and birds. The popular clothes market at Xiushui is just east of the Friendship Store.

Among the stores are the Lufthansa Centre in the Kempinski Hotel, and the New World Shopping Center at Fuchengmenwai, with some 200 stores. Both centers sell international goods including photographic and computer equipment and designer clothes. Fast-food outlets abound, and you can buy imported food from the supermarkets.

"I climbed the Great Wall" is the ubiquitous T-shirt slogan

SECONDHAND STORES
An interesting diversion for the jaded shopper is a visit to Commission Shops, which deal in secondhand goods and can provide the occasional bargain. Try the one at 113 Dongdan Beilu or at 119 Qianmen Lu.

Liulichang, a short distance south of Tiananmen Square, is renowned for its antiques shops

Peking Opera is an ingenious and colorful combination of elements from many sources: traditional music, poetry, singing, recitation, dancing, acrobatics, and martial arts. In China there are over a hundred types of traditional theater, with singing their common feature—it is a kind of singing drama, yet has little in common with Western opera.

Peking Opera: fascinating as a spectacle, it can sound unusual to Western ears

LACKLUSTER STAR
One of the greatest practitioners of Peking Opera was Mei Lanfang, who died in 1961. As a student he felt that his eyes were insufficiently lustrous for stardom. To remedy this, he exercised his eyes relentlessly by gazing at the flickers of an incense flame in a darkened room, by staring at soaring kites against a blue sky and by keeping pigeons so he could follow their flight. This, he concluded, gave him a pair of bright, keen, expressive eyes.

History Each type of Chinese opera uses the dialect of a particular area; Peking Opera is one such and grew out of several types of opera being staged in Beijing some 200 years ago. The demands made upon the performer are great—he or she must be attractive in make-up, of pleasing physical proportions, and have a pair of expressive eyes, and a rich variety of facial expressions. A professional must train for up to 12 years.

Gestures and symbols Symbolism is all-important in Peking Opera, because the stage is generally bare. Gestures signify the opening of a door, entering or leaving a room, climbing a mountain or crossing a stream. Riding in a carriage is suggested by attendants standing on each side of the performer and holding flags painted with a wheel design. Walking in a circle indicates a long journey; a spotlight on two men somersaulting represents a fight at night, and so on. A Chinese proverb goes: "Small as the stage is, a few steps will bring you far beyond heaven."

The action is accompanied by relentless percussive music from the wings. The main instruments are gongs and drums, and clappers of hardwood and bamboo. A distinctively strong rhythmic pattern is produced; and the drummer, who is also the conductor, is able to suggest any emotion in coordination with the performer.

The stringed instruments are the *jinghu* (Beijing fiddle) and the *erhu* (fiddle); the *yueqin* (moon-shaped mandolin); the *pipa* (a four-stringed lute); and *xianzi* (three-stringed lute). Sometimes a horn and a flute are used.

The words are both spoken (stylized) and sung (high-pitched). The spoken parts use Beijing dialect for clowns, frivolous female roles, and children, and the dialect of Hubei and Anhui for grander, more serious roles. The melodies are set to a fixed pattern and are adapted from provincial folk songs, arranged to suit the action.

Roles The characters are classified according to age and personality. Female roles are *dan* and subdivided into "quiet and gentle," "vivacious or dissolute" and so on. Male roles are *sheng* and subdivided into "old," "young," and "warrior." The third role is *jing* (the painted face), people who are rustic and simple, or devious or dangerous. These are subdivided into principal, minor, civilian, and warrior and are distinguishable by the colors and patterns used in their distinctive make-up (rather heavy because originally opera was an open-air event) and costumes (based on those of the Ming dynasty). The clown (*chou*) is depicted by a dab of white on his face. Thus the moral standing of the characters is known immediately. In fact the plot is insignificant—the appeal of the drama lies in the spectacle and in the skill displayed by the performers.

Action Some Westerners may find Peking Opera hard to endure at first. The spectacle is impressive and the reactions of the audience fascinating (there is no formality and much movement and comment), but the singing can seem unmelodious to the untrained ear. It is not without its subtleties, however, and is an integral part of the drama itself. Peking Opera is special in another way, too, because in many of the dramas the action is presented by spectacular tumbling acrobatics.

Where to see Peking Opera
Performances are held frequently in Beijing at the Liyuan Theatre, in the Qianmen Hotel; also at Prince Gong's Palace, the Lao She teahouse on Qianmen Dajie and at the ancient wooden theater, Zhengyici Daxilou, on Xiheyan Dajie.

STATUS SYMBOL
In Peking Opera, an umbrella draws attention to an important or prestigious character. Attendants hold umbrellas over the heads of emperors, and officials sit under them when conducting their affairs of state. Even fairies carry umbrellas for aesthetic reasons. Curved handles have more status than straight ones.

Yuxian paper cut: a traditional opera figure as portrayed in folk art

Poster for a Chinese movie being shown with English subtitles, starring Gong Li. Zhang Yimou is China's most famous movie director

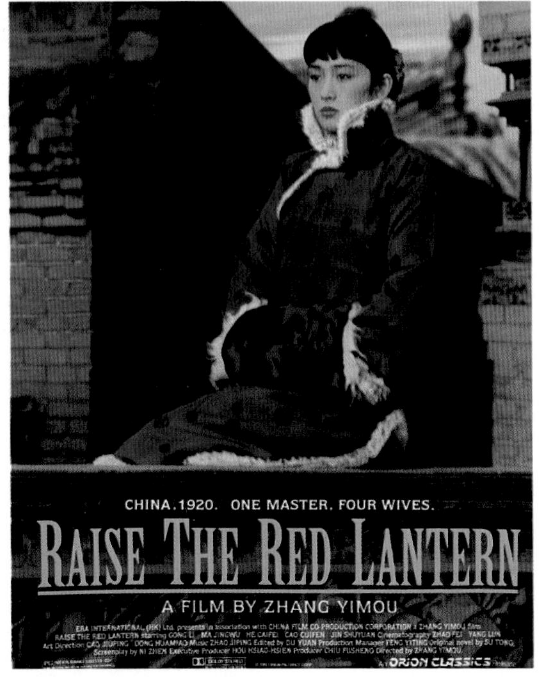

CHINA.1920. ONE MASTER. FOUR WIVES.
RAISE THE RED LANTERN
A FILM BY ZHANG YIMOU
ORION CLASSICS

Entertainment and practical matters

Entertainment Beijing is not famous for its evening entertainment, although the situation has improved greatly over the last few years. For the casual visitor interested in sampling traditional culture, however, there is plenty to satisfy. To find out what is going on you should look in *The China Daily* (the English-language newspaper) or refer to three new publications—the quarterly *Welcome to China, Beijing*; the monthly *Beijing This Month*; or the weeklies *Beijing Weekend* and *Beijing Scene*, available at your hotel.

There are many theaters in Beijing, although the Guanghe Theater at 24 Qianmen Dajie is the only old one. Performances are inexpensive, likely to cost just a few *yuan*, particularly if tickets are bought directly from the theater itself. At any one time Beijing's theaters are likely to have on offer Peking Opera (frequently in the Zhengyici Daxilou and the theater of the Qianmen Hotel); a dance drama, in which a traditional story is told in dance and music; concerts ranging from classical Western music to ethnic music and dance, Chinese pop music, or a mixture of all of the above. Acrobatics (highly recommended and presented nightly at the Poly Plaza on Baoli Dasha Juyuan) and puppetry are also on offer. A new feature is a revival of a Chinese music hall at the Tianqiao Happy Tea Garden. The cinema is popular and some of the movies produced in China have received international acclaim, among them *Yellow Earth* (1984), *Farewell My Concubine* (1993), *Red Sorghum* (1987), and *Raise the Red Lantern* (1991). Sometimes the International Club shows Chinese movies with English subtitles, and the Friendship Hotel sometimes shows old foreign movies.

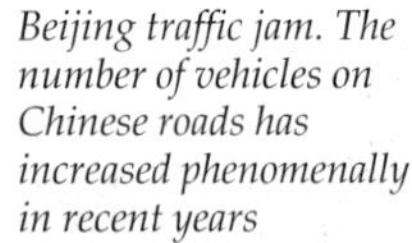

Beijing traffic jam. The number of vehicles on Chinese roads has increased phenomenally in recent years

Most of the major hotels have discothèques, and karaoke bars abound. Other discos include Poachers Inn on an island in Tuanjiehu Park, JJ's at 74 Xinjiekou Bei Dajie and the Oriental Number One, at the Asian Games Village on Anding Lu. Independent bars are springing up along Wangfujing and especially along Sanlitun Lu, many of which offer live music. The International Club has tennis courts, a swimming pool, billiards, and ping-pong. There is a golf club near the Ming Tombs and a rifle range.

Practical matters The best way to get around is by taxi. There are different price scales more or less according to size—but those with the lowest fares are the so-called "xiali" taxis. Hail and make sure that the meter is in use. You are advised not to use the pedicabs, certainly not without agreeing on a fare in advance. To obtain a taxi in advance, telephone the Capital Taxi Company at 557461. To rent a car with driver, telephone 863661 or the Beijing Car Company at 594441. The local bus service is comprehensive and inexpensive, but the buses are often very crowded (numbers 1, 4, 37, 52, and 57 run east–west along Chang'an Avenue). Also, special double-decker buses travel continuous routes around downtown. The subway has only three lines but is often less packed than the buses. The most useful is the circle line with stops at Beijing Train Station, Qianmen (Tiananmen), the zoo, and the Lama Temple.

Renting a bicycle is feasible but it is advisable to spend a little time observing the traffic first.

Emergency numbers are 110 (Police), 119 (Fire), and 120 (Ambulance). Many hotels have clinics, and there is a First Aid Centre on Xuanwumen Dong Dajie. Among several hospitals the best is the Beijing Union Medical Hospital (Xiehe Yiyuan), 53, Dongdan Beidajie, tel: 6529 6114. Asia Emergency Assistance, 1 Xingfu Sancun Bei Jie, tel: 6462 9100, offers 24-hour medical treatment.

Although most mail can usually be taken care of in hotels, some services may require a post office—the main one is on Yabao Lu, north of Jianguomen overpass.

The office of China International Travel Service (CITS) now known as Beijing Tourism Group, is at 28 Jianguomenwai Dajie, tel: 6515 8562.

MEDICAL WARNING
One of the less savory stories to come out of money-mad Peking in the 1980s was one concerning nurses who, it was alleged, were extorting high payments from patients before offering treatment. This situation has now changed, but do check in advance how much you may be expected to pay.

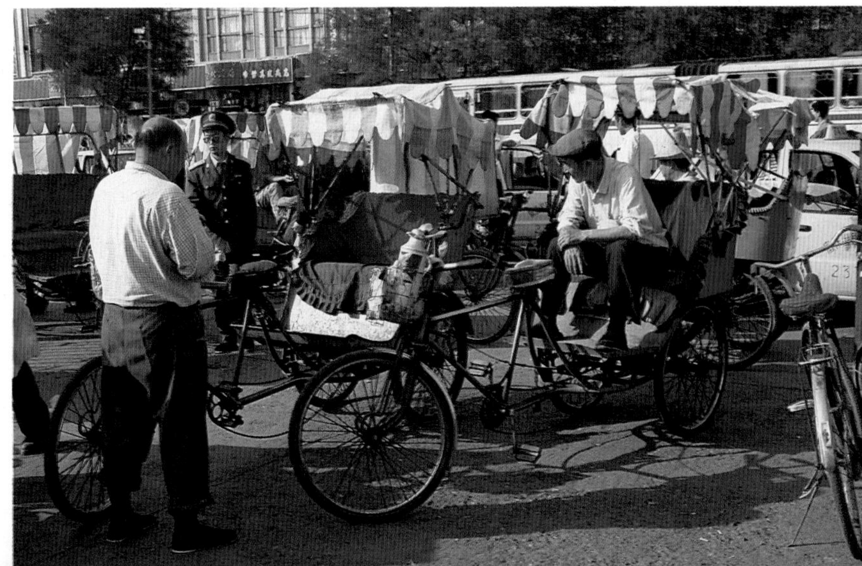

Pedicabs, prolific in most Chinese cities, can be useful in heavy traffic but be sure to agree on the fare in advance

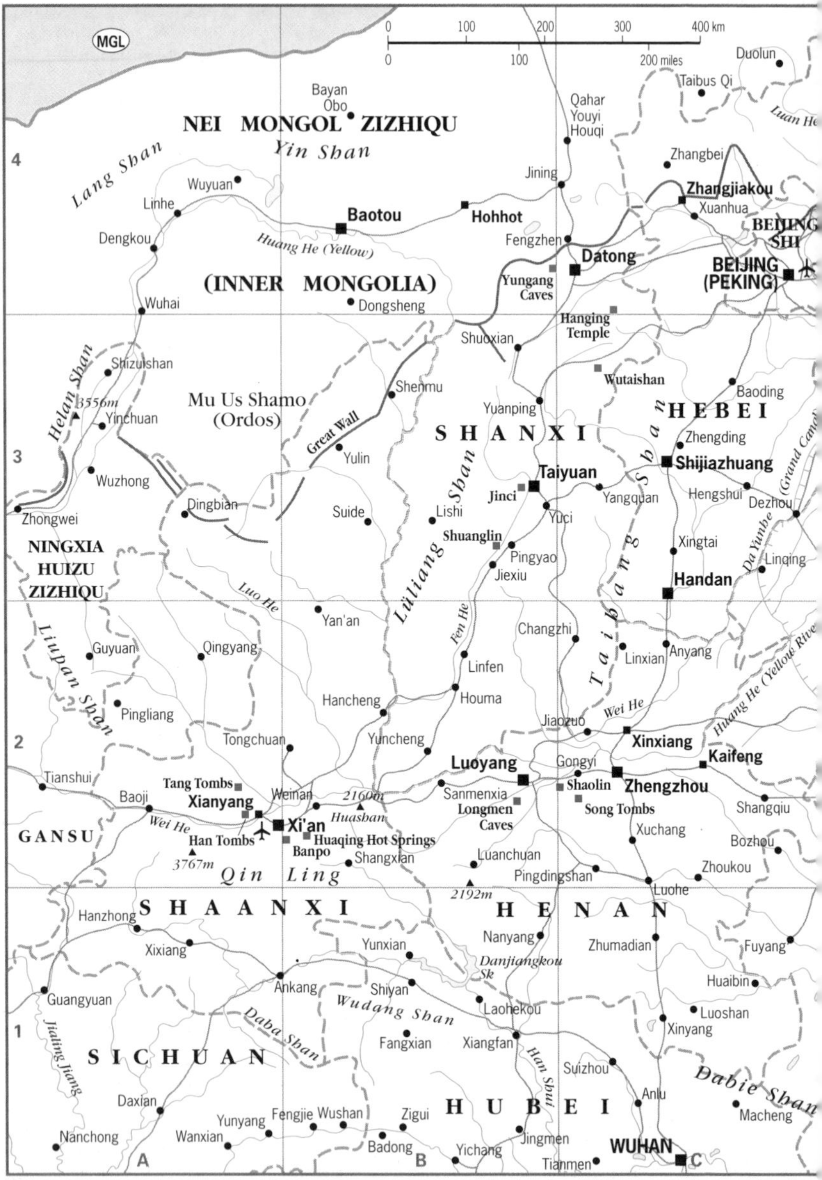

▶▶▶ REGION HIGHLIGHTS

Chengde Palace *page 85*

Longmen Buddhist Caves *page 93*

Taishan *pages 98–99*

Terra-cotta Warriors *pages 108–109*

Xi'an *pages 105–107*

Yungang Caves *page 86*

The North

LIAONING
Chifeng
Weichang
Laoha He
Chaoyang
Fuxin
SHENYANG
Fushun
Benxi
Liao He
Jinzhou
Anshan
Chengde
Jinxi
Yingkou
Liaodong Wan
Yalu Jiang
Dandong
KP
Liaodong Bandao
Great Wall
Qinhuangdao
Shanhaiguan
Beidaihe
Xinjin
Tangshan
TIANJIN
TIANJIN SHI
Jinzhou
Dalian
Tanggu
Bohai Wan
Bo Hai
Cangzhou
Longkou
Yantai
Chengshan Jiao
Weihai
Dongying
Laizhou Wan
Shandong Bandao
Rongcheng
Laiyang
Zibo
Weifang
Qingzhou
Jinan
Laoshan
Taishan
Zhucheng
Qingdao
Tai'an
SHANDONG
Qufu
Shijiu
Jining
Linyi
Huang Hai
Zaozhuang
Weishan Hu
Lianyungang
Xinyi
Binhai
Xuzhou
Da Yunhe (Grand Canal)
Huaibei
Qingjiang
Suzhou
Hongze Hu
JIANGSU
Guo He
Xinghua
Bengbu
Gaoyou Hu
Dongtai
Fengyang
Huai He
Huainan
Yangzhou
Taizhou
ANHUI
Zhenjiang
Nantong
Nanjing
Changzhou
Hefei
Wuxi
SHANGHAI
Ma'anshan
Chaoxian
Suzhou
Lu'an
SHANGHAI
Chao Hu
Wuhu
Yixing
Tai Hu
SHI
Tongcheng
Huzhou
Jiaxing
Chang Jiang (Yangtze)
Tongling
ZHEJIANG
Hangzhou Wan
Anqing
Hangzhou
Zhoushan
D
E

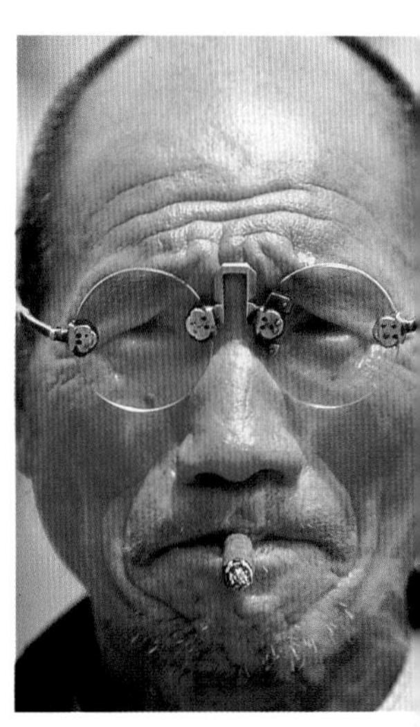

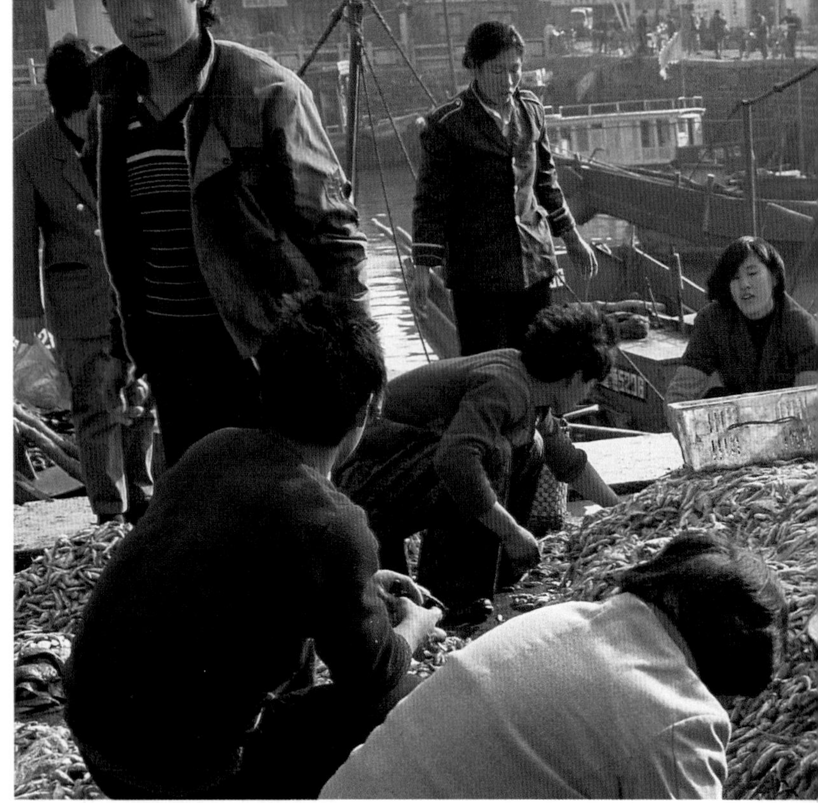

SLOW BUT SURE
Stone tortoises bearing stelae were first used in the 6th century AD. Symbols of longevity, their use was restricted to the highest grades of officials. When such stelae were surmounted with dragons, they were still more potent.

CHINA'S HEARTLAND
I love this wretched country,
This age-old country,
This country that has nourished what I have loved:
The world's most long-suffering
And most venerable people.
—A Qing, *The North* 1938

THE NORTH China—not counting Tibet, Xinjiang, and Inner Mongolia—can be broadly divided into two: the area north of the Yangtze and that south of the Yangtze. Since the geographical and cultural reality is more complicated than that, "the north" is generally taken to mean the area comprising the floodplain of the Yellow River (Huanghe), where Chinese civilization is believed to have started. The Yellow River is known as "China's Sorrow" because of its tendency to produce drastic floods. The north's boundaries are the Yangtze Valley in the south, Inner Mongolia to the north, Manchuria to the northeast and Gansu province, which is the corridor to the desert areas, in the northwest. It is composed of the provinces of Hebei, Shanxi, Henan, Shaanxi, Shandong, and parts of Jiangsu and Anhui.

CROPS AND THE CLIMATE Climatically, the region is one of extremes. Summers are very hot, with average temperatures of 77°F during July (over 100°F is not uncommon). Winters, however, are long and cold (state housing is provided with heating in the north, but not in the south), with average January temperatures well below freezing. Snow is a rarity, but in spring northerly winds bring in sand from the Mongolian Gobi. The short fall from September through October is the most pleasant time to visit.

Despite the heat, rice is not grown in the north because of the absence of water—instead wheat, millet, and barley are cultivated, and cotton is grown after the harvest of winter wheat in June. Other crops include sorghum, corn, sweet potatoes, and seasonal vegetables, especially cabbages, eggplants, beans, peppers, leeks, and onions. Mulberry bushes are grown for the manufacture of silk, tobacco is an important cash crop, orchards are noted for apples, persimmons, pears, and pomegranates, while rape, sunflower, sesame, and peanuts are grown for oil.

Houses are traditionally of one story with all the windows facing onto a courtyard. In the cities these have largely been replaced by high-rise apartment buildings, but in the countryside many traditional-style homes survive and are still being built.

THE CHARACTER OF THE REGION The northern areas of China are still mostly Han (or ethnic Chinese)—with the exception of the Muslim Hui people, there are no minorities in the region. The north, with the capital Beijing, is still the center of political power in China. Compared to the south, which has had links with the outside world for centuries, the north is highly resistant to change.

But the north shares many characteristics with the rest of China because the culture of the Han Chinese has been remarkably successful in maintaining continuity over the entire area of China for many centuries. That character was formed in the north of China, and it was under the leadership of a northern state, the Qin, that China was unified. It was further shaped by the constant threat of the barbarians from beyond the northern frontiers and by the fickle nature of the Yellow River.

Penglai, Shandong province: early morning shrimp harvest…

…and temple guardian figure

THE LAST IMPERIAL GENERAL
Yuan Shikai, who tried to restore the Qing dynasty with himself as emperor in 1915, is buried just outside Anyang. A traitor through and through, he betrayed the 1898 One Hundred Days of Reform movement to the Dowager Empress Cixi and then, realigning himself with progressive factions, was appointed President in 1911, before declaring himself Hongxian Emperor. He died in 1916. His tomb is in the style of that of Ulysses S. Grant.

▶ Anyang *80C2*

Anyang, in the north of Henan province, is close to the site of the last capital of the Shang dynasty and has a well-preserved old quarter with alleyways, courtyards, and low-eaved houses. In 1899, ancient oracle bones with engraved marks, which were used to predict the future, were found here, and later excavations confirmed the existence of a 3,000-year-old city. There are few upstanding remains at the site of **Yin**—just the merest outline of a city—but the original excavations produced much from the tombs. A possible excursion from Anyang is to the **Red Flag Canal**. Built by hand during the Cultural Revolution as part of a project to irrigate the region, the 900 mile canal was also intended to show the feasibility of a self-reliant China.

▶ Beidaihe *81D4*

China's foremost beach resort is a five-hour train ride from Beijing. It first became famous at the end of the 19th century when it was patronized by foreigners living in Tianjin's concession areas or the legations of Beijing. Much of the architecture, with its European-style villas, reflects the period. Kiessling's restaurant still exists, serving desserts and bread. The sea water is clear and the **three beaches ▶** (formerly divided into one for foreigners, one for Communist Party officials, the third for everyone else) are clean. There are a number of scenic spots in the area with unusual rock formations and views. The train from Beijing stops about 9 miles from the resort, but there is a bus link.

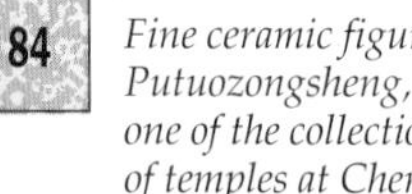

Fine ceramic figure on the Putuozongsheng, one of the collection of temples at Chengde, the Qing emperors' summer palace

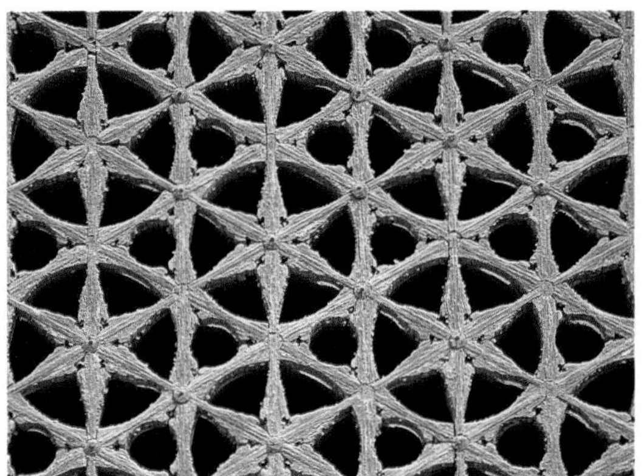

Window screen detail, Puning Temple, Chengde

A GLUT OF PALACES
The Manchu rulers of the last imperial Chinese dynasty were spoiled for choice as far as summer palaces were concerned. There were the two on the outskirts of Beijing as well as Chengde, also called the Summer Palace. The first two were favored toward the end of the dynasty, but during the 17th and 18th centuries the court spent most of the summer at Chengde. Local tours cost much less than those arranged from Beijing.

▶▶ Chengde *81D4*

Sometimes known as Jehol, Chengde was the 18th-century summer palace of the Qing emperors, close to the mountains and forests of their northern homeland. It has the largest imperial gardens in China and is six hours by train from Beijing. It is now a UNESCO World Heritage site.

At first a country seat, it soon became an important center of government. Many of the pavilions were built in the style of the religious architecture of the minority peoples in China—especially the Mongolians and Tibetans—partly to impress their envoys and partly to use Lamaism to control these potentially troublesome peoples.

In the mid-19th century, Jehol witnessed many dramatic events as hostilities between China and the foreign powers increased. It was abandoned as a summer retreat in 1820 following the death of the Jiaqing Emperor, but in 1860 as the British and French forces approached Beijing, the Xianfeng Emperor fled here accompanied by his favorite concubine, the ambitious Cixi. Concerned that the emperor might die without naming their son as heir, she forced her way into his bedroom to extract the promise that was to make her the most powerful person in China. The emperor died shortly afterward.

The palace▶▶▶ (*Open* daily 8:30–6:30. *Admission: moderate*) consists of a villa within a park and several outer temples. The entrance through the Lizhengmen (main gate) takes you to the Front Palace, now a museum of imperial memorabilia. Beyond is the Misty Rain Tower (Yanyulou), an imperial study. The Wenjin Chamber (Wenjinge) housed the Sikuquanshu (Complete Library of the Four Treasures of Knowledge), an anthology of literature and philosophy. Outside the main park are the **Eight Outer Temples** (*Open* daily 8–5:30. *Admission: inexpensive*), built between 1750 and 1780. The largest and most impressive is the Putuozongsheng, a miniature facsimile of the Potala in Tibet, although the most interesting is the Pule, built for Mongolian envoys in a style that is partly Buddhist and partly Islamic.

Tibetan-style roof ornament at Chengde

Yungang Caves: the broken-hearted son of Emperor Daiwu, represented as a Buddha in Cave 20

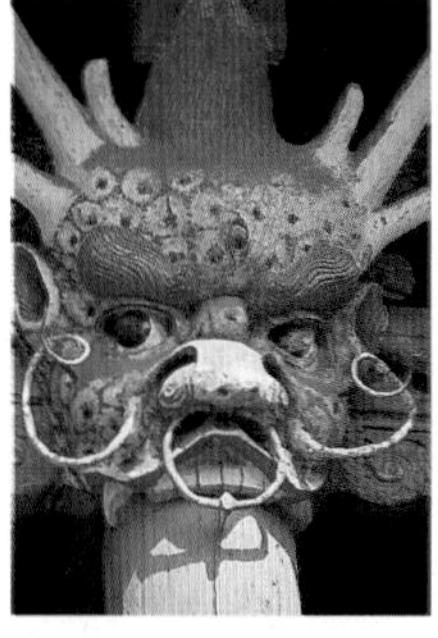

Detail on Yungang cave facade of a mythical creature supposed to warn sinners

►► Datong *80C4*

Datong is a grimy coal town in Shanxi province. It lies west of Beijing, not far from the Mongolian border on the route of the Great Wall (of which there are several decaying remains in the vicinity) and the railroad track to Mongolia and Siberia. This poor industrial city is interesting because of its Buddhist shrines, created in the 5th century AD when Datong was briefly capital of the Northern Wei. During this period the town prospered and the Buddhist religion, actively fostered by the Wei rulers, flourished, producing some of China's finest Buddhist art. More than 51,000 stone carvings still exist.

The **Yungang Caves►►►** (*Open* daily 8:30–5:30. *Admission: moderate*) are 10 miles west of the city. Originally the entrance to each was concealed by pagoda-like buildings. The idea of sculpting the rock into Buddhist shrines came from India, and there is plenty of evidence of Indian, Persian, and even Mediterranean influence in the decorative features of the caves. The peculiarly Chinese styles are seen in the bodhisattvas, dragons and apsareses (angel- or wraith-like creatures). The original caves were carved with images of the first Northern Wei emperors, but the site was abandoned after the imperial capital was moved to Luoyang. Caves 5 and 6 are the most impressive, the first with a 56-foot Buddha, the second with the life story of Buddha carved on the east, south, and west walls. The statue in Cave 19 is of the Daiwu Emperor, a one-time champion of Buddhism who later rejected it in favor of Taoism, persecuting Buddhists in the process. Cave 20 offers the best view of a Buddha statue, supposed to represent the son of the Daiwu Emperor, who died of a broken heart as a result of the misdeeds of his father.

Datong has an interesting **old center►**, one of the better preserved ones in China, worth a stroll even if you are not interested in the two monasteries or the dragon screen. The **Huayan Monastery►►** (*Open* daily 8:30–5:30. *Admission: inexpensive*) is the more interesting of the monasteries, with an atmosphere of antiquity lacking in some others. Its main attraction is the Bojiajiaocang Hall with architecture and 31 clay figures from the Liao period (AD 907–1125). The **Shanhua Monastery** (*Open* daily 8:30–8. *Admission: inexpensive*) has Ming sculpture in its main hall. **The Nine Dragon Screen**, built in 1392 on Dadong Jie and one of only three in

ANCIENT PAGODA

Not surprisingly there are few original wooden pagodas still standing in China today. The earliest is the Yingxian pagoda some 40 miles south of Datong. It was built in 1056 and is 220 feet high.

China, was supposed to have offered protection to the mansion of the 13th son of the first Ming emperor, Hongwu, who was viceroy of Shanxi.

The **Datong Locomotive Factory**▶▶▶ was, until 1989, the only one in the world still making steam locomotives; now it produces diesel and electric engines. The museum has seven steam locomotives. Contact CITS for a tour of the factory (*Tours: expensive*). The **Mass Graves Exhibition Hall** commemorates Japanese atrocities in the 1940s.

A worthwhile day trip from Datong is to the **Hanging Temple** (**Xuankongsi**)▶▶ (*Open* daily 8:30–4:30. *Admission: moderate*), constructed on the side of a cliff, about three hours' drive from the city. The temple's precarious location is spectacular enough, but the loess landscape and the villages passed through en route are also worth seeing.

▶ Gongxian/Gongyi City

80C2

Gongxian County, now called Gongyi City, is famous for the Buddhist caves at the foot of Dalishan dating back to AD 517 and, above all, the **Song Tombs** (*Admission: inexpensive*) of seven of the nine Northern Song emperors. Here, 700 stone statues of animals, and military and court officials line the sacred avenues that lead to the ruined tomb buildings, scattered over an area of 12 square miles. Stylistically, there are several clear distinctions, varying from Tang influence to the naturalistic features of the later Song.

IMPERIAL CAPITAL

Although Datong's heyday was during the Wei period, it was also the capital under the Liao rulers, a Mongol people who gave up their nomadic lifestyle and controlled the extreme north of China in the 10th to 12th centuries. Although they attempted to overthrow the Song dynasty, they were eventually conquered by the Jin rulers, ancestors of the Manchus.

The gravity-defying Hanging Temple (Xuankongsi), well worth the three-hour journey from Datong

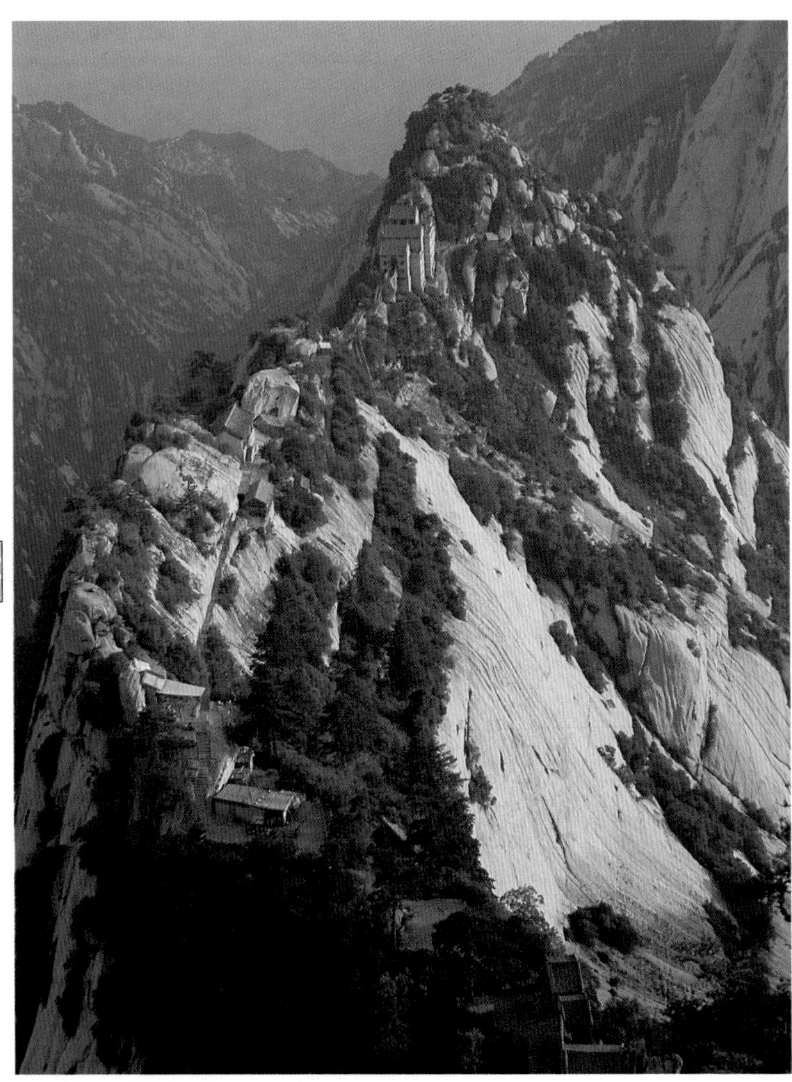

Huashan Mountain is one of China's five holy Taoist mountains

▶ Huashan 80B2

Open: daily. Admission: moderate

Huashan (Flowery Mountain), 7,218 feet high, 70 miles east of Xi'an, is one of the five mountains in China sacred to Taoism and, to some extent, later adopted by the imported religion of Buddhism. There are three routes to the top which can be followed in a day, as well as a cable-car. Accommodations can be found also at the summit. The mountain is composed of five peaks; the Middle Peak has the best view of the "Sea of Clouds" at dawn.

▶ Jinan 81D3

As capital of Shandong province, Jinan is an important political and industrial center. It is well known for its springs—Gushing-from-the-Ground Spring, Black Tiger Spring, Pearl Spring, and Five Dragon Pool—surrounded

by gardens. The **Shandong Provincial Museum**▶▶ (*Open* daily 8–11AM, 2–5PM. *Admission: inexpensive*) has a fine collection of sculptures and artifacts from Longshan, and an exhibition of musical instruments.

The **Four Gate Pagoda (Simenta)**▶, the oldest stone pagoda in China, dating back to the 7th century, is 22 miles from Jinan. Beyond Simenta is the Song dynasty **Dragon Tiger Pagoda** (**Longhuta**), which is surrounded by a small forest of *stupas* (burial chambers) built as a memorial to the monks who lived at the nearby Shentong Monastery. The **Thousand Buddha Mountain** (**Qianfo shan**), served by a cable car, has good views and statues from the Sui dynasty.

Lively detail from the glazed tiles that face the Iron Pagoda in Kaifeng

▶▶ Kaifeng *80C2*

An imperial capital during the Northern Song dynasty, Kaifeng is particularly interesting because of the presence of a Jewish community, one of several in China before the establishment of the foreign concessions in the major ports in the 19th century. Although the presence of Jewish residents in Kaifeng is well documented, their origins are a mystery. The heart of the Jewish quarter was **Beitun Jie**, where some of the streets bear Jewish names. In the center of the old town a street of Song-style buildings has been constructed.

One of Kaifeng's principal attractions is the **Xiangguo Monastery** (**Xiangguosi**)▶▶ (*Open* daily 8:30–5. *Admission: inexpensive*), founded in AD 555. The current buildings date back only to 1766. The original buildings were destroyed in the deliberate flooding of the Yellow River in 1642 in an attempt to stop the Manchu invasion. There is a magnificent bronze bell and a gingko wood statue of Guanyin of a Thousand Arms and Eyes.

The **Iron Pagoda** (**Tieta**)▶▶ (*Open* daily 8:30–4:30. *Admission: inexpensive*), built in the year 1049 and 177 feet high, is said to house relics of the Buddha.

The **Dragon Pavilion** (**Longting**), a fine Qing hall on the site of the old imperial palace, was the only building not destroyed by the flood of 1642.

The **Yuwangtai** (**King Yu's Terrace**), southeast of the old wall, was the haunt of Tang musicians and poets. The nearby **Fan Bo Pagoda**, built in 977, is the oldest building in Kaifeng. Just northeast is **Long Temple**, containing an Iron Rhinoceros from 1466, supposed to guard against flooding.

Near the **Liuyuankou Ferry** is a lookout point across the Yellow River, 5 miles to the north of the city.

The metallic sheen of the glazed bricks that cover the Iron Pagoda in Kaifeng give it its name

The Yellow River (Huang He) is 3,410 miles long and the second longest river in China. The birthplace of Chinese civilization, this temperamental waterway—named after the color of its silty waters—has earned itself the epithet "China's Sorrow."

OLD TRICK
Almost 300 years after the Ming officials at Kaifeng deliberately breached the Yellow River to halt the Manchus, the nationalist leader, Chiang Kaishek, did the same at Zhengzhou, when he tried, but failed, to prevent the Japanese invad-ers from utilizing the railroads in 1937. Hundreds of thousands of Chinese died.

Riverside ox at Zhengzhou, meant to placate the river

Route The Yellow River emerges from the Bayan Har Mountains in Qinghai. When it reaches Lanzhou it is already of considerable size; then it winds across north China, bunches up into Inner Mongolia, returns to China proper, and emerges into the Gulf of Bo Hai in the Yellow Sea.

Heavy water The Yellow River is infamously temperamental. The quantity of water that it carries varies drastically from season to season and from year to year, a reflection of the strongly seasonal rainfall of north China, three-quarters of which occurs from June through August. The rainfall is supplemented by snow melting in Qinghai as late as June. The river's characteristic hue is produced by thick deposits of filtered soil (loess) picked up in Gansu, Shaanxi, and Shanxi, blown there from the deserts of Central Asia. When the river reaches the sea, the water is colored in all directions by the same ocher paste, and indeed the coastline is constantly expanding farther northeast as the silt finally settles.

No ships Despite its size, the Yellow River has never been important as a waterway. The density of the silt, the erratic water flow, and the difficulty of mapping the shifting shoals have made this impractical. Even in areas quite close to the mouth, the river is shallow, and in the severe northern winters it often freezes. So it tends to be used for local fishing, ferries from bank to bank, and some commerce over short, sure distances. This lack of commercial potential has been compensated for by the smaller **Huai** River to the south, which is navigable; the man-made **Grand Canal**; and the **Wei**, the Yellow River's principal tributary, navigable almost as far as Xi'an.

Temperament The Yellow River has been most important as a source of irrigation, but at a price. When it floods, it does so with a vengeance. Whole towns have been washed away, and even now it is not remarkable to see the bodies of animals, and occasionally of humans, bobbing through the middle of Lanzhou. On the whole, however, the construction of dikes has kept the river in check.

In 1855, severe flooding altered the course of the river near its mouth, shifting it some 220 miles to the north. For 500 years previously it had joined the Huai in Jiangsu province, to flow with it to the sea. This change, which had the effect of almost emptying stretches of the Grand Canal, was not the first, for from the 7th century BC until AD 11 the river in its lower reaches

became a series of divided channels, all of which flowed into the sea to the north of the mouth today. Construction of dikes at that time created a single major channel and reduced the frequency of floods but accelerated the deposit of silt. This made the floods, when they came, far worse because the water between the dikes was higher than the surrounding plain. Records indicate that the river burst its banks on 1,500 occasions during the last 3,000 years.

The silt (80 pounds carried in every cubic yard of water) made the area attractive to the first Chinese cultures. Traces of neolithic settlements are legion along the river's banks, and the first recorded dynasty, the Shang, had an early capital near Zhengzhou.

In recent years flooding has not been the only problem. On the contrary, there have been water shortages and in 1997 the Yellow River ran dry 600 miles short of the sea for nine months.

Ferry crossing point at Zhongwei in the Autonomous Hui Region of Ningxia

The Yellow River at Huaxuankou near Zhengzhou. Mao's words "Control the Yellow River" are inscribed on the wall

Laoshan water

DROPPING OUT
During the 12th century, Luoyang was famous for the "Seven sages of the Bamboo Grove," a group of scholars who abandoned politics in favor of a bohemian lifestyle: discussing Taoism, writing poetry, playing music, and drinking wine. According to legend, one of them was constantly shadowed by a servant bearing wine flagons and a spade for his burial in case he dropped dead.

The residence of the former German governor in Qingdao

▶ Laoshan *81D3*

Open: daily. Admission: moderate
To the east of Qingdao, in Shandong province, Laoshan is an attractive mountain area famous for its mineral water, which is used in the production of China's best-known beer, Qingdao (Tsingtao). The mountain is also noted for its **Taiqing Palace**, a Taoist monastery from the Song Dynasty. A cable car can take you halfway up.

▶▶ Luoyang *80B2*

Although a major city historically and industrially, Luoyang is comparatively little-visited. There is, however, plenty to see in the vicinity. The site, strategically placed with hills on three sides and bisected by four rivers, was inhabited from neolithic times. In 771 BC, it became the main Zhou capital, and legend has it that Confucius studied here and Laozi was the keeper of archives. Capital again under the Later Han, it was the starting point of the Silk Road. Buddhism was introduced into China from India via Luoyang, and it hosted a number of Chinese inventions, including paper.

After the fall of the Han, the city remained capital for several dynasties and was the scene of a cultural flowering. The Northern Wei dynasty moved its capital from Datong to Luoyang and carved its monuments to Buddhism at nearby Longmen. But the Wei rulers suddenly abandoned the city in 534; it lay in ruins for about 70 years before becoming the capital again, under the Sui. It was a secondary capital under the Tang, too, after which the focus of Chinese life moved elsewhere, and Luoyang, though capital of Henan province, became a backwater until its industrial revival after 1949.

Luoyang is not beautiful, but a walk in the old town, around **Zhongzhou Donglu**, with its well-preserved timbered houses and market atmosphere, pleasantly evokes the past. Luoyang is famous for its peonies, which bloom in early April particularly in Wangcheng Park or Zhiwuyuan. It is said that in AD 800 Empress Wu Zetian, angry that peonies refused to bow to her command to bloom in the snow, banished them from Xi'an.

Most of what has been uncovered of Luoyang's past is in the **museum**▶▶ (*Open* daily. *Admission: inexpensive*), near Wangcheng Park, where there are some fine examples of work, notably the famous Tang polychromatic figures

and models of the Sui dynasty grain silos discovered north of the old town. From the park, a pair of Han tombs and one from the Jin with interesting murals have been moved to the **Museum of Ancient Tombs** (*Open* daily 9–4:30. *Admission: inexpensive*), on Jichang Lu.

The **Longmen Buddhist Caves▶▶▶** (*Open* daily 6–8. *Admission: expensive*) are among the finest in China. On a splendid site by the Yi River, outside the town, the earliest caves were carved soon after AD 493, although the majority date from the Tang. There is a spectacular array of niches, statues, carved pagodas, and inscriptions, among which the most striking is the 56-foot-high Buddha flanked by statues of leering guardians.

The Han dynasty **Baimasi** (**White Horse Temple**)**▶**, 6 miles from Luoyang, is China's earliest Buddhist temple. Its foundation during the first century AD dates back to a journey made by envoys of the Han who went west in search of Buddhist scriptures, and who returned with them on the backs of a pair of white horses. The structures you see now date from the Ming and Qing Dynasties (*Open* daily 8–5:30. *Admission: inexpensive*).

Heavenly guard and demon warrior on Fengxian Temple; Longmen Buddhist Caves near Luoyang

▶ Qingdao *81D2*

See following page for town map and walk

China's interesting fourth port was no more than a fishing village in 1897 when the Germans annexed it to compete with other Western powers. It was returned to China only in 1922. It is a popular beach resort and is home to China's most famous **brewery▶** (*Open* daily. *Admission: expensive*), which can be visited via CITS. There is a modern Qingdao but the well-preserved old **German Concession▶▶**, with its cathedral, and the former German governor's residence are worth a visit for their European atmosphere. The **Qingdao Museum▶** has a good collection of paintings and large stone Buddhas. There are also several parks. A day excursion to **Laoshan** from Qingdao is possible by boat or by bus.

China's premier export beer is brewed in Qingdao (Tsingtao) using Laoshan mineral water

The heart of Qingdao

Begin at the No. 1 Bathing Beach and walk toward downtown along the waterfront. Pass the **Marine Museum and Aquarium▶** and Lu Xun Park and continue to the pier with the Huilan Pavilion perched at the end.

Opposite the pier is Zhongshan Road, the main street. Walk along it for a short distance and turn left on Guangxi Road to see the busy station and famous reconstructed clock tower.

Retrace your steps to Zhongshan Road, continue past the many stores, visit the **Catholic Cathedral** on the right, and then continue past the skyscraper department store opposite the Jianglinglu alley to Jingchen market on the right.

Walk through the market and bear right up a rising street; then bear left and then right. Once at the main street turn left, and at a junction by an old church turn right into the heart of the old but well-preserved **German Concession area**.

Continue downhill, keep to the left of a small park and then at a clearing bear to the right toward another church and then left before you reach it, down Longkou Road.

Cross another junction which has an ancient Chinese wall on the left, climb up the hill, and then bear right by some trees.

Take the road as it curves left around a building with a tower, and then right keeping the tower on your left. This road will eventually bring you back to the waterfront.

▶ Qufu *81D2*

Qufu is famed as the birthplace of Confucius and as the home of his clan, the Kong. The **Kong Mansion▶▶** (*Open* daily 8–4:30. *Admission: moderate*), built during the Ming dynasty, was home to the clan until 1948 and is one of the finest examples of an aristocratic mansion in China.

The **Kongmiao** (**Temple of Confucius**)**▶▶** (*Open* daily 8–4:30. *Admission: inexpensive*) dominates the town. Across the moat is the Guiwenge, which used to contain the Confucian library. In the Great Courtyard is a tree, allegedly planted by Confucius, the Xingtan Pavilion, and the Dachengdian, built during the Qing dynasty and one of the largest wooden structures in the world.

The **Konglin▶▶▶** is the family graveyard, set amid trees just outside the town, which contains Confucius' simple and dignified grave. Confucius' birthday is celebrated on September 28th in Qufu. South of Qufu is **Zouxian**, birthplace of the philosopher Mencius.

One of the residential rooms in the Kong Mansion, Qufu, family seat of Confucius' clan, the Kong

POPE'S VIEW

The master's fame reached far and wide. "Superior and alone, Confucius stood. Who taught that useful science, to be good."—Alexander Pope, "The Temple of Fame" 1715.

Confucian wine improves the mind. Wine from Qufu

POLITICALLY INCORRECT

The opinions of Confucius, who was himself fairly high-born, on women and the lower classes would be given short shrift these days. "Women and people of low birth are very hard to deal with," he said. "If you are friendly with them, they get out of hand, and if you keep your distance, they resent it."

China's railroad system is of particular interest for a number of reasons, not least because China's withdrawal from the world stage for so many years aroused curiosity among train buffs, who tend to have an insatiable desire for detail.

Traveling "hard seat class" in Inner Mongolia

REVOLUTION AND THE RAILROADS
It is possible that the railroads in China played a contributory role in the downfall of the last dynasty. Railroad construction in the decade up to 1911 had been financed largely by foreign organizations in cooperation with provincial governments, but it was less profitable than before. The Chinese government, already badly short of funds, was compelled to service railroad debts and consequently took control of the system. Resentment of this action in the provinces led to rallies among all enemies of the state, sparking the 1911 revolution.

A difficult start China's railroad system is interesting for several reasons: the expansion of the railroad network; the fact that until 1989 steam locomotives were still being manufactured in China (and are still used); and because the train service is a good way to meet the Chinese.

The history of China's early railroad system is characterized by Chinese intransigence and imperial maneuverings. The first attempt to introduce railroads to China was made by a consortium of Chinese and foreign companies in 1863, but the application was refused because of the Taiping Rebellion. In 1864, a further application was made to the governor of Jiangsu, Li Hongzhang, a man aware of the advantages that dealing with foreigners could bring to China. But he felt that the time was not yet right, despite agreeing with the Europeans that the railroads were a key to prosperity. This did not stop the illegal laying of a track from Shanghai to Wusong in 1876 (after negotiations with landowners and families whose ancestral graves were likely to be affected), which was subsequently torn up.

Official approval The Chinese were slowly coming around to the idea, and the next line to be built, with official approval, was for a coal mine near Tianjin. The train was initially pulled by mules, but the Beijing government soon turned to steam traction, recognizing its military possibilities. Indeed, it was fear of Russian and Japanese aggression that led to plans for new lines in Manchuria and between Beijing and Guangzhou (Canton).

Henceforth railroad construction became increasingly entangled with the fates of the Western powers, whose presence in China was increasingly unwelcome.

Foreign pressure Some Western powers felt that China was fated to be carved up among them, others disagreed. The result was several spheres of influence, each economically dominated by one power. China constantly found itself caught in the middle of their struggles. In some ways this was to China's advantage. Railroads were built, but usually under some sort of foreign pressure, because the Chinese government had no money. The first contract was signed in 1896, with France, for a railroad near the Vietnamese frontier, and this was followed by more with other countries. The eagerness to build railroads was founded less on the desire to make money (they were hardly profitable) than on the need of each power to obtain concessions before any of the others did.

Shortfall After the Boxer Rebellion the Chinese enthusiasm for railroads increased, and various agreements with foreign powers were ratified. In 1911, major lines were removed from provincial to central imperial government control. Sun Yatsen strove to standardize the railroad systems, which reflected the technology current in the countries involved in their construction. Apart from the logistical challenge, standardization was difficult because of China's great climatic and geographical extremes.

Wars For the next 40 years, despite civil war and invasion by the Japanese, the railroads continued to function. With the help of private Chinese capital and the Boxer Indemnity Fund, but mostly using revenues generated by the railroads themselves, the system was improved. However, the resumption of civil war after the Japanese withdrawal brought everything to a halt.

With the communist victory in 1949 railroads became a priority. Collaboration with the U.S.S.R. produced many more lines as well as the construction of the railroad bridge across the Yangtze at Wuhan. After the split in 1960, concern for defense led to the construction of still more lines and the Yangtze Bridge at Nanjing. Today electrification and new lines to remoter areas (for example between Kunming and Dali, andKunming and Nanning) are a priority.

Until 1989 steam locomotives were produced just for the home market
Opposite, top: a steam train in the desert at Dongsheng
Above: Manchurian steam in Heilongjiang

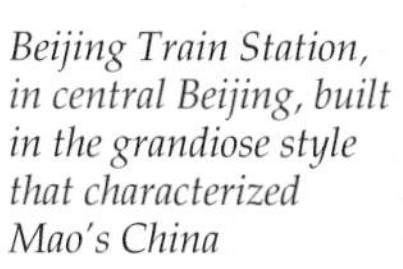

Beijing Train Station, in central Beijing, built in the grandiose style that characterized Mao's China

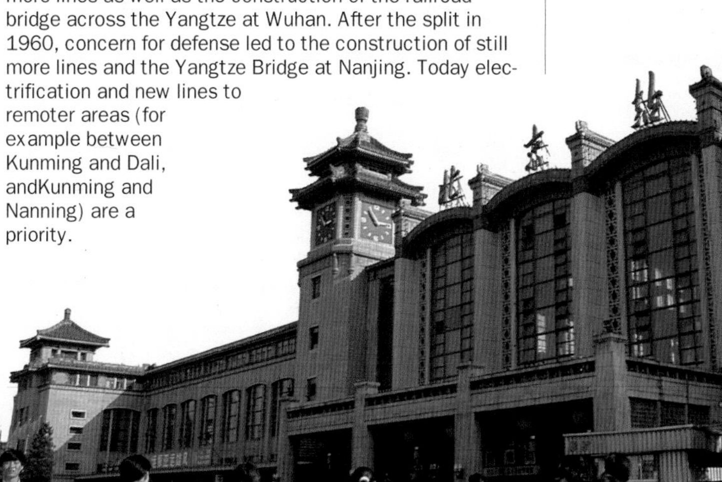

The 17th-century town gate of Shanhaiguan, inscribed "First Pass Under Heaven"

SACRED PEAKS
The five holy mountains represent the five directions sacred to the Chinese (north, south, east, west, and center), hence the link with the emperor who was viewed as the son of heaven and who lived at the center of his kingdom.

▶ Shanhaiguan (The Pass between the Mountains and the Sea) *81D4*

Shanhaiguan is where the Great Wall meets the East China Sea. The 1639 **town gate** is inscribed "First Pass Under Heaven." A temple about 4 miles out of town is dedicated to Meng Qiangnu. The wife of a man conscripted under the Qin to build the Great Wall, she followed him only to find that he had died. Her tears brought the wall down to reveal his skeleton within.

▶ Shaolin *80C2*

The **Shaolin Monastery▶** (*Open* daily 8:30–5:30. *Admission: moderate*), west of Zhengzhou, was founded in AD 495. It was said to have been visited by the founder of Zen Buddhism, Bodhidharma, in AD 527. Having crossed the Yellow River on a reed, he contemplated a wall for nine years. He rejected doctrine for meditation, and Shaolin is best known for the practice of *gong-fu* by its monks, a martial art developed to enhance meditation that has found fame in movies. Shaolin is also noted for its Ming frescos, as well as its forests of *stupas* (burial chambers) and its collection of stelae, one of which dates back to 683. Kung fu classes are possible at the Shaolin Monastery Wushu Institute.

The "Forest of Stupas," or ancient burial chambers, near the Shaolin Monastery, Shaolin

▶ Shijiazhuang *80C3*

The capital of Hebei province is an important railroad crossing and the burial place of the Canadian doctor Norman Bethune, honored by the Chinese communists. He arrived in China in 1938 and died that year.

About 8 miles north is Zhengding, site of the **Longxing Temple**, famous for its 72 foot bronze of Guanyin. A further 25 miles southeast is China's oldest bridge, the Zhauzhou Bridge (Zhauzhou Qiao), which was built 1400 years ago.

MASSACRE OF MISSIONARIES
Taiyuan was a major center for antiforeign Boxer activity in 1900. Xenophobia reached a climax when the local governor rounded up all the foreign missionaries in the area and publicly executed them.

▶▶▶ Taishan *81D2*

Open: daily. Admission: moderate

Taishan is perhaps the holiest of the five Chinese holy mountains devoted to Taoism and the cult of the emperor. Of the two possible routes to the summit, the middle one is the most popular. Make your way through the **Daizongfang** and begin the five-hour, 4,970-foot climb up the 5,500 steps. You can also take a bus to Zhongtianmen, about halfway up, where there is a cable car to the top. There is a hotel at the summit.

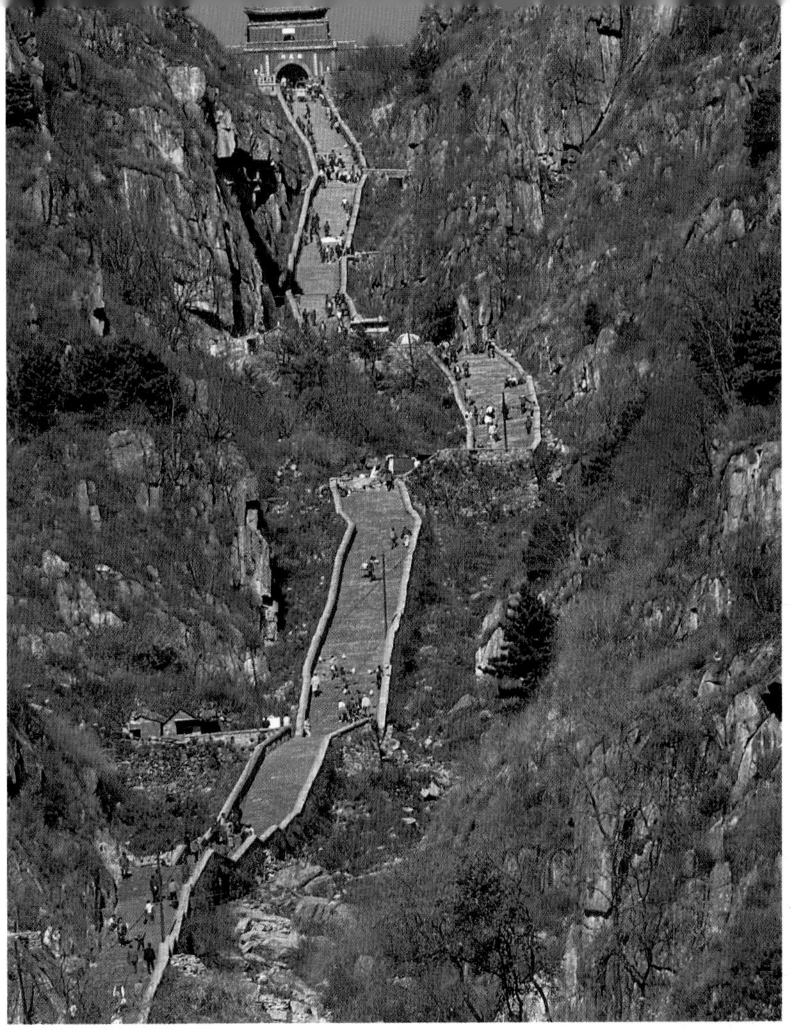

The mountain is covered with temples, scenic spots, and tourists or pilgrims. A circuitous western route back also offers excellent views over the mountainside.

The **Taishan Temple** at the foot of the mountain is one of China's great, ancient palace-style buildings.

Visitors to the mountain of Taishan, the holiest of China's holy Taoist mountains, must climb thousands of steps to reach the summit

▶ Taiyuan *80B3*

The capital of Shanxi province is an industrial city with several interesting features. The **Shuangta Temple▶▶** (*Open* daily 8–5. *Admission: inexpensive*) is one of China's finest examples of Ming architecture, while the **Chongshan Temple▶** (*Open* daily 8–5. *Admission: inexpensive*) was once part of the largest Buddhist monastery in China. The **Shanxi Provincial Museum▶** (*Open* daily 9–6. *Admission: inexpensive*), has reopened in a former Confucian Temple. Other temples include the **Jinci▶▶**, 15 miles southwest of Taiyuan, with some fine examples of Song architecture. Also dating from the Song-dynasty, 56 miles south, is the **Shuanglin Monastery▶▶** (*Open* daily. *Admission: inexpensive*) while only 1.5 hours southwest of Taiyuan is Pingyao, one of the few remaining towns with a complete city wall.

YELLOW EARTH

The provinces of Shanxi and Shaanxi not only have similar names but are both covered in thick deposits of yellow loess, sometimes to a depth of over 325 feet. In some places, troglodyte cave-houses have been cut into the perpendicular valley sides. Though primitive, the cave-houses are cool in the summer and warm in winter.

"Qi" in Chinese denotes a vital breath within us that also animates the cosmos. Although it is a loose term, according to Chinese philosophy—notably Taoism—the secret of inner strength lies in harnessing this mysterious force.

Gong-fu *is about self-discipline, both as a form of exercise (above,* taijiquan*) and as a martial art*

Natural alliance The secret of outer strength lies in using *qi* to unleash latent power that depends not on physical strength but on knowledge. *Gong-fu* is the cultivation of *qi* and its use as a fighting technique.

Taoism claims to be able to demonstrate its superiority through movement, based on the notion that the human body is the universe in miniature. But the movements themselves are to be based on acquiescence, not confrontation, with nature.

In martial arts there are two categories of movement, external and internal. Both forms aim to tap into the flow of *qi*. Of the former, karate, concerned with bodily skills of self-defense, is a well-known example. Internal forms are more concerned with the body as a vehicle of spiritual development; among these *taijiquan*, or shadow-boxing, is the best known.

Meditation Meditation concentrates the mind so movements made are in tune with it. Meditation in action is considered essential by Taoists because it involves the whole human being, body and soul. The practitioner must be aware of his or her actions, so the weapon, whether it be hand or sword, is directed to strike but does so almost intuitively, having sensed in advance the movement of an opponent. The mind is flowing, and this is *qi*. The relationship between the two types of breathing, physical and spiritual, is vital. Perhaps this could be described as "tranquil," but the word is inadequate

because it fails to imply the level of alertness essential for success. *Taijiquan* is supposed to be able to teach both the calmness necessary in everyday life and the added awareness needed for fighting.

Rhythms In *taijiquan* the spine should be erect, the abdomen relaxed and the center of gravity lowered. The breath must be allowed to find its source in an area an inch or so below the navel and identify with the inner breath of *qi*; to concentrate on control of physical breathing alone is to inhibit one's natural, instinctive strength. There must be no strain, for to strain is to go against nature. Energy should be stored and only unleashed at the right moment, as the arrow from the bow. Observing the Chinese people will show that these lessons have been absorbed and used in ordinary life, for the Chinese are rhythmical in everything they do until speed is called for, in which case the reaction is intense and accurate.

In some ways *qi* might be thought of as the combination of concentration and self-discipline. But for Taoists, *qi* is something more; it is the essence of essences, an innate, though invisible, power shared by all human beings.

The martial artist's concentration of *qi* should produce the innocent mental state of a child—no preconceptions, focused only on the immediate circumstances but within the larger framework of the universe. This state is illustrated by the following account of a *gong-fu* contest taken from Peter Ralston's *Consciousness and the Martial Arts*: "For example I would start to move and my opponent would throw a kick and I would realize that I was moving out of the way of a kick. But I was doing it before I knew why! I just moved, and they would throw a kick and miss!"

Gong-fu *as an aid to meditation: sculptures in the temple at Shaolin Monastery and (top, opposite) a wall painting portraying 13 monks practicing their art before the Tang Emperor Li Shimin in the 7th century* AD

A WORLD OF SHADOW-BOXERS

David Rice, in his book *The Dragon's Brood: Conversations with Young Chinese*, describes Chinese shadowboxing: "From five o'clock in the morning, in every street-corner park, in front of every apartment block, and in the woods around the Temple of Heaven, there were thousands of people, some in groups, some alone, all performing what seemed to be slow-motion ballet, making strange, slow, graceful movements with limbs and torso."

Tianjin's foreign concessions

A stroll through the foreign concessions reveals a surprising degree of Westernization. Walk from the east train station toward the river. Cross Liberation Bridge and continue along Jiefang Road, passing the old Imperial Hotel on the right. Continue through the former **French Concession** to the Fine Arts Museum. Yingkou Road marked the beginning of the **British Concession**, but continue along Jiefang Bei Road to the Astor Hotel and the former Victoria Park. Turn left to the river and return along the waterfront, passing the old French and British consulates and the Customs House.

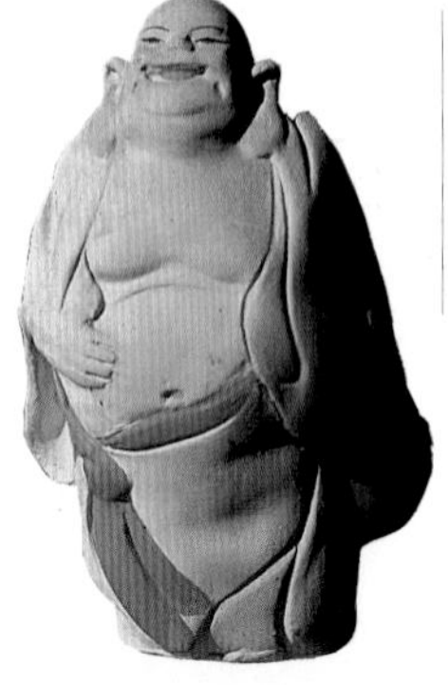

►► Tianjin (Tientsin) *81D3*

Tianjin was one of the treaty ports controlled by the Western "great powers" from the 19th century. In 1976, it was hit by an earthquake, but has since recovered to become China's third-largest city, with the status of autonomous municipality (as Beijing, Chongqing, and Shanghai), which is similar to that of a province.

Tianjin has retained much of its European atmosphere, although the various concessions granted to the foreign powers in 1860 never merged, as they did in Shanghai, to form an International Settlement. Each concession preserves a distinctive flavor, particularly the British, French, and German ones. The old Chinese town is to the north of the city, the concessions to the south.

Other than the **concessions▶▶** there are several places of interest. The **Dabeiyuan** (**Great Compassion Temple**) (*Open* daily 8–5. *Admission: inexpensive*), is a Buddhist temple that used to contain the cranium of Xuanzang, the 7th-century monk who made a celebrated journey to India. **Wenhua Jie** (**Ancient Culture Street**)▶ is an area of restored traditional Chinese stores, just west of the river. It is close to the **Tianhougong** (**Hall of the Heavenly Empress**), originally a temple, now a **Folk Museum▶** (*Open* daily 9–4:30. *Admission: inexpensive*) with many examples of the mud craft peculiar to Tianjin and of the woodblocks made in the nearby village of Yangliuqing. The **Fine Arts Museum▶** at 77 Jiefang Bei Road has old and new paintings. The 18th-century **Great Mosque** (**Qingzhen Da Si**)▶ is in the old Chinese city. The old **French cathedral▶** is interesting. Also worth a look is the southern-style **Guangdong Guildhall** (**Guangdong Huiguan**)▶, built in the 1920s as a center for traders from that province. Tianjin is famous for its annual Kite Festival, and its fascinating, daily **antiques market** on Shenyang Dao. The **TV Tower** (**Dianshi Ta**), which you can climb for 100 yuan, was built in the 1990s.

HIDDEN AGENDAS
China has always had secret societies that, dedicated to the overthrow of the government of the day, were often no more than criminal gangs. Tianjin in the 19th century was the headquarters for many, including the White Lotus, which was influenced by Buddhism and Manichaeism. These societies were active in the early 20th century, setting fire to Esso storage tanks in 1929. It is said that they still exist today.

French Concession architecture along the former rue de France, Tianjin's old banking district

▶ Wutaishan *80C3*

Wutaishan in the north of Shanxi province is one of the four holy mountains of Chinese Buddhism. It is a cluster of five peaks, the highest reaching just over 9,800 feet. There is an abundance of temples, many concentrated at the town of **Taihuai**. The Yuan dynasty **Nanshan Temple** is decorated with frescos of the classic "Journey to the West" made by the monk Xuanzang, who traveled to India. The **Luohou Temple** contains an imposing wooden lotus flower on a mechanism that, when rotated, opens the petals to reveal carved Buddhist figures.

STRENGTH THROUGH WISDOM
Wutaishan is supposed to have been the home of the Bodhisattva Manjusri, the god of wisdom. Riding on the back of a lion, he carries a sword used to fight ignorance.

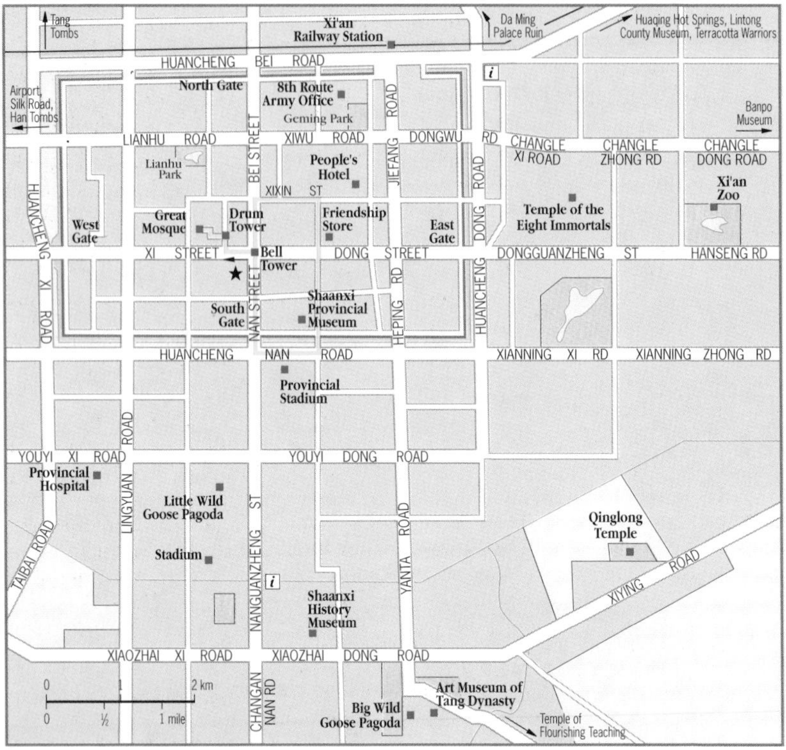

Tang Tombs
Xi'an Railway Station
Da Ming Palace Ruin
Huaqing Hot Springs, Lintong County Museum, Terracotta Warriors
HUANCHENG BEI ROAD
Airport, Silk Road, Han Tombs
North Gate
8th Route Army Office
Geming Park
Banpo Museum
LIANHU ROAD
XIWU ROAD
DONGWU RD
CHANGLE XI ROAD
CHANGLE ZHONG RD
CHANGLE DONG ROAD
Lianhu Park
BEI STREET
People's Hotel
JIEFANG ROAD
XIXIN ST
Xi'an Zoo
HUANCHENG XI ROAD
Great Mosque
Drum Tower
Friendship Store
East Gate
DONG ROAD
Temple of the Eight Immortals
West Gate
XI STREET
Bell Tower
DONG STREET
DONGGUANZHENG ST
HANSENG RD
HUANCHENG
South Gate
NAN STREET
Shaanxi Provincial Museum
HEPING RD
HUANCHENG NAN ROAD
XIANNING XI RD
XIANNING ZHONG RD
Provincial Stadium
ROAD
YOUYI XI ROAD
YOUYI DONG ROAD
Provincial Hospital
Little Wild Goose Pagoda
LINGYUAN
Qinglong Temple
TAIBAI ROAD
Stadium
NANGUANZHENG ST
YANTA ROAD
XIYING ROAD
Shaanxi History Museum
XIAOZHAI XI ROAD
XIAOZHAI DONG ROAD
0 1 2 km
0 ½ 1 mile
CHANGAN NAN RD
Big Wild Goose Pagoda
Art Museum of Tang Dynasty
Temple of Flourishing Teaching

104

Xi'an, taking in the Muslim quarter

The Bell Tower near downtown is a good place to start. From here, head west along Xi Street until you arrive at the **Drum Tower** at the beginning of the Muslim quarter. Turn right beneath the tower, turn left on a narrow, stall-lined street and follow it as it bears right, and then turn left again to the **Great Mosque**. After that return to the main road and walk left along it, passing a number of attractive traditional houses. At the top bear right along Xixin Street until you finally come to the old main square. A little farther on is the People's Hotel. Return to the square and turn south, walk past the Friendship Store and continue on until you get to the Shaanxi **Provincial Museum**. Turn right to the South Gate and then right back to the Bell Tower.

Worshiper at the Great Mosque in Xi'an's Muslim quarter

The Bell Tower stands in a pivotal position at the center of Xi'an's Ming period street plan

▶▶▶ Xi'an *80A2*

One of the greatest cities in the history of civilization, Xi'an (Sian) had declined to a provincial backwater before the discovery of the Terra-cotta Warriors in 1974. Since then it has become one of the most important tourist destinations in the world. Its history is long and illustrious. A capital during the early Zhou dynasty, it became the first capital of a united China under the First Emperor, Qin Shihuang. During the Tang dynasty Xi'an became the center of the greatest flowering of Chinese culture. It is thought that the population may have reached two million, at a time when commerce with the outside world reached unprecedented levels. The modern city, however, is based on the Ming street plan.

Although the **Terra-cotta Warriors▶▶▶** (see pages 108–109) must be the highlight of the visit, there is much else to see in and around the city. The **city wall and moat▶▶▶** (*Open* daily 8AM–10PM. *Admission: inexpensive*), over 9 miles in perimeter, dates from the early Ming. Made of rammed loess on a base of earth, lime, and glutinous rice, faced with gray brick, it was completely restored during the 1980s and is an awesome sight, particularly in the misty early morning or at dusk. It is possible to mount the wall, 40–45 feet wide at the top, at different points.

The old **Shaanxi Provincial Museum** was housed in the former Confucian Temple at the foot of the wall in the south of the city. Part of it still is; the rest is now in a new museum on Xiaozhai Donglu. The **old museum▶▶** (*Open* daily 8:30–6. *Admission: inexpensive*) houses the famed Forest of Stelae, a collection founded in 1090 of inscribed stone tablets, some dating back to the Han. Some have pictures of scenery or illustrations; others carry the text of the 13 Classics. One testifies to the arrival in Xi'an of a Nestorian Christian priest and the foundation in 781 of a chapel.

The **new museum▶▶▶** (*Open* daily 8:30–5:30. *Admission: moderate*) has a display of locally discovered Zhou bronzes, fine Tang ornaments, and a variety of stone sculptures including four of the carved horse reliefs from the tomb of Li Shimin, founder of the Tang dynasty. Two of these are now in the Metropolitan Museum in New York.

FOLK ART

The brightly colored quilted jackets embroidered with stylized designs that are now for sale all over China originate from the countryside around Xi'an. A more recent development is the art in naïve style from Huxian, a nearby town. The vivid paintings of agricultural themes became popular in the late 1950s and are now widely sold in the area.

INFORMATION AGE

For many years CITS (China International Travel Service) was regarded as more of an obstacle than an aid to obtaining information about China. Things have improved only slowly but in Xi'an there is now a Tourist Information Center (Tel: 745 5043; *open* daily 7:30AM–8PM) close to the train station which offers helpful and friendly service.

Part of the Forest of Stelae in Shaanxi Provincial Museum

THE JOURNEY WEST
The "Journey to the West" (*Xiyouji*) is the name of a fable written during the Ming dynasty. The fable is based on the pilgrimage to India made by the Tang monk Xuanzang, in honor of whom the Xi'an Big Wild Goose Pagoda was built. In the story of his adventures, he is accompanied by a pig, symbol of intelligence and greed, and a magician monkey. There are many stories based on the characters, some of which appear in a television series.

The city's symbol is the 197-foot **Big Wild Goose Pagoda (Dayanta)▶▶▶**(*Open* daily 8:30–5:30. *Admission: inexpensive*), first built in AD 652 to house the sutras collected from India by Xuanzang, the wandering monk. The top offers fine views across the city. The **Little Wild Goose Pagoda (Xiaoyanta)▶** (*Open* daily 8:30–5. *Admission: inexpensive*) is a similar, smaller, more delicate structure from 707.

Xi'an's Muslim population numbers 30,000, a legacy of the Silk Road. On Huajue Xi'ang in the Muslim quarter is the **Great Mosque (Qingzhensi)▶▶** (*Open* daily 8–7:30. *Admission: inexpensive*). It was founded in 742, though the heavily restored present buildings are in Ming style. It is a charming place, particularly the garden and prayer hall.

Near the Mosque is the **Drum Tower▶**, and its twin, the **Bell Tower▶**, just to the southeast. Moved here in 1582, Bell Tower was built in 1384 and originally stood at the center of the Tang city, two blocks west. Music performances take place daily (*Towers open* daily. *Admission: inexpensive*).

The route to the Terra-cotta Warriors takes visitors past several places of interest. The area around Xi'an has been

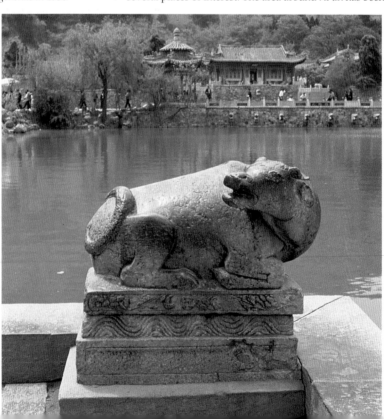

Ancient guardian of Huaqing Hot Springs, near Xi'an, where Chiang Kaishek was captured by his own generals in 1936

important from the earliest times. **Banpo▶▶▶** (*Open daily 8–6:30. Admission: inexpensive*), discovered in 1953, is a covered excavation that clearly shows the layout of a neolithic village of the Yangshao culture. The foundations of several dwellings (thatched roofs supported by timber columns) and kilns and graves, some of which were filled with urns containing the bones of children, can all be viewed. The pottery discovered there shows an interesting progression of pattern from representations of man and fish to more abstract geometric design.

The **Huaqing Hot Springs▶** (*Open daily. Admission: moderate*), a scenic spot in the shadow of Li Mountain, have been patronized for their mineral content since the Zhou dynasty, but they are particularly associated with the Tang emperor Xuanzong and his concubine Yang Guifei, whose fate is a perennial subject of Chinese art. The baths are being reconstructed in the Tang style. The springs are also associated with the "Xi'an incident" of 1936. Chiang Kaishek had come to Xi'an to continue his offensive against the communists, ignoring pleas for a united front against the invading Japanese. A warlord, Zhang Xueliang, though allied to Chiang's nationalists, saw the urgency of the situation and captured him here, chasing him from his office (which still stands just above the spring) up the hillside. Chiang was forced into an alliance, though he later obtained his revenge on Zhang by imprisoning him.

Not far from Huaqing is **Lintong County museum▶**, frequently overlooked by tourists but with an interesting display of Buddhist relics discovered on Li Mountain and other sites in the area. Close to Xi'an is **Xianyang museum▶** (*Open daily 8–6. Admission: inexpensive*), housing 3,000 miniature soldiers excavated in 1965.

There are several worthwhile sites not normally included in a visit to Xi'an. The **Han dynasty Tombs▶** (none of which have been excavated) lie 22 miles west of Xi'an. The most interesting is that of Huo Qubing, which has a series of fine stone animals that would once have graced the spirit (or royal) way and are now under cover. There is a museum devoted to items discovered in the area. Nearby is the tomb of the Tang concubine Yang Guifei. The main **Tang Tombs▶▶**, however, are some 50 miles northwest of Xi'an. The grandest is **Qianling** (unexcavated), the tomb of the third Tang emperor and his wife Wu Zetian, one of the three notorious women rulers of Chinese history, who assumed power on the death of her husband.

The location of the tomb, on a natural hill, is impressive. It is approached along a "spirit" or royal way running between two mounds, flanked by a succession of winged horses, birds, human figures, and stelae. Beyond is a congregation of headless statues—the foreign envoys who attended the emperor's funeral. Nearby are several lesser tombs, some excavated, notably those of Princess Yongtai and Prince Zhanghuai, and covered with beautiful court paintings. East of Qianling is the **Zhaoling** group of tombs—it was from the tomb of Taizong, the second Tang emperor, that the famous horse panels now displayed in the provincial museum were taken.

The **Temple of Flourishing Teaching (Xingjiaosi)▶**, 16 miles southeast of Xi'an, is spectacularly sited on the side of a hill, overlooking a village and a tree-studded plain. It is famed as the burial place of the monk, Xuanzang.

A COSMOPOLITAN CAPITAL

Despite the magnificent city walls, which date from the Ming dynasty, Xi'an's greatest days were already long past by then. During the Tang the city was much larger—an array of markets was closely controlled by a sophisticated government bureaucracy while the inhabitants lived in walled districts which were closed at night. Life in Xi'an was international—the city was filled with traders from as far away as the Middle East, perhaps even Rome, who came to deal in horses, jewels, exotic fruit, silks, and porcelain, and who had their own mosques, and Manichaean and Zoroastrian temples.

Detail: Little Wild Goose Pagoda, Xi'an

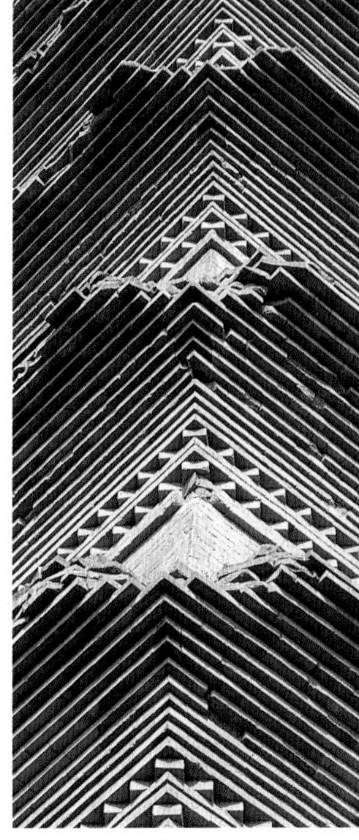

The discovery of the Terra-cotta Warriors in 1974 by local farmers who were digging a well turned out to be one of the most significant archeological finds of the 20th century.

FROM EMPEROR TO QUEEN
Such is the beauty of the bronze chariots exhibited at the site of the Terra-cotta Warriors that Queen Elizabeth II was given an exact copy of one of them when she visited in 1987. She is also one of the few foreigners ever to have been allowed to stand in the pit among the warriors.

Construction The First Emperor, Qin Shihuang, whose as yet unexcavated mausoleum lies beneath a hill one mile from the site, was a figure of almost legendary stature. The scale and nature of this find reveals a level of material civilization remarkable for its self-confidence.

Work was begun on the mausoleum in 246 BC, as soon as the First Emperor became ruler of Qin, and involved the labor of nearly 750,000 conscripts. According to historical records, the mausoleum itself was filled with models of palaces and a China in miniature where the "waters" of the Yellow and Yangtze rivers were made of mercury and could even be made to flow by means of a special mechanism. The site was protected by automatic crossbows. Outside the mausoleum there was a perimeter fence and villas once occupied by guards.

The army So far interest has focused on the army of life-size terra-cotta soldiers arrayed in pits to the east. The largest, Pit 1, is now protected under a vast hangar. It consists of 11 parallel underground corridors from which earthen ramps lead to the surface. Each was paved with bricks and protected by a wooden roof covered in straw matting and clay. The mausoleum was sacked by rebel soldiers after the First Emperor's death, probably as a result of the telltale mounds of excavated earth.

The soldiers stand in military formation in infantry battle order facing east. They have some armor but no helmets (which were reserved for officers). The vanguard at the east end consists of bowmen who are

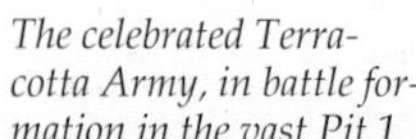

The celebrated Terra-cotta Army, in battle formation in the vast Pit 1

separated from the foot soldiers by chariots, and mobile infantry unarmored for rapid deployment. Armor was unnecessary since ferocity and bravery were considered sufficient protection for infantrymen. Thus in the narrow north and south corridors soldiers guarding the flanks face outward, shieldless. The Terra-cotta Warriors did, however, carry real arms, made of bronze, many of which were removed by the rampaging rebel army.

Sculpture The statues themselves were made of local clay. No two faces are alike—each is a personal portrait. Each body was made separately. The legs are solid, but the torsos are hollow. Hands and head were added later. Individual details such as beards and ears were sculpted last, then the whole statue was brightly painted. It is uncertain why so much trouble was taken, but one theory is that the different faces, many of which belong to what have become minority races, are a celebration of the first unification of China. Another argues that the warriors demonstrate the power of the ordinary citizen, a view that smacks more of 20th-century Marxism than serious empirical analysis. But certainly these men were clearly highly esteemed by the First Emperor, even if their presence here represents no more than the egotism of a powerful man.

Exhibitions Pit 2 contains a unit of cavalry and war chariots; Pit 3 contains a war chariot, 68 warriors, and numerous bronze weapons; and Pit 4 is empty. Pits 1, 2, and 3 are currently open to the public (*Open* daily 8:30–5:30. *Admission: moderate*).

Separate exhibition halls display examples of the soldiers under glass, and in yet another hall you can see a pair of scaled-down bronze chariots of remarkable precision, discovered in 1980 just west of the tomb itself.

It is forbidden to photograph or video the exhibits in Pits 1, 2, and 3, a rule that is vigorously enforced. Photography is permitted elsewhere, however. There is an interesting market outside the site gates.

Each of the life-size warriors is said to be an individual portrait

ROYAL RAGE

The First Emperor was a driven man. In about 218 BC he found crossing the Yangtze difficult because of a gale. He blamed the river goddess whose temple was on a nearby mountain and so, to punish her for inconveniencing him, he ordered 3,000 slaves to fell all the trees on its slopes.

A deserted back street near the waterfront in the old part of the port city of Yantai, Shandong province

▶ Yan'an (Yenan) *80B2*

Yan'an (Shaanxi province), the communists' headquarters during the Anti-Japanese War, holds an honored place in Chinese history as it was also the end point of the Long March. The area is notable for its cave architecture, and for **Qingliangshan** (*Open* daily 7–8. *Admission: inexpensive*), a park with the Ten Thousand Buddha Cave, the name given to any

shrine filled with Buddhist statuary. Miraculously, many of the statues survived the Cultural Revolution.

▶ Yantai *81E3*

Known as "Chefoo" to 19th-century foreigners, Yantai is a fishing port, notable for its **Fujian Guild Hall and museum▶** (*Admission: inexpensive*), built by traders from Fujian in 1884.

▶ Yulin *80B3*

This small town in Northern Shaanxi has interesting architecture and an almost complete Ming wall.

▶ Zhengzhou *80C2*

The capital of Henan province is thought to have been a Shang dynasty capital. A city of middling importance for the next 3,000 years, it only recently regained its stature, but as a rather ugly manufacturing center. Here in 1938 Chiang Kaishek breached the Yellow River dikes to hold back the Japanese, killing vast numbers of Chinese in the process. There is a commemorative tablet at Huaxuankou on the road to the Yellow River. The new **Provincial Museum▶▶** (*Open* daily 9–4:30. *Admission: moderate*), located in Nongye Lu, has a remarkable display of local finds from the neolithic to Ming periods. The Ming dynasty **Temple of the City God (Chenghuangmiao)▶** is dedicated to the city protector, a tradition said to date back 4,000 years. At the east end of the same street are the remains of the **Shang city wall**.

RAILROAD STRIKE
In Communist folklore, Zhengzhou is inextricably linked to the revolution because of the strike which started on the railroads in 1923. This arose because of the local warlord's opposition to the establishment of a united trade union, not least because the railroad line was vital, he felt, to the movement of his troops. Thirty-five workers were shot, and the strike that followed is considered to be one of the first major steps taken by the Workers' Movement.

In 1930, Mao Zedong, with the assistance of Zhu De, founder of the Chinese Red Army, and others destined to play a considerable role in the New China, founded a Chinese soviet republic in the mountains of Jiangxi, in south-east China.

Breakout Chiang Kaishek, aware of the growing threat to his nationalists posed by the communists in southern China, mounted five campaigns against them in the years 1931–1934. Only on the fifth occasion were Mao's forces compelled to break out. The communists decided to retreat from Jiangxi to Yan'an, a remote town in the northwest, in Shaanxi province. From October 1934 for two years almost 100,000 marchers lived off the country-side, making their way over mountains and difficult terrain to Yan'an, a distance of almost 8,000 miles. Peasants were converted to the cause en route, but the ordeal and battles with local warlords took their toll, and only a fraction of the original number completed the journey.

The march, however, was an important milestone in Mao's career—it enabled him finally to achieve the leadership he sought, and in 1935 he was elected chairman of the Party's Central Committee. Simultaneously, the march temporarily benefited the nationalists because much of the burden of fighting was passed on to the warlords. At the same time there was a good deal of factional fighting among the communists themselves; it was only Mao's emergence as leader that settled those differences once and for all. Once the communists had arrived in Yan'an, it became their capital until 1945.

Revolutionary base areas

1934
1935
1936
Guerrilla zones

Long March routes

First Front Army
Second Front Army
Fourth Front Army
Sixth Army Group
25th Army Corps

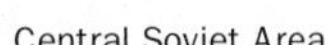

1 Central Soviet Area
2 Hunan-Jiangxi
3 Hunan-Hubei-Sichuan-Guizhou
4 Sichuan-Shaanxi
5 Fujian-Zhejiang-Jiangxi
6 Hunan-Hubei-Jiangxi
7 Hubei-Henan-Anhui
8 Hubei-Henan-Shaanxi
9 Shaanxi-Gansu-Ningxia

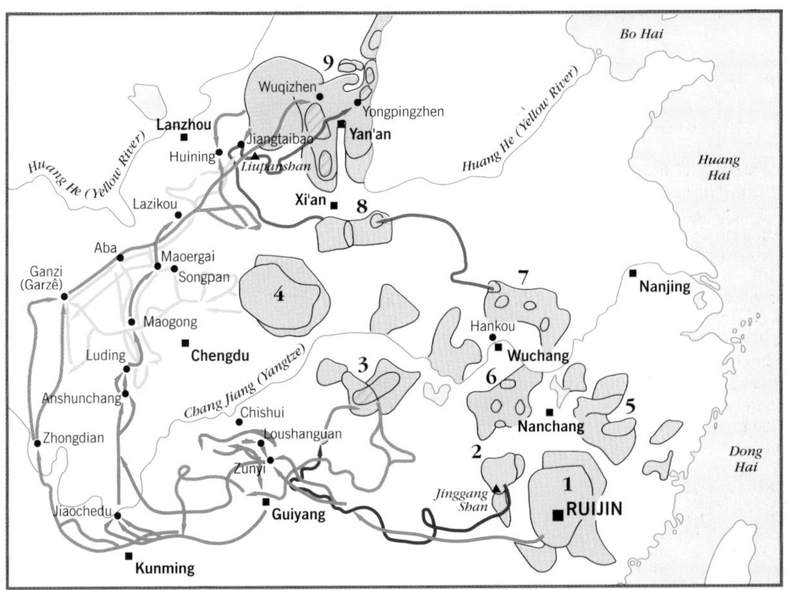

112

Women workers shovel snow off the streets of Harbin

Right: the Throne Room of the Manchurian Imperial Palace, Shenyang

The Northeast

►►►REGION HIGHLIGHTS

A detail from the walls of the Imperial Palace, Shenyang

THE NORTHEAST Although the northeast region of China has much in common with north China, it nevertheless has its own character, a mixture of China, Manchuria, Siberia, and Korea.

This is partly because the frontier here has fluctuated considerably over the centuries. Indeed it is only during the last 25 years that agreement has finally been reached between the Chinese and the Russians to prevent the sniping across the banks of the Heilong Jiang (Amur) River that had previously been a characteristic of the region. Residents of this region may now go about their daily business without fear of invasion, and foreigners also benefit since they may travel more freely here.

The region is the northernmost part of China proper and consists of the provinces of Liaoning, Jilin, and Heilong Jiang. It borders Siberia in the north, Korea in the southeast, and Chinese Inner Mongolia in the west, and is washed by the Yellow Sea to the south. The area is a marked contrast to the rest of China because of its freezing winters, fir-clad hills and mountains, rivers, and lakes, as well as its minority peoples. These days its major cities are vital components in China's industrial life.

MIGHTY MANCHUS
Such was the Manchus' prestige when they took control of China in 1644, that the then Dalai Lama journeyed in person from Lhasa to Beijing to acknowledge the suzerainty of the new Qing dynasty. He ordered the building of the White Dagoba there in 1651 (it still stands today in Beihai Park).

OFF THE BEATEN TRACK From the visitor's point of view, the northeast is usually considered a fringe attraction. This does not mean, however, that it is devoid of interest, only that it demands more research and more effort. For the nature lover, particularly, the northeast has much to offer; but the determined traveler can discover much else. After all, China was ruled by people from this region for the last 300 years of its imperial history.

Its history, as might be expected in frontier country, is a checkered one and rather obscure. Of the many peoples to have made their home in the northeast the best known are the Manchus or Manchurians, who gave a political shape to the region. They, it seems, were originally a Jürchen tribe of Tungusic stock. The Tungus inhabited the northeast, living by a mixture of hunting and agriculture. The Manchu dynasty arose out of the Aisin Gioro clan, which held the hereditary chieftainship of one of the Jürchen tribes. By the usual tactics of marriage into and alliance with other tribes, Nurhaci, the leader of the Manchus (whose son subsequently inaugurated the Qing dynasty), developed a power base in the Liaodong peninsula and created a united front against the Chinese, with whom relations had for long been uneasy.

By the time Nurhaci was sufficiently powerful to invade China he had inculcated a sense of statehood into his people. The economy was solidly based on ginseng and horses, while the state bureaucracy, no doubt influenced by that of China, was conducted using a new script based on the Mongol alphabet. Shenyang became the capital of the new Manchurian state, which was then absorbed into China.

The Manchurian state was later reincarnated briefly and ingloriously in the 1930s as Manchukuo, a spurious attempt by the invading Japanese to give legal substance to their own ambitions.

The ginseng and the horses remain, and so do some 10 million Manchurians, one of China's 55 minority peoples. The northeast is not China's heartland but is nonetheless an integral part of the modern Chinese state.

CHINA IN A MODERN WORLD

A fascinating aspect of China is its contradictions: a Third World country that makes its own nuclear weapons; a socialist country that encourages its citizens to earn more; a country that pioneered great inventions (gunpowder, the magnetic compass, printing) yet lags behind modern technology; and a country that has strict measures for population control yet relies on manual labor for agricultural production.

A winter vendor of yams in Harbin where January temperatures plummet to –20°F, or lower

FEATURE FILM
Changchun is advertised as the cradle of New China's movie-making industry but most of the movies that have come to international attention in recent years have been made elsewhere. *Yellow Earth* and *Red Sorghum*, made in the Xi'an studios, received widespread acclaim in Europe and America, while *Farewell My Concubine*, made with Chinese talent and Hong Kong money, was nominated for an Oscar in 1994.

ASSIMILATED RULERS
China's last dynasty, the Qing, were Manchurians, from the part of China known as Dongbei, or the Northeast. Like the Mongols, they were foreign conquerors but with a crucial difference—they did not impose their own traditions on the Chinese, but instead adopted the Confucian customs and structures of Han China. At the same time the Manchu maintained their own identity, by continuing to wear their traditional dress and insisting that men wear their hair in a long braid. They also protected their power base by employing both Chinese and Manchu in influential political posts.

▶ Anshan *112A1*

Anshan produces over 20 percent of China's steel but has little aesthetic appeal. To the southeast, some 6 miles away, are the **Tanggangzi Hot Springs**, where Puyi, the Last Emperor, used to go to bathe with his empresses. About 12 miles to the southeast is **Mount Qian (Thousand Lotuses Hill)▶**, a well-known beauty spot of green peaks and Taoist and Buddhist monasteries dating back to the Ming dynasty.

▶▶▶ Changbaishan *112B1*

Open: daily. Admission: expensive
China's largest nature reserve, a vast area of dense forest and tundra, is noted for its varieties of plant and animal life, from wild ginseng to Manchurian tigers. It is within the Yanbian Korean Autonomous Prefecture, and its most famous beauty spot is the volcanic crater lake of **Tianchi (Heavenly Lake)▶▶**, at a height of over 6,500 feet. With an average depth of 670 feet, Tianchi is the deepest lake in China. Formed by an eruption in 1702, it glistens in the shadow of wild peaks and is a one- or two-hour climb from a 200-foot waterfall, the point where most visitors arrive. There is hiking from late June through September. At other times of year the area is only accessible by snowmobile.

▶ Changchun *112B2*

Between 1933 and 1945, Changchun, the capital of Jilin province, was the capital of Manchukuo, the artificial state created by the Japanese to be ruled over by the puppet Last Emperor, Puyi (see pages 118–119). His former **imperial residence▶▶** (*Open* daily 9–3:45. *Admission: inexpensive*) has become a museum and exhibition hall. Otherwise, Changchun is famous for its car factory (which produced the Red Flag limousine used by

Dalian is one of China's most important ports. The maritime climate here means that the waters never freeze

Party dignitaries) and for its movie studio. Tours of both can be arranged by CITS.

▶ Dalian *112A1*

Formerly known as Dairen and Luda, Dalian is the only real port in the northeast. It is clean and uncrowded and, as an Open Coastal City, has an air of prosperity not commonly found in most of the rest of China. Strategically important because of its deep-water, ice-free harbor, it was a rival to Hong Kong under the Japanese. Before that Dalian was of interest to the Russians, who wanted to build a thriving alternative to Vladivostok, which becomes icebound. Under the terms of the Yalta Agreement in 1945, the Japanese gave up Dalian to the Soviet Union, whose occupation ceased only in the 1950s. The occasional Russian street sign is a reminder of that time, and there are some interesting examples of neoclassical architecture, like the People's Cultural Hall on Zhongshan Square.

It is not an exciting place to visit, however. A tour of the port is possible, and there are some excellent beaches at Jinshitan and Fujiazhuang. The shopping streets are lively, and the **Natural History Museum▶** (*Open* daily. *Admission: inexpensive*) is of interest, but Dalian's main attraction is its fish restaurants. Specialties include sea-cucumber stew, yellow croaker in sweet-and-sour sauce, pike in soy bean sauce, soft-fried sea conches, and phoenix shark's fin.

About 125 miles to the northeast of Dalian is the **Bingyu (Ice Valley)▶▶**, which winds through a 12,000-acre primeval forest, and a river meanders through a landscape of sheer rock formations. Places of interest in the valley include the Skylark Peak, Xiaoyu (Small Valley), the Yingna River, and the Longhua (Dragon Splendor) and Huaguo (Orchard) Mountains.

ORE DOWN UNDER

Iron was first discovered in China in about 600 BC, followed quickly by the development of cast iron. There was a flourishing iron and steel industry by the Han dynasty. China still has huge reserves of untapped iron ore, mostly of low quality with an iron content of about 30 percent. A great deal of high-grade ore is imported from abroad. To secure supplies, the China Metallurgical Import and Export Corporation bought a 40 percent stake in a mine at Channar in Western Australia.

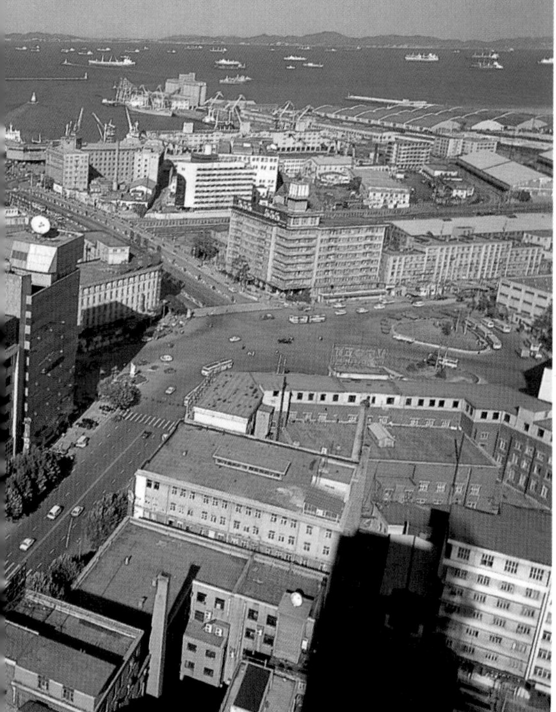

Steel works at Anshan, Liaoning province. The smoking furnaces highlight China's serious pollution problem

The tragi-comic life of the Last Emperor has been colorfully brought to world attention by the Italian director Bernardo Bertolucci in his movie The Last Emperor. *Puyi's story was a travesty, but in many ways he personified the decline and fall of a once-great civilization.*

REFORMATION
For the Western reader the first part of Puyi's autobiography (on which the movie was largely based) is fascinating for its insight into the way of life inside the Forbidden City. The second part, dealing with the Last Emperor's reeducation, is less colorful. Nonetheless, it too is of interest because it shows how Puyi was used as an example to the people: the book closes with the words, "Only today, with the Communist Party and the policy of remolding criminals, have I learned the significance of this magnificent word ['man'] and become a real man."

One man's life, two ways of living

From Emperor to Citizen
NOW THE SUBJECT OF A MAJOR FILM
THE AUTOBIOGRAPHY OF PU YI
THE LAST EMPEROR OF CHINA

Early start Puyi was born in Beijing on February 7, 1906, in the mansion of his father, Prince Chun, who inherited the title from Puyi's grandfather, the seventh son of the Emperor Daoguang (reigned 1821–1850). He was not yet three when, in November 1908, he was made emperor at the behest of the dying Dowager Empress Cixi, in whose shaky hands the destiny of China had lain for several lackluster decades.

Puyi ascended the throne as the tenth and last emperor of the Qing dynasty on December 2. On February 12, 1912, he was forced to abdicate by the newly installed revolutionary government, but his retirement was not to be a quiet one.

Premature retirement The years after his abdication are of greater interest than those of his juvenile reign. His life under the Republic was at first governed by the Articles providing for the Favorable Treatment of the Great Qing Emperor after his Abdication. His title of dignity was to be retained; he was to receive an annual allowance of four million taels; he was to continue to live, temporarily, in the Forbidden City; the sacrifices at his ancestral temples and imperial tombs would be maintained forever; the uncompleted tomb of the Emperor Guangxu would be finished according to the original plan; although no further eunuchs were to be engaged, all persons of imperial grade would continue to be employed at the palace; the former emperor's private property would enjoy the protection of the state; and the existing palace guard would become part of the Republican Army.

Palatial existence Puyi remained in the Forbidden City, complete with imperial retinue, until 1924 when the nationalists, concerned at the threat of restoration, forced him to leave. It was as if he lived in a continuous theatrical production—outside, the China that had sustained dynastic rule for 2,000 years was attempting to come to terms with notions of incipient democracy, something altogether at odds with Chinese tradition; while, simultaneously, Puyi lived a barely diluted imperial existence in the palace. Everywhere he went—whether to study, carry out imperial duties or to stroll in the garden—he was pursued by his staff of eunuchs and attendants. He called this "the daily pomp."

Restoration There was surprisingly widespread support for the monarchy in early Republican China, and Puyi was restored to the throne for just 12 days in 1917. The idea of restoration was never entirely relinquished, particularly by the Japanese, who thought that popular support for an emperor might play a useful role in their own ambitions for a Pan-Asian empire.

After his expulsion from the Forbidden City in 1924, Puyi took refuge in the Japanese Legation. He was later made puppet emperor of Manchukuo, the artificial empire created in northeast China by the invading Japanese. After the war he was captured by Soviet troops and lived in Russia until Mao's victory in 1949. After his return he underwent political indoctrination before becoming a gardener in the Botanical Gardens in Beijing. He was publicly humiliated during the Cultural Revolution, and died in 1967.

Above: Scene from the movie The Last Emperor, *directed by Bernardo Bertolucci*

The much-decorated last representative of 2,000 years of imperial rule looks out at a rapidly changing world

SUN DRIED
The name "Harbin" comes from the Manchu language and means "a place for drying fishing nets in the sun," which is an indication of the city's lowly status before being discovered by the Russians, when it was no more than a remote village.

▶ Dandong 112B1

A border town with North Korea, Dandong, in the province of Liaoning, is one of the most important ports in the region and is also an important center of light industry. A visa is required to visit North Korea, however, it is possible to see North Korea without a visa by taking a speed-boat ride along the Yalu River, or by going up the hill in Jinjiangshan Park. A visit to the town's Museum to Commemorate U.S. Aggression (*Open* daily 8–5:30. *Admission: inexpensive*), offers an insight into the Cold War. About 30 miles from Dandong is **Fengcheng**, where the 2,756-foot Fenghuang Mountain is dotted with temples from various dynasties.

Fall mists on Taoist Fenghuang Mountain, near Dandong

▶▶ Harbin 112B2

Architecturally speaking, Harbin, in Heilongjiang province, is unique in China. This is because of Russian influence—not from the alliance with the Soviet Union in the 1950s, but from the days when Harbin was an important junction on the Russian Manchurian Railroad. As a result Harbin's skyline is shaped by the onion domes and traditional roofs of a prerevolutionary Russian town, although these are gradually being eclipsed by high-rise buildings.

Before the 1890s Harbin was a moderately sized fishing village on the Sungari (Songhua) River. The construction of the railroad brought many Russian engineers and merchants, followed by Chinese in search of work. After 1917, the population swelled to 200,000 as refugees from the revolution in Russia escaped over the border.

There are still a few Russian residents left in Harbin, but their numbers are dwindling fast, to be replaced by crowds of Russian citizens who cross the border to go shopping. Their influence can be seen most clearly in the

Continued on page 122

BEAR NECESSITY
One of China's rarest and most famous dishes is perhaps found only in Harbin. This is Bear's Paw, often associated with the 4th-century BC philosopher Mencius who said: "Fish I love; bear's paw I love; If I cannot have both I'll forgo fish for bear's paw."

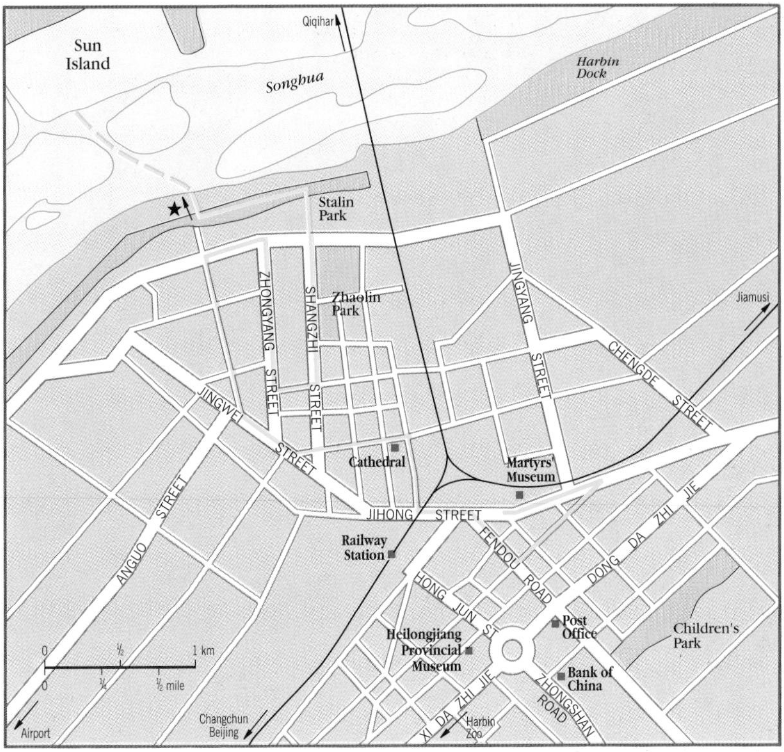

Sun Island
Songhua
Harbin Dock
Qiqihar
Stalin Park
Zhaolin Park
ZHONGYANG STREET
SHANGZHI STREET
JINGYANG STREET
CHENGDE STREET
Jiamusi
JINGWEI STREET
Cathedral
Martyrs' Museum
JIHONG STREET
ANGUO STREET
Railway Station
FENDOU ROAD
DONG DA ZHI JIE
HONG JUN ST
Heilongjiang Provincial Museum
Post Office
Bank of China
Children's Park
ZHONGSHAN ROAD
XI DA ZHI JIE
Harbin Zoo
0 ½ 1 km
0 ¼ ½ mile
Airport
Changchun Beijing

Walk

Harbin

Take a ferry to **Sun Island** and then return, walking eastward through the Stalin Park, noting the **Flood Control Monument**, to Shangzhi Street on the right. Walk on with Zhaolin Park on the left. At the intersection turn right, then right again up Zhongyang Street with the Modern Hotel on your right. At the top turn left, then take the first left to the intersection with Jingwei Street. Take the second left for the **cathedral**, then head south to Fendou Road and Dong Da Zhi Jie in the downtown area.

Harbin: winter in China's far north

One of the glowing ice sculptures, London's St. Paul's Cathedral, created for Harbin's extraordinary ice festival held in Zhaolin Park every year

Continued from page 120

Daoliqu▶▶ area, near Zhongyang Dajie, which is also of interest for its stores and markets on the banks of the river. Nearby is the restored Church of St. Sophia.

During World War II Harbin was home to a Japanese Germ Warfare Experimental Base, which is now a museum, some 20 miles away in the town of Pingfang. The museum (*Open* daily 8:30–11:30AM, 1–4PM. *Admission: inexpensive*), shows the sadism of the experiments carried out on Chinese, Soviet, British, and Korean prisoners of war who suffered unspeakable horrors.

A more cheerful reason to visit Harbin is for the **ice festival▶▶** in January–March. Artists create ice and snow sculptures that are wrapped around lanterns so dragons, bridges and traditional pavilions glow in the dark. The sculptures are concentrated mostly in Zhaolin Park. There is also a ballroom dancing competition, a food sampling fair, as well as the chance to ride on sleds and snowmobiles.

Sun Island is a sandbank on the Songhua River that is popular with sunbathers in the summer. A snow-sculpture competition is held there in January. It also has parks and gardens, including **Siberia Tiger Park** (*Open* daily. *Admission: moderate*), where Siberian tigers are bred.

▶ Heilong Jiang (Heilong or Black Dragon River) *112B3*

This river, which has given its name to the province, is more familiar by its Russian name—Amur. It forms the border between China and Russia and has been the scene of border disputes and skirmishes. Now that the border has been settled once and for all, the area is open to foreign visitors. Boat tours run between **Heihe**, **Huma**, and **Tongjiang**. This is a region of minority peoples: the Hezhen, numbering about 1,500 at the last count, live by fishing and, like their Inuit cousins, use dog sleds. Nowadays, however, the Hezhen wear woven clothing

COLD COMFORT

Although the people of Harbin are well known for their warmth, the city has a typical Siberian climate. In the winter temperatures fall to –36°F but in the summer can climb to more than 85°F.

instead of animal hides. Another minority people, with a population of just over 4,000, are the shamanistic Oroqens, who also live across the border in Inner Mongolia. Although many lead settled lives now, they are by tradition nomadic forest hunters, raising reindeer and making their utensils from birch bark.

Mohe is China's most northerly town, from which the aurora borealis can be viewed.

▶ Jiamusi *112C3*

A large manufacturing town, Jiamusi is of interest for the farms where ginseng is grown and also where red deer are bred for their antlers, which are used in Chinese medicine.

▶ Jilin *112B2*

A major chemical center with a population of over a million, Jilin (formerly Kirin), although not of particular interest, has nearby ski slopes, a **ginseng farm▶**, and a **museum** (*Open* daily 9–4:30. *Admission inexpensive*) containing a large meteorite that fell in 1976. There is also an ice festival in January. The **Wen Confucian Temple** (*Open* daily 8–5. *Admission inexpensive*) with an exhibit about the old imperial examinations, is worth a visit.

Songhua Lake is 8 miles southeast of Jilin, in a scenic area of 210 square miles.

▶ Jingpo Lake *112B2*

Some 70 miles from the town of Mudanjiang is this S-shaped lake surrounded by high mountains. A good place for fishing (equipment may be rented), it is 56 miles square and the result of a volcanic lava flow that dammed up a gully. The area is a **national park▶▶**, with volcanic craters, karst caves, and waterfalls, including the 130-foot-wide Diaoshuilou. Sadly the area is beginning to be spoiled by the trappings of insensitive tourism development but visits in spring or fall are comfortable and comparitively tourist free.

A NORTHEASTERN TREASURY

The three treasures of the northeast are antlers, furs, and ginseng. There is also frog oil, which is extracted from the female frog's ovary and, when served in soup or with chicken, is supposed to have curative properties.

Manchurian ginseng and tree fungus, used in traditional Chinese medicine

▶▶ Shenyang *112A1*

Now a city of six million and the capital of Liaoning province, at the beginning of the 17th century Shenyang was the capital of the Manchurian Empire. In that same century the Manchus overran China, making Beijing their capital, relegating Shenyang (formerly known as Mukden) to a secondary position. At the beginning of the 20th century it was a Russian railroad town; then it alternated between China and Japan during the first Russo-Japanese War (1904–1905). During the next 45 years it was in the hands of various warlords, the Japanese, the Russians, the Guomindang, and finally the communists. Nowadays Shenyang has an industrial output that rivals Shanghai's—its many industries include aircraft and textiles.

Stately birds and elegant lotus blossoms adorn an ornamental feature in the Imperial Palace in Shenyang, Liaoning province

The city's main sites are the **Imperial Palace▶▶**, the **Qing tombs▶▶** and the **Shisheng Temple▶**. The **Imperial City** (*Open* daily 8:30–4:30. *Admission: moderate*) is a Manchu version in miniature of the Forbidden City in Beijing. It was originally named the Palace of the Prosperous Capital (Shenjing Gong), but it was renamed the Traveling Palace of Upholding Heaven after Beijing became the capital in 1644. The palace was completed between 1625 and 1636, and additions were made during the 18th century. Contained by its walls are some 300 rooms and 10 courtyards, all arranged on three axes—

Map of Shenyang

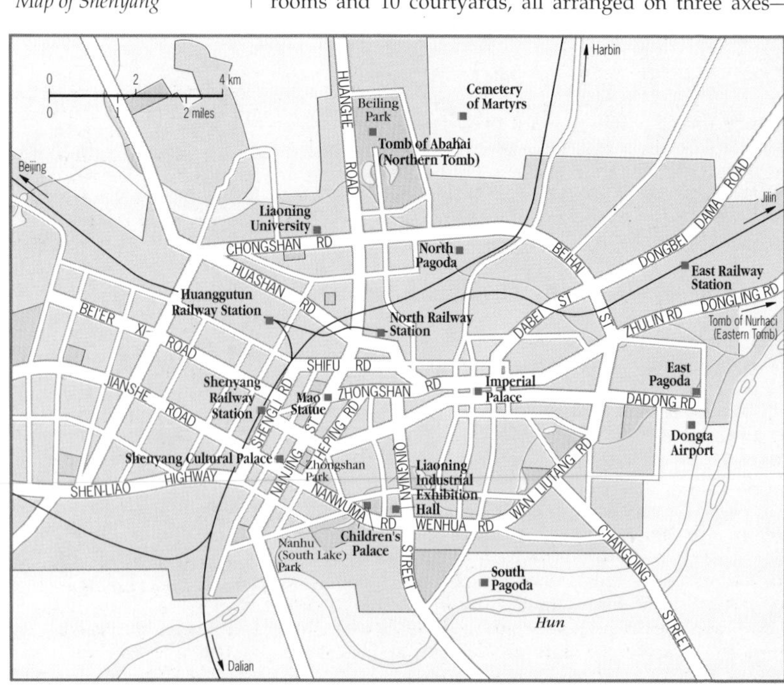

Roofscape, Imperial Palace, Shenyang

middle, eastern, and western. The arrangement of the buildings on the eastern axis is most typically Manchu. On the western axis is the Wensuge (Hall of the Source of Culture), built in 1782 to house a manuscript edition of the 3,450 classical works that made up the Complete Library of the Four Treasures of Knowledge.

The **Tomb of Nurhaci (Dongling or Fuling)**, founder of the Manchu tribal group, is northeast of Shenyang. An avenue of stone animals leads to a wall enclosing a tower and a mound, in which are buried the emperor and his empresses and concubines (*Open* daily. *Admission: inexpensive*).

Beiling or **Zhaoling** (*Open* daily 7:30–5:30. *Admission: inexpensive*), in a wooded park in the northern part of the city, is the tomb of Huang Taiji, son of Nurhaci, and his wife. It is better preserved than Dongling—there are stone horses and lions, bridges, and a fine *pailou* (canopied gateway) in black stone, as well as a stele bearing Abahai's calligraphy.

The **Shisheng Temple**, on Heping Lu, was built in 1638 and was the main Lamaist temple in the city.

▶ Wudalianchi *112B3*

This nature reserve comprises five linked lakes, formed in 1720 when volcanic activity forced lava into the Bei River. The mineral springs are said to cure almost any ailment.

▶▶ Zhalong *112B3*

(*Open:* daily. *Admission: expensive*)

Zhalong is at the edge of a vast area of marshland that lies on a bird migration route from the Arctic to southeast Asia. Some 180 species of birds pass through from April through October, among them the almost extinct red-crowned crane, the traditional Chinese symbol of longevity.

STOCKS AND SHARES

In 1986, Shenyang was the first city in China since 1949 to boast a stock exchange. In the same year, a Shenyang company declared bankruptcy, unheard of in a socialist economy.

CHARISMATIC CRANES

For the Chinese, animals are to be either eaten or worshiped. Such was the reverence accorded the red-crowned crane by Duke Yi of Wei that he paid them a salary and allowed them to travel in carriages. This irritated the Wei generals, who asked, "Since the cranes are so highly honored, why not let them do the fighting?"

For Westerners, traditional Chinese medicine is invariably associated with acupuncture, but acupuncture is only one of several applications, all of which are based on the precepts of Taoism.

A Yunnan herbalist passes on his knowledge to his son

SLOW BUT SURE
Chinese medicine usually comes in the form of a variety of pills and potions with a plethora of bewildering instructions. Tempting though it is to ignore them, patience and careful observance of the directions often leads to good results. Chinese medicine does not act as quickly as its Western counterpart.

In the pharmacy of the Hospital of Traditional Chinese Medicine, Tianjin

Vital essence Chinese medicine is considered unscientific and imprecise by some Western practitioners. But a Chinese doctor might well argue that its imprecision—or flexibility—is in fact its strength. The Chinese refer to organs, but when they do so it is not the organs themselves that are important but their function in the distribution of vital essence (or *qi*) throughout the body. The 11 "organs" by which health is judged are the bladder, circulation, gall bladder, heart, kidney, large intestine, liver, pancreas, small intestine, stomach, and something called the "triple burner," which has no material existence at all but is a driving force. Over the centuries, hundreds of points were located on the body, linked to these organs. By joining them together, meridian paths were drawn that traced the flow of *qi*.

Harmony There are 12 meridians, each corresponding to one of the five Chinese elements (metal, earth, fire, water, wood) and each best treated at a certain time of day. A further eight meridians are important in Taoism but of less importance to clinical medical treatment. What concerns Chinese medicine is not the state of the heart itself but the invisible motor that drives the heart to beat. Illness results from a disharmony between mind and body, which can arise when emotional strain, for example, distorts nature's balance.

Diagnosis The Chinese doctor examines the state of the flow of *qi* through the body's meridians by checking the pulse. He or she uses three fingers to read the six different pulses in each wrist that correspond to the 12 meridians. By applying different levels of pressure with the fingers, he or she will notice irregularities. Having read the pulse, the doctor will ask questions of the patient to decide upon the appropriate treatment.

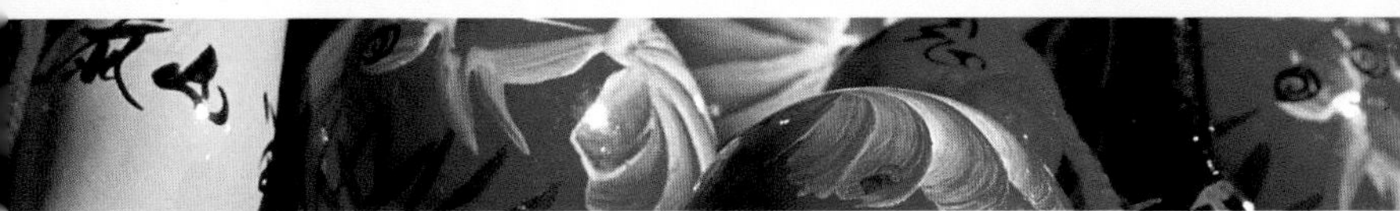

Treatment The aim is to stimulate the flow of *qi* in the blocked meridian using acupuncture (*zhenjiu*), acupressure (similar to acupuncture), heat treatment with needles in conjunction with the burning leaves of mugwort (moxibustion), or massage (*anmou*). The most precise and efficacious of these is acupuncture, which is particularly good for relieving pain.

Diet is considered vital to health and partly explains the Chinese obsession with food. Taoist teaching recommends abstinence from a variety of foods and stimulants from aubergines to vinegar, although a less rigorous version of the diet suffices for most. Only food that relates to the organs and the elements associated with them is eaten, so, for example, hot foods are recommended for the lungs.

Much of this, although not scientifically expressed according to Western terminology, does correspond to Western ideas, and there is no doubt that Chinese medicine, even if based on amorphous theories, is extremely effective for some diseases. Some aspects, like the use of talismans and incantations, are less likely to win over sceptics, but Chinese medicine in general deserves serious consideration.

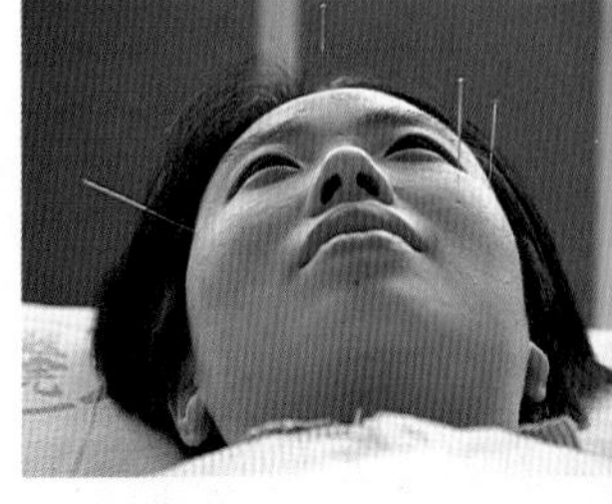

Above: acupuncture
Top: medicinal gourds

SKIN TONIC
Taoists believe that following a strict diet for three years will result in the regeneration of skin tissue throughout the body; after 10 years the teeth and bones will be renewed.

A medicine market

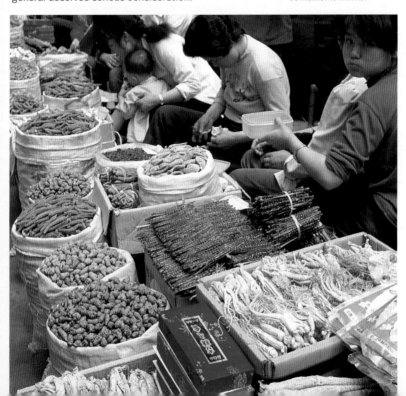

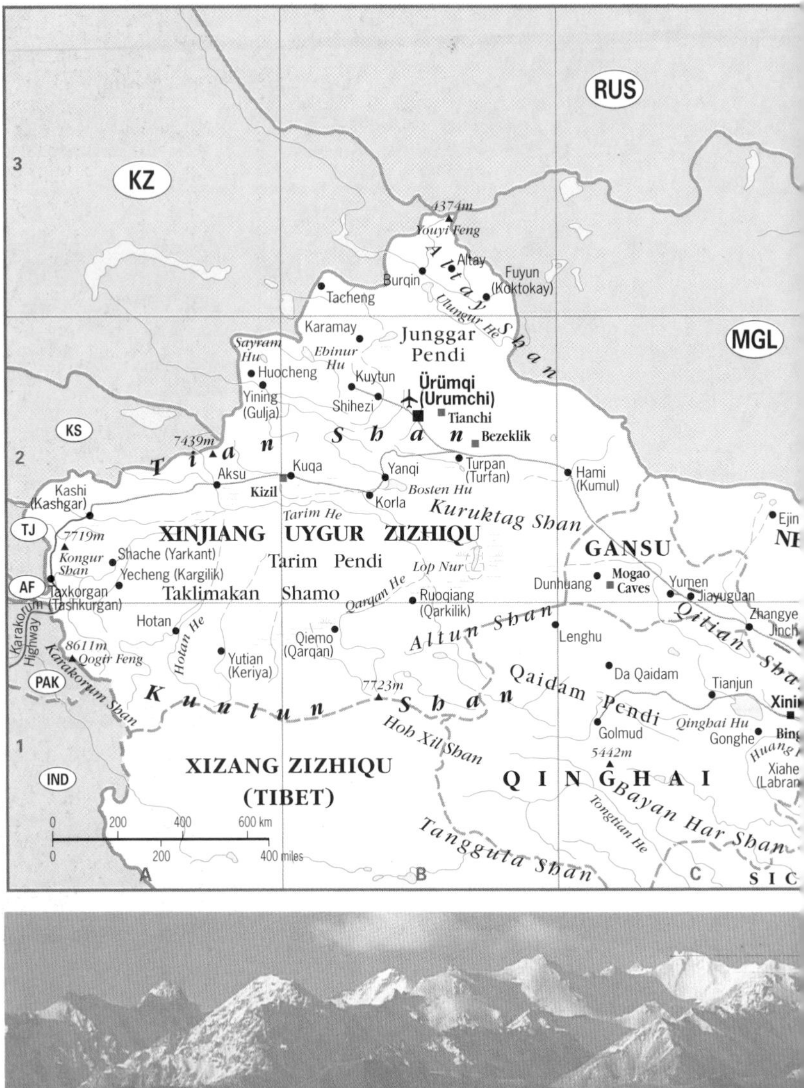

RUS
KZ
MGL
KS
TJ
AF
PAK
IND
4374m
Youyi Feng
Altay Shan
Altay
Burqin
Fuyun
(Koktokay)
Tacheng
Ulungur He
Karamay
Junggar
Pendi
Sayram
Hu
Ebinur
Hu
Huocheng
Kuytun
Ürümqi
(Urumchi)
Yining
(Gulja)
Shihezi
Tianchi
Bezeklik
7439m
Tian Shan
Aksu
Kuqa
Yanqi
Turpan
(Turfan)
Hami
(Kumul)
Kizil
Bosten Hu
Korla
Kashi
(Kashgar)
Tarim He
Kuruktag Shan
XINJIANG UYGUR ZIZHIQU
GANSU
7719m
Kongur
Shan
Shache (Yarkant)
Yecheng (Kargilik)
Tarim Pendi
Taklimakan Shamo
Lop Nur
Dunhuang
Mogao
Caves
Yumen
Jiayuguan
Taxkorgan
(Tashkurgan)
Qarqan He
Ruoqiang
(Qarkilik)
Zhangye
Hotan
Altun Shan
Lenghu
Qilian Shan
Karakorum Highway
8611m
Qogir Feng
Hotan He
Qiemo
(Qarqan)
Yutian
(Keriya)
Da Qaidam
Tianjun
Karakorum Shan
Kunlun Shan
7723m
Qaidam Pendi
Golmud
Qinghai Hu
Gonghe
Hoh Xil Shan
5442m
XIZANG ZIZHIQU
(TIBET)
QINGHAI
Bayan Har Shan
Tongtian He
Tanggula Shan
0 200 400 600 km
0 200 400 miles
A
B
C
1
2
3

Inner Mongolia and the Silk Road

REGION HIGHLIGHTS

MINORITIES AND NOMADS
The Xinjiang province is usually associated with the Uyghurs, but there are also the nomadic Kazaks of the mountains, fine horsemen who live in yurts; and the Kirgiz, also nomadic, who keep herds of camels. The Xibo Manchus, who live near the Russian border, are descended from Qing dynasty garrison troops.

Wrestlers in the grasslands outside Hohhot. Mongolian wrestling expresses joy in manhood

INNER MONGOLIA (NEI MENGU) AND XINJIANG Although these vast areas have separate histories, there is a tendency to place them together, along with the province of Gansu, gateway to the Silk Road oases, and the autonomous region of Ningxia. Maybe this is because of their location on either side of the Gansu corridor; or because both, like Tibet, are outside the mainstream of Chinese life (much as Beijing would like to believe otherwise); or perhaps because there is a tendency for tour companies to combine the two as a package.

As far as the peripheral regions of the Chinese Empire are concerned, the world's attention has been focused on Tibet. But the peoples of the Mongolian grasslands and the Muslims of the northwest chafe at Chinese rule from time to time as well (several protestors were killed in Yining in 1997 as the authorities quelled riots). The former Mongolian People's Republic (known in the past as Outer Mongolia and now simply as Mongolia) is a sovereign state that may yet yearn for reunification with Chinese Inner Mongolia. The Muslims of the northwest have plenty of close relatives across the border in the former Soviet republics—the growing Islamic movement may strengthen ties with the old oasis towns of the Silk Road.

CHINESE RULE Both areas are comparatively recent acquisitions by China. After the fall of the Mongolian Empire at the end of the 14th century the Mongol tribes returned to their nomadic, tribal ways, but under the Qing dynasty the Mongol homelands were absorbed into the Chinese Empire, the Chinese at last allaying their fear of the barbarians across the Wall. This huge area was difficult to subjugate, and the Russian empire lopped off the northern, "outer" part of Mongolia as a protectorate. Inner Mongolia remained part of China until 1911 and the

Struggling up the "singing sands"—dunes near the oasis town of Dunhuang, Gansu province

Hui Muslim from Ningxia

fall of the last dynasty. The two Mongolias were reunified for eight years. China then reclaimed Inner Mongolia while Outer Mongolia declared itself the Mongolian People's Republic in 1924. The Japanese occupied much of the area during the 1930s, but after World War II the Chinese declared Inner Mongolia an autonomous region within China. China recognized Outer Mongolia as a separate state in 1946. Inner Mongolia has a population of 20 million, of which a mere two million are ethnic Mongolians.

Xinjiang ("New Territory") was brought under Chinese rule at various times during the Han and Tang dynasties, but it was the acquisitive Qing dynasty that brought the region to heel in the 18th century. The Muslims never accepted Chinese rule and, with the fall of the dynasty in 1911, the region came under the control of a succession of warlords. An attempt in 1945 to form an independent Turkestan Republic failed, and the communists absorbed the area into China with little difficulty in 1949. Now more than half its population of 13 million is Han Chinese.

In both regions, although some concessions have been granted to cultural differences, on the whole Chinese rule is paramount. Nonetheless, daily life for many of the natives of these areas is quite different from that of their compatriots behind the Great Wall, a fact that is still very much in evidence, particularly in the towns of the Silk Road or at the annual Naadam Fair in Mongolia.

OVER THE BORDER

In the mid-1980s a little-reported phenomenon was taking place in the remote border regions of the Mongolian People's Republic and China, for many years a sensitive area because of their traditional enmity. The infrequent trains between the two were crammed with Chinese men and women who had been living in Mongolia and who, as a result of tension between the two countries, were being sent back to China. Belongings and food were piled high in the compartments, only to be confiscated at the border.

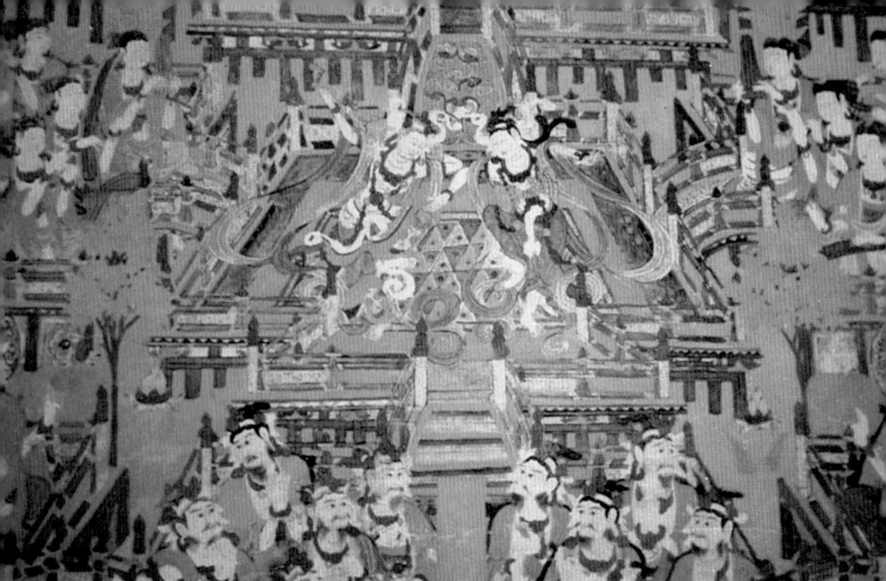

Buddhist dancers depicted in the Mogao caves (Cave 112)

►►► Dunhuang *128C2*

A small oasis town in Gansu province, Dunhuang (which means "blazing beacon") is the most important site on the Silk Road itinerary because of the magnificent array of early Chinese Buddhist paintings in the **Mogao caves►►►** (15 miles away). Dunhuang was made a prefecture in 117 BC by Emperor Han Wudi, and some of the beacons made of yellow earth that were part of the Han extension of the Great Wall are visible between the town and the railroad station at Liuyuan, the nearest point of arrival.

The cave paintings, accumulated over several centuries, were the legacy of the pilgrim monks on their way to India and of merchants and nobles who made their own artistic contributions as a blessing for their caravans and salvation for their souls. The painters were sometimes locals, sometimes masters brought in for the purpose. The cave temples were excavated by monks from AD 366; their walls were covered in mud and then layers of dung, plaster, and animal hair, and kaolin was added to provide a suitable surface on which to paint. As the Silk Road declined, the caves became less important, and in the 10th century they were sealed. In 1900, they were rediscovered by a monk who made it his life's work to return them to their former glory. Soon after, the Anglo-Hungarian explorer Sir Aurel Stein persuaded the monk to part with a remarkable collection of manuscripts and silk paintings, now displayed in the British Museum and the Bibliothèque Nationale, Paris.

The caves (*Open* daily 8:30–10, 2–5. *Admission: expensive*) were made a national monument in 1961. Of the 1,000 caves, about 40 are thought worth visiting. A morning and afternoon visit is necessary to fully appreciate the caves, while a torch is an essential accessory.

The earliest caves date back to the 4th century AD (Northern Wei dynasty). A good example is Cave 257, famous for paintings on the west wall depicting the story of the Buddha who, as Deer King, was betrayed by a man whose life he had saved. It also features a very early landscape. The later Western Wei is represented in Cave 249, with some beautiful landscape paintings.

SUTRAS AND DOCUMENTS

Sir Aurel Stein's finds at Dunhuang consist mainly of manuscripts written out as acts of devotion, as well as the Diamond Sutra (now in the British Museum), claimed to be the world's earliest known printed book (AD 866); some of the documents were of a secular nature—tax and census returns, and bills of sale, for example—which appear to have been sealed in the caves for safekeeping, and there is also a manuscript fragment containing musical notation for the lute.

Cave 428 was decorated during the Northern Zhou with portraits of figures who had sponsored sacred paintings—these are beneath the story from the life of Buddha on the east wall.

The finest caves of the Sui dynasty are 150, 244, 410, 420 (with a spectacular temple painted on the ceiling), and 427. By this time foreign influence (Indian, Central Asian) had been replaced with a purer Chinese style.

Dunhuang's art peaked during the Tang dynasty, when religious traditions were combined with observations of real life. Murals vary from scenes from the sutras to portraits of individuals. The finest examples are in Caves 1, 16, 17, 51, 70, 96, 130, 139, 148, 172, 202, 209, 320, 321, 323, 328, 329, 332, 365, and 387.

The **Crescent Lake▶▶** (4 miles south) is a spring-fed pool (*Open* daily. *Admission: moderate*) surrounded by giant sand dunes (called "the singing sands") that can, with difficulty, be climbed. Camels and drivers are available to take you, for a fee, to the dunes.

The "old city movie set," a Song-dynasty-style town constructed for the Sino-Japanese movie *Dunhuang*, is in the desert to the southwest.

Dunhuang Museum▶ (*Open* daily 8–12, 3–6. *Admission: inexpensive*) on Yangguan Donglu, has exhibits from some of the caves at Mogao and also from the old fortresses at Yangguan and Yumen.

GUARDIAN OF THE CAVES
Sir Aurel Stein bought most of his documents from the Taoist Abbot Wang Yuanlu, who devoted much energy to obtaining funds for the restoration of the caves. According to Stein, his efforts were not very successful: they showed "only too plainly how low sculptural art had sunk in Dunhuang." However, Stein admired the efforts of the abbot, "whose devotion to this shrine and to the task of religious merit which he has set himself in restoring it, was unmistakably genuine."

A Tang Dynasty "Apsara," celestial angel, in Cave 44

Perfect statuesque tranquillity at Dunhuang: seated Tang Buddha in Cave 328

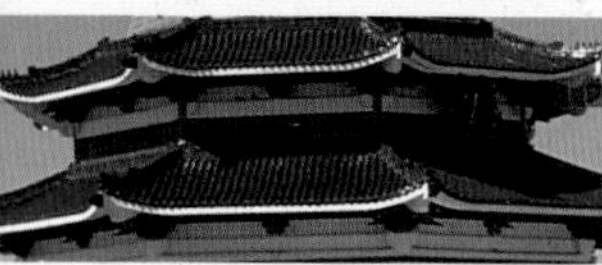

Inner Mongolia (Nei Menggu) was absorbed into the Chinese Empire in the 18th century. The history of the Mongolian people before that is long and occasionally illustrious.

Above: the tomb of Genghis Khan

BENEATH THE GRASSLANDS
The attractions of Mongolia for the Chinese are concealed below the earth's surface. It is the best place in the country for rare earth minerals, and there are at least 60 verifiable mineral ores in 500 different locations, including coal, iron, chromium, copper, lead, zinc, gold, mica, salt, and mirabilite.

The Lamaist Wudangzhao Monastery, north of Baotou

Nomads For centuries the Mongols were a loose confederation of nomadic tribesmen based on the banks of the Onon River, and a constant threat to the Chinese, who constructed the Great Wall to keep them out. In the early 13th century, the various tribes united under Genghis Khan and conquered most of the known world. The Mongols ruled China (the Yuan dynasty) for over 100 years, but with Kublai Khan's death in 1294 the empire disintegrated. Although minor khanates remained in isolated parts of the former empire, the Mongols returned to their homeland and their nomadic ways.

Grasslands Something of the traditional Mongol way of life is still evident on the grasslands. Round felt tents, or "ghers," and herdsmen on horseback can sometimes be seen but visitors are discouraged from discovering the grasslands for themselves, other than through sanitized tours organized by CITS. Foreign travel companies organize interesting specialized trips, or you might try to rent a taxi or jeep to take you out to the grasslands.

Highlights Inner Mongolia has its own atmosphere, and there are several places worth visiting, particularly in summer. The capital is **Hohhot** (**Huhehaote**) where the main attractions are the **Inner Mongolia Museum▶▶** (*Open* daily. *Admission: inexpensive*), which displays artifacts of traditional Mongolian life and a locally discovered mammoth; the **Old Town▶▶**, with its low houses and markets and temples and mosques; and the **Five Pagoda Temple▶** (*Open* daily. *Admission: inexpensive*), unique in China for its Classical Indian style. Tours can be arranged to the grasslands.

The Five Pagoda Temple, Hohhot

Xilinhot has little to recommend it but is a good center from which to arrange a visit to the grasslands.

Baotou is the largest city of Inner Mongolia. Its main attraction, apart from the steel mill and a small locomotive museum, is the 13th-century **Wudangzhao Monastery▶▶** (*Open* daily. *Admission: inexpensive*), 45 miles to the north and the best example of a Tibetan-style monastery in the region. On the side of a hill, the monastery consists of temples, houses, a hostel, and lamas' living quarters. It is worth the drive from Baotou.

About 40 miles south of Baotou you can visit **Yimeng Xiang Shawan**, or the resonant sand gorge, filled with dunes up to 270 feet high.

Hailar, on the banks of the Heilong Jiang (Amur River), is another good starting point from which to visit the grasslands. Manzhouli is even better; from here you can also visit Dalai Lake, one of the largest lakes in China.

From Dongsheng, south of Baotou, it is possible to reach **Genghis Khan's Mausoleum** (*Open* daily. *Admission: moderate*) via Ejin Qi. The mausoleum dates from 1954, when the Khan's ashes were returned from safekeeping in Qinghai. He remains an object of veneration to Mongolians.

Perhaps the best time to visit Inner Mongolia is in the summer, usually the month of August, during *Naadam* (the word means exhibition or game or joke). In recent years it has come to mean the national festival, a celebration of archery, wrestling, and horsemanship.

A harsh climate makes for tough people: Mongolian wrestlers at the annual Naadam *fair*

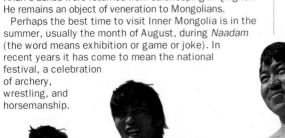

NEWS FROM KASHI
Perhaps the most entertaining account of Kashi before 1949 is to be found in Peter Fleming's *News from Tartary*, for many the ultimate travel book. He stayed in the former British Consulate, "a pleasant house with a lovely garden, standing on a little bluff outside the city. From its terrace you looked across the green and checkered valley of a small river toward the too seldom visible mountains." The bazaar was filled with "Kirghiz and bearded Tadjiks from the hills [who] moved with a hint of swagger among the self-effacing Turkis."

Traditional Kashi cloth in vibrant colors

►► Jiayuguan *128C2*

This small town is at the far end and narrowest point of the Gansu Corridor, marking the western extremity of the Great Wall and the traditional boundary of Han China. "One more cup of wine for our remaining happiness. There will be chilling parting dreams tonight," wrote a 9th-century poet of a parting at Jiayuguan. Just outside the town is an imposing **Ming fort►►►** (*Open* daily 8–8. *Admission: inexpensive*), built in 1372 in a dramatic setting between two ranges of mountains that crowd in on the pass. It rises in spectacular fashion—crenellated walls 33 feet high surmounted by towers with elegant roofs—from an area of flat-stone desert. The **Heishan rock carvings►**, reputedly made by the Huns about 1,500 years ago, are 12 miles northwest. Some 4 miles north of the fort is a reconstructed section of the Great Wall, with fabulous views of the Valla Mountains.

►►► The Karakorum Highway *128A2*

The route between Pakistan and China was opened in the mid-1980s using what was once a branch of the Silk Road. It is a magnificent way of leaving or entering China. From Kashi, a day's drive through awesome mountain scenery, passing rippleless lakes and crumbling caravanserai, takes you to Tashkurgan (an uncomfortable overnight stop). From Tashkurgan, the road winds up to a height of nearly 16,000 feet before it crosses the border into the mountain valleys of Pakistan.

►►► Kashi (Kashgar) *128A2*

Conjuring up a host of magical images, Kashi, or Kashgar as it is more widely known, manages to meet expectations in many ways, despite steady historical decline, Chinese indifference to local culture and creeping modernization. Its importance grew from its location as an oasis at the point where the northern and southern arms of the Silk Road converged, forming a natural gateway to the mountain passes leading to India and Russia. Kashi was held by the Chinese periodically from AD 78, but by the 10th century it was firmly in the Islamic world, where it remained until the Chinese reconquered the area in the 18th century. Kashgar became a focal point for the rivalry between Russia and Britain, a tussle for hegemony in Central Asia known as "the Great Game." Kashgar became a haven for spies of these empires, both of which opened consulates (the former British one stood at the back of the Chini Bagh Hotel grounds, the former Russian one is the Seman Hotel).

There are several places to see. The **Id Kah Mosque►** (*Open* daily. *Admission: inexpensive*) is the largest in Xinjiang, with room for at least 6,000 worshipers. Founded in the mid-18th century, its present appearance dates from 1838. The **Abakh Hoja Tomb►►**, in the eastern suburbs, contains 72 tombs of the family members of Abakh Hoja, a saintly man of the 18th century whose daughter was the legendary "fragrant concubine" (so-called because she was supposed to have naturally secreted perfume) who was abducted by the Emperor Qian Long. She defied the emperor and was forced to commit suicide by the emperor's mother.

The **market►►** in the center of town is a colorful daily event and worth lingering in for a couple of hours. Try to be in Kashi for the **Sunday Bazaar▶▶▶**, a meeting point for all the farmers in the area who come, much as they have done for centuries, to sell their wares, from melons to horseflesh. Hot and dusty, it provides a fascinating glimpse into local life.

Since 1999 there has been a railroad link with Ürümqi which, some fear, marks the beginning of the end for "old" Kashi.

THE FINAL FRONTIER
The Inner City of Jiayuguan town, the last Chinese outpost on the Silk Road, with its 33-foot-high wall, was a citadel that housed the Chinese military commander. Beyond were the "barbarian" tribes. Outside the west gate is a stele inscribed with the characters: "The Greatest Barrier Under Heaven."

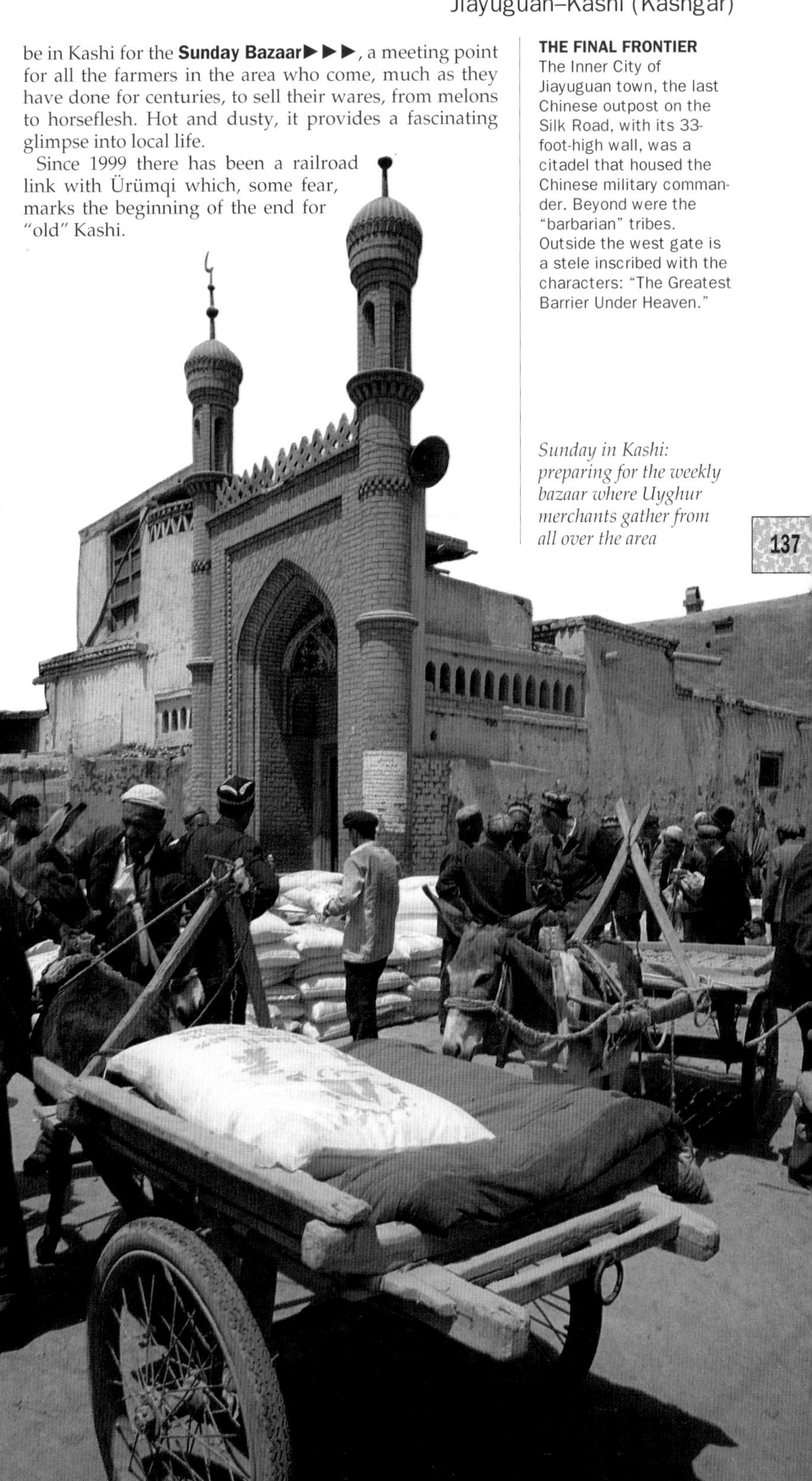

Sunday in Kashi: preparing for the weekly bazaar where Uyghur merchants gather from all over the area

PARADISE LOST
The Kingdom of Kuqa was an extraordinary place, exciting the wonder of seasoned travelers such as the 7th-century Tang monk, Xuanzang. It measured 312 by 200 miles and was blessed with luxuriant oases where even corn and rice grew. The orchards were filled with grapes and pomegranates, the ground with gold and copper. Above all the air was soft, and the people, who were gifted above all others in the playing of the lute and pipe, were honest.

The 88-foot-high Tang dynasty Future Buddha in Bingling Buddhist caves, Gansu province

▶▶▶ Kuqa *128B2*

Kuqa is the second largest town in the central part of Xinjiang and was once the capital of an ancient feudal state, the Kingdom of Qiuci. The ruins consist mostly of sand-brick walls but convey a little of the region's past glories. Taken by the Chinese in the 7th century, it was an important center for Buddhism and the home of Kumarajiva, one of the greatest translators of Sanskrit works into Chinese. Kuqa had its own Indo-European language, lost for more than 1,000 years until the script was discovered by the sinologists Paul Pelliot and Albert Von le Coq on items in the caves at Kizil at the turn of the century. The manuscripts found here, on palm leaves, paper, bark, and wood, were removed and deciphered in Paris.

Kizil▶▶▶ (*Open* daily 9:30–8. *Admission: expensive*) is just over an hour's drive from Kuqa. The caves in cliffs above the Muzart River were decorated between AD 500 and 700, before Chinese stylistic devices had reached this far, and the paintings are both Indian and Iranian in style. Of the 236 caves, about 70 are reasonably preserved. Many of the best frescos were removed by Albert Von le Coq to Berlin, where some were destroyed during World War II. Others can still be seen in Berlin's Museum of Indian Art.

▶▶ Lanzhou *129D1*

The capital of Gansu province lies on the upper reaches of the Yellow River. A former staging post on the Silk Road, it has become an industrial city of remarkable ugliness. The city has a few items of note. The **Gansu Provincial Museum▶▶** (*Open* Mon–Sat 9–12, 2:30–5. *Admission: inexpensive*) contains the finest display of Yangshao (early neolithic) pottery in China, and bronzes from the Han-dynasty tomb of General Zhang, including the famous

"flying horse," its hoof poised on a swallow's wing. It is now a widely used symbol of the area.

The **Five Springs Mountain (Wuquanshan) Park▶** attempts to reconcile concrete with traditional Chinese architecture, with some success. In the park (*Open* daily. *Admission: inexpensive*) is the Chongqingsi, a 14th-century temple with a 13th-century iron bell. From here there is a chairlift (*Open* 9AM–10PM. *Admission: inexpensive*) to **Lanshan Park**, high up in the Lanshan mountains.

The **White Pagoda Mountain Park▶** (*Open* daily 6:30AM–10PM. *Admission: inexpensive*) consists of several temples including the Yuan dynasty **White Pagoda**.

The main reason for a stop in Lanzhou is to visit the **Buddhist caves at Bingling▶▶▶** (*Open* daily—except during low-water periods, usually in winter. *Admission: expensive*), 60 miles from the city. Organized tours are recommended as trips to the caves are dependent upon the unpredictable river-water level and involve a two-hour bus journey and a further two hours by boat. En route you may visit the **Liujia Gorge Dam**, one of the largest in China.

The 34 caves at Bingling contain several hundred statues (the largest of which in Cave 172, is a Tang Future Buddha, about 88 feet high) and many paintings. The earliest caves date back to the Northern Wei period, but painting continued through the Tang, the period of greatest activity, to the Qing. Some of the best work is in Caves 4, 10, 11, 82, 114, and 169.

It is also possible to visit **Xiahe** and the **Labrang Monastery** (described on pages 146–147) from Lanzhou, although the journey will take seven hours. Xinglongshan, 30 miles from Lanzhou, is a mountain covered in Han dynasty temples.

TREACHEROUS WATERS
The Yellow River carries heavy deposits of silt down from the loess region of the northern steppe. For centuries the silt has caused severe flooding and drainage problems. Construction of the dam at Sanmenxia in Gansu province began after 1949, but later the reservoir became clogged with the river's sediment and had to be rebuilt.

View across the Yellow River over the city of Lanzhou from White Pagoda Mountain

Ningxia Huizu Zizhiqu is the Autonomous Hui Region of Ningxia and is very similar to Gansu province, of which it was once a part. Its landscape varies from the arid and mountainous south to the northern desert region (the Tengger Desert, part of the Gobi), bisected by the Yellow River.

NORTHWESTERN BORDER TROUBLE
The Western Xia (Xixia) were a northern Tibetan (Tangut) tribe who became the dominant force in their homelands. They invaded the Chinese northwest in 1040, at first with considerable success, but the sheer size of the Chinese army and its sophisticated hardware, which included early hand grenades, in the end was too much for the Xia. The Song dynasty nonetheless was compelled to pay tribute to the Xia, as well as to the Khitan (another tribal state threatening Chinese stability) as the price of peace. The Xia were finally vanquished by Genghis Khan in 1227.

Discussing religion at a Ningxia mosque. The Hui, whose ancestors came from the Middle East, are an Islamic people

The Hui Ningxia is one of the poorest and most underdeveloped areas of China—even now, maybe half the population earn less than the equivalent of U.S.$20 per year. In this region of parched soil, everything depends on rainfall and there is even a relocation program to move people who can no longer make a living from the land.

Ningxia has a population of four million, of whom about one third are Hui people. The Hui are Muslims. With Chinese features, althoughdarker skinned, they are descended from Arab and Iranian traders who came to China along the Silk Road during the Tang dynasty and intermarried with the local population. Their numbers swelled during the Yuan (Mongol) dynasty, when more arrived from Central Asia. During the Muslim Uprisings of 1862–1878, the Hui played a major role, but they were mercilessly punished by the imperial troops. Ningxia was created as an administrative region in 1928, was absorbed into Gansu in 1954, and reemerged as an autonomous region in 1958.

Highlights Ningxia is not a major center for tourism, but it is not without interest. The provincial capital, once the capital of the 11th-century Western Xia dynasty, is **Yinchuan▶▶**. Set amid irrigation canals used since the Han dynasty, the city has little to offer, except in the old town, which houses the 400-year-old Yuhuang Pavilion, the Drum Tower, several mosques, the West Pagoda, the North Pagoda (which dates back to the 5th century but was rebuilt in 1771), the South Gate, a Catholic church built at the turn of the century, and Ningxia Museum.

More enticing is **Gunzhongkou▶▶**, 10 miles west of Yinchuan, among the Helanshan mountains, which reach over 11,000 feet in height. Here are the Twin Pagodas and the Western Xia Mausoleum, constructed by the founder of the Western Xia dynasty, Li Yuanhao.

Below: sheepskin coracle on the Yellow River
Below and top, opposite: details from Gao Temple, Zhongwei

About 60 miles from Yinchuan, near **Qingtongxia▶▶**, is the group of 108 white Dagobas built during the Yuan dynasty—mysteriously in the shape of a triangle.

Zhongwei▶ is a small but ancient town which has the **Gao Temple** (*Open* daily 8–6. *Admission: inexpensive*), an unusual edifice in wood constructed for use by Buddhists, Confucianists, and Taoists. East of the town are remains of the Great Wall and, on the edge of the Tengger Desert at Shapotou, the **Desert Research Centre** (*Open* daily. *Admission: inexpensive*). Its original aim in 1956 was to find ways of preventing the desert sands from encroaching onto the railroads, and it seems to have met with some success. Like Yinchuan, Zhongwei is watered by ancient irrigation canals. Rafts made of sheep leather, a traditional method of transportation on the Yellow River, can sometimes still be seen at work.

Guyuan, in southern Ningxia, has more than 130 caves cut into the mountains. The caves contain fine Buddhist work up to 1,400 years old.

Maijishan: The name means "Corn Rick Mountain"

▶ Linxia 129D1

Another former Silk Road town in Gansu province, which is interesting because of its minority inhabitants: the Hui, Dongxiang and Uyghur peoples.

▶▶ Maijishan 129D1

The Buddhist caves (*Open* daily 9–5. *Admission: moderate*) on Maijishan, a mountain 20 miles southeast of Tianshui in the south of Gansu, rank with those at Datong, Dunhuang, and Luoyang as the most important in China. Joining a group with a guide is advisable, and a flashlight is useful. The caves are reached by a network of precipitous stairways.

The earliest date back to the 4th century AD. Some 200 remain, many of those on the west side untouched since the Song dynasty—notable are Caves 100, 133, and 165. On the less well-preserved east side, the most interesting caves are 4, 7, 13, 72a, 102, 133, and 191. At **Gangu**, west of Tianshui, is a 75-foot Tang-dynasty Buddha overlooking the Wei River.

Clay sculptures outside the spectacular Maijishan Buddhist caves

▶▶▶ Turpan (Turfan) 128B2

Turpan, which is served by train from Daheyan, 40 miles away, is perhaps the most delightful town along the Chinese Silk Road, in part for its interesting sights, but chiefly because it still exudes, with its trees and traditional Uyghur mud-brick houses, a tranquil, old-world atmosphere rare in China. Although most of the inhabitants are Uyghur, much of Turpan's historical importance is pre-Islamic. The Uyghurs, originally nomads from Siberia and Central Asia, settled in the area after the 9th century, when they were converted to Islam. They retain much of their way of life, wearing traditional clothes, building trellised courtyards and small kilns for drying the famous grapes from the area, and following a diet—mutton, flat bread, dried fruit, pilau rice—quite distinct from that of Han China.

Most of the places of interest lie just outside the town, but there are a few things of worth within its walls. Turpan's **market**▶▶ with its dried fruit, exotic medicines, and gleaming rolls of cloth, is endlessly fascinating. The **Imin Minaret**▶▶ (*Open* daylight hours. *Admission: inexpensive*), part of a former mosque, was built in 1778 and is made of beautifully decorated brick in the tapering Iranian style.

Outside the town are some remarkable ruins, graves and caves, many of which were disturbed by turn-of-the 20th-century archeologist adventurers. The **Cave Temples at Bezeklik▶▶** (30 miles northeast) (*Open* daily 8–11, 3–6. *Admission: inexpensive*), part of a monastery that existed between the 6th and 14th centuries, were carved out of the cliff face above the Murtuk River in a desert setting. There are some fine paintings remaining (in an Indo-Iranian style with Chinese influence) but many were removed by Von le Coq to museums in Berlin, and some were subsequently destroyed by Allied bombs.

To the west of Turpan is the abandoned town of **Jiaohe▶▶▶**, and to the southeast the ruined city of **Gaochang▶▶▶** (*Open* daily 8–11, 3–6. *Admission: inexpensive*) and the ancient graveyard of **Astana▶▶** (*Open* daily 8–11, 3–6. *Admission: inexpensive*). Jiaohe was originally a Han garrison town, taken by the Uyghurs and abandoned in the Yuan dynasty possibly because of a lack of water or because of Muslim fanaticism toward Buddhist remains. It is both poignant and spectacular in its clifftop setting, as is Gaochang, another Han garrison town, that was the Uyghur capital from 840 to 1209. It was abandoned at the beginning of the Ming dynasty.

Astana is a graveyard used between the 3rd and 8th centuries. Well-preserved bodies have been discovered here as well as documents, coins, and pottery, now displayed in Turpan and Ürümqi museums. Three of the graves are open, one showing two of the occupants, the others with charming Tang wall paintings.

Also nearby are the **Flaming Mountains▶**, which glow at sunset, and **Grape Valley▶**, center of grape production.

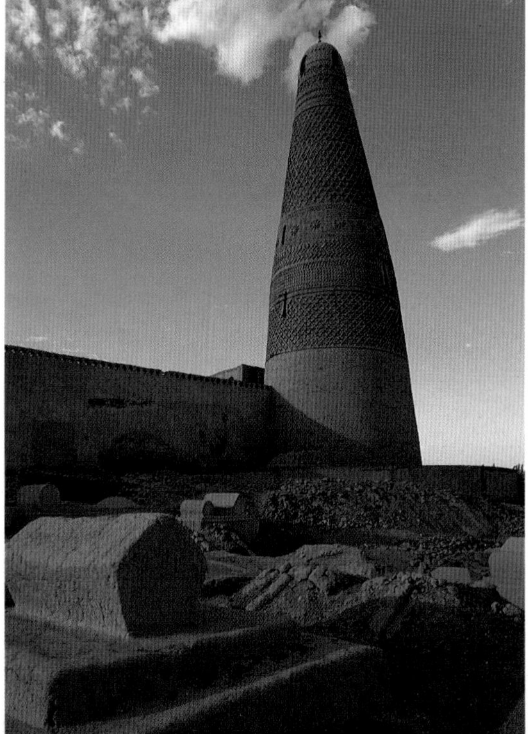

Every evening the Flaming Mountains outside Turpan reflect the desert heat

LOW LAND

Turpan lies in the Turpan depression (Turpan is a Uyghur word meaning "lowland"), one of the lowest landfalls on earth, descending to 500 feet below sea level at its deepest point. Depressions such as this are a characteristic feature of the northern part of western China. Encircled by mountains, the oases high up are fed by melting snow in summer, while the centers remain true desert.

WELL-WATERED DESERT

Turpan is noted for its underground water channels, which are known as *karez*. These carry water formed by the melting snow from the nearby mountains and prevent it from evaporating in the intense heat of the summer. The system is thought to have been imported from Persia 2,000 years ago.

The Imin Minaret, Turpan, built in 18th-century Iranian style

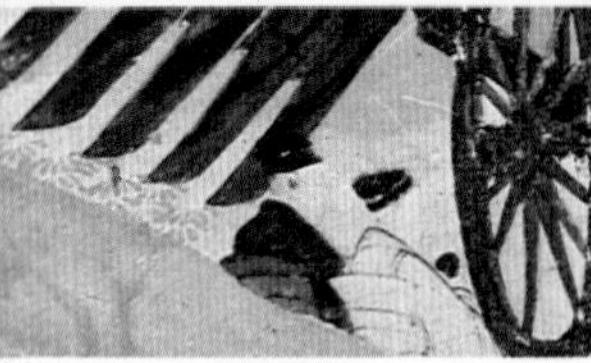

The Silk Road is the collective name given to a number of trade routes linking the Chinese and Roman empires. Many commodities passed along it, but silk was for centuries one of its mainstays because silk production remained a mystery outside China (see pages 182–183).

Detail from a mural in Mogao Caves, Dunhuang

FLYING HORSES
General Zhang Qian's mission west took 13 years, during which time he was taken prisoner twice by the Xiongnu tribe. One of his most significant discoveries was the existence of the so-called "flying horses" of Ferghana, in Uzbekistan, which were altogether more powerful than the horses familiar to the Chinese and which were taken in large numbers to build up the Chinese cavalry.

Exploration The Silk Road opened up during the reign of Emperor Han Wudi, who in 138 BC dispatched General Zhang Qian on a mission to seek an alliance with peoples west of China against the northern tribes. The information he brought back about Central Asia led to the westward extension of the Great Wall along the oasis towns of the Gobi and Taklimakan deserts, which were to become vital links in Silk Road trade. Beyond China much of what was to be dubbed the Silk Road had been in use for centuries, since communication between the fringes of the great civilizations of Egypt, Mesopotamia, and northern India was already possible, if not commonplace. When Alexander the Great marched east, many Western ideas found their way east as well, and vice versa. Zhang Qian's mission formed the final link in the chain. The Romans unified the Mediterranean area, which was linked to Central Asia by means of the imperial highways of the Persian Empire. The Silk Road was to remain in constant use until about the mid-14th century.

Merchants The traffic went in both directions—China imported grapes, glass, amber, saffron, and, during the cosmopolitan Tang dynasty, a variety of alien faiths including Manichaeism and Nestorianism, as well as Buddhism from India and, later, Islam. The starting point for Chinese exports was the imperial capital of Xi'an (or Chang'an as it was then). Few merchants would have accompanied their merchandise all the way to its final destination. Goods were transported by camel through Gansu and Xinjiang from oasis to oasis, through middlemen, most notably in the Middle East. In Xinjiang the route went north or south of the Taklimakan, meeting at Kashi, from where it went west via Balkh or Samarkand and Bukhara.

Kashi market: trade still flourishes along the Silk Road

Tea shop selling tea and traditional snacks, on the road between Turpan and Kashi

Foreign influence The centuries passed, and governments, rulers and dynasties changed—the Parthians and the Sassanians succeeded the Persian Empire; the Roman Empire fragmented and Byzantium emerged in its place, along with the kingdoms of western Europe—but the Silk Road continued as a commercial artery. The greatest upheaval was the gradual expansion beginning in the 7th century of Islam throughout Central Asia to the borders of the Chinese heartlands, a movement that had the effect of binding a vast area together in faith. The Silk Road was probably most open to trade between China and the West under the Mongols during the 13th century, the period when Marco Polo's great journey to China was made.

Decline By the 16th century the Silk Road had lost its significance, as the great empires declined and as maritime trade took the place of caravans. The desert swallowed some towns; radical Islam made travel difficult for infidels; and the Chinese became more inward-looking after the Tang. Oasis towns along thousands of miles, whose existence had depended on trade, were left to bask in the desert sun until their rediscovery by 19th-century adventurers and the current generation of travelers.

JUST DESERTS
The Taklimakan ("go in, not come out") Desert in Xinjiang province, which separates the northern and southern arms of the Silk Road, was conquered by the archeologist-explorers Sir Aurel Stein and Sven Hedin in the late 19th century.
A hundred years later, Taklimakan has again been subjugated, this time by an Anglo-Chinese expedition led by Charles Blackmore in 1993–1994. The expedition discovered many lost towns previously hidden under the sands.

Modern-day tourist caravan at the Singing Sands, Dunhuang

INFAMOUS WARLORD
After 1911, Xinjiang was for several decades ruled by a succession of warlords. The most infamous of these was Yang Zhengxin. His legendary ferocity led him to behead his enemies at banquets to which he had cordially invited them in a spirit of reconciliation. In the end he was shot at a banquet in 1928.

▶ Ürümqi (Wulumuqi) *128B2*

The capital of Xinjiang, with a population of about one million inhabitants, is somewhat uninspiring in appearance, but there are good reasons for going there. Its position as capital and transportation hub make a visit almost inevitable. Despite an unprepossessing exterior and a lack of any precise center, the city is of interest for its "minority" quarters, where Hui and Uyghur peoples live with their own markets and restaurants. The excellent **Minority Peoples' Museum▶▶** (*Open* Mon–Fri, 9:30–6:30; Sat–Sun, 10–4:30. *Admission: inexpensive*) on Xibei Lu imaginatively explains the ways of life of the various nationalities in the area and is well worth a visit. There is also **Hongshan Hill** with its Qing pagoda and view; factories that produce carpets, jade, and musical instruments; and the Eighth Route Army Office Museum.

Ürümqi's main attraction lies outside the city—**Tianchi (Heaven's Lake)▶▶▶** (*Open* summer, daily. *Admission: moderate*) is cradled 62 miles away at an altitude of 6,560 feet among the Tian Shan (Heavenly Mountains), which rise to nearly 20,000 feet. It is a magnificent (and popular) sight, well worth the journey; if you have the time and the inclination, you can go on horseback with a Kazakh guide to the snowfields above and spend the night in a yurt.

From Ürümqi, it is also possible to visit the beautiful **Nanshan grasslands** (Baiyanggou) 45 miles south, where it is also possible to stay overnight in a yurt.

▶▶▶ Xiahe and the Labrang Monastery *128C1*

Xiahe is almost 10,000 feet above sea-level in eastern Gansu, some 100 miles from Lanzhou and within striking distance of the old Tibetan northeastern province of

Kazakhs in the summer meadows of the Heavenly Mountains, Baiyanggou

Monks at Labrang Monastery, Xiahe

Amdo. It is a place of exceptional interest, home to one of the six major Tibetan monasteries, the **Labrang Tashi Khyll (Labulengsi)▶▶▶** (*Open* daily 8AM–noon, 2–6. *Admission: moderate*), an important place of pilgrimage for Tibetans who flood here in their distinctive finery.

The monastery was built in 1709 by Jamyang Zhepa (a renowned abbot of Drepung Monastery in Lhasa). At one time there were 4,000 monks (reduced to 1,700 now) filling the six institutes of Esoteric Buddhism, Medicine, Law, Astrology, and Higher and Lower Institutes of Theology, and the various halls and residences. On religious holidays, followers of Tibetan Buddhism pour in to mix with the monks in religious celebrations. The Great Prayer Festival (Monlam) takes place just after the Tibetan New Year (based on the lunar calendar and therefore variable) either in February or March, and there are some fascinating celebrations on the 13th, 14th, 15th, and 16th days of the relevant month. In the vicinity of Xiahe there are beautiful areas of grassland, at Ganjia and Sangke, where yaks are grazed.

▶ Yining *128A2*

Yining, center of the Ili Kazakh Autonomous Prefecture, and the scene in recent years of clashes between the authorities and Uyghur separatists, is a town near the Russian border that has only recently opened to foreign tourists. Nearby, in the Ili Valley, is **Almalik**, thought to have been the capital of the empire (today's Xinjiang) inherited by Chaghatai, the second son of Genghis Khan, in 1227. The northern arm of the Silk Road ran through here on the way to the great oasis towns of Central Asia.

There is little to see in Yining unless you are lucky enough to witness a **traditional celebration by Kazakh horsemen▶▶▶** in the nearby pastures, a performance of high-spirited horsemanship that includes competitive games and a peculiar chase on horseback with a dead goat.

The countryside is beautiful though, particularly in the region of the **Sayram Lake▶▶▶**, on the road to Ürümqi, where the waters are the color of sapphire.

BORDER PARTY

The border of Kazakhstan (in the former U.S.S.R.) is very close to Yining. Since the 1950s, Westerners have been forbidden to cross it, but in 1985 an international group of tourists was allowed across in celebration of 2,000 years of the Silk Road. A bar was set up on the Soviet side of the border (after customs) and Beatles music was broadcast across the wilderness. The travelers were met by a prancing dragon on the Chinese side.

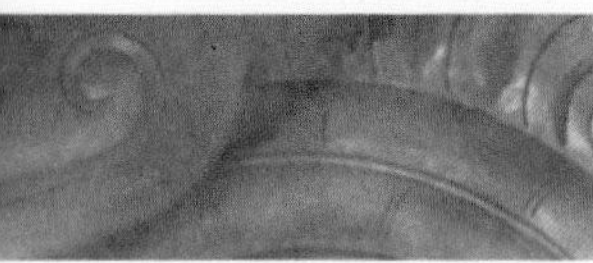

Jade ("yu") is the stone most often associated with China. Usually thought of as a deep green color, in fact it has an unexpectedly wide range of hues, ranging from creamy white to almost black.

TOAD GREASE
The oily substance that blends the abrasive mixture used in jade cutting is called "toad grease," and, according to Chinese texts, was produced from toads killed in a special way. In fact, the grease is tallow from mutton or lard from pork.

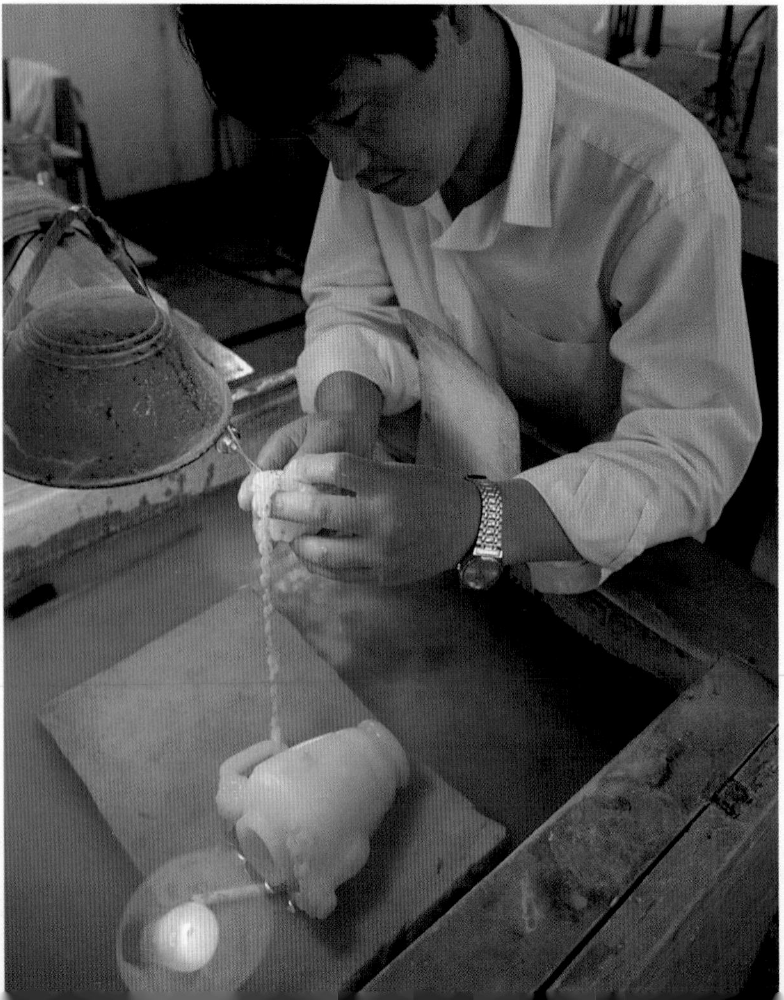

A jade craftsman in Yangzhou, Jiangsu

History The point just outside Dunhuang where the northern and southern arms of the Silk Road divided was known as Yumenguan or "the Jade Gate," and jade has long been associated with both imperial and magic powers and known for curative properties, particularly for kidney diseases. It was one of the principal items of tribute payable by tribal princelings to the Chinese emperor.

Nature Just what is jade? And how do you tell good from bad, or even good from less good? The oldest jade is a calcium-magnesium-aluminium silicate with a hardness of 6.5 on the Mohs' Scale. It is classical nephrite, found most particularly in Hotan, the old Silk Road town of

Khotan. In the 18th century, the brilliant green jadeite from Burma became popular. Other stones, particularly serpentine, are sometimes also called jade. What passes for jade in stores in Hong Kong is often no more than fluorite, a soft stone that, compared with jade, is of little value. Jade's hardness is one of its distinguishing features and what makes it valuable to the Chinese.

Colors Nephritic jade was originally found in the form of pebbles from alluvial deposits in Chinese Turkestan (Xinjiang) and was first mined from rock in the 12th century. Curiously, for a mineral so treasured by the Chinese, it is not found in China proper at all. "Its fascination derives from its subdued smooth brilliance which can be redolent of the deep waters of a mountain lake or of the mistiness of a distant summit." White jade, which is slightly opalescent and translucent, is known in China as "mutton-fat" jade. Nephritic jade occurs in a wide variety of colors because of the presence of metallic oxides or silicates, usually iron, that endow it with shades from gray to, rarely, black. Ferrous silicates produce shades of green ranging from pale to almost black and, very occasionally, blue, while ferric silicates bring browns and oranges and, most prized of all, yellow. Streaks in the jade are caused by trace elements—manganese, for example, produces pale jade with threads of pink or purple. The most common shade—and widely considered the loveliest—is the pale smoky green, called Cabbage Jade by the Chinese. Jade can also change with age, giving added depth to the color.

Hard dark-green jade, similar to an emerald of the deepest hue, is more likely to be jadeite. Although very similar in appearance to nephritic jade, jadeite has a different chemical composition and was for long considered by the Chinese to be of inferior value. Jadeite can also be a brilliant red, because of the presence of chromium, which is never found in nephritic jade; the presence of manganese produces a lilac color.

Heaven Jade is still commonly used in the manufacture of jewelry and ornaments, but its use for tribal objects goes back to neolithic times—the jade *pi* will be seen in many Chinese museums. This flat disc, with a large central hole, is often said to represent Heaven and is thought to derive from ancient sun cults. The oldest known example dates back to 2000 BC. What is most remarkable is its perfectly formed central hole, suggesting that the Chinese already knew how to use a primitive lathe.

APPEASEMENT
The Chinese believed that various earthly spirits remained in the body after death, once the Celestial Spirit had departed. It was feared that such spirits might become angry, leave in a huff and torment the relatives. To prevent this, the body orifices were plugged with jade, and offerings were made to encourage the spirits to leave peacefully.

A jade "pi" with decorated surface. A "pi" was a ritual disc that symbolized heaven

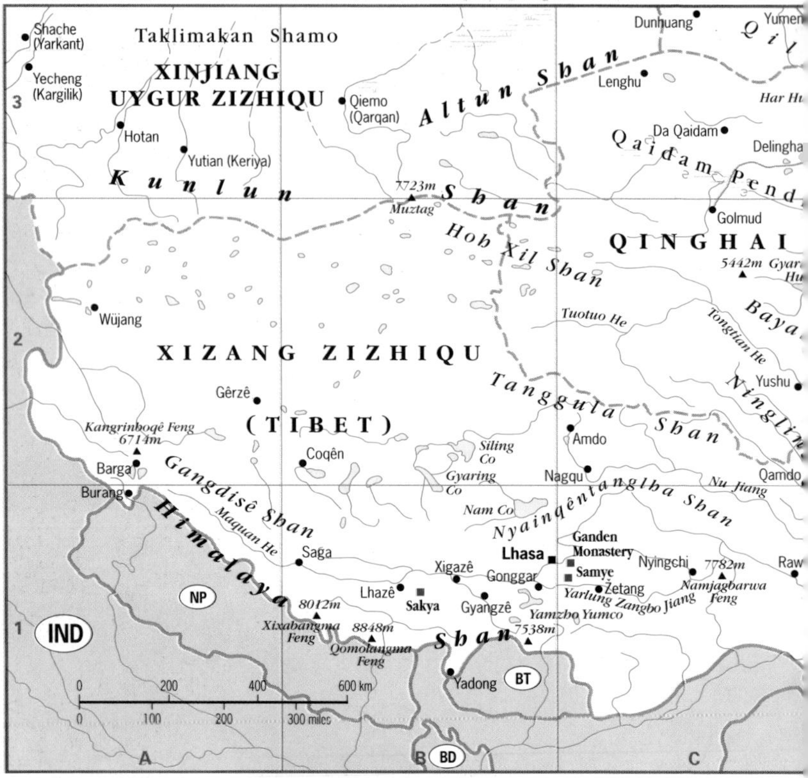

Shache (Yarkant)
Taklimakan Shamo
Dunhuang
Yumen
Yecheng (Kargilik)
XINJIANG UYGUR ZIZHIQU
Qiemo (Qarqan)
Altun Shan
Lenghu
Har Hu
Hotan
Yutian (Keriya)
Da Qaidam
Qaidam Pendi
Delingha
Kunlun Shan
7723m Muztag
Golmud
Hob Xil Shan
QINGHAI
5442m
Wüjang
Tuotuo He
Tongtian He
XIZANG ZIZHIQU
Gêrzê
(TIBET)
Tanggula Shan
Yushu
Kangrinboqê Feng 6714m
Amdo
Barga
Coqên
Siling Co
Gyaring Co
Nagqu
Qamdo
Burang
Gangdisê Shan
Nam Co
Nyainqêntanglha Shan
Nu Jiang
Maquan He
Himalaya Shan
Saga
Ganden Monastery
Lhasa
Samye
Nyingchi
7782m
Raw
Xigazê
Gonggar
Zetang
Namjagbarwa Feng
Yarlung Zangbo Jiang
NP
Lhazê
Sakya
Gyangzê
Yamzho Yumco
8012m Xixabangma Feng
8848m Qomolangma Feng
7538m
IND
Yadong
BT
0 200 400 600 km
0 100 200 300 miles
A
B
BD
C
1
2
3

The terraced rice fields of western Sichuan, gateway to Tibet

▶▶▶ REGION HIGHLIGHTS

Sichuan and the Tibetan Plateau

An endless cycle – the "wheel of life," often found at the entrance to Tibetan monasteries

SICHUAN AND THE TIBETAN PLATEAU It may seem odd to place a province (Sichuan) that is part of China proper in the same chapter with Tibet, which, although part of the modern state of China (as the "autonomous" region of Xizang), remains quite separate as far as way of life, culture, and attitudes are concerned. There are two reasons, one practical, the other geographical and historical. First, the majority of visitors to Tibet enter on direct flights from Chengdu in Sichuan. Secondly, Sichuan is situated at the foot of the Tibetan Plateau, and in fact much of the western mountainous area of the province forms part of it. Furthermore, in the distant past some of what is now Sichuan was ruled by Tibetan tribes, and consequently traces of Tibetan culture remain in the area. Chongqing and Dazu, however, are discussed in the Yangtze Valley chapter (pages 170–173) since they are usually visited only by those making the journey through the Yangtze Gorges.

Sichuan, the largest and most populous (over 100 million people) of China's provinces, is quite distinctive. The vast Chengdu plain is one of the country's most important rice-producing regions. Sichuanese food—some of the best in China—is hot and spicy. Most famously, Sichuan is associated with the giant panda—a few are found in neighboring provinces, but Sichuan is their preferred home. The cultivated valleys give the province a particular beauty, and there is an astonishing array of flora. Its mountainous nature has allowed it to enjoy a degree of independence during the centuries of Chinese rule. Although linked to China since the 4th century BC, it previously enjoyed an advanced civilization of its own, affiliated to the cultures

Writing on the wall: "Fu," the character for "happiness" or "luck," Baoguang Temple, Chengdu

THAT OLD GANG OF MINE
The architect of China's recent prosperity and democratic reforms, such as they are, was Deng Xiaoping, who was a Sichuanese. In fact, so many of the people associated with his period of rule are from Sichuan that they are sometimes referred to as the Sichuan Gang.

A Tibetan woman in Songpan, northern Sichuan, heavy with amber, coral, and turquoise jewelry

of Southeast Asia. Sichuan, now one of China's fastest growing areas, continues to retain an independent spirit.

TIBET Dogged by the tag of Shangri-la and shielded by its isolated location among the highest mountains in the world and its determination to exclude outside influence, Tibet, until recently, remained an enigma. Its history before the early 7th century AD is obscure, but in AD 625 Songtsen Gampo became the first king of a unified Tibet, his empire spreading into China and India. The fact that he married Buddhist princesses (as well as Chinese ones) seemed to strike a chord in the Tibetan mind—for within a century, following a debate between an Indian sage and Bon priests, the native Bon religion had been ousted in favor of Buddhism. After years of internecine struggle, the notion of the reincarnation of religious leaders was introduced, but Tibetan Buddhism remained divided into three rival schools. Finally, in the 14th century unity was established by the Gelukpa (yellow hat) sect, which built the great teaching monasteries.

In 1720, the Chinese took Tibet and, despite British interference, more or less held it until 1911. Tibet then became independent until 1951, when the Chinese re-established control. Repression followed, and the current Dalai Lama fled to India in 1959. The Cultural Revolution saw the destruction of hundreds of monasteries, and although the material existence of Tibetans has now improved, there is still repression. But Tibetan traditions continue, some of the monasteries still function, and Tibet remains one of the most naturally beautiful places on earth.

MONKEY BUSINESS
There is an interesting explanation of the origins of the Tibetans. It is said that the Sakyamuni Buddha, observing that there were no humans in Tibet, elected to confine his work to India. The responsibility for dealing with Tibet was passed to Avalokitesvara, who assumed the form of a monkey and descended onto a mountain in Tsetang. After he mated with a demoness, six offspring were born, half human and half monkey, the first Tibetans.

"PURE LAND"
The most popular form of Chinese Buddhism is called *jingtu* (Pure Land), and is unknown in India or Central Asia. It teaches that the Pure Land is a kind of heaven or nirvana that can be achieved by chanting the name "Amitabha Buddha" (the Buddha of the future). Most of the Buddhist temples stIll operating in China today are of this type.

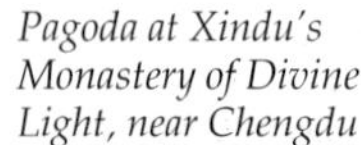

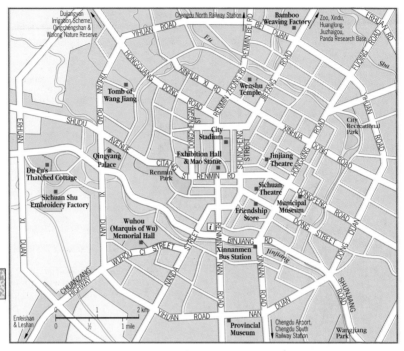

Pagoda at Xindu's Monastery of Divine Light, near Chengdu

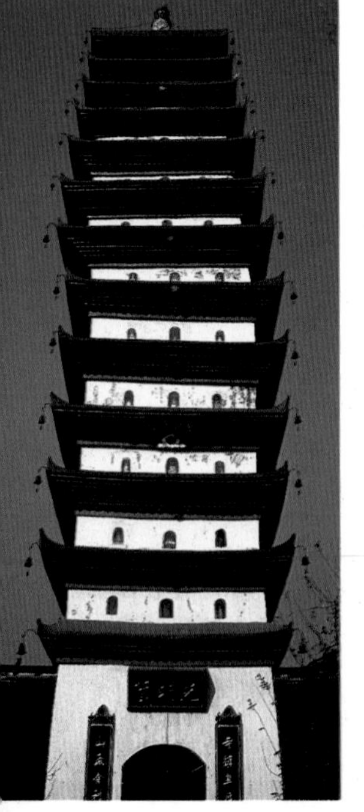

►► Chengdu 151E1

The capital of Sichuan combines modern tree-lined avenues with narrow streets of traditional half-timbered houses and is one of the fastest growing cities in China. Renowned for its prosperity from silk, lacquer, and precious metals, it has always been outside the mainstream of Chinese life, perceived as a place of refuge by poets and rulers alike. Chengdu's main attractions include a sense of well-being unusual in modern Chinese cities, and the streets themselves, which still have much character, although many of the older ones are due to be demolished. There are also several places to visit outside the city.

Du Fu's Thatched Cottage►► (*Open* daily 7AM–11PM. *Admission: inexpensive*) is a memorial to one of China's greatest poets, Du Fu, a minor official under the Tang Dynasty who was forced to flee from Chang'an (Xi'an) after a rebellion. He spent four years in Chengdu, where he wrote many of his best poems. He is highly regarded because his poetry was compassionate in an age when compassion was rare. The memorial, constructed 200 years after his death, is set in a pretty bamboo garden where there is a museum containing early versions of his poetry.

Of the several temples in Chengdu, the most interesting (and much patronized by locals) is the **Wenshu►►** (*Open* daily 6AM–8:30PM. *Admission: inexpensive*), which has four halls and a teahouse in the garden. The **Provincial Museum►** (*Open* daily 10–5. *Admission: inexpensive*) is important for its displays of Sichuanese culture. **Chengdu Zoo►►** (*Open* daily 8–8. *Admission: inexpensive*) has a large number of giant pandas. Even better is the **Giant Panda Breeding Research Base►►►** (*Open* daily 8–6. *Admission: inexpensive*), which opened in 1995.

There are several excursions from Chengdu. About 10 miles away is **Xindu▶▶** a town associated with colorful basketware and the **Monastery of Divine Light (Baoguangsi)** (*Open* daily 8–5:30. *Admission: moderate*). The monastery dates from the Tang dynasty, but it was reconstructed in the 17th century. It has some pretty gardens and courtyards, a 13-story leaning pagoda, a fine tablet from AD 540 bearing a frieze of 1,000 Buddhas, and an Arhat hall with 500 Buddhist statues.

Also of interest is the ancient **Dujiangyan Irrigation Scheme▶▶** at Guanxian, about a two-hour drive west of Chengdu. Begun in 256 BC by the governor of the state of Shu to tame the Min River, it is a remarkable precursor to modern dams—the original stone and bamboo dike divided the river into an "inner" and "outer" channel while a second dike was built to divert water in case of flood. The system now irrigates over three million acres. The best view is from the nearby Subdued Dragon (Fulong) Temple, or the Two Kings Temple (Erwangmiao), reached via a chairlift; below the latter is the Anlang chain bridge.

Also worth a visit is the **Qingchengshan Taoist Mountain▶▶** (*Open* daily. *Admission: moderate*) which can be climbed in one day. Its highest temple (Shangqinggong) stands at over 4,925 feet. The going is not too tough, and the Taoist belief in harmony with nature gives a rustic feel to the buildings en route. Alternatively, there is a cable car.

Finally there is the **Wolong Nature Reserve▶▶** (*Open* daily. *Admission: expensive*), a day's drive from Chengdu, established in the 1970s for panda conservation and now China's largest reserve. To enjoy a visit here, time and a willingness to trek are essential.

SPICE OF LIFE

Sichuanese food is famed for its spicy qualities. One of the best dishes is Ma-Po Doufu (bean curd), a red-hot stew made famous by a pockmarked female (*ma-po*) chef-peddler. Another is Bang-Bang Chicken, cold chicken topped with spiced sesame sauce.

A MEETING

How long does youth last?
Now we are all gray-haired,
Half of our friends are dead,
And both of us were surprised when we met.
—Du Fu (712–770)

Bamboo culture: tea house at the People's Park, Chengdu

Prayer flags on the summit of Emeishan

FLORA AND FAUNA
Emeishan is attractive not only for pilgrims searching for "the way" but also for its wide variety of animal and plant life. Aside from the monkeys there are the famous bearded frogs, 200 species of butterfly, silver pheasants, lesser or red pandas, medicinal herbs, tea bushes, rhododendrons, and an array of colorful flowers.

Kumbum stupa at Palkhor Monastery, Gyangzê

▶ Dêgê *151D2*

This town on the road from Chengdu to Lhasa is famous for its 250-year-old **Bakong Scripture Printing Lamasery** (*Open* daily. *Admission: moderate*), which houses the last surviving copy of a woodblock history of Buddhism in 555 plates.

▶▶▶ Emeishan ("Lofty Eyebrow Mountain") *151D1*

Open: dawn to dusk. Admission: expensive

One of the holy mountains of Buddhism, the abode of Samantabhadra the Bodhisattva of pervading goodness, Emeishan, in the southwest of Sichuan province, rises to well over 10,000 feet. The pair of peaks with a green fir coat, and frequently a topcoat of dense mist at various levels makes a magnificent sight. From the base to the summit is a distance of some 30 miles but, although it may require two days to complete the pilgrimage (ascent or descent), no special climbing skills are necessary. A minibus goes from the Baoguo Monastery up to Jieyindian, at 7,875 feet, and from there you can continue either on foot or by cable car to the summit (or even on the back of a porter). You can descend the whole way on foot, spending the night in one of several temples *en route* that offer accommodations (for example, the Hongchun or the Qingyin). Unfortunately, inclement weather often obscures the spectacular view, but many like to stay the night here to see the sunrise, others to enjoy the rainbows and fantastic shadows, called "Buddha's Glory," which sometimes appear on the clouds below during the late afternoon. Lower down is the famous Xixiangchi (Elephant Bathing Pool), where the elephant belonging to Samantabhadra was believed to have bathed; here the moon is supposed to cast an eerie light. The mountain is famous for its monkeys (especially on Xianfeng, or Fairy Peak), which can be fierce and should not be approached.

It is also possible to combine a visit to Emeishan with one to **Leshan** (see page 160), only a short distance away.

▶▶▶ Ganden Monastery *150C1*

About 25 miles east of Lhasa lie the remains of what was once one of the most important monasteries in Tibet. Ganden, "the Pure Land of Tushita," where Maitreya the Future Buddha resides, was founded by the great 14th-century reformer Tsongkhapa (or Je Rinpoche), who is generally depicted wearing monk's robes and a yellow hat. The main hall of the monastery was not consecrated until 1417, and its founder died here in 1419. The head of the monastery, the Ganden Tripa, is also the head of the Gelukpa order. By 1959 there were 5,000 monks, but the Cultural Revolution reduced the monastery to ruins. Located on the slopes of Mount Drokri, it is being painstakingly reconstructed. Among the most interesting buildings are Tsongkhapa's Golden Tomb and the Amdo Khantsen. A path leads behind the hill, offering breathtaking views. Pilgrim buses for Ganden leave early each morning from Lhasa.

▶ Ganzi (Garzê) *151D2*

The capital of the Ganzi Tibetan Autonomous Prefecture (as distinct from the Tibetan Autonomous Region), in remote Sichuan, is home to the Ganzi Lama Monastery, from where there are splendid views of the Ganzi Valley.

▶▶ Gyangzê (Gyantse) *150B1*

A small Tibetan town (once the center of the wool trade) at a height of 12,390 feet and about 50 miles east of Xigatse, old Gyangzê forms a street of traditional Tibetan houses dominated by the **Palkhor Monastery**▶▶▶, which was built in 1429. Once much larger, the monastery now has only the main temple and a nine-story stupa, Tibet's largest, decorated with the stern eyes of Buddha outside and fine murals within. It is overlooked by the **old fort** (*Open* daily. *Admission: inexpensive*) set astride a pinnacle. In 1904, Gyangzê witnessed one of Britain's lesser military exploits, when Francis Younghusband, sent to enforce a trade agreement, allowed the massacre of 700 Tibetans. The fortress was captured and a trade mission was then established.

▶▶ Jiuzhaigou *151D2*

Open: daily. Admission: expensive

This little-known scenic area in the Aba Autonomous Prefecture of Sichuan, far north of Chengdu, rivals Guilin for its beauty, with the added attraction of Tibetan and Qiang minority settlements. It is an area of lakes, mountains, and waterfalls not yet spoiled by tourism, although more roads and accommodations are being built ready for large numbers of visitors. An important transit point for Jiuzhaigou is Songpan, a pretty town set in dazzling scenery.

IN A STUPA

Stupas (known as "chorten" in Tibet) probably evolved in India as prehistoric burial chambers for local rulers, but under Buddhism they acquired a sacred status as the symbol of Buddha himself. Subsequently, they became burial places for the ashes of saints or repositories of holy scriptures or relics. In Tibet stupas have square bases (earth), surmounted by a globe (water), a triangle (fire), and a crescent moon (air) and sun (infinite space).

The Five-Color Pool, Jiuzhaigou

Although the giant panda has received the most publicity over the years, China is also home to a number of other endangered species.

HAIRY MONSTER
Not strictly speaking an endangered species, the yak is found in any numbers only in the Tibetan region. It is so well adapted to high altitudes and the bitter cold that it could not survive in mild, lowland areas. Bulky yet nimble, it needs a daily supply of fresh water, snow being an inadequate substitute.

Giant panda Although it is impossible to know just how many pandas remain in the wild, it is thought that the number is no higher than 1,000, insufficient to guarantee their survival. The giant panda is found mostly in Sichuan, but there are a few in the neighboring provinces of Shaanxi and Gansu; in these provinces 13 reserves have been established to preserve the panda (no easy task where even the death penalty fails to deter rapacious poachers from trapping and skinning pandas). Live pandas were discovered in 1896, although remains dating back over 600,000 years have been found. The animals prefer altitudes of between 6,560 and 10,000 feet, consume 45 pounds of a specific variety of bamboo per day, and are very sensitive to their environment. When supplies of bamboo failed in the 1970s, up to 200 pandas were estimated to have died of starvation. Their mating habits are mysterious—captive breeding has met with limited success, and the birth rate in the wild is not much better. The future for the giant panda remains bleak.

Above: giant panda, sensitive to its environment
Top: Père David's deer, now found only in captivity

A Manchurian (or Siberian) tiger. The tiger is a Chinese symbol, yet is almost extinct

Père David's deer The outlook is more optimistic for some of China's other rare animals, since efforts are now being made to ensure their survival. One of the most intriguing is the Père David's deer, first discovered in the imperial hunting parks by the French priest and zoologist Père Armand David in 1865, when they were already extinct in the wild. They are thought to have come from Manchuria and Kokonor. By 1900 there were none left in China, even in the parks, but the species survived at Woburn Abbey in England, where a breeding herd was established by the dukes of Bedford. In 1985, 20 of the creatures were presented to the Chinese government to live at Chengde, but it is unlikely that they will ever be reestablished in the wild.

Tiger China has three subspecies of tiger—the South China tiger, the Manchurian (or Siberian) tiger, and the Bengal tiger. The South China tiger, unique to China, may no longer exist in the wild, because at the last count there were only 50 left, an insufficient number to prevent its seemingly inevitable extinction. The Manchurian tiger's chances of survival are even lower according to a recent survey, which recorded less than 30 individuals, although there are a few more in Siberia. The Bengal tiger, which is still found in Yunnan, is not much better off, although exact statistics are hard to come by.

Unfortunately for tigers, some parts of their anatomy are thought to have properties crucial to Chinese virility; trade in these organs is so lucrative that the law banning it is almost impossible to enforce.

Others There are other animals and birds in the same precarious position: the golden monkey, the Yangtze alligator (a smaller cousin of those in the U.S.A.), the red-crowned crane, and the Yangtze River dolphin. Efforts are being made by the Chinese in cooperation with the Worldwild Fund for Nature and others to ensure their survival, but sadly many Chinese accord them low priority, and the future for many of these creatures is grim.

MOSQUITO BOAST

Despite its climate, China is remarkably free of mosquitoes. This is one of the success stories of the Communist Party, which initiated a determined program to eradicate malaria. Similar efforts were made to decrease the sparrow population, which had risen to alarming proportions. It is said that Chairman Mao exhorted citizens regularly to go outside with garbage can lids and make such a racket that the birds would never return. Although sparrows were the target, millions of other birds were, literally, scared to death, too.

ACCLIMATIZING TO TIBET
Since Tibet lies at an average altitude of about 13,000 feet, you can expect to suffer from shortness of breath because of the thin oxygen supply. This affects everyone to a greater or lesser degree, regardless of age or levels of fitness. To minimize the discomfort, you are advised to rest for a few hours after your arrival, no matter how healthy you feel. This gives your body time to acclimatize gradually. Increase your fluid intake by drinking plenty of water or tea, but avoid alcohol.

RIPPLING WATERS
Lhasa's original name was Rasa, from "ralasa," the sound made by the wind and the waves ruffling the waters of the lake around which the city was built. The lake was filled up and covered by the Jokhang in the 7th century.

The Buddha's head, of cathedral-like proportions, at Leshan

►► Kangding *151D1*

Sometimes known as Dardo, Kangding stands at an altitude of 9840 feet, but it is dwarfed by mountains of up to 25,000 feet. Tibetan in flavor, the town has several working monasteries and some excellent walking in the area. You can also trek along the nearby **Hailuogou Glacier**, said to be the lowest in Asia, or visit the beautiful grasslands at Tagong.

►►► Leshan *151D1*

Open: daily. Admission: moderate

One of the most impressive places in Sichuan (five hours by road from Chengdu and 90 minutes from Emeishan), this small town has old cobbled streets and considerable charm although tourism and modernization have already made a significant impact on it. Its principal attraction is the colossal **Grand Buddha (Dafo)►►►**, carved out of the cliffs at the confluence of the Min and Dadu rivers. In a sitting posture, the position favored by Maitreya the Future Buddha, it is the largest Buddha in China, towering to over 225 feet—one of the toes alone is 28 feet long. Narrow twisting stairs to the right of the figure take you up on to the Buddha's head, and above the right shoulder are the **Grand Buddha Temple►** and Song dynasty **Lingbao Pagoda►**. A boat ride past Dafo is especially recommended (boats operate 7–5). There is a temple at the statue's head from where a staircase takes you to its feet.

The **Wuyou Monastery►►**, dating back to the Tang dynasty, is situated on Wuyou Hill and is a short ferry ride away from Leshan dock. Opposite the temple, on the same bank as the Grand Buddha, are several tombs and a crudely fashioned Buddha that dates from AD 159, about the time that Buddhism was introduced to China.

The **Orient Buddha Park** (*Open* daily 8:30–5. *Admission moderate*) contains a newly carved reclining Buddha, at 557 feet, the longest in the world.

The Potala Palace seen from Chokpuri through prayer flags

▶▶▶ Lhasa *150B1*

The Tibetan capital since the unification of the country in the 7th century, dominated by the magnificent Potala, Lhasa has been shabbily treated by the Chinese but still manages to convey much of its unique character if only because of its remote, ethereal location—the name Lhasa means "Ground of the Gods." For the 600 years, between the end of the first Yarlung dynasty in the 9th century and the beginning of the era of Dalai Lamas in the 15th, Lhasa was capital in name only, as Tibet was torn by civil war and religious schism. Since the arrival of the Chinese in 1951 there have been many more changes, very few aesthetically for the better.

Lhasa has a wealth of things to see, most of them concerned with Tibetan religious life. The first place to visit is the **Barkhor (Intermediate Circuit)▶▶▶**, the oldest part of the city and a quadrangle of streets surrounding the Jokhang Temple, the most revered and ancient of Tibetan temples. The Barkhor teems with religious and commercial activity—pilgrims doing clockwise circuits, frequently on their hands and knees, and street vendors selling their wares from stalls. This is the heart of old Tibet and, although about one-third of it has recently been gutted in order to build shopping malls, it nevertheless still manages to retain something of its old flavor.

The **Jokhang (Shrine of Jowo)▶▶▶**, facing the newly built "plaza," is open from 9 to noon (enter via a side door in the afternoons). Only some woodwork on chapel doorways and the statue of Jowo Sakyamuni, given to King Songtsen Gampo by his Chinese wife and believed by Tibetans to have been made by the celestial artist Vishvakarman, date back to the shrine's founding in the 7th century. The atmosphere here is similar to, but more intense than that of any other temple in Tibet—the smell from the thousands of flickering candles fills the gloomy air, and pilgrims prostrate themselves before altars. The main chapel, and the most elaborate, is the Chapel of Jowo Sakyamuni,

The endless knot, Tibetan Buddhist symbol of eternity, adorns the roof of Jokhang Temple, Lhasa

THE LAST PANCHEN LAMA
The last Panchen Lama, who died in 1989, was the tenth in his line. In 1959, when the Dalai Lama fled to India, the Panchen Lama found himself in China, unable to escape, and remained in the hands of the Chinese government from that time on. Although many saw him as little more than a traitor, his pro-Tibetan statements led to his imprisonment and probable torture during the Cultural Revolution. Subsequent Panchen Lamas have been the "incarnation" of the Chinese State and therefore unrecognized by Tibetans.

The Time Wheel dagoba at Taer Monastery, Huangzhong, Qinghai

CHINA'S GULAG
Qinghai is a bleak and in many ways forbidding place, a reputation not helped by the fact that the Chinese government has built labor camps here for criminals from all over China. Nobody knows for certain how many criminals are imprisoned in them, but it is alleged that the Chinese undercut most of the world's export prices with the aid of cheap labor both in these camps and in many others all over China.

whose statue is laden with brocade and jewelry. There are dramatic views across the city from the roof.

The **Potala Palace▶▶▶** (*Open* daily 9–1. *Admission: expensive*), named after a holy mountain in India, was first built on this site in the 7th century, but the current structure dates from 1645. It was the home of successive Dalai Lamas and has been their winter home since the construction of the Summer Palace in the 18th century. It is of an ineffable beauty—the best view is from the Kyichu River. Several chapels, part of the living quarters, and the tombs are open to the public.

The **Norbulingka (Summer Palace)▶▶** (*Open* Mon–Sat 9–noon, 3:30–5:30. *Admission: moderate*) in the west of Lhasa has been used as a summer palace since the time of the 8th Dalai Lama. More of a park than an estate, it has a tranquil, bucolic air. Architecturally less imposing than the monasteries and the Potala, the palace's domestic atmosphere allows an insight into the more homey aspects of theocratic rule. It is from here that the Dalai Lama escaped in 1959.

Other principal monasteries here are the **Sera▶▶** (*Open* daily 9–4:30. *Admission: moderate*), 3 miles north of Lhasa, and the **Drepung▶▶** (*Open* daily 9–4. *Admission: moderate*) located 5 miles west, both of which deserve extended visits.

▶▶ Qinghai Province *150C2*

Formerly the Tibetan province of Amdo, Qinghai forms part of the Tibetan Plateau but has provincial status separate from the Tibetan Autonomous Region. An area of high grassland, mountain ranges, and salt marshes in the northwest, it includes the sources of three important rivers: the Yellow River, the Yangtze, and the Mekong. The largest town in the province is Xining, interesting only for a 14th-century **mosque▶**, the largest in the region, and the excellent **West Gate market▶▶**. Some 15 miles southwest is one of the most venerable of Tibetan monasteries, the

Taer at Huangzhong▶▶▶ (*Open* daily. *Admission: moderate*), noted for its yak-butter sculptures.

Qinghai's main attractions are the scenery, the peoples and—perhaps most spectacularly—**Kokonor (Qinghai Lake)▶▶▶**, China's largest saltwater lake and a bird lover's paradise. Huge flocks of migrating birds land here, particularly from March through June, the mating season.

▶▶ Sakya *150B1*

About 85 miles southwest of Xigazê is the focal point for the Sakyapa sect, which was founded in the 11th century. There are two monasteries: the northern one was virtually destroyed during the Cultural Revolution while the southern monastery, an imposing fortresslike building, still stands, complete with assembly hall and fine chapels.

▶▶▶ Samye *150C1*

Open: daily. Admission: moderate

The first monastery built in Tibet (AD 770) is in a marvellous position on the north bank of the Brahmaputra River (Yarlung Tsangpo), 25 miles northwest of Zêtang. An irregular ferry takes 1.5 hours to make the river crossing and a truck takes you to the monastery. It is worth the effort.

▶▶▶ Xigazê (Xigatse) *150B1*

Tibet's second town, and the site of one of its greatest monasteries, the **Tashilhunpo▶▶▶** (*Open* daily 9–noon, 2–5. *Admission: moderate*), is the spiritual home of the Panchen Lama (the incarnation of Buddha Amitabha), second to the Dalai Lama. The monastery dates from 1447 and is outstanding architecturally, though not spiritually, particularly under the last Panchen Lama, who died in 1989 and was widely regarded as a Chinese puppet. Since then, there has been a standoff between the Chinese government and the Dalai Lama over the election of a successor.

Sakya rooftops, excellent for drying crops and yak dung and for hoisting prayer flags

Taking the ferry to Samye across the Yarlung Tsangpo (the Brahmaputra)

SUPPRESSION OF A CULTURE

Traditional Tibetan culture may never recover from the damage inflicted by the Chinese after the revolt of 1959. The Cultural Revolution of the 1960s and 1970s saw the brutal suppression of religious life and the destruction of many of Tibet's cultural treasures. During the 1980s, there were demonstrations and violent clashes against Chinese rule. Material aspects of life have improved, however, although the Tibetans' appetite for Western pop music and movies further undermines their traditional unique way of life, which can never now be reestablished.

Buddhism took root in India and spread throughout Asia. In Tibet, Buddhism competed with the native shamanistic religion (Bon), which it eventually absorbed while retaining some Bon symbolism.

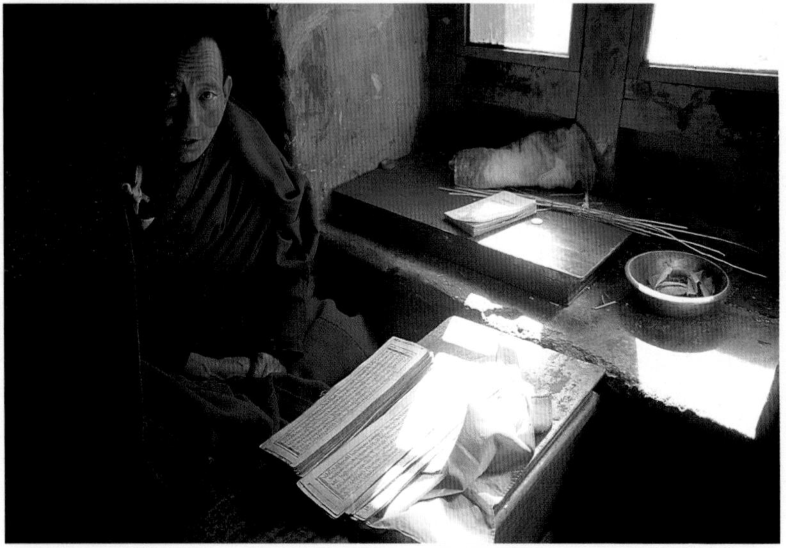

Monasteries (above, Ganden) hum with the recitation of sutras

Jewels Buddhism is the following of the path to self-awareness and enlightenment, a way of dissolving the existential confusion within ourselves that is seen as the source of human strife. The Buddhist must commit himself to the "Three Jewels"—to the Buddha (Sakyamuni, the manifestation of the ideal of enlightenment); to the Dharma (the way revealed by Buddha); and to Sangha (the religious community). And in Tibet there is a fourth "jewel," devotion to a spiritual teacher, or lama.

Vehicles There are three types of Buddhism. The first is known as Hinayana ("the lesser vehicle"), which presents the basic teachings of the Buddha himself; its practice requires a high degree of moral discipline combined with meditation. As the number of devotees grew, so the monasteries expanded, requiring more complex

MONK BUSINESS
Monks who choose to follow the full course of philosophical training are required to study a range of subjects over a period of up to 20 years. The basic course lasts two or three years, followed by further study of the five main subjects of Buddhist philosophy, eventually leading to the degree of Geshe, or Doctor of Divinity. The remaining years are devoted to tantric studies.

Devotees prostrating themselves in front of Jokhang Temple, Lhasa

administration on the part of the monks, which in turn had political implications. Gradually Tibetan government became theocratic, a process reinforced by the custom whereby families made a contribution to the Buddhist order by offering a son as a monk.

Mahayana ("the greater vehicle") is based on Hinayana but asserts that enlightenment (nirvana) cannot be attained on one's own but instead necessitates the liberation of all humanity. Compassion is one of the central themes of Tibetan Buddhism, embodied in the "bodhisattva," the disciple who refrains from entering nirvana in order to save others. In Tibet the most important bodhisattva is Chenrezi, manifested in human form as the Dalai Lama. You can see Chenrezi in many temples, sometimes with four arms, sometimes a thousand, and as many faces. The vocal expression of compassion is "Om mani padme hum," which you hear murmured everywhere you go. Sometimes the chanting is accompanied by the beating of a drum to ward off the supplicant's ego, for his quest is to know emptiness, to be free of all prejudice in his interpretation of himself and of the world around him.

The third type is Vajrayana ("the diamond"), also based on the twin objectives of compassion and enlightenment but through the teaching of Buddhist tantras. Sutras are the words spoken by Buddha for all, but tantras are vouchsafed only to a select few. Tantric Buddhism sees the human condition as more than making moral choices. Internal energy if misdirected adds to the store of human misery, but, by channeling it in the correct way, you achieve nirvana. Studying the tantras helps speed up the way to enlightenment.

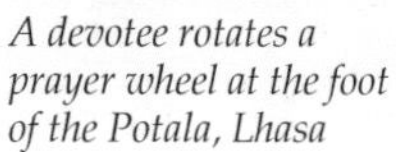

A devotee rotates a prayer wheel at the foot of the Potala, Lhasa

Tashilhungo Monastery: its size and site reflect the significance of monasteries in Buddhist culture

Temples Tibetan temples are filled with images. Mandalas are a series of colored squares within a circle and are used as an instrument of meditation. You must shed all preconceptions about reality, and imagine you are a deity and that the mandala is your world. The wheel of life, often seen at temple entrances, represents the eternal universe, seen by Tibetan Buddhists as an infinity of systems inhabited by humans, animals, giants, ghosts, devils, and celestials. Existence without enlightenment is a meaningless cycle of reincarnation from one to the other. Liberation is achieved by breaking out of this cycle.

TANTRAS AND TANGKAS
Buddhist terminology can be confusing for the uninitiated. It is easy, for example, to confuse tantras with tangkas, although they are very dissimilar. While tantras are prayers and teachings, tangkas are painted scrolls, usually depicting lamas and deities and various events from their lives, that serve as an aid to meditation.

LAMAS AND MONKS
Lamas and monks are not necessarily one and the same. A lama does not need to be a monk, for a lama is someone spiritually qualified to lead others on the path to enlightenment.

GANSU
SHAANXI
HENAN
HUBEI
SICHUAN
GUIZHOU
HUNAN
J
Hanzhong
Xixiang
Nanyang
Zhumadian
Fuyang
Yunxian
Danjiangkou Sk
Huaibin
Ankang
Shiyan
Wudang Shan
Laohekou
Luoshan
Xinyang
Guangyuan
Daba Shan
Fangxian
Xiangfan
Jiangyou
Mianyang
Jialing Jiang
Han Shui
Suizhou
Dabie
Daxian
Baidi Cheng
Anlu
Machen
Fu Jiang
Nanchong
Yunyang
Fengjie
Wushan
Zigui
Jingmen
Wanxian
Daixi
Yangtze Gorges
Badong
Sanxia Dam
Yichang
Tianmen
WUHAN
Shibaozhai
Chang Jiang (Yangtze)
Gezhouba Dam
Ezhou
Jiangling
Shashi
Xiantao
Hong Hu
Huangshi
Enshi
Wuxue
Hechuan
Fengdu
Dazu
Jinshi
Shishou
Puqi
Neijiang
Zigong
Chongqing
Qianjiang
Datong Hu
Yueyang
Mufu Shan
Luzhou
Dayong
Changde
Wuling Shan
Dongting Hu
Daozhen
Dalou Shan
Yiyang
Jiuling Sha
Tongzi
Yuan Jiang
Jishou
Changsha
A
B
C
1
2

大光明钟表商店

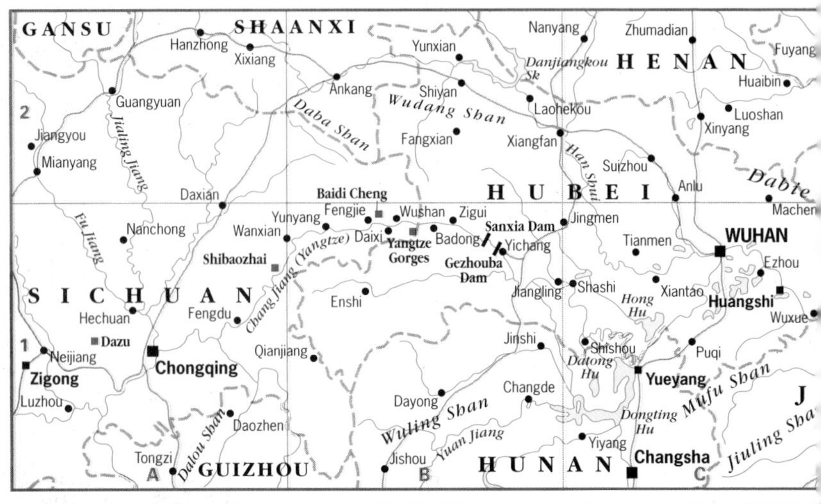

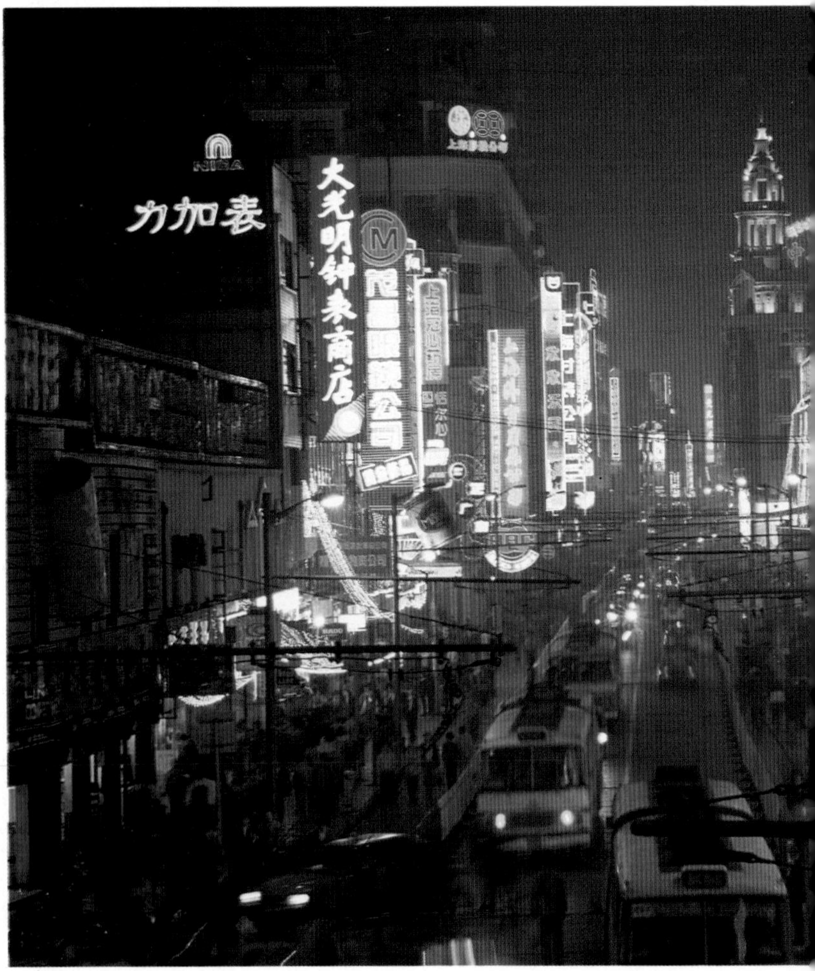

The Yangtze Region

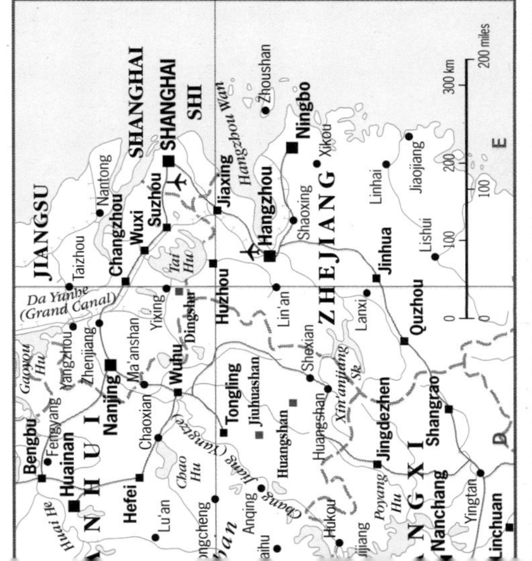

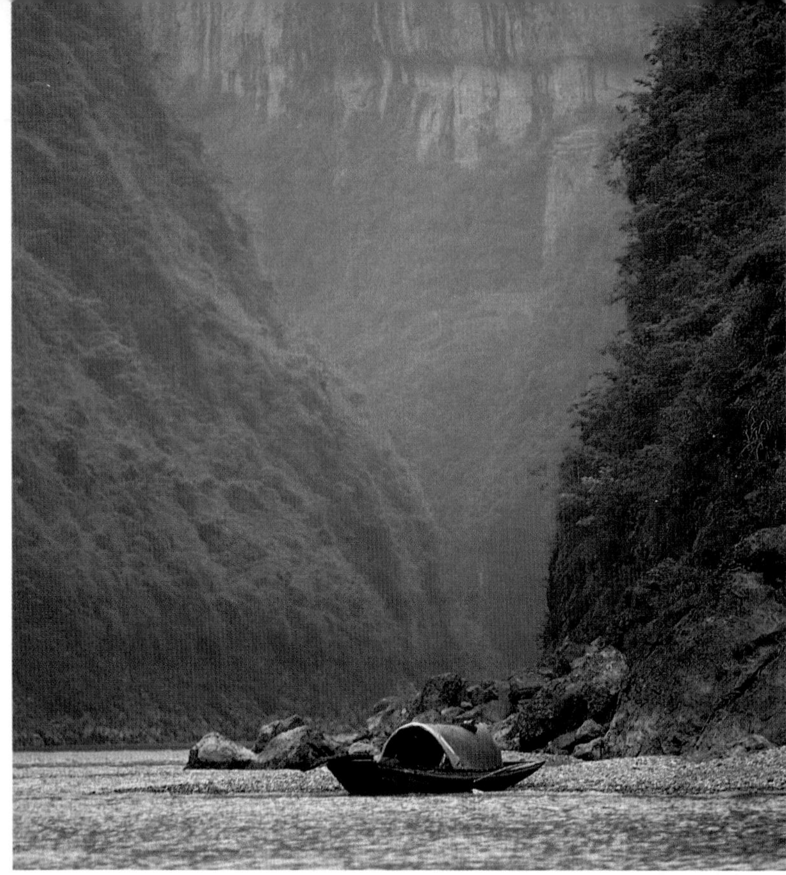

The Yangtze River, the heart of China: one of the three lesser gorges along the Daning River

MARCO'S MISCHIEF
It has always been assumed that Marco Polo, the Venetian traveler, actually went to China. Yet, although he was allegedly the governor of Yangzhou, there is no mention of him in any Chinese records. This is surprising given that few Westerners would have had contact with China in the 13th century. Also, there are certain aspects of Chinese culture that would have made an impact on a Westerner—calligraphy, for example—of which Polo makes no mention. Some scholars believe that his book was a fictionalized autobiography based on the medieval conception of the Orient.

THE YANGTZE REGION In a sense, this region does not exist. The course of the Yangtze River neatly divides China into north and south, passing through eight very separate provinces, but the reason for creating this artificial region and for classing so many heterogeneous places together is simple: they are all destinations that are likely to be visited on the same trip, their common link being the Yangtze River.

The Yangtze (Yangtze is a corruption of a local, Yangzhou-area pronunciation of Chang Jiang, which means "the long river"), 3,940 miles in length, is the third-longest river in the world after the Nile and the Amazon. It rises in Qinghai province, part of the Tibetan Plateau, and disgorges into the Yellow Sea. It is joined by some 700 tributaries along its course and is divided into three sections. The Upper Reaches, possibly the most spectacular part, run from its source across the Sichuan Basin, through the Three Gorges (discussed on pages 194–195), to Yichang in Hubei province. The Middle Reaches are between Yichang and Hukou at the mouth of Boyang Lake in Jiangxi province, where the river, wide and sluggish, flows through flat, low land, fed by waters from the Dongting as well as Boyang Lake. The Lower Reaches run from Hukou to the estuary, a landscape characterized not only by its flatness, but also by the network of canals that crisscross it. Known as the "Land of Fish and Rice," it is home to a third of China's population, producing some

40 percent of national grain output (including 70 percent of paddy rice), 33 percent of cotton, 50 percent of freshwater fish, and 40 percent of industrial output.

NAVIGATION Although the river was once a vital navigation artery of the Chinese Empire, the arrival of the railroads almost emptied the Yangtze of the traditional sampans ("three planks"), wupans ("five planks"), and junks that used to throng its length as far as Chongqing. Nowadays ocean-going vessels penetrate upriver as far as Wuhan, and local traffic is much in evidence. Not so long ago boats had to be pulled by trackers through the treacherous rapids, gruelling toil that was little better than slavery. Instructions were relayed to the harnessed trackers, heaving on ropes, by means of a beating drum. Some craft could require as many as 400 trackers to pull them. Isabella Bird, the indefatigable Victorian English traveler who, at age 64, made a journey along the Yangtze in 1896, observed 300 trackers dragging a junk without making perceptible progress in two hours. "Suddenly the junk shivered, both tow ropes snapped, the lines of trackers went down on their faces, and in a moment the craft was spinning down the rapid; and she flew up into the air as if she had exploded." The towpaths carved into the rocks are still visible here and there. The main obstacles to safe navigation were blown up after 1949.

After 1861 annual tea races were held on the Yangtze, when competing clippers from foreign companies raced to bring the freshest tea from China to Britain, the United States, and Russia. After the China tea trade collapsed, the Yangtze impinged on Western consciousness only in 1949, the year of the Yangtze incident. The *Amethyst*, a British frigate, was fired on by the communists, who were about to launch a final offensive on the nationalists. The ship's daring nocturnal escape is now part of British naval folklore.

The Yangtze, the greatest river in China, remains a powerful symbol of Chinese civilization, and much that is most fascinating about the country is still to be seen in this region.

DONGTING LAKE
Dongting Lake was once China's largest freshwater lake. Now, because of the accumulation of silt from the four rivers that feed it, it is only the second largest. Flood-prevention projects (over 6,000 irrigation or drainage channels and 15,000 sluices) mean that the surrounding area is productive year-round, and the lake acts as a reservoir for flood-water in the summer. At its center is an island where Junshan Silver Needle Tea is grown. The tea was once presented as tribute to the emperors.

▶▶▶ REGION HIGHLIGHTS

Dazu *pages 172–173*

Grand Canal *pages 176–177*

Huangshan *pages 178–179*

Nanjing *pages 179–181*

Shanghai *pages 184–189*

Suzhou *pages 190–191*

Yangtze cruise *pages 194–195*

The Yangtze demands careful navigation

Cable car across the Yangtze at Chongqing

THE HAN RIVER
The Yangtze's longest tributary is the Han (956 miles), which rises in the Qingling mountains in Shaanxi province. Like the Yellow River, it is temperamental and prone to flooding. In 1488, it changed its course, separating Hanyang from Hankou (two of the cities that make up modern Wuhan).

Red Plum Pavilion at Changzhou, one of the less-visited towns on the Grand Canal

►► Changzhou *167E2*

The old center of Changzhou has much to commend it. On the Grand Canal, with a network of smaller canals spanned by little stone bridges and a labyrinth of narrow streets and alleyways, it has an atmosphere of its own. The restored **Tianningsi (Temple of Heavenly Tranquility)►►**, founded 1,300 years ago, is a beautiful example of temple art, with its elegantly curving eaves and shining plum-colored lacquer. Behind the temple is the **Red Plum Park (Hongmei Gongyuan)►**, which has two pagodas and a teahouse. The **Ma Garden (Mayuan)►** is worthy of a visit, and the **Mooring Pavilion (Yizhouting)** has literary associations with the Song-dynasty poet Su Dongpo. An exploration of the main streets, Dong Dajie and Nan Dajie, will be rewarded. Tours around Changzhou's ornamental comb factory are also possible.

►► Chongqing *166A1*

Most people who journey through the Yangtze Gorges usually start or finish at Chongqing. It is perched high on the cliffs overlooking the confluence of the Yangtze and

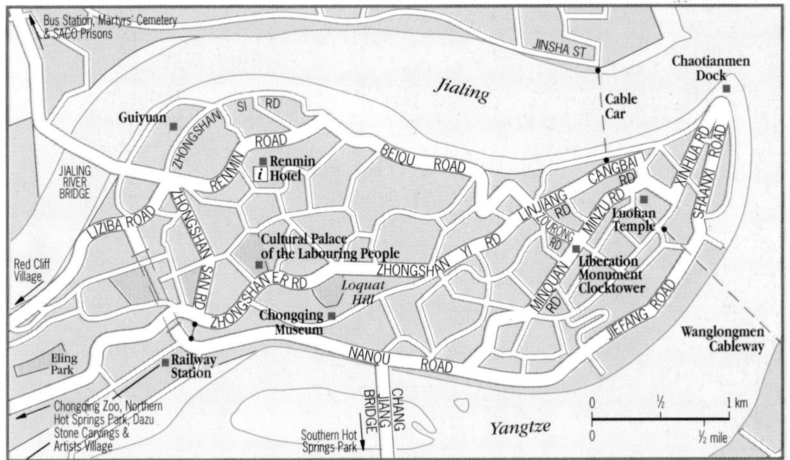

the Jialing rivers and although it is not a beautiful city, its position lends it an air of grandeur. Now an important industrial and mineral center (which gained special municipality status in 1997), it has always been Sichuan's trade outlet with the rest of China. One of the farthest flung of treaty ports (opened to foreign trade in 1890), Chongqing came to prominence as the nationalist capital in 1938, after the Japanese took Nanjing. Filled with spies, it was the object of continuous bombing missions by the Japanese during World War II.

Chongqing has few specific attractions but plenty to enjoy. The best park, and the city's highest point, is on **Pipashan (Loquat Hill)▶▶**, entrance on Zhongshan Erlu, (*Open* daily 6AM–10PM. *Admission: inexpensive*), with panoramic views across the city. **Chongqing Museum▶** (*Open* daily 9–5. *Admission: inexpensive*) is in the park—Han-carved tomb bricks, dinosaur remains and some excellent paintings are on display. Farther down, at the end of Xinhua Lu, Shaanxi Lu, and Minzu Lu, by the docks, is **Chaotianmen▶▶**, the meeting point of the two rivers and a hub of activity. Overhead, to the left, is the cable car, which gives spectacular views over Chongqing's rocky promontory (Cangbai Lu and Jinsha Jie are the two stations). Another cable car, at Wanglongmen, spans the Yangtze to the south.

South of Minzu Lu, near the junction with Cangbai Lu, is **Luohan Temple▶** (*Open* daily 8–5. *Admission: inexpensive*), founded in the Song dynasty and well known for its hall of 500 lifelike arhats. The main shopping streets are at the corner of Zourong Lu, Minquan Lu, and Minzu Lu, around the Liberation Monument Clock Tower.

Just north of the Renmin Hotel, on the south bank of the Jialing River, is **50 Zengjiayan** where Zhou Enlai (China's Foreign Minister during the Maoist era) lived and worked.

The **Red Cliff Village (Hongyan cun)** (*Open* daily 8–5:30. *Admission: inexpensive*) to the west of the city illustrates China's modern history. This was the residential area for the representatives of the Communist Party during the Guomindang Communist alliance of World War II. There is a good museum of revolutionary history here.

AIR RAIDS AND FLOWERS
The writer Emily Hahn was in Chongqing during World War II. "Chungking. What does the name evoke in my mind? Air raids. Oranges. Szechuan food, good, full of strong pepper, probably to warm up the blood on the cold, wet, muddy days...Yet Chungking is a place of flowers. You can have roses in your garden all the year round. I am not kind in my description... but I liked it."

Taking home a new washing machine, Chongqing docks

Vision of Hell, a Buddhist carving at Baodingshan, Dazu, bears remarkable similarities to contemporary Christian visions of hell

Classic Purple Sand tea-ware from Yixing. The teapots, it is claimed, retain both the color and the flavor of the tea

▶▶▶ Dazu *166A1*

Dazu is famous for its Buddhist **stone carvings▶▶▶**. Set in lush, picturesque countryside, and less formal than the other major groups at Datong and Luoyang, thousands of the sculptures and reliefs exhibit a colorful liveliness peculiar to Sichuan, in which the storytelling element is as important as orthodox religious iconography. The carvings are in two principal areas—Beishan (North Hill) and the more interesting Baodingshan (Precious Summit), where the carvings were completed according to a plan and follow the area's contours. Mostly Buddhist, the carvings also carry elements of Taoism and Confucianism.

The carvings at **Beishan** (*Open* daily 8–5. *Admission: moderate*), 1.25 miles north of Dazu, were begun in the 9th century. The work continued for about 250 years, and some 10,000 statues were made. The earliest caves are numbers 2, 3, 5, 9, and 10. Cave 245 contains over 600 figures and many scenes of everyday Tang life. In Cave 113, a divine Avalokitésvara (who became Guanyin in Chinese Buddhism) gazes in rapture at the moon's reflection. In 136, the largest cave, Samantabhadra (Bodhisattva of pervading goodness) rides an elephant, with Manjusri (Bodhisattva of wisdom) on a lion, while Sakyamuni is surrounded by representations of Guanyin, goddess of mercy and bringer of sons. Other caves of interest are 101, 113, 125, and 279.

Baodingshan (*Open* daily 8–5. *Admission: expensive*) lies 9 miles northeast of Dazu. There are two groups of carvings here—Xiaofowan and Dafowan. Dafowan is the more colorful, with lively scenes from Buddhist scriptures. The carvings were completed between 1179 and 1249 and are in a horseshoe-shaped gully reached down a flight of stairs by some reconstructed temple buildings. "A fierce tiger coming down the mountain" greets you at the bottom right. Niche

3 reveals the Wheel of Life with the founder of the site, Zhao Zhifeng, at its center; above him is the Pavilion of the Western Paradise, flanked by the animals that represent stages of rebirth. Niche 8, the Dabei Pavilion, contains the figure of the 1,000-arm Avalokitésvara, the largest ever carved in China. In niche 11 is the famous reclining Buddha, 98 feet long, whose posture symbolizes entry into nirvana. Try to make time to see niches 14 (Buddha Teaching), 15 (Requital of Parental Kindness), 21 (Eighteen Layers of Hell), and 30 (Cowherds with Oxen, a symbolic story of taming the passions).

▶▶ Dingshu *167D2*

About 45 miles to the west of Wuxi is Yixing county, dotted with tea plantations, bamboo groves, and miniature lakes. The area is famous for its pottery and underground caverns. Although the hotels are in Yixing town, the place of greatest interest is **Dingshu (or Dingshan)▶▶▶**, which has specialized in the production of glazed ceramics since the Han dynasty. Its Purple Sand pottery is seen all over China, particularly as teapots. The stores are filled with modern pottery at very low prices, and a stroll around the streets is well worthwhile. Factory tours are usually possible, while the **Exhibition Center** displays older and more sophisticated examples of Dingshu ware. The Ceramic Research Institute is worth visiting and the Ceramic Museum, on the road to Yixing, has examples of Yixing pottery from 6,000 years ago to the present day.

Excursions are also offered to the three groups of **caves▶▶** (*Open* daily. *Admission: moderate* [Shanjuan, Zhanggong]; *inexpensive* [Linggu]; wear shoes with a good grip and take waterproof jackets and flashlights. The **Shanjuan** group is 16 miles southwest of Yixing. You leave the caves by boat along a subterranean stream. The **Linggu**, 16 miles south of Yixing, is the largest group. **Zhanggong Cave** is 11 miles south of Yixing.

LOST ART
Despite claims to the contrary, it seems that the Chinese have almost lost the art of making beautiful porcelain. Cheap, practical, occasionally interesting porcelain is manufactured by the ton, but little has any true beauty. It is possible to find exact replicas of famous museum pieces in stores aimed at the foreign tourist and in museum shops, and these are bargain purchases.

TANTRIST SCULPTURE
Zhao Zhifeng, who founded the Buddhist site at Baoding (Dazu), was from the nearby village of Miliang. From 1179 to 1249 he supervized the carving of thousands of images in the mountain face representing the teachings of Buddhism, making Baoding one of the most important centers of Tantric Buddhism in China.

Wheel of Life, Dazu, with Zhao Zhifeng at the center

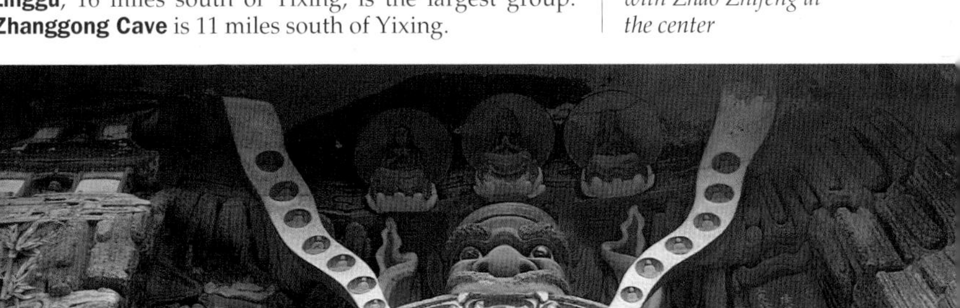

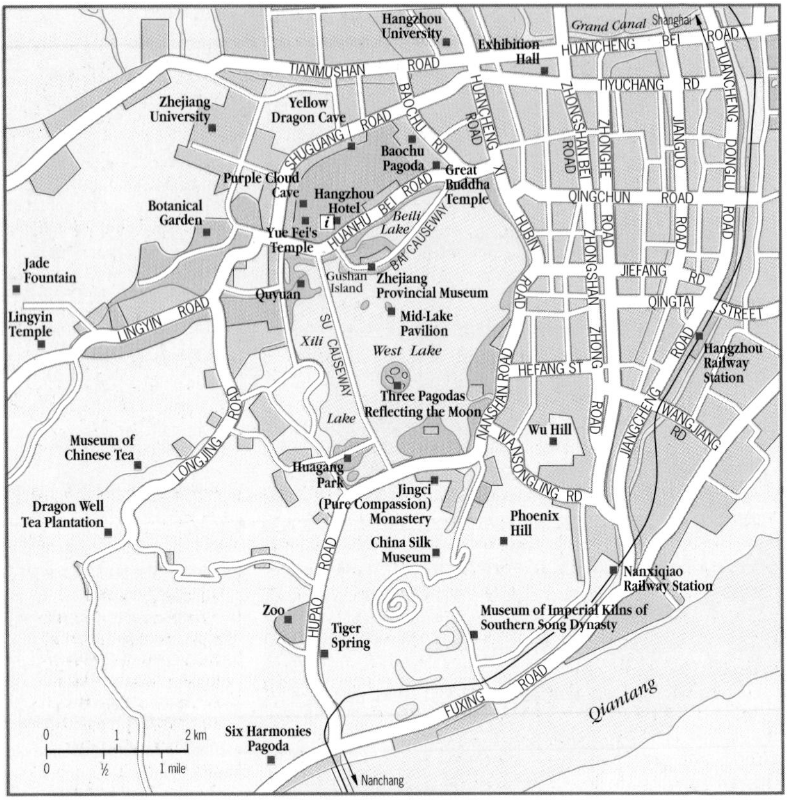

West Lake, Hangzhou, an "earthly paradise," is a traditional destination for honeymooners

►► Hangzhou *167E1*

The capital of Zhejiang province, Hangzhou lies on the banks of Qiantang River, about 60 miles from the sea. Famous above all for the West Lake, it is also the southern terminus of the Grand Canal (see page 176), which reached Hangzhou during the Sui dynasty and is a testament to the former importance of this now comparatively provincial town. Renowned for its scenic beauty, Hangzhou is a favorite destination for newlyweds. Its reputation as a place for leisure and sensual pleasures goes back to the Song dynasty, when it succeeded Kaifeng as capital of the Southern Song. Marco Polo wrote about its captivating women and the loveliness of its temples and gardens. Under the Qing, Hangzhou remained one of the richest towns in China, but in the mid-19th century, during the Taiping Rebellion, much of it was razed. Although many historic buildings have been destroyed, parts of the town have not changed for centuries, and the lake and surrounding hills retain their reputation as one of China's best-known beauty spots.

West Lake (Xihu)►►► was originally a shallow inlet off Hangzhou Bay. In the 4th century AD silt deposits from the Qiantang River built up, creating a barrier and forming the present lake. Two sections of the lake are enclosed by two causeways, the result of water-control work during the Tang and Song dynasties.

The Bai Causeway encloses the Beili Lake and runs from

near the Hangzhou Hotel on the north bank to Gushan Island and then back to the north bank farther east. This makes a good walk with fine views from both the Duanqiao (Broken Bridge, so-called because snow melts first at the bridge's hump, giving the impression of a gap) and from the top of Gushan. A Qing pavilion houses the **Zhejiang Provincial Museum▶▶** (*Open* daily. *Admission: inexpensive*), which includes one of the hollow bricks (complete with ancient printed sutra found within) from the collapsed Leifeng Pagoda, the oldest finds associated with rice and silk culture in China, and ancient maps of the city. At the eastern end, the Pavilion of the Autumn Moon on a Calm Lake is, unsurprisingly, perfect for watching the moon, and it doubles as a teahouse.

Detail from the Lingyin Temple

The Su Causeway links the north shore with the south (at the Huagang Park, filled with fish pools) and encloses the Xili. Near the north end is the **Tomb and Temple of Yue Fei▶**, a much venerated Song general.

No visit to Hangzhou is complete without a boat excursion around the lake. Steamers depart from Gushan, the east shore (Hubin Lu), and Huagang Park for tours of the islands, including the renowned **Three Pagodas Reflecting the Moon (Santanyinyue)** island, which contains four miniature lotus-covered lakes.

The **Lingyin Temple▶▶** is a celebrated Chan (Zen) Buddhist temple, founded in AD 326. The current structure dates from the late Qing dynasty. Its highlights are the Great Hall, with its 65 foot camphor-wood statue of the Buddha, and the Feilaifeng (Peak Flying From Afar), a hill opposite the temple covered with inscriptions and reliefs carved into the rock dating from the 10th to the 14th centuries, the most important such site in south China. A cable car rides to the top of the nearby northern peak.

Other places worthy of attention are the **Six Harmonies Pagoda▶**, the **Dragon Well Tea Plantation▶**, and the **Silk Spinning Factories▶** as well as the China Silk Museum on Yuhuangshan Lu (*Open* daily. *Admission: inexpensive*).

HEAVENLY WALK

Hangzhou is a delightful town in which to stroll. Aside from the obvious walk around the lake, you can explore the hills by following a path behind the Yuefei Temple, or wander along the canals on the eastern side of town.

A carved laughing Buddha, here with entourage, on the "Peak Flying From Afar"

The Grand Canal (above and opposite) has been in constant use for over a thousand years

▶▶▶ The Grand Canal (Da Yunhe) *167E2*

A cruise along the Grand Canal is one of the easiest and best ways of seeing what makes China tick. In half a day you can travel between Wuxi and Suzhou (or vice versa) through a jostling floating hubbub that has barely changed in over a thousand years.

The Grand Canal, which in parts dates back to 400 BC, is still the world's largest man-made waterway. The early sections were built in the north for the movement of troops but it was the Sui Emperor Yangdi who undertook the construction of the main canal in the 7th century AD, with the labor of 5.5 million conscripted men—in some places this meant all the commoners between the ages of 15 and 55. They worked under the supervision of 50,000 police, and those unable to finish their work quotas were flogged or forced to wear neck weights. The Sui emperor celebrated the completion of the canal by arriving amid a flotilla of beautifully decorated dragonboats pulled by teams of the loveliest girls in the empire.

The emperor's original aim in building the canal was to link his two capitals, Xi'an and Luoyang, but he decided to extend the canal as far as Hangzhou, so as to connect the four major trading rivers—the Yangtze (which it crosses by means of locks), the Yellow, the Qiantang, and the Huai—thus linking the rich area of the Yangtze Valley, the rice-bowl of China, with the more heavily populated north. Normal trade was not its only function—it was also used to convey tribute to the imperial court: "nine thousand barques conveying

WATER-BORNE
One of the features of the Grand Canal is the string of barges following each other nose to tail. In the past, entire families lived aboard, but apparently nowadays factories own most of the boats and allocate apartments to the boatmen they employ. However, judging by the family atmosphere on some of the barges—children, pets, and cooking all in evidence—it is more than likely that the new liberal approach to the economy is encouraging the reemergence of old habits.

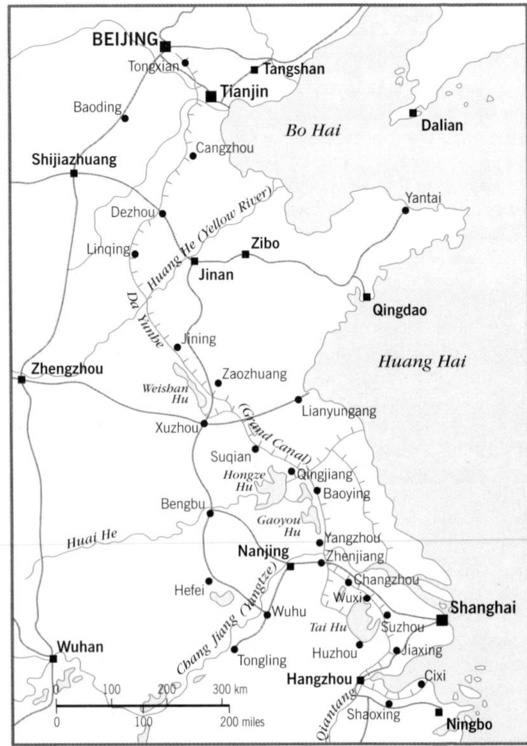

The Grand Canal

tribute to the emperor," as a contemporary wrote to convey the frenetic activity on the canal.

During the 12th century, China's economic focus moved to this region, and the towns bordering the canal grew in status. During the Mongol dynasty, the canal's importance was such that it was extended to the new capital, Beijing. Although the decadent Qing dynasty liked to suppress shipments of grain in favor of imperial pleasure barges, the canal did not lose its supremacy until the beginning of the 20th century, when the course of the Yellow River altered, the railroads proved more efficient, and coastal shipping began to be used more widely. In 1793–1794, the first British embassy to China, under Lord Macartney, returned to Macau from Beijing by way of the Grand Canal (and several rivers), a journey of 2,000 miles of which a mere 80 had to be traveled over land. In 1896, the traveler Isabella Bird described the canal as "wonderful even in its dilapidation"; after arriving at Tianjin (Tientsin) from Tungchow her boat "took two days and a half to make its way through the closely jammed mass of cargo and passage boats at the terminus."

Since the 1950s the Grand Canal has undergone a renaissance. The southern stretch between Zhenjiang and Hangzhou is navigable year-round, and cruise boats, some equipped in imperial livery, ply the waters. An overnight service also operates between Suzhou and Hangzhou.

CHINA'S CULTURE
One of the commodities commonly carried along the Grand Canal is bamboo. China's culture is sometimes said to have been founded on bamboo, a sentiment illustrated by the following remark by the poet Su Dongpo (1036–1101): "I would rather eat a meal without meat than live in a place with no bamboos. Without meat one may become thin: without bamboos one becomes vulgar."

LOOKING TO THE FUTURE
There are plans afoot to improve the northern stretches of the Grand Canal, which have been silted up for centuries, by diverting water from the Yangtze to the more arid regions of the north and dredging some sections to enable navigation by vessels of up to 2,000 tons.

MOON MAN
A famous drunk, the poet Li Bai met a most romantic end, or at least one in keeping with his philosophy ("With three cups I penetrate the Great Tao. Take a whole jugful—I and the world are one"). He drowned while drunkenly leaning overboard trying to embrace a reflection of the moon.

▶ Hefei 167D2

Hefei is the capital of Anhui, a comparatively poor province created in 1662. The town has an excellent **museum▶▶** (*Open* daily. *Admission: inexpensive*) its highlight being a Han-dynasty jade burial suit. It is the nearest point of departure for a visit to the tomb of China's most eminent poet, Li Bai (701–762), who is buried near the place where he drowned. Some 60 miles northeast of Hefei, near Fengyang, are the **remains of the capital built by the first Ming emperor▶** close to his birthplace before he realized that Nanjing was a better site. The foundations and, nearby, the impressive "spirit" (or royal) way to the tomb of the emperor's parents are visible.

▶▶▶ Huangshan (Yellow Mountain) 167D1

Open: daily. Admission: expensive

One of a range of 72 peaks in south Anhui, the highest reaching 5,900 feet, Huangshan is considered the most beautiful mountain in China. It is located amid gorgeous rural landscapes and its slopes are covered with pine trees and swathed in cloud. It is a strenuous but not difficult climb to the summit. There are several routes, but the best way is to take the eastern, shorter route up and the longer, more spectacular western route down (just possible in 10

Huangshan, featured in innumerable paintings and even on stamps

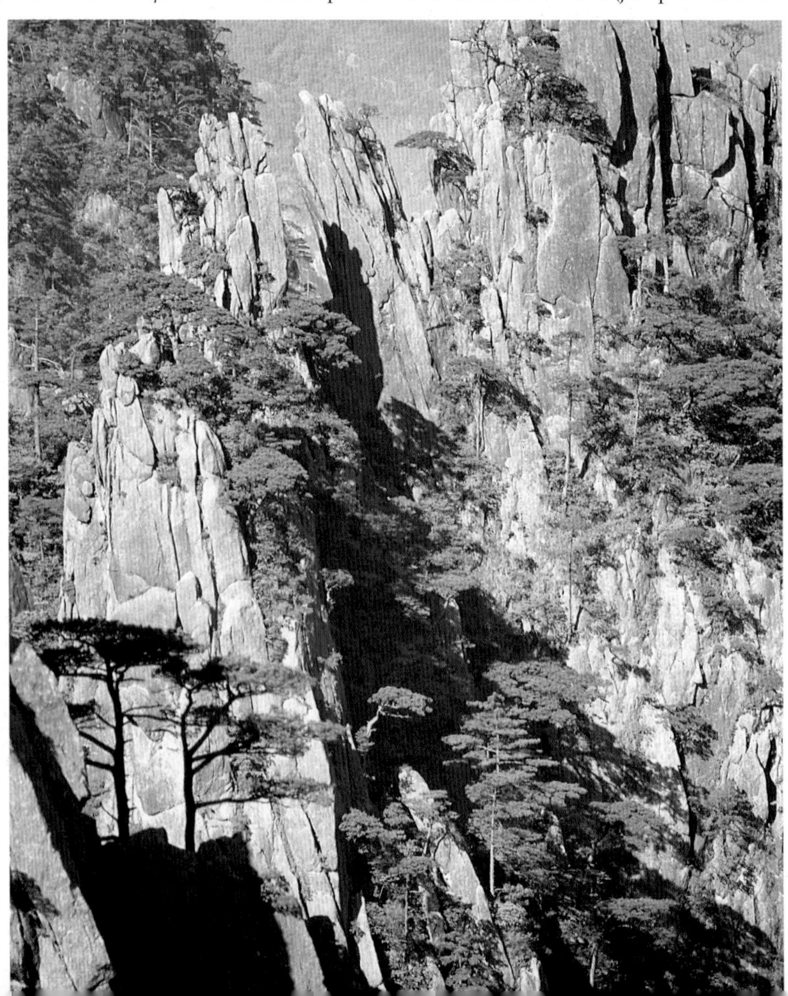

hours). A bus takes visitors to the main path, which starts from the lower cable car terminal and provides the quickest way to the summit (cable car service runs from 5:30AM). South of Huangshan (44 miles away) is Shexian, which is well known for its Ming-dynasty houses.

►► Jiuhuashan *167D1*

Jiuhuashan, the southern holy Buddhist mountain in Anhui province, is revered as a place of pilgrimage for the bereaved. Not as stunning as Huangshan, but still a splendid sight, the 4,600-foot climb can easily be accomplished in a day or ride the cable car which takes visitors up part of the way. You can get to Jiuhuashan from Nanjing by bus (7 hours), from Wuhu (4 hours) or from Huangshan (6 hours).

►►► Nanjing (Nanking) *167D2*

The capital of Jiangsu province lies on the south bank of the Yangtze and is one of the most delightful Chinese cities, despite the sprawl of modern buildings. Downtown retains its Ming street plan, the old city wall is largely intact, and an air of dignified calm, absent elsewhere in China, pervades the city's tree-lined streets.

It has been a capital at various times during the last 2,000 years—of the kingdom of Wu after the collapse of the Han, of local dynasties when China later fragmented, of imperial China under the early Ming, and of Republican China under the nationalists between 1911 and 1949.

Nanjing is an even mix of imperial and revolutionary China. Downtown is the area around Zhongshan Lu and Hanzhong Lu. But let us start with the **Ming city wall►►►**, which ignores the usually rigid rectangle, by necessity following instead the natural contour of the land for 20 miles, making it the longest city wall in the world. Much of it is still complete and can be seen from the park surrounding the **Xuanwu Lake►**, or it can be examined in detail on the road to the **Purple and Gold Mountains Observatory►** (*Open* daily. *Admission: inexpensive*), the largest in China. The **Zhonghua City Gate►►**, made of stone and clay bricks (each stamped with the name of its maker), has three inner gates designed to trap would-be attackers who breached the first gate in a compound. Steps lead up to the ramparts, which command fine views over the city. Often there are people selling the local polished stones (which are a Nanjing specialty) around the foot of the gate.

Just back into the city from Zhonghua Gate, along Zhonghua Lu, are the **Taiping Museum►** (*Open* daily 7:30–5. *Admission: inexpensive*) and the **Confucian Temple** (*Open* 8AM–9PM. *Admission: inexpensive*). The museum is housed in the residence and garden of one of the leaders of the Taiping Heavenly Kingdom Rebellion (1851–1864) (see page 42), and exhibits maps, coins, weapons, documents, and other artifacts relating to

Astronomical instrument at the Purple and Gold Mountains Observatory, Nanjing

The Yangtze River Bridge, Nanjing, a 3-mile feat of engineering that took eight years to complete

TOMB OF THE KING OF BORNEO

In 1408, the king of Borneo arrived in Nanjing, along with his extensive family, to pay tribute to the Ming court. His mission was evidently not entirely successful, because he died there the same year and is buried just to the south of the city walls.

the Taiping movement. Taiping wall paintings have recently been found at 74 Tangzi Jie. The area around the Confucian temple, called **Fuzimiao**, has become a lively area of restaurants, sideshows, and stores.

The **Provincial Museum▶▶** (*Open* daily 9–11:45AM, 1:30–4:45PM. *Admission: inexpensive*) at 321 Zhongshan Donglu, in an attractive building constructed in traditional style, is noted for its Han jade burial suit—jade squares linked by silver thread. Other display items include ceramics and bronzes from prehistoric times to the Qing dynasty.

The ruins of the **Ming Palace▶** (*Open* daily. *Admission: inexpensive*), on which Beijing's Forbidden City is modeled, rest under the trees near the Provincial Museum, a little farther west along Zhongshan Donglu. Two sets of five marble bridges, part of the old Meridian gate, and a crop of carved pillar bases remain. On the other side of the road there are a few scale-version buildings which give an idea of what the original palace would have been like.

With the exceptions of the **Ming Bell** and **Drum Towers▶** (in the center on Beijing Xilu), Nanjing's other attractions lie on the outskirts of the city. The magnificent **Yangtze River Bridge (Nanjing Changjiang Daqiao)▶▶▶** (*Open* daily. *Admission: moderate*), always cited as an example of what the Chinese could do when the Russians said it was impossible, is to the northwest of the city and links south with north China. Before its opening in 1968, trains crossed the river on a special ferry, taking two hours for each journey. The bridge is a double-decker (rail and road) and, between its extreme points, is over 1.25 miles long, making it one of the longest bridges in China. An elevator takes you up to a viewing tower on the south side from where there are excellent views of both the bridge itself and the river.

To the east of the city a road weaves through bamboo groves to the **Tomb of Zhu Yuanzhang▶▶** (*Open* daily. *Admission: inexpensive*), the first Ming emperor. The tomb is not open, but you can walk down the spirit (or royal) way lined with statues, less grand than its counterpart in Beijing but also less spoiled by commercialism. At the end farthest from the tomb the road curves to the right, but walk straight ahead to see the large brick arch, part of the wall that used to surround the tomb.

Farther on, east of the Ming tomb and embedded in the slopes of the Purple and Gold Mountain (Zijin Shan) is **Sun Yatsen's Mausoleum▶▶▶** (*Open* daily 8–5. *Admission: inexpensive*). Founder of Republican China, he died in 1925 in Beijing where he was laid out in the Biyun Temple. The competition for the design of his mausoleum was won by Y. C. Lu, who was influenced by the shape of the Liberty Bell in Philadelphia. The tomb itself is in the uppermost pavilion, reached by several flights of stairs. Sun Yatsen's remains are covered by a marble effigy.

East of Sun Yatsen's Mausoleum is the **Linggu Pagoda▶**, built by an American in 1929. Nearby is the fine **Beamless Hall▶▶** (*Open* daily. *Admission: inexpensive*), made entirely of brick without any wooden beams. It was part of a temple that existed on the site of the first Ming emperor's tomb.

THE RAPE OF NANJING
Between 1937 and 1945, during the Japanese occupation, it is estimated that at least 400,000 civilian residents of Nanjing were murdered or raped with appalling brutality. In the 1980s, a school history textbook was published in Japan that gave only a passing mention to this massacre. The Chinese government protested until changes were made.

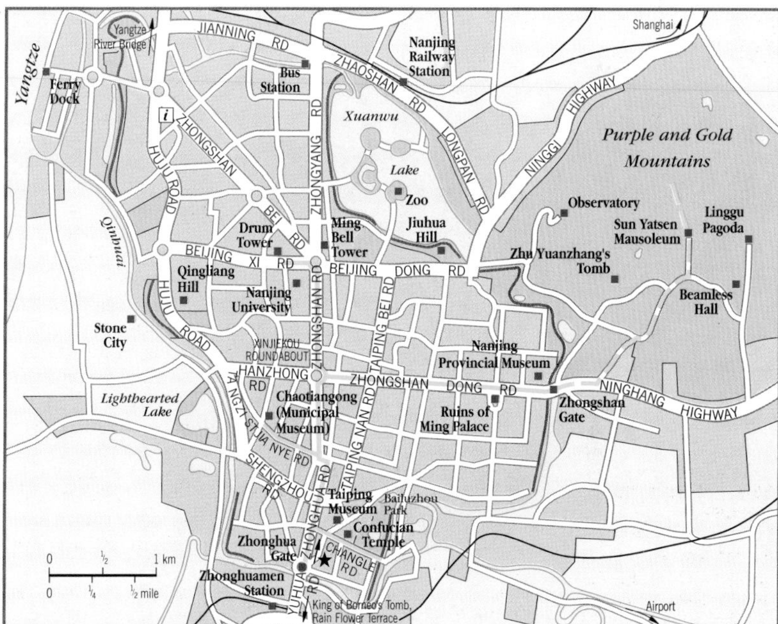

Walk

or bicycle ride—Nanjing

Start from the pretty, old wooden-fronted houses outside Zhonghua City Gate and head north up Zhonghua Road. Turn right on Changle Road to Bailuzhou Park which leads you to an interesting area of alleyways and old houses. Go back to Zhonghua Road, past the Taiping Museum and ornamental gardens and then turn left on Jianye Road to Chaotiangong, one of the oldest parts of the city and home to the Municipal Museum. Return to Zhonghua Road, go to the Xinjiekou circular road and up Zhongshan Road to the Drum Tower. East from the Xinjiekou circular takes you to the Ming Palace site and the Nanjing Provincial Museum. You can continue on to the Purple and Gold Mountains (Zijin Shan) by bicycle.

Nobody knows the precise date of the discovery of silk, but Chinese tradition ascribes it to the Empress Xi Ling who harnessed the natural skills of the silkworm for the benefit of humanity in the year 2640 BC.

Sericulture The Chinese kept the secret of silk for 3,000 years until, it is said, perfidious princesses and cunning missionaries exported it to the West and throughout the Orient. The word "sericulture" derives from the Greek word for silk, *serikos*, and refers to the raising of silkworms and the production of raw silk. Farmers breed the silkworms and then deliver the cocoons to spinning factories, where raw silk is drawn on to bobbins, ready for commercial use.

The silkworm is the caterpillar of the moth *Bombyx mori*, a native of China. One moth may lay 500 eggs, which are hatched in incubators or open trays at about 70°F. The caterpillars are black or gray, later turning creamy white, and are interested only in eating. Mulberry leaves, their preferred diet, are supplied to them every three to four hours. After five weeks the caterpillars are 3 inches long and are extremely sensitive to smells or noise; when full-grown they reject food and become restless, a sign that they are ready to make their cocoons. Small straw frames are then placed on the trays for this purpose.

The silk is produced by a pair of tubular spinning glands, each of which secretes a single fiber. One fiber is joined together with the other by muscular contraction, producing a thread up to 300 feet long. A gummy secretion holds it all together in its cocoon shape. This process takes about ten days, after which 90 percent of the cocoons are sent to the factory, while the farmer keeps 10 percent for breeding purposes.

The factory Once at the factory the cocoons are sorted to reject any that are flawed, and the remainder are then steamed to kill the live chrysalis. The threads from six or seven cocoons are needed to produce a fiber strong enough for weaving. The cocoons are immersed in hot water to loosen the threads, which are then extracted from the water and reeled together as one by machine. The cocoon case left behind is used as an ingredient in traditional medicine.

Top: silkworms and cocoons
Above: a silk-embroidered double-sided peony, on display in Suzhou Silk Museum

Old fabric, new style

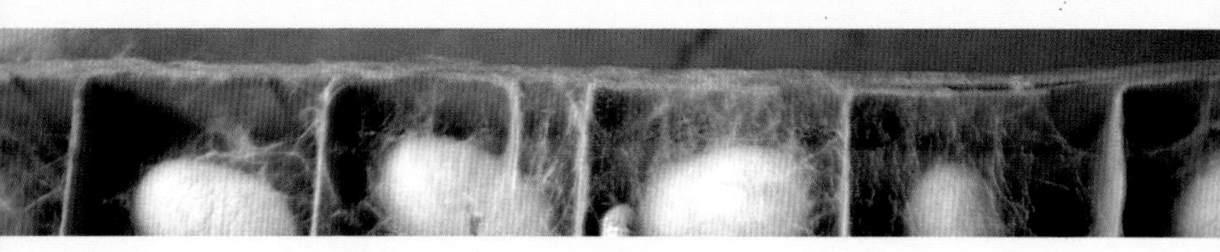

The newly created thread is then transformed into a yarn suitable for weaving by a process of doubling and twisting, known as "throwing," which gives it durability and strength. The amount of throwing varies according to the use to which the yarn will be put. After a certain point, silk loses its sleekness and is left with a granular surface, known as crepe.

The twisting is done mechanically—rows of machines transfer the yarn from one bobbin to another, with each bobbin moving at a different speed in order to achieve the amount of twist required.

From here the silk goes to dyeing factories and then to weaving factories to be made into cloth or carpets, or perhaps to institutes that specialize in the production of silk embroidery. The most famous of these is in Suzhou, and there are others in Guangdong and Sichuan.

SILK MARKETS

Much of China's 45,000-ton silk production is exported. China has 90 percent of the world market for raw silk and is attempting to increase its 40 percent share of the finished silk market.

Separating the silken strands from cocoons at a factory in Suzhou

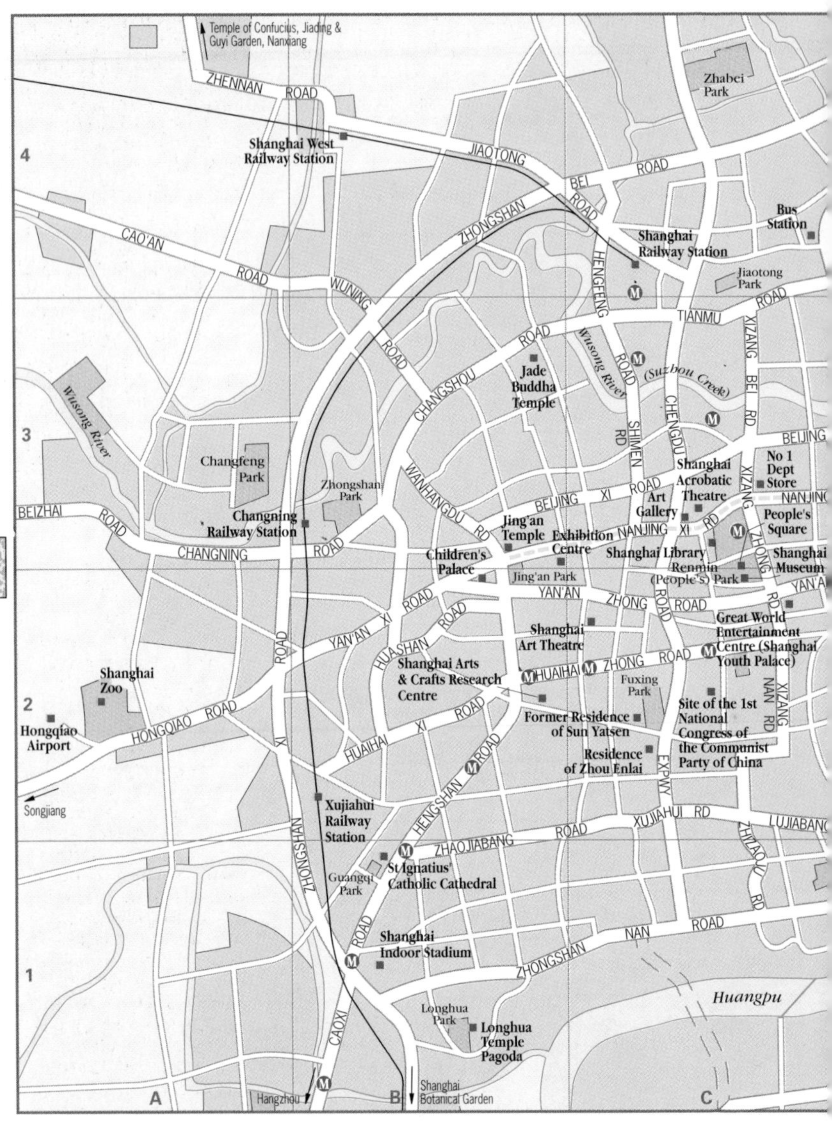

CITY SLICKERS
In pre-1949 Shanghai, stockbrokers dashed between offices in the financial districts as the rates fluctuated, in low-slung, four-wheel carriages, drawn by little Mongolian ponies. Each sported a coachman dressed in all his finery.

▶▶▶ Shanghai *167E2*

Shanghai, with a population of more than 13 million, is one of China's largest cities and, as one of China's four municipalities (along with Tianjin, Beijing, and Chongqing), is under direct central government control. It was a town of reasonable importance from the 13th century, when it became a county seat and was located in the area now known as the old town, which until the early part of the 20th century had its own wall. In the 19th century, the foreign powers recognized Shanghai's potential as a harbor, located as it is on the banks of the Huangpu, only 17 miles from the mouth of the Yangtze. The Treaty of Nanjing in 1842 (which concluded the Opium Wars) ceded areas of Shanghai first to the British and then to the French and Americans, forming what was known as the "Foreign Concessions." The British and Americans then combined to form the International Settlement, while the French Concession remained separate. The rules governing these enclaves were complicated, but essentially foreign nationals were not bound by Chinese law, but were subject to the jurisdiction of their own consuls. Up until 1949, foreigners dominated commerce and industry, amassing huge fortunes, as did a number of Chinese.

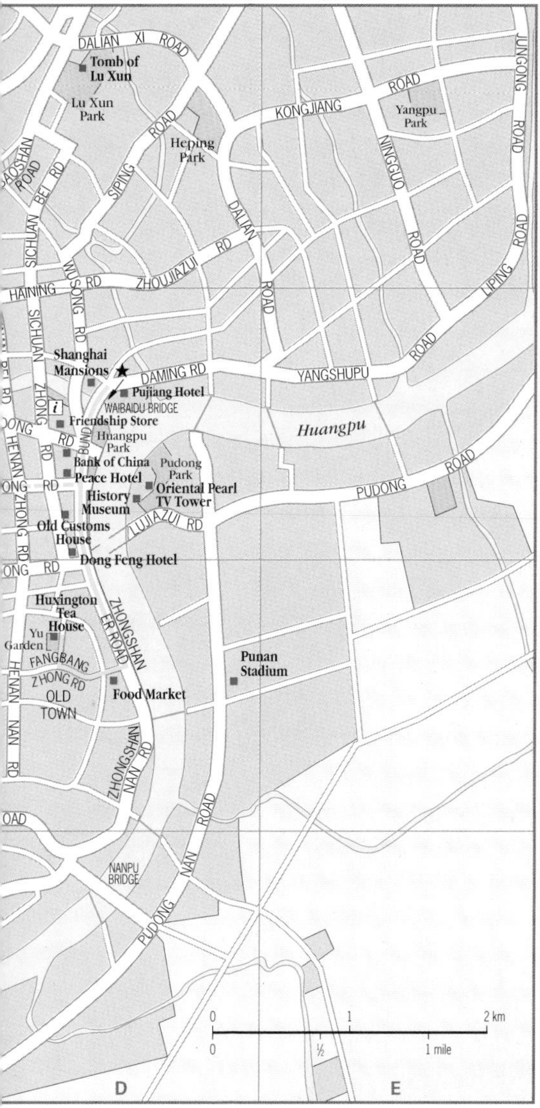

The colonial legacy is a bizarre one. Although Shanghai is a vital part of Chinese industry, and despite visible signs of change, it looks like a European city in a Chinese setting. A walk around the Bund and its neighboring streets is a good way to soak up its atmosphere.

Early morning dance lessons in Shanghai

THE GREAT WORLD

On the corner of Yan'an Lu and Xizang Lu is an extraordinary building resembling a wedding cake. The building was formerly called the Great World. Inaugurated in 1917, it was a cross between bazaar and freak show. Open from noon until late at night, each floor was devoted to different attractions from the burlesque to the vile: sing-song girls (see page 189) and peep shows, a stuffed whale and imported lavatories with a resident expert on their use. It is now open again in the evenings with fairground amusements and live performances of opera, trick-cyclists, and other entertainments.

THE GREAT MALOO

The Nanjing Road was originally cobbled and is named after the Nanjing treaty of 1842, which ceded areas of Shanghai to foreign control. For the Chinese it was always the Great Maloo, or Great Horse Road, since it was built for horsemen. It was noted by the writer John Steinbeck as one of the most interesting streets in the world.

FAR-SEEING JESUITS
Shanghai was dominated by foreigners by the second half of the 19th century, but 300 years earlier the Jesuits had already begun to exert an influence there. Occupying the area called Xujiahuie, they set about converting the locals to Catholicism, building a cathedral and observatory on land bought from one of their converts.

For superb views across the city, go to the viewing platform of the **Oriental Pearl TV Tower▶** (*Open* daily. *Admission: expensive*), one of the tallest buildings in Asia. The tower stands opposite the Bund in the Pudong area. The Shanghai History Museum is also due to be moved here.

The **Jade Buddha Temple (Yufosi)▶▶** (*Open* daily. *Admission: inexpensive*), on Anyuan Road, has a restored main hall and the remarkable Jade Buddha, brought back from Burma by a local abbot. The temple is lively on the first and fifth days of the lunar month. Shanghai's two other active temples are the **Jing'an▶** on Nanjing Xi Road and the **Longhua▶**, Longhua Road. The **Shanghai Museum▶▶▶** (*Open* daily 9–5. *Admission: inexpensive*), has a fine collection of Chinese art and porcelain. Of the many parks, the most interesting are the Renmin, the Hongkou, and the Jing'an.

The Shanghai Bund and its neighborhood

See highlighted map, pages 184–185.
The **Bund▶▶▶** (derived from the Anglo-Indian word meaning quay), about a mile long, is the city's fulcrum. Ideally, a half day should be devoted to a walk through the area—the Bund and the nearby streets, and the Friendship Store (China's largest)—or a day, if you combine the walk with a harbor cruise to the Yangtze mouth (boats leave near the Peace Hotel). At the far end of the Bund, just the other side of Suzhou Creek, is **Shanghai Mansions Hotel,** a 22-story brick ziggurat, in what would have been the American Concession.

Opposite, on the other side of Zhongshan Dong Road, is the **Pujiang Hotel**, formerly the Astor House, and opposite that the **Russian Consulate**.

Cross the Waibaidu Bridge back to the Bund. The former **British Consulate** (1870) at No. 33, set in manicured lawns, now has commercial offices. The Bund proper, known as Revolution Boulevard during the Cultural Revolution, consists almost entirely of pre-1949 buildings in grandiose style. No. 29 was originally the Banque de l'Indochine and No. 31 the former offices of Jardine, Matheson & Co., upon whose opium deals the prosperity of Shanghai was founded.

The outstanding buildings this side of the Nanjing Road are the **Bank of China**, with its New

Huxinting teahouse

York facade and Chinese roof, jostling for supremacy with the **Peace Hotel**. The Peace Hotel was originally the Cathay, built by Sir Victor Sassoon as the finest in Asia. Redolent of the 1930s, it sounds like the 1940s, because an old jazz band still thumps out nostalgic tunes in the bar at night.

Nanjing Road▶▶ is one of the busiest streets in China with a huge variety of merchandise on sale, though it is now somewhat upstaged by **Huaihai Lu**, the main street of the old French Concession. It leads through the heart of the city to the old **Racetrack** (now **Renmin Park**), the department stores, the Jing'an Temple, and the opulent villas of the former foreign residents.

Continue along the Bund past the old **Customs House** at No. 14, with some fine mosaics in the lobby ceiling and surmounted by **Big Ching**, a clock that used to chime like Big Ben in London. Number 12 is the former premises of the **Hong Kong and Shanghai Banking Corporation**, built in 1921, now the Pudong Development Bank. Number 3, the Dong Feng Hotel, was originally the famously snobbish **Shanghai Club** (the British Club), watering hole of the taipans (bosses of the foreign trading companies) and home to the longest bar in the world.

Yan'an Road was formerly Avenue Edward VII, the boundary between the International Settlement and the French Concession. The waterfront strip (Zhongshan Er Road) was the Quai de France. Walk along here to the former Chinese Bund, which runs in front of the **Old Town▶▶▶**. Turn right on Dongmen past Waixiang Guajie on the left, site of a local **food market** and worth a visit. Continue on to Fanbang Zhong Road until, on the right, you meet the Ming gateway to the **Temple of the City God** (**Chenghuangmiao**), and beyond it the tea-house and the Yu Garden.

Pass through the gateway and into the heart of the old town, a maze of quaint stores and restaurants reminiscent of old China. In the middle is a small lake. The zigzag bridge leads to the 18th-century **Huxinting tea-house▶▶**, a midlake pavilion and an excellent place for a refreshing pot of green tea.

The nearby Ming dynasty **Yu Garden▶▶** (*Open* daily 8:30–4:30. *Admission: inexpensive*) is a fine example of miniature landscaping, built in 1559. The first pavilion is the ceremonial Three Ears of Corn Hall, followed by the Hall for Viewing the Grand Rockery. Turn right as you come out of here, follow the pond shore, then keep right past a series of pavilions, halls, and gardens to reemerge in the old town behind the tea-house.

The skyline of the Shanghai Bund

Shanghai is a legend. A generation after the last "Shanghailanders" relinquished their privileges, the name continues to evoke nostalgia for a way of life that can never be the same again.

The Peace Hotel Jazz Band, still thumping out 1940s classic tunes

FOX-HUNTING MEMORIES
Part of the charm of pre-1949 Shanghai was its absurdity. It was an oasis of unreality in a world that was all too real beyond the boundaries of the Foreign Concessions. For the British, memories of home were reinforced by such events as the paper hunt. A pack of foxhounds would set off in pursuit of a chemical trail with the odoriferous qualities of a fox. Horses and huntsmen galloped across the countryside not far behind, with the last man in the field being responsible for mollifying any outraged farmers.

The old Cathay Hotel, now the Peace Hotel, where Noël Coward wrote Private Lives

A unique city The European man's pre-1949 Shanghai seemed to be "life itself." It was an extraordinary mix of the very seedy and the very decadent, immense wealth and terrible poverty. It has even given its name to a verb—according to the dictionary, to be shanghaied is to "be drugged and shipped as a sailor, when unconscious."

The city's oddities were due to the peculiar circumstances of the city's existence. Written into the Treaty of Nanjing was the notion of extraterritoriality, which meant that foreign nationals in Shanghai were outside Chinese law, which was of Medieval severity. Of course each of the concessions had its own laws, but in practice almost anything went. Shanghai became a magnet for the dispossessed, seekers of wealth, and adventurers.

Shanghailanders Most of what is left of concession Shanghai dates from 1920 to 1949. The character of the two concessions (the French and the International Settlement) was quite different—not only did you change buses at Edward VII Avenue but also electricity systems. The International Settlement was a combination of the British and the American Settlement. Each concession reflected different national personas and atttracted different characters. And Shanghai was full of characters: wealthy Baghdad Sephardic Jews like Sir Victor Sassoon, owner of the Cathay Hotel (today's Peace Hotel), with his stable of greyhounds—greyhound racing was a passion among expatriates—whose names coincided with his initials ("Very Slippy," "Veiled Secret," "Very Soon"); Silas Hardoon, the wealthiest man in Shanghai, who owned an estate (now covered by the old Russian-style Exhibition Center) in the city where he kept his Eurasian wife and

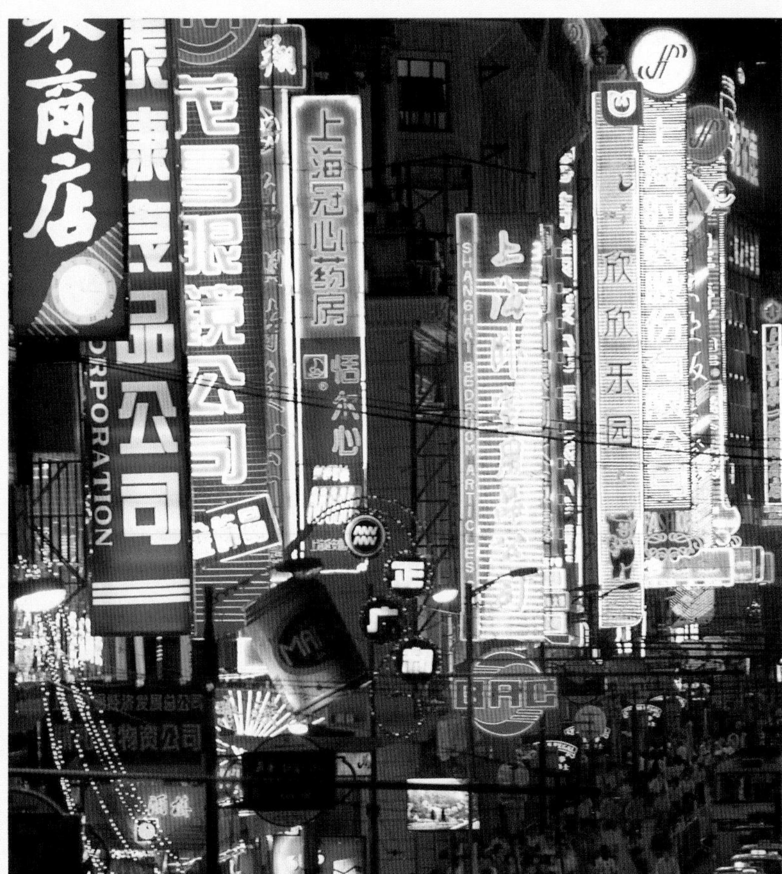

After years of darkness, Shanghai's famous night-life has returned

colony of adopted children; and underworld criminals, such as the notorious Pockmarked Huang and Big-Eared Du, who ran the city from the safety of the French Concession. The mixture of propriety and duplicity that was Shanghai is exemplified by the careers of these two—Huang was the Chief Detective of the French Sûreté, and Du would threaten those who spurned his offers of protection by delivering a coffin to their front door.

Nightlife Above all, Shanghai was a nocturnal city. Night started with the tea-cocktail hour, "tea for propriety and cocktails for pep," and perhaps finished at dawn at Blood Alley (Xikou Lu). Taxi-dancing was an institution—hostesses were for hire in vast dance halls but required that a drink be bought, invariably cold tea but billed as champagne or whatever the lady requested. Then there were the sing-song girls, who provided entertainment at restaurant dinner parties. Although they were not above prostitution, their main accomplishment was seductive singing, accompanied by a man playing the *erhu*, a two-string Chinese violin. The sing-song girl was easy to identify in her highly polished lacquer rickshaw; a bell announced her presence while a lamp at her feet was angled to highlight her face and the lotus in her hair.

AFTER DARK

The Russians arrived in the wake of the 1917 Revolution and were an important and volatile element in the make-up of pre-1949 Shanghai. They are credited with the development of the cabaret. Young Russian women teamed up with Filipino dance bands to perform in Chinese-owned cabarets and were frequently cited in scandalous divorce cases. As a contemporary guidebook pointed out, "There are three classes of cabaret—high class, low class, and no class."

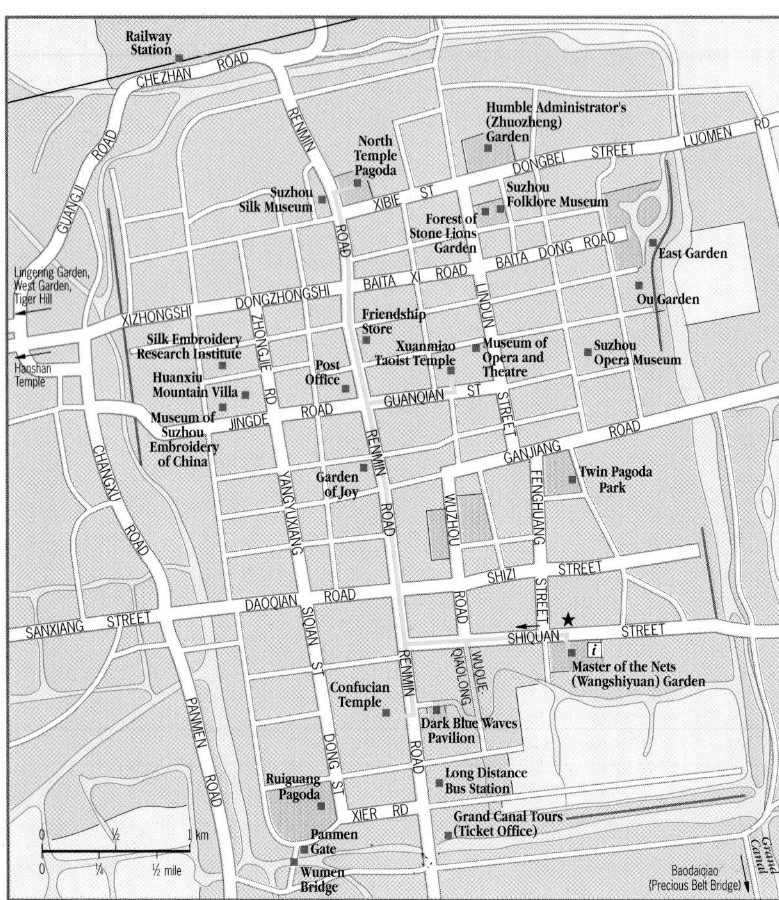

Walk

Suzhou's gardens and temples

A short walk introduces you to some of Suzhou's principal sights. On Wangshi Xiang, an alley off Shijin Jie close to the Suzhou Hotel, is the **Master of the Nets Garden** (**Wangshiyuan**)▶▶▶, a miniature garden built around a pool and first laid out in 1140. It has several small halls carved in lattice and fretwork on the principle of "framing a view."

From Wangshiyuan turn left to Shiquan Street and then take the first left onto Wuqueqiaolong until you reach the **Dark Blue Waves Pavilion** (**Canglangting**)▶▶, which dates back to the 10th century.

Back on Shiquan Street turn left and walk until you reach the junction with Renmin Road, then turn left again and continue to the **Confucian Temple**▶ where you will find a street plan of Suzhou, the earliest such map extant in China.

Return to Renmin Road, retrace your steps northward and turn right onto Guanqian Street, to reach the Song-dynasty **Xuanmiao Taoist Temple**▶ (*Open* 9–6. *Admission: inexpensive*). Continue north along Renmin Road past the Friendship Store (No 504) to the impressive **North Temple Pagoda**▶▶ (*Open* 8:30–4. *Admission: inexpensive*), set in a pretty garden.

▶▶▶ Suzhou *167E2*

A comparatively small town in Jiangsu province, Suzhou is one of China's most charming cities, recognized for centuries for its loveliness. Its fame rests on its silk and its gardens, and the pretty houses overlooking narrow canals spanned by traditional bridges—once a standard feature in this area—are now attractions in their own right.

Suzhou's history dates back to the 6th century BC when it was founded on a network of canals built to control the Yangtze floodwaters. Its subsequent prosperity was due to the construction of the Grand Canal and the growth of the silk industry, which flourished under the Tang and became even more important under the Song with the establishment of the capital at Hangzhou. Later it was known as a great cultural center, but it has remained relatively unaffected by the convulsions of Chinese politics.

The wealth of Suzhou's officials, scholars and traders was invested in their **gardens** (*Open* daily 7:30–5:30. *Admission: moderate*). The greatest, the 10th-century **Humble Administrator's Garden (Zhuozhengyuan)▶▶▶**, is also the largest, occupying a 10-acre site; the poetically named 19th-century **Lingering Garden (Liuyuan)▶▶▶** is small with delightful rock gardens. The **Forest of Stone Lions Garden (Shizilin)▶▶▶**, about one acre in size, has four lakes, rocks, bridges, and hills and is considered one of Suzhou's finest gardens. The **Yi Yuan (Harmony Garden)**, on Renmin Lu, is a Qing dynasty garden featuring colored pebbles and rock gardens.

At the **Silk Embroidery Research Institute▶▶▶** you can watch craftsmen creating their painstaking masterpieces (sometimes embroidering with a strand that is a mere one-fortieth of a silk thread) as well as buy samples of their work. **Suzhou Silk Museum▶▶** (*Open* 9–5. *Admission: inexpensive*), near North Pagoda on Renmin Lu, offers a fascinating insight into the story of silk with live silkworms and a collection of silk looms.

Outside the city is **Tiger Hill (Huqiushan)▶▶▶** (*Open* daily. *Admission: moderate*), a scenic spot, with a Song-dynasty leaning pagoda with some Tang features and built in brick to imitate wood architecture. In 1957 workers discovered sutras there and a record of its construction date (959–961). The low, long **Precious Belt Bridge▶▶** affords excellent views of life on the canals.

BRIDGES OVER CANALS

Handsome bridges spanning the canals are a feature of Suzhou. One of the most impressive is the Maple Bridge, near the Hanshan Temple, the subject of a poem by the Tang poet Zhang Ji entitled "Anchored by night at the Maple Bridge." Another, offering a classically picturesque view, arches across the old moat near the Panmen Gate.

Wangshiyuan, the Master of the Nets Garden

Luohan Hall in the "Temple of the Return to the Fundamental Principle," Guiyuan Temple, Wuhan

▶▶ Wuhan *166C1*

Wuhan, capital of Hubei province, is an iron and steel city on the Yangtze made up of the three former cities of Wuchang, on the south bank, Hanyang, and the former treaty port of Hankou on the north. Wuchang was briefly capital of the state of Wu in the 3rd century AD, and Hanyang was founded during the Sui dynasty. Hankou was little more than a fishing village until the Western powers established concessions there from 1861. Wuhan was the center for the revolutionary activity that culminated in the 1911 uprising and overthrow of the Manchu dynasty.

Wuhan tends to be seen merely as an embarkation or disembarkation point for the Yangtze River cruises, but the old downtown area, improved recently, has some attractions. The most striking of these is the **Yellow Crane Pavilion (Huanghelou)▶** on Sheshan (Snake Hill) in Wuchang, by the river bridge. Recently restored, it was originally built in the 3rd century AD. Commemorated in many poems, it gets its name from the story of a Taoist priest, Wang Zian, who alighted here on a yellow crane on his journey to become one of the Immortals. If you have time to explore Sheshan a little farther, you will find the **Shengxiang Baota** lama stupa, embossed with interesting carvings, and the **tomb of Chen Youjing**, who declared an independent state at the end of the Yuan dynasty, both worth a visit.

Farther east is the **East Lake (Donghu)▶**, a spacious, pleasant place for a boat trip or stroll. Nearby is the remarkable **Provincial Museum▶▶▶** (*Open* daily 8:30–noon, 2–4. *Admission: inexpensive*), mostly devoted to the finds excavated from the tomb of Marquis Yi of the state of Zeng, who died in 433 BC, and important because it demonstrates the extraordinary richness of Chinese cultural life well before China became a single, unified state. The highlight is a set of 64 bronze bells on racks, supported by bronze soldiers, used daily in concerts of ancient music. The crawling dragon motif is repeated on many of the ritual lacquerware

REBEL HEADQUARTERS

From 1926 to 1927 Wuhan was the headquarters of a faction of the Guomindang that opposed Chiang Kaishek. The faction commander was Wang Jingwei, who at the time allied himself to the communists. In 1927, in an abrupt *volte-face*, Chiang Kaishek turned on them, murdering 100,000 of their supporters in the Wuhan district. He was eventually to lead a Japanese puppet government in Nanjing in 1940 and to die in Tokyo in 1944.

vessels that were also discovered in the tomb. There is a fine collection of ritual bronzes, as well as other ancient musical instruments.

In Hanyang the **Guiyuan Buddhist Temple▶▶** (*Open daily 8:30–5. Admission: inexpensive*) on Cuihui Jie, built in the Qing dynasty on the site of a Ming garden, is celebrated for the 500 figures sculpted by two artists between 1822 and 1831. **Guishan (Tortoise Hill)▶** was once covered in temples and pavilions, some of which have been reconstructed, including the Song-dynasty **Guqin Terrace (Guqintai)**. It was built to commemorate two Han-dynasty musicians, Yu Baiya and Zhong Ziqi, who used to play together here. One year Yu arrived to find that his friend had died; after playing a farewell tune on his lute, he broke the strings, vowing never to play again.

Hankou▶▶, like Shanghai, is interesting for its European atmosphere, a legacy dating from 1861 to 1949 when the foreign powers were established here. The British Concession extended from Jianghan Dadao to the train station; then, in sequence, were the smaller Russian, French, German, and Japanese concessions.

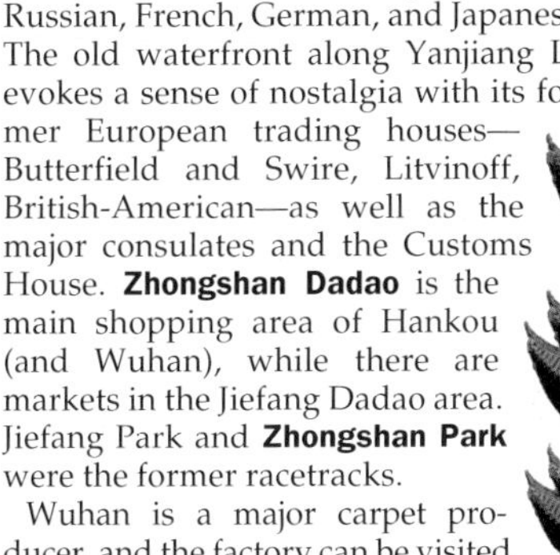

The old waterfront along Yanjiang Lu evokes a sense of nostalgia with its former European trading houses—Butterfield and Swire, Litvinoff, British-American—as well as the major consulates and the Customs House. **Zhongshan Dadao** is the main shopping area of Hankou (and Wuhan), while there are markets in the Jiefang Dadao area. Jiefang Park and **Zhongshan Park** were the former racetracks.

Wuhan is a major carpet producer, and the factory can be visited by appointment.

The Yangtze River Bridge was completed in 1957. Over a mile long, it carries both trains and road traffic. A second bridge was completed in 1995.

CHAIRMAN MAO TAKES A DIP

During the Cultural Revolution, Wuhan was the scene of Chairman Mao's famous swim in the Yangtze River. Mythology recounts that he swam from bank to bank, an unlikely feat when you look at the width of the river at this point; what he did was to go in and allow himself to be carried by the current a little way. Mao's villa, near East Lake, is open to the public.

The Yellow Crane Pavilion, overlooking the Yangtze, Wuhan

Although the river itself and the life along its banks are fascinating in themselves, the focal point of the cruise along the Yangtze is the dramatic journey through the Three Gorges.

YANGTZE GORGES
The Three Gorges were formed about 70 million years ago when earth movements caused a vast inland sea draining east to cut into lime-stone faults in zigzag fashion, creating the perpendicular cliffs and sharp curves of the gorges.

Transportation For most people the journey along the Yangtze begins or ends either at Wuhan or Chongqing (downstream takes 3 days and 2 nights, upstream 5 days). Between the two cities are the gorges themselves and a host of towns and villages. As well as the luxury ships run by CITS and those chartered by foreign tour companies, there are local steamers that have basic accommodations ranging from fairly unpleasant dormitories to two-berth cabins of an acceptable standard with a small lounge. They have restaurants that serve, on the whole, execrable food. Some of them have upgraded cabins with private bathrooms and air-conditioning. If you can secure a cabin, eat the food, and tolerate the booming whistle, a trip on one of these ships is a worthwhile experience.

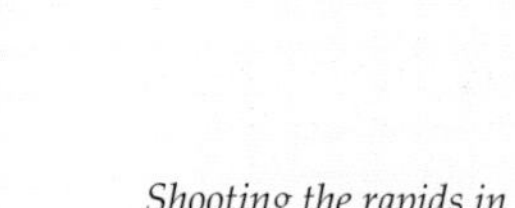

Sights The Yangtze is lined with evocatively named rocks and hills. About 886 feet east of Chongqing is the **Stone Treasure Stronghold (Shibaozhai)**, a 100-foot rock said to resemble a jade seal, with a brilliant red pagoda against the side. At its summit is an early 18th-century temple. About 30 miles beyond, **Wanxian** is a typical settlement, high on the banks and reached by a long flight of steps. An established trading center, it is crammed with market stalls piled high with fruit, nuts, and traditional basket-ware. There is also a silk-weaving factory. At **Yunyang**, the Zhang Fei Temple is dedicated to a Three Kingdoms general renowned for his honesty. Next is **Fengjie** with its Ming walls, then **Baidi Cheng** followed by the Gorges.

The Gorges The Gorges are a spectacular sight. The first is the 5 mile **Qutangxia (Bellows Gorge)**. As you enter it,

Shooting the rapids in one of the Yangtze's three "Lesser Gorges" along the Daning River

Red Shoulder Mountain appears on the north side, pockmarked with square holes, ancient burial places said to have been used as bellows by the god of carpenters, Lu Ban. On **White Salt Mountain**, on the south bank, are the remains of a 6th-century city. Clinging precariously to the rock-face high up on the north side of the gorge is the old towpath. The gorge ends at the town of **Daixi**.

Boats often moor at **Wushan** in order to visit the three beautiful small gorges along the Daning River. A fee is charged for this extra boat excursion.

Next comes the 28-mile **Wuxia (Witches Gorge)** lined by 12 peaks, six on either side, each with a poetic name based on the legend of Yao Ji, daughter of the Queen of the West, and her 11 sisters. **Zigui** was the home of the 3rd-century BC statesman Qu Yuan of the state of Chu, whose suicide, when his advice to resist the rise of the state of Qin was ignored, is commemorated in the annual Dragon-boat races. Finally comes the 47-mile **Xiling Gorge**, which comprises seven smaller gorges. The main ones are the **Gorge of the Sword and the Manual on the Art of War** (named after Zhuge Liang, a 3rd-century AD minister said to have hidden his treatise on military strategy here); and then the **Ox Liver and Horse's Blood Gorge**, the **Kongling Gorge**, and the **Shadowplay Gorge**, all named after colors and shapes of rocks.

A former treaty port, Yichang is now famous for its **Gezhouba Dam**, completed in 1986 (see panel).

Though the waters are rising, the gorges remain a most spectacular sight

SUNKEN GORGES

Work has begun, recent scandals concerning funding notwithstanding, on the Chinese authorities' latest dam project on the Yangtze, which will submerge the gorges forever. The Sanxia Dam, due to be completed by 2008, will create the world's largest reservoir. The aim of the project—which will involve the relocation of about two million people—is three-fold. It will ease shipping, prevent flooding, and provide hydroelectric power to China's interior.

Visits can be arranged to the Gezhouba Dam (it produces 14 billion kilowatt-hours annually), the White Horse Cave, and Three Visitors Cave. Both caves have fine rock formations.

Traditional Huishan clay figurine "fatties," still made in Wuxi

FIGURES OF CLAY
Wuxi is not only known for its rocks and silk, it also produces the famous Huishan figurines made of local clay. Depicting characters from traditional fairy-tales, operas, and plays, they may not be to everyone's taste, but even if they do not appeal to you, a visit to the factory to watch them being made is worthwhile.

ATTRACTION OF OPPOSITES
In *Behind the Wall*, Colin Thubron describes the rocks of Lake Tai as "a frozen turmoil" that "concentrated the wild energy of nature." In traditional garden, rocks represented the hard, masculine "yang" principle, in contrast to the water, next to which they were usually placed, which was soft, feminine "yin." "Water was stone's antithesis. It was the blood of the earth, drunk by the kings of old legend in search of immortality."

►► Wulingyuan

This mountainous, lush area in northwestern Hunan is home to several minority peoples and is the site of Asia's largest cave. Trails provide some excellent hiking and it is possible to go rafting. An airport has been built to serve the area.

►► Wuxi and Lake Tai *167E2*

Wuxi town is a convenient access point for **Lake Tai (Taihu)►►**, one of the largest freshwater lakes in China. It is famous for its ornamental limestone rocks pierced with holes by the action of the waters, which were highly prized and often adorn traditional Chinese gardens.

Wuxi, one of the principal ports on the Grand Canal, has one of the fastest growing economies in the country. Although an old town (it got its name, which means "no tin," during the Han dynasty when the tin mine on Xishan dried up), its economic expansion dates only to the turn of the 20th century when wealthy Shanghai entrepreneurs established new factories and developed the silk industry. A visit to the **Number 1 Spinning Mill►►** is worthwhile.

There are accommodations at the lakeside (some distance out of town) and downtown—which has a lively port atmosphere. The city is dominated by Xihui Hill and Park, where one of the most noted gardens in China, the **Jichangyuan (Attachment to Freedom Garden)►►** (*Open* daily. *Admission: inexpensive*), stands on the site of an ancient monastery. Such was its fame that the Emperor Qianlong replicated it as the Garden of Harmonious Interest in the Summer Palace in Beijing. Xihui Park was created in 1958 by linking the Hui Mountain, with its nine dragon peaks and spring water, its temple, and its Song-dynasty bridge with Xi Mountain and its 16th-century Longguang Pagoda and Temple. There is another garden, the **Liyuan** (**Wormy Garden**), near the lakeside Hubin and Shuixu hotels. **The Meiyuan (Plum Garden)►**, on the road to the Taihu Hotel, is particularly pretty in the early spring, when its thousands of plum trees are in blossom (*Open* daily. *Admission: inexpensive*).

Opposite the Taihu Hotel is **Tortoise Head Promontory (Yuantouzhu)►** (*Open* daily. *Admission: moderate*), a beauty spot populated with teahouses in a lakeside setting. From here, boat trips to Sanshan Island are sometimes possible. There are infrequent boat services across the lake and by canal to Yixing (Dingshu), Hangzhou, Changzhou, Suzhou, and Xidongtingshan, where the ornamental rocks are prepared. In Wuxi town on the main streets of Renmin

Zhonglu, Jiefang Xilu, and Zhongshan Lu some older houses or restaurants (serving the delicious local specialties, whitebait or Wuxi spare ribs) still survive.

►► Yangzhou *167D2*

Yangzhou, Jiangsu province, has a cultured past that has bequeathed many poets and painters, gardens, a local opera style, and the still-live tradition of recitation of novels in the street.

The Xu Garden (Xuyuan)►►, on the west side of the Narrow West Lake, is noted for the beautiful carved woodwork inside the pavilions. Three other **traditional gardens (Xiyuan, Yechunyuan, Hongyuan)►►** cluster around the moat to the west of the Xiyuan Hotel.

The **Geyuan►►** (*Open* daily), on Dongguan Jie, was the 19th-century home of a salt merchant, one of several merchant houses in this area. Another attractive garden is the

Eternal China: view through a moon gate, "Five Pavilion Bridge," Yangzhou

Heyuan►► (*Open* daily. *Admission: inexpensive*) on Xuningmen Jie, small but ingeniously contrived. The **Museum►** (*Open* daily 8–5. *Admission free*) is located on Yanfu Xilu in a Qing temple. To the northwest are traces of the Tang city walls and the **Fajingsi Temple**. The **Slender West Lake** (**Shouxi Hu**)**►►** has the famous Five Pavilion Bridge (Wutingqiao). Another unusual point of interest is the **Tomb of Puhaddin** (Puhaddin was a Yuan-dynasty Muslim preacher and descendant of Mohammed), which overlooks the Grand Canal.

The current **Daming Monastery (Monastery of Great Brightness)►** (*Open* daily 8–4:30. *Admission: moderate*) was built in 1934 on the foundations of a much older monastery. The original temple, established more than a 1,000 years ago, was founded by the Tang dynasty monk Jianzhen, who spent many years in Japan as a missionary. The temple's Jianzhen Memorial Hall is based on the great hall of the Toshodai Temple in Nara, Japan.

DESIGN DIFFERENCES
Yangzhou gardens tend to be smaller than those of Suzhou—sometimes indeed the residential area is larger than the garden area. The gardens furthermore seem to have absorbed a mixture of influences ranging from southern architectural motifs like curved gable end walls to the more restrained northern style.

YANGZHOU ECCENTRICS
Europeans associate Yangzhou with Marco Polo, who is supposed to have been governor here, but for the Chinese it brings to mind the "eccentrics of Yangzhou," a group of painters who incurred imperial disapproval. Also known as the Eight Eccentrics, they specialized in simple, dramatic works and one, Gao Qipei (1672–1734), is especially remembered for painting with his finger and fingernail.

▶ Zhenjiang 167D2

Zhenjiang's prosperity was founded on silk and the Grand Canal. Industrial now, in the 19th century it was a treaty port, and the **museum▶** (*Open* Fri–Wed 9–5. *Admission: inexpensive*) is housed in the former British Consulate in an area which leads down to the river. Jinshan is dominated by the **Jinshan Temple▶▶** (*Open* daily 6–6. *Admission: inexpensive*), with its stunning, renovated Main Hall of Golden Buddhas and the **Cishou Pagoda▶**. **Jiaoshan▶** is bamboo-forested and home to the **Dinghui Temple** and remains of the gun batteries. On **Beigushan▶** are the 11th-century **Iron Pagoda** (**Tieta**), the **Sweet Dew Temple (Ganlusi)** and the **Soaring Clouds Pavilion** (**Lingyunting**).

Hall of the Golden Buddhas at the Jinshan Temple, Zhenjiang, one of the oldest temples in this region

Chinese gardens are works of art that mirror the Taoist principle of harmony with nature. Imperial parks aside, wealth could not buy the large country estates that it did in Europe, so the Chinese garden was a city retreat for the cultivated scholar-official whose yearnings for rural tranquillity were sublimated in the gentle art of gardenscaping.

Balance The most famous Chinese gardens are the miniature gardens of southern China, where ponds become lakes, rock gardens mountains, and where bridges and pavilions provide the human element. But not all gardens need be small—to the Chinese, the Summer Palace in Beijing is a garden where the pond really is a lake, the pavilions are palaces, and the rock gardens are dwarfed by hills. It is the natural world in microcosm, an expression of both the wealth and majesty of the emperor and the variety of the world at large.

Top: Taihu rock in the Forbidden City

Below: the zigzag pathway in the Master of the Fishing Nets Garden, Suzhou, illustrates the concept of never revealing the whole garden at once

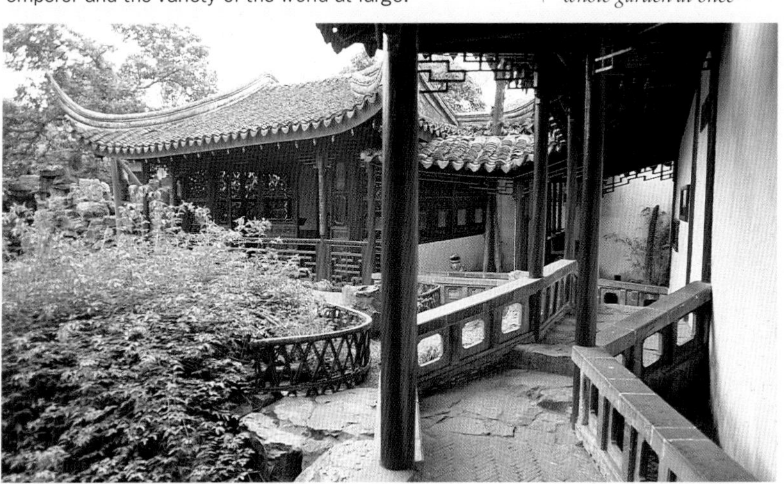

Harmony In a Chinese garden all the emotions experienced in the natural landscape should be aroused. Lofty mountain peaks are evoked by rocks and stones piled up together; ponds reflect clouds and shadows, mirroring the sky; sunlight gives way to shade, and paths lead from high to low. The garden expresses the physical Taoist precepts of balance and harmony and the coexistence of the natural and the man-made.

Bamboo, pine and plum-blossom, pots of flowers, scented shrubs, and intricately cut gateways giving tantalizing glimpses of what is to come complete the tranquil scene. The cultivation of the garden was an accomplishment for the cultured scholar-official equal to painting and poetry-writing. It was a place for recreation, contemplation, and philosophizing, to be enjoyed in all weathers.

NATURE AND NURTURE
Although the Chinese garden intends to imitate, if miniaturize, nature, the human touch is considered an integral part of a garden landscape. Calligraphy is frequently inscribed on rocks or over doorways, and the fanciful names that are given to pavilions are usually taken from literary sources and supposed to enhance enjoyment of the garden.

SICHUAN
HUBEI
Han Shui
Suizhou
Anlu
Dabie Shan
Lu'a
Tongchen
Macheng
Daxian
Yunyang
Fengjie
Wushan
Wanxian
Badong
Jingmen
Tianmen
WUHAN
Taihu
Chang Jiang (Yangtze)
Yichang
Jiangling
Shashi
Hong Hu
Xiantao
Ezhou
Huangshi
Enshi
Wuxue
Huko
Jiujiang
Guling
Lushan
Poyan Hu
Jinshi
Shishou
Datong Hu
Puqi
Qianjiang
Yueyang
Mufu Shan
Boyang
Dayong
Changde
Wuling Shan
Dongting Hu
Nanchan
Daozhen
Yuan Jiang
Yiyang
Jiuling Shan
Jishou
Changsha
Gan Jiang
2942m
Shaoshan
Xiangtan
Linchuan
Wu Jiang
Tongren
HUNAN
Zhuzhou
Yichun
Huaihua
Lengshuijiang
Loudi
Liling
Pingxiang
Nancheng
Shaoyang
Ji'an
Zhenyuan
Hengyang
Jiang
Guangchang
GUIZHOU
Hongjiang
Xiang
JIANGXI
Kaili
Jingxian
Dong'an
Leiyang
Duyun
Yongzhou
Suichuan
Wu
Miao Ling
Ruijin
Rongjiang
2142m
Ganzhou
Dushan
Quanzhou
Chenzhou
2081m
Daoxian
Dayu
Nan Ling
Guilin
Lechang
Rongshui
Shaoguan
Longnan
Hechi
Yangshuo
Jianghua
Lianxian
Pingle
Lianping
Meizhou
Liuzhou
Li Jiang
GUANGDONG
GUANGXI ZHUANGZU ZIZHIQU
Bei Jiang
Huaji
Heshan
Pingnan
Qingyuan
Conghua
Heyuan
Wuzhou
GUANGZHOU (CANTON)
Lianhua
Binyang
Zhaoqing
Lufen
Guigang
Nanning
Xi Jiang
Foshan
Huizhou
Rongxian
Yulin
Luoding
Jiangmen
Shenzhen
Yunkai Dashan
Zhongshan
Kaiping
Macau
HONG KONG
Yunwu Shan
Qinzhou
Yangjiang
VN
Maoming
Beihai
Zhanjiang
Leizhou Bandao
Haikang
Beibu Wan
Xuwen
Nan Hai
Qiongzhou Haixia
Haikou
Wenchang
HAINAN
Hainan Dao
Changjiang
Qiongzhong
Dongfang
1867m Wuzhi Shan
Xinglong
Tongshi
Sanya
Xincun
Luhuitou

A
B
C
1
2
3
4
5

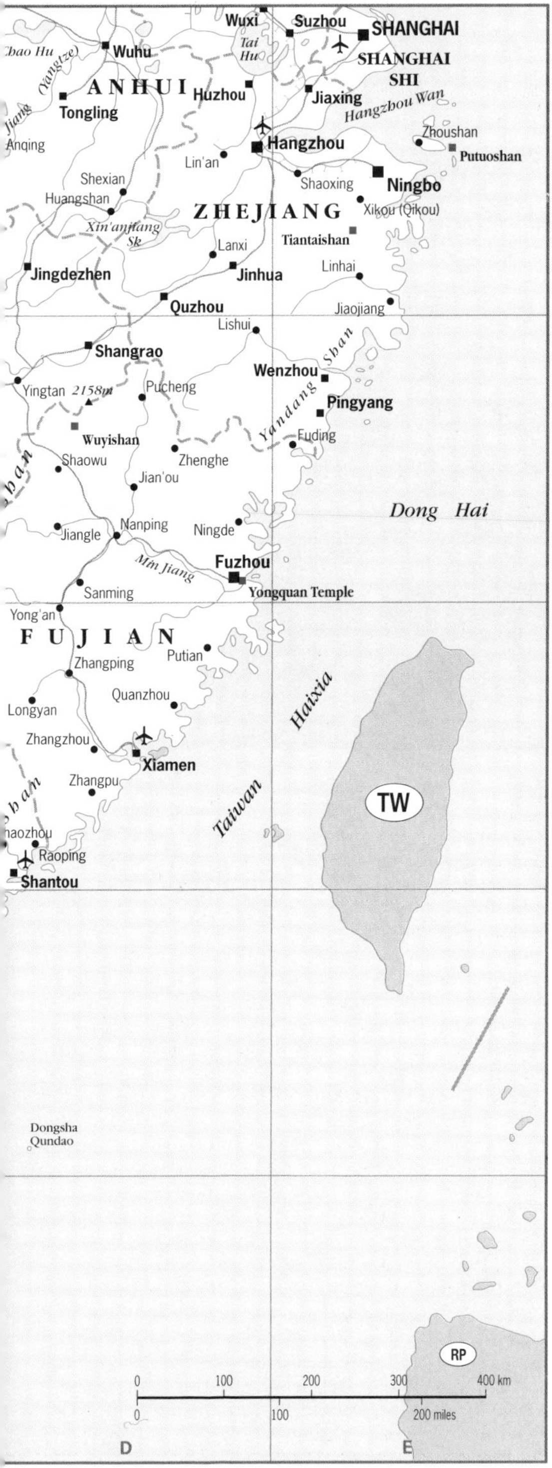

South China

▶▶▶ REGION HIGHLIGHTS

BIG WIND
Typhoons (from the Chinese "da feng," or "big wind") strike China more frequently than any other country, at a rate of about seven a year. By Chinese standards a gale of force 8 to 11 is regarded as a typhoon. Generally speaking, they arrive July through September and can, though rarely, penetrate as far as 248 miles inland and last several days. On the whole, however, they fizzle out after a few hours.

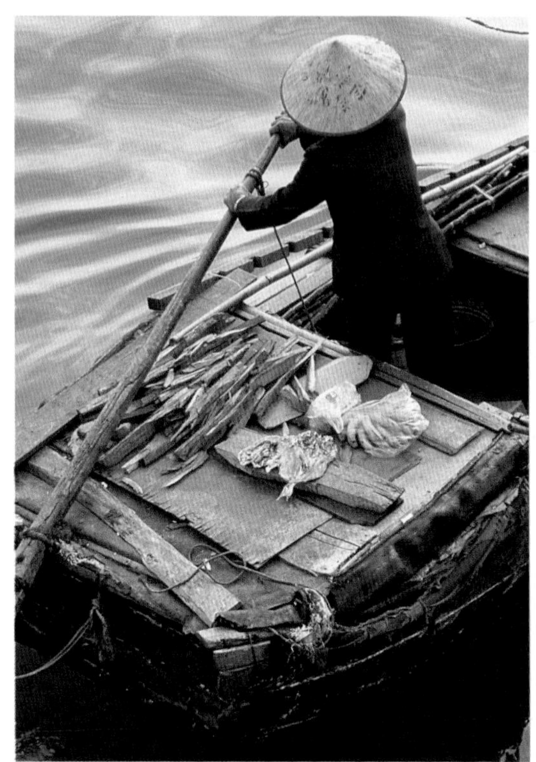

A traditional sampan, an increasingly rare sight in modern China

CRUDE CONFLICT
One area not mentioned in this section are the Spratly Islands. This group of islands in the South China Sea are claimed by China, Brunei, Malaysia, the Philippines, and Vietnam, but would be of little importance were it not for their oil reserves. Though the existence of oil is unproven, the lure of its potential wealth is enough to make all the countries concerned unusually protective. In November 1998, the Philippines warned off a pair of Chinese naval ships from the area, accusing China of creeping colonialism.

SOUTH CHINA Broadly speaking, south China is the area south of the Yangtze excluding southwest China as well as a number of towns and cities already included in the Yangtze region, for demographic, historical, or geopolitical reasons. What is left is a relatively homogeneous area quite different from the north. The provinces included are Hunan, Guangdong, Hainan Island, Fujian, parts of Jiangxi, and Zhejiang, as well as Hong Kong and Macau.

Two thousand years ago the south was populated by indigenous tribes that were only incorporated into a larger China when the first Qin emperor unified the country in 221 BC. Even then the area remained marginal—Chinese settlements were sparse and uprisings frequent. It was only in the 12th century, as the threat from northern tribes became more urgent, that the Chinese headed south in greater numbers, slaughtering the native tribes or driving them into mountain strongholds, or forcing them still farther south onto Hainan Island or into Indo-China. The merchant classes, formerly despised, began to prosper in the bountiful south, and the entrepreneurial spirit, often associated with the Chinese, became very much a southern characteristic. By the early 13th century, with the Southern Song capital at Hangzhou, the focus of Chinese life shifted south, albeit temporarily since under the Mongols the north was preferred once again, and the Ming dynasty that followed established its capital at Beijing. The south, therefore, although quite obviously part of China, has maintained a separateness that is still evident today.

The major visual differences between south and north are color and topography. The north is brown and yellow (the colors of earth, sand, dust, and silt), the landscape is generally flat, and any hills or mountains are dry and arid. The south is green, with a wet, steamy climate. Its rolling hills are layered with terraces. Like the north, the south has hot summers, with July averaging between 77°F and 85°F. Winters are mild, with frost a rarity in many areas and in some parts unknown. Rainfall is between 40 and 100 inches per year, and although summer is the wettest season, rain is spread more evenly throughout the year than in the north. Along the coast the summer is also the season of typhoons. The south's most important crop is rice, except in the mountainous province of Fujian where fishing and forestry traditionally take priority. As in the north, the pig is the main meat source and fish are also widely eaten; the water buffalo, not seen in the north, is used as a draft animal everywhere. Architecture differs, too—courtyards are less popular and two-story houses are more common, often with the upturned eaves and roof decoration that typify traditional Chinese architecture.

Most important are the cultural dissimilarities between north and south. Although the dialects of the more northerly parts of the region are based on Mandarin, and although Chinese characters are universal, the dialects of the south are compounded of many distinctive words, a plethora of tones and implosive consonants. Finally, unlike the insular north, the indented coastlines of Fujian and Guangdong, with their excellent natural harbors, have a tradition of foreign trade that dates back to the arrival of Arab merchants during the Tang dynasty.

Commerce is the lifeblood of the south

Sanya Harbor, Hainan Island: China's "Water People" have lived on boats for generations

YOUNG MAO
It is difficult to reconcile the Mao of later years with the young man in Shaoshan who threatened to commit suicide when faced with an arranged marriage, or the student who failed his art examination by drawing a circle and calling it an egg. However, while a student in Changsha in 1917 he became "student of the year," simultaneously organizing student societies, an experience that would stand him in good stead in later life.

▶▶ Canton

See Guangzhou, page 206.

▶ Changsha *200B4*

The capital of Hunan province, Changsha is of interest for its provincial museum and its relative proximity to Mao Zedong's birthplace 60 miles away at Shaoshan (see page 224). The excellent **museum▶▶** (*Open* Mon–Fri 8–noon, 2:30–5, Sat–Sun 8:30–5. *Admission: inexpensive*) has a fine collection of neolithic pottery and bronzes from the Shang and Zhou dynasties. But its most famous attraction is the mummified body of the wife of the Marquis of Dai, prime minister to the king of Changsha in 193 BC. The body was well-preserved when unearthed, its skin still supple. Other links with Mao include the **Hunan No.1 Teacher Training College** (*Open* daily. *Admission: inexpensive*).

▶ Foshan *200B2*

Foshan, famous for its Shiwan ceramic ware since the Han dynasty, is 15 miles from Canton (Guangzhou). The **ceramic factory** may be visited by appointment. In the south of the town is the **Zumiao** (**Ancestral Temple**)**▶▶** (*Open* daily 8:30–4:30. *Admission: inexpensive*) founded in the Northern Song dynasty, a Taoist temple devoted to the worship of the demon-slaying Emperor of the North, with complex wooden carving and ceramic roof decoration.

Fuzhou is one of the foremost centers for Taiwanese investment in China

▶ Fuzhou *201D4*

Fuzhou's importance as a trading port goes back to the Tang dynasty, although its heyday began in the 10th

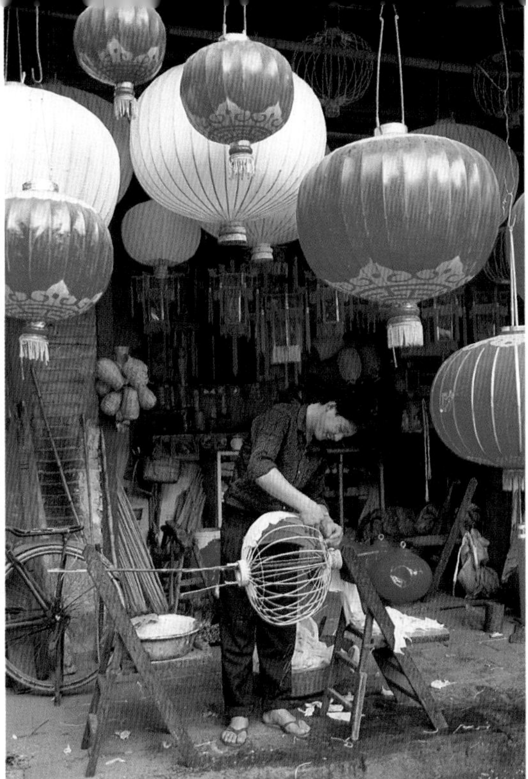

OLD HABITS
Lin Zexu's efforts to deal with the opium trade in the 1830s by confiscating smokers' equipment, forcing addicts to enlist for cures and severely punishing dealers, have present-day parallels. Liberalization of the economy has resulted in increased drug trafficking, and a government crack-down on those involved. Dealers are shot, and suspected addicts are sent on compulsory three-month rehabilitation courses.

A lantern maker in Fuzhou. Although much of old China has disappeared, the traditional skills are still alive and well

century. Its cosmopolitan nature attracted foreign settlers, and it became known as a center for Nestorian Christianity. Under the Treaty of Nanjing in 1842 it was one of the first cities opened to Western residents. Marco Polo described Fuzhou as "a veritable marvel," and reminders of its trading past still remain here and there.

Fuzhou sits astride the scenic Min River. Its center is the streets of Wuyi Lu, Gutian Lu, and Dong Dalu.

The **Fujian Provincial Museum▶▶** is in Xihu Park, site of an artificial lake dug in AD 282 for irrigation purposes. The museum includes ceramic figures from a tomb dating to the 10th century, a full-size boat-coffin 3,500 years old, a collection of Nestorian crosses, and examples of the locally produced Song-dynasty black ceramics.

The most noteworthy of Fuzhou's temples is the **White Pagoda▶** on Yushan, first constructed in AD 904, although its brick exterior dates from 1548. Nearby is the **Dashi Hall**, once a shrine where city officials prayed for good fortune and now the **city museum▶▶**. The main exhibit is a Song-dynasty tomb, with its male and female occupants on view in a tank of formaldehyde.

West of Dashi Hall is the **Black Pagoda**, a little way off Bayiqi Beilu. Built in AD 799, it bears some fine carvings.

Other sights include the **Lin Zexu Memorial Hall**, on Xiamen Lu, devoted to the memory of a minister who protested to Queen Victoria about the opium trade. The former **Foreign Concession area▶▶** is on the south bank in the Nantai area across the ancient stone bridge. Halfway up Gushan, a 3,480-foot mountain some 5 miles from Fuzhou, **Yongquan Temple▶** has two ceramic pagodas.

The delicate art of Foshan paper cutting

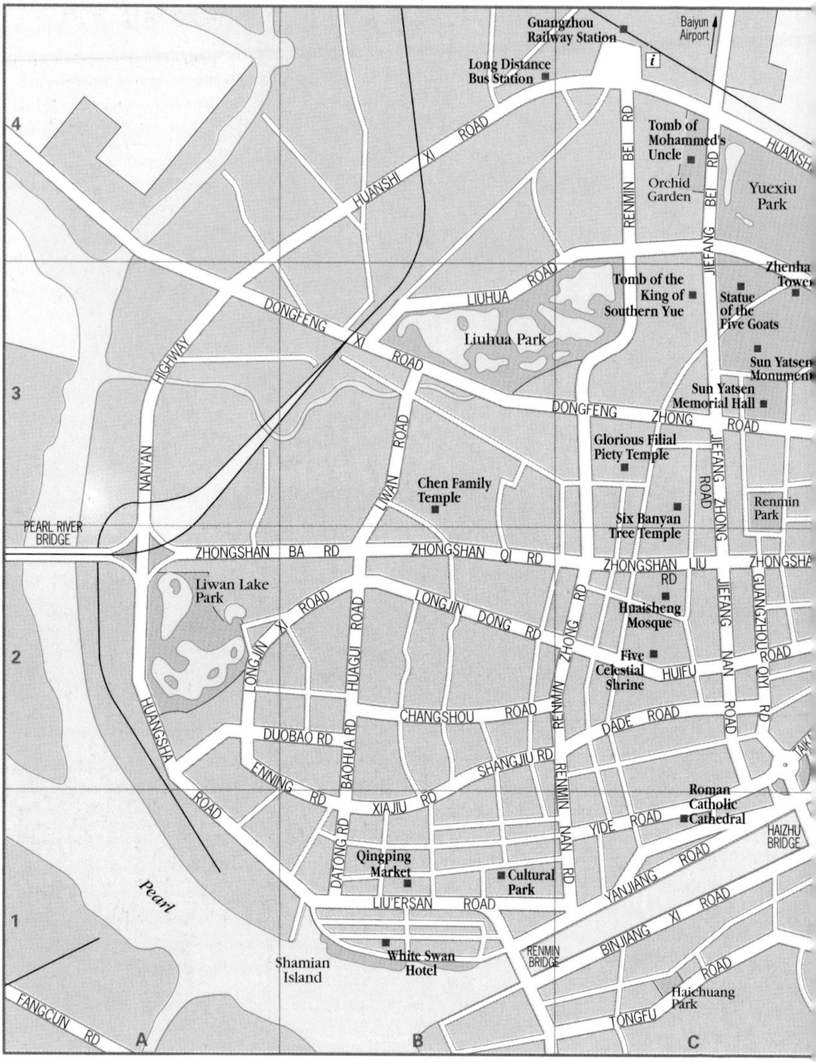

►► Guangzhou (Canton)

200B2

Guangzhou, or Canton, the capital of Guangdong province, is a major city and port located on China's fifth river, the Pearl. It is also the city most used to dealing with Europeans, because they have been trading here for over 400 years. Colonized by the Qin in 221 BC, Guangzhou came under Chinese control during the Tang dynasty and became a major port, attracting foreign traders from as far afield as the Middle East and Central Asia. The Portuguese were the first Europeans to trade here (from 1516), followed by the Dutch and the British.

Perversely, Guangzhou is a city that does not receive its fair share of appreciation from contemporary foreign visitors, since for many it is merely a transit stop. As a Special Economic Zone fuelled by foreign and Chinese investment, it is vibrant and lively. Famous for its

CANTON OR GUANGZHOU

The origin of the name given to Guangzhou (the Mandarin Chinese name for the city) by foreigners from the 17th century is unclear. It may derive from the English meaning of "cantonment" as a lodging assigned to troops. A more likely explanation is that it is a corruption of Guangdong, which is the name of the province, not the city.

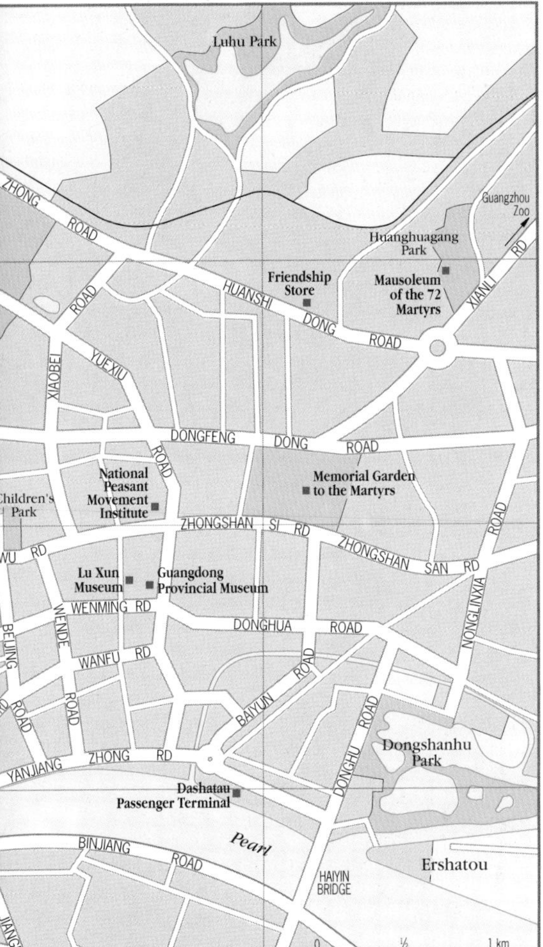

cooking, its restaurants and stores spill out onto its old colonnaded streets, shaded beneath banyan trees with their distinctive hanging, stringy roots. Furthermore, there are several points of interest.

Canton's center is the area along the riverfront (Yanjiang Road) and the main shopping streets behind—Jiefang, Zhongshan, and Beijing. Also on the waterfront, behind the unmistakable White Swan Hotel, is the former foreign enclave of **Shamian Island▶▶**. Before its acquisition by the British as a concession area following the Second Opium War, foreign traders were restricted to the city shoreline, their families compelled to live in Macau. Shamian, which was shared by the French and the British, remains a small village, with European buildings in grandiose colonial style that are gradually being restored, and which once housed the French and British consulates,

SOUTHERN APPETITE
Although Cantonese cooking is admired throughout China, the northern Chinese are contemptuous of the Cantonese people, perhaps a legacy of the Confucianist disdain for trade. The attitude is neatly summed up by an old Chinese saying: "The Cantonese will eat anything that flies except an airplane and anything with four legs except a table."

Snake, it is said, warms you in winter. Try some at Jianglan Lu Snake Restaurant, in Guangzhou

Colonial architecture on Canton's Shamian Island

FAIR CANTON
Although present-day China is comparatively open, from the early 1960s, and particularly during the Cultural Revolution when China's borders were effectively sealed, the Canton Trade Fair was the only conduit available to Western traders, journ-alists and intelligence agencies through which to glean an idea of what was going on in the country.

CHINESE HOROSCOPE
The horoscope is represented by 12 animals, with one animal governing each year in a 12-year cycle. Each animal represents one of the Twelve Earthly Branches in Chinese astrology. Traditionally the Chinese remember their ages by the animal sign to which the person belongs and calculate their date of birth from there. The 12 animals are: rat, ox, tiger, rabbit, dragon, snake, horse, sheep, monkey, rooster, dog, pig. In 1999 it was the year of the rabbit, 2000 was the year of the dragon, 2001 is the year of the snake, and 2002 will be the year of the horse.

banks, and Protestant, and Catholic churches. Walk across the island directly from the White Swan, cross the bridge to Liu'ersan Road, turn right, and you will see on your left the narrow entrance to **Qingping Market▶▶▶**, one of the most fascinating in China. It sells everything imaginable in the way of foodstuffs, spices, and live animals. Considering the Cantonese reputation as omnivores, this market may not be for the squeamish, but it is the purest Guangzhou, quintessential southern China.

The **Pearl River▶▶** is the city's pulse. To enjoy a simple and brief encounter with it, take a ferry to the other shore, or take a cruise on one of the pleasure boats that regularly leave from near the Renmin Bridge. During the summer, night cruises sometimes operate.

Sun Yatsen, born in Zhongshan county, was a Cantonese, and his **Memorial Hall▶** on Dongfeng Road is in the form of an octagonal theater, built in a garden that was the site of the residence of the Qing governors of Guangdong and Guangxi.

Parks and gardens are one of the charms of Guangzhou. If you are here in February, before the humid season, visit the **Orchid Garden (Lanpu)▶▶** (built on the site of the Muslim burial ground) when the orchids are in flower. A haven of tranquility with its bamboo groves, pools, and pavilions, it can be enjoyed at any time. Just behind the garden is the tomb of Mohammed's uncle (Muhanmode Mu), who is thought to have founded the Huaisheng Mosque on Guangta Road, said to be the oldest mosque in China.

To see something of the south bank, go to **Haichuang Park▶** with its remains of the Ocean Banner Monastery. Guangzhou's largest park is the Yuexiu, which includes the **Zhenhai Tower▶**, built in 1380, the only part of the city wall to remain and now housing the city museum. Nearby to the south is the **Sun Yatsen Monument**, with his bequest to the nation engraved on its side; and to the west the **Statue of the Five Goats**, the city's symbol. The **Cultural Park (Wenhua Gongyuan)▶** on Liu'ersan Road was constructed in 1956 and built with mass entertainment in mind. Here you can watch rollerskating, carousels, open-air theater, and opera performances, among other events. Another attractive park with revolutionary connotations is the **Memorial Garden to the Martyrs (Lieshi Lingyuan)▶** on Zhongshan Road, commemorating a massacre of communists by the Guomindang in 1927.

Canton also has its fair share of temples. The most interesting exemplifying local architectural styles is the **Chen Family Temple (Chenjiaci)▶▶**, which now houses an exhibition of the best of local craftwork. Built in 1890–1894 with monies collected among the Chen clan, it has a long front hall behind which extend several other halls, separated by courtyards. The facade and roof of the entrance hall are crowded with figures of deities and with colorful and fanciful interpretations of operatic tales. The **Six Banyan Tree Temple (Liurongsi)▶▶** (*Open* daily. *Admission: inexpensive*) is a working temple on Liurong Road and was founded as a home for the Buddha's ashes in AD 537. Its name was conferred on it by the Song-dynasty poet Su Dongpo, who was enchanted by the banyan trees (no longer there) in the courtyard. There are panoramic views from the pagoda, the tallest in the city, parts of which date to the 11th century, while in the Hall of the Sixth Patriarch (of the Chan Buddhist sect) is an AD 989 bronze figure of the patriarch. **Glorious Filial Piety Temple (Guangxiaosi)▶**, on Guangxiao Road, was founded in the 4th century AD, though most of the buildings date from 1832. It has a fine main hall and a pair of ancient pagodas, one reputed to be built over a hair of the Sixth Patriarch.

The **Roman Catholic Cathedral (Shishi Jiaotang, or "stone house")▶**, on Yide Road, is a reminder of the 19th-century European presence in Canton. Begun in 1860 by a French architect, it is built of granite on the site of the office of the Chinese governor of Guangdong, which had been destroyed by the French and British during the Opium War. Its four bronze bells were cast in France.

One of Canton's highlights is the **Tomb of the King of Southern Yue (Nanyuewang Hanwu)▶▶▶** (*Open* daily 9–5:30. *Admission: inexpensive*). Before unification under the first Qin Emperor in 221 BC, southern China was a loose confederation of the "Hundred Yue" nationalities known as Lingnan. After the fall of the Qin Empire, a breakaway general established the independent kingdom of Yue with its capital in Canton. It lasted until 111 BC, spawning five kings before the Han re-established dynastic control over southern China. This is the tomb of the second king, Chao Mei. The chief attractions are the seven-chamber tomb's burial goods, including swords, jade ornaments, *pi*-discs, gold seals, musical instruments, cooking utensils, bronze mirrors, and silver boxes.

Guangzhou's Qingping market—freshness is everything

GOAT CITY

The symbol of Guangzhou, a herd of five goats, is based on the myth of the city's foundation, a myth that itself aptly reflects the fertility of the surrounding countryside. The legend relates that five celestial beings arrived in the area riding five goats. The goats were bearing bundles of rice, symbols of a promise that the region would never suffer famine.

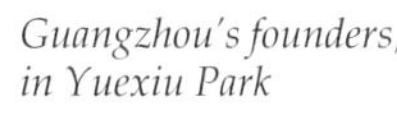

Guangzhou's founders, in Yuexiu Park

►► Hainan Island *200A1*

A large tropical island off the south coast, Hainan has several minority tribes, beautiful scenery, and reasonably good beaches, but it has traditionally been regarded by the Chinese as a pit of disease and poverty. Since 1978 Hainan has been an important military center, but nowadays its main industry is tourism.

Hainan was made a province in 1988. The rather run-down capital, **Haikou►**, has a bustling atmosphere that compensates for its lack of cultural attractions. The liveliest street is Jiefang Lu, crisscrossed by alleys and lanes. Xinhua Nanlu is lined with buildings in Portuguese colonial style. Outside the town you may visit the **Tomb of Hai Rui►**, a Qing official, or the **Five Officials Memorial Temple** (*Open* daily 8–6. *Admission: inexpensive*), while the best beach is Shuiying. Also noted for its beaches (and coconut groves) is **Wenchang**, about 45 miles from Haikou.

However, the finest beaches are on the south coast, where the main town is **Sanya►►**. East of Sanya is the resort of Luhuitou, and nearby is the attractive but crowded **Dadonghai Beach**, and **Yalong Wan** (**Asian Dragon Bay**).

There are good bus services along Hainan's two principal roads: around the east coast and across the mountainous center via Tongshi, the capital of the Li and Miao autonomous prefecture. The hill villages here are home to the Li and Miao minority peoples, who still follow a traditional way of life, although this is increasingly under threat. Farther north is **Qiongzhong►►** with a lively market and nearby 984-foot waterfall.

Xincun, on the southeast coast, populated by Danjia people, is the center for the pearl industry and departure point for **Monkey Island►** (*Open* daily 9–5. *Admission: moderate*), a reserve for Guangxi monkeys. **Xinglong** is famous for its fruit, hot springs, and especially its coffee.

THE EDGE OF THE WORLD
Just as Jiayuguan was "The Last Barrier under Heaven" and Shanhaiguan the "First Pass under Heaven," so Sanya was known as "Heaven's Limit." Mountains in the center of Hainan Island rise to 5,900 feet, and the subtropical climate allows coconuts, palm oil, rubber, and pepper to be produced.

A beach on China's tropical island, Hainan

▶▶▶ Hong Kong *200C2*

A few years ago the contrast between Hong Kong and the rest of the People's Republic of China was remarkable. The differences are now no longer so marked, largely because parts of mainland China are becoming more like Hong Kong in the wake of the 1997 handover of sovereignty (see pages 214–215).

There is almost nothing old in Hong Kong. Its pull is its frantic, relentless modernity. Its nature is perfectly illustrated by the fate of the old Repulse Bay Hotel. A charming colonial-style building in white, with upstairs veranda open to the sea, it was demolished only to be replaced by an exact replica a couple of years later.

For all that, Hong Kong is a powerful magnet that continues to exert a fascination. Although the island is now linked to the mainland by a modern subway system (MTR), it is worth crossing by the old-fashioned **Star Ferry▶▶▶** to or from Kowloon at least once to take in the magnificent skyline of gleaming skyscrapers.

Originally the name Hong Kong ("Fragrant Harbor") referred only to the main island, but it now usually covers Kowloon, the New Territories, and the Outlying Islands as well. The busiest areas are Hong Kong Island and Kowloon. Standard tours include the main sights: **Aberdeen▶▶**, a harbor area crowded with junks and sampans; **Stanley▶▶**, with its market specializing in factory outlet clothes; and the less well-known **Tin Hau Temple** on Stanley Main Street, the oldest on the island, founded by the pirate Chang Po Chai in about 1770; and **Victoria Peak▶▶▶**, the island's highest point, which has spectacular views on a clear day and can be reached either by road or by the old funicular railroad, the lower station of which is served by minibus from the Star Ferry.

Hong Kong is home to over six million people

ECCENTRIC VIEW
In 1847, Robert Fortune wrote a book entitled *Three Years Wandering in the Northern Provinces of China*. His journey enabled him to form an opinion of Hong Kong. In light of its subsequent history, his verdict is ironic: "Viewed as a place of trade, I fear Hong Kong will be a failure."

SUZIE WONG
Hong Kong is invariably associated with Suzie Wong, the entrancing prostitute made famous in Richard Mason's book, *The World of Suzie Wong*. Her world no longer really exists, for many of the bars of Wanchai have closed and those that remain deal mostly in overpriced drinks.

The Bank of China building, Hong Kong. Devotees of modern architecture will find much to interest them in Hong Kong, where a building is old almost as soon as it is built

If you are in front of the Excelsior Hotel in Causeway Bay, one of the main shopping areas, at noon, you will still hear the firing of the midday gun, an event that was immortalized in the Noël Coward song "Mad Dogs and Englishmen." Going west by streetcar along the north coast of the island will take you through **Wanchai**, the shabby bar and disco district, to **Central**, the main area of multinational companies and designer stores. Hidden among the skyscrapers are smaller, more intimate streets—those off Des Voeux Road and Li Yuen, Wing On and Wing Sing streets—filled with market stalls and local stores. On Hollywood Road is the **Man Mo Taoist Temple▶▶**, one of the oldest in Hong Kong.

There are several museums—the **Flagstaff House Museum▶▶▶** (*Open* Thu–Tue 9–5. *Admission free*) on Cotton Tree Drive in one of the few remaining buildings of distinction, built in 1844, houses a fascinating collection of tea paraphernalia, while the **Fung Ping Shan▶▶** at the university has a fine collection of Chinese art, ceramics, and bronzes. The **City Hall** has an art museum also. The **Botanical Gardens▶**, are a haven of quietness. Nearby is another ghost from the past, **Government House**, the former residence of Hong Kong governors. There is an excellent **aquarium** at Ocean Park (*Open* daily 10–6. *Admission: expensive*) on the south of the island.

The **Tsimshatsui area▶▶** of Kowloon, served by the Star Ferry, is a mecca for those wanting jewelry and electronic goods. **Ocean Terminal** is filled with an amazing

THE STORY OF CHINA TEA
Tea is thought to have been first used in the Chinese southwest. It was known during the Han dynasty but became popular only during the Tang dynasty, when the creation of the perfect pot of tea became almost an art form. Rituals developed and tea drinking became a ceremony in itself. While the ceremonial aspect has all but disappeared today, teahouses remain full. Drivers keep their tin mugs or glass jars on the dashboard all day, half-filled with leaves. Brewed in the cup like this, the second infusion is considered the best, but the leaves can be used again and again.

array of stores but prices are not usually negotiable. If you want to bargain, you need to patronize the stores along and off Nathan Road. One of the most famous landmarks of Kowloon is the Peninsula Hotel, now hidden from the water by more recent constructions but still expensively elegant. Opposite is the Hong Kong Cultural Centre, which contains an excellent Museum of Art and the fascinating Space Museum.

North of Tsimshatsui is **Yaumatei** with the dubious jade market on Kansu Street and Temple Street night market. The **Lei Cheung Uk Museum▶** is a Han tomb found in 1954. Going farther north still takes you into the rural New Territories bordering China, an area of paddy fields, hills, and little walled villages that originally belonged to single clans. Ram Tin is the best place to see these.

Ferries from piers in Central will take you to the majority of the 250 or so Outlying Islands, where life generally is very much quieter than elsewhere. This will eventually change, at least on **Lantau▶▶**, the largest island and the site of the new airport. Lantau is twice the size of Hong Kong Island and has two small towns (Tai O and Mui Wo Bay) and an excellent beach at Cheung Sha. Lantau Peak rises to almost 3,300 feet, there are scenic walks and it is possible to find basic accommodations at either the Buddhist or Trappist Monastery.

The other islands of note are **Cheung Chau▶▶** and **Lamma▶▶**, which have pleasant beaches, tranquil paths, and good, less expensive, seafood restaurants.

STROLL
Although most of old Hong Kong has been destroyed, there are a couple of areas that provide relief from the chromium-plated present—along and around Hollywood Road, for example, or Caine Road and Robinson Road, or the streets off Queens Road East. Another interesting place is the Yaumatei Typhoon Shelter in the New Territories, home to many Tanka and Hokla boat people.

Skyscrapers notwithstanding, Hong Kong still exudes a certain exoticism

Since the 1970s, when the issue of Hong Kong's sovereignty arose as China re-emerged from the Cultural Revolution, its future, and by extension the future of Macau and Taiwan, has been of prime concern.

UNREST IN HONG KONG
Considering the controversy engendered by the expiry of Britain's lease in 1997, there has been remarkably little civil unrest in Hong Kong. In 1956, there were riots when communist supporters confronted the Guomindang. In 1966, the year the Cultural Revolution began, mobs rioted in protest at a small increase in the first-class fare of the Star Ferry; and in 1967, a series of labor disputes culminated in a siege of the governor's residence by workers wielding Mao's *Little Red Book*.

Top: Shenzhen, just across the border
Below: Government House, symbolically dwarfed by change

Democracy Hong Kong, which was Britain's last significant colony, remains one of the world's foremost centers of capitalism. As a European colony on Chinese soil until 1997, Hong Kong was an historical anomaly. It was ceded to the British "in perpetuity" under the Treaty of Nanjing in 1842; in 1860, Britain acquired the Kowloon peninsula and then, in 1898, the New Territories on a 99-year lease. In 1984, Britain agreed to transfer full sovereignty of the islands and New Territories to China in 1997, subject to Chinese assurances that Hong Kong's economic freedom and capitalist lifestyle would be preserved for at least 50 years—the "two systems, one China" agreement. Under this agreement, Hong Kong would become a special adminstrative region within China, with its own laws, budget, and tax system, and would retain its free-port status and authority to negotiate international trade agreements. The West feared however, that once the lease expired, the six million citizens of Hong Kong would be unable to withstand undemocratic decisions from Beijing deleterious to Hong Kong's financial standing.

Negotiations between the governments of China and Britain were long and difficult. Some of the problems were of Britain's own making. Proper representative democracy had never been accorded to the average Hong Kong citizen, although Britain introduced indirect elections to select a proportion of the new legislative council in 1984, and direct

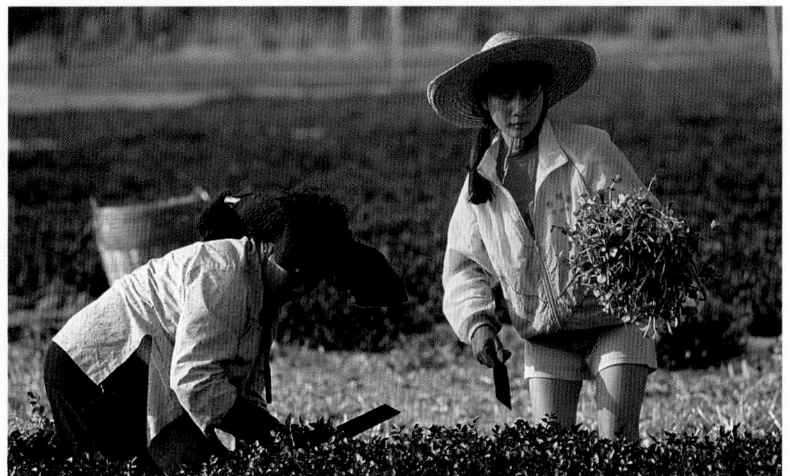

elections for seats on local councils in 1985. The last British governor of Hong Kong, Chris Patten, courted controversy throughout his tenure because of his attempts to increase the level of democratic representation. Opposition from Beijing culminated in the dissolution of the Legislative Council immediately prior to the handover, followed, on July 1, 1997—the first day of Chinese rule—by the establishment of a new legislative council composed of Hong Kong representatives appointed from Beijing.

In the months leading up to the handover the heightened sense of expectation brought a flood of anti-British propaganda from the Chinese government, and much agonizing and reflection on the part of the British. On June 30, the date of the ceremonial handover, it rained unrelentingly. The atmosphere was an odd mixture of elation, apprehension, and forlorn fatalism. Finally, Chris Patten's departure, accompanied by the lowering of the Union Jack, was a dignified and low-key affair. And then, following a fireworks display in the continuing rain, Hong Kong returned to work.

The future Although some changes have been made (Chinese replaced English as the official language; the Union Jack has been replaced with a red flag emblazoned with a white Bauhinia flower and five red stars), on the whole not much has altered, so far. A glimpse into southern China, in particular, where Special Economic Zones such as Shenzhen are almost indistinguishable from Hong Kong, proves that the contradiction between communism and capitalism can be, to some extent, reconciled.

Taiwan and Macau China's relationship with Taiwan is improving. Until recently, contact was rare but there is talk of direct flights between the two Chinas, and they will inevitably draw closer in many other ways, although Taiwan's free elections in 2000 elicited angry threats from Beijing. Under the "Macau Pact" of 1987, Portugal agreed to hand over sovereignty of Macau to the People's Republic on December 20, 1999 under similar terms to the "two systems, one China" agreement. The transition has been made and so far there is little sign of change.

Cultivation on an outlying island, where space is still plentiful

POISONED BREAD
In 1857, Cheong Ah Lum, the baker who provided bread to the British, thought he could wipe out the British by putting arsenic in the loaves. The attempt failed because his mixture was too strong and the victims vomited the bread up before digesting the poison.

Hong Kong's old trams provide low-cost transportation

PEAK-TOP VILLAS
Twenty-one of the finest villas on Lushan are currently being restored by the American architect Piero Patri. Controversially, they will then be sold to private investors, mostly Chinese businessmen who left China at the time of the revolution and made their fortunes abroad. However, the leases are good for only 50 years, after which the villas revert to the state.

Lushan, an "oriental Switzerland" in the middle of China

►► Jingdezhen *201D5*

This small town in Jiangxi has excellent local clay and has been famous since the Han dynasty for its porcelain. The imperial kilns were established here from the Ming dynasty and produced ceramics for the court and the blue-and-white ware exported to Asia and Europe from the 16th century. The town's prosperity is still based on porcelain—there are kilns everywhere and they may be visited by appointment. The **Ceramic Exhibition Hall (Taociguan)►** on Lianshe Beilu has a good display (*Open* daily. *Admission: inexpensive*). Also interesting is the river area at the west end of Juishan Donglu, the town center around Juishan Donglu, Zhonghua Beilu, and Zhongshan Beilu, and the **Ceramic Research Institute►** (*Open* daily. *Admission charge*) in a Ming house west of the river. Around the town are artificial hills created by the waste from ancient kilns.

►► Lushan *200C5*

Lushan, a beautiful 4,920-foot peak in Jiangxi topped by the hill town of Guling, was much favored by foreign residents during the 19th century, and later by Chiang Kaishek, Mao Zedong, and Harry Truman as a refuge from the heat. There is little in particular to see but plenty to enjoy if you walk around the town, made up of European-style villas, and then out to Lulin and Ruqin lakes via the Three Ancient Trees, Dragon Head Cliff, and Fairy Cave. At Lulin Lake is a museum commemorating the Politburo meeting here in 1970, when Lin Biao, later to die in mysterious circumstances, clashed with Mao.

▶▶ Macau *200C2*

The oldest former enclave in Asia, Macau was first established as a missionary trading post in 1537 and was leased to Portugal in 1557. It reverted to China in 1999. About 40 miles from Hong Kong, Macau comprises the tip of a peninsula and the offshore islands of Taipa and Coloane (which has fine beaches). Most of the population is Chinese with a sprinkling of Portuguese and Macanese, an intermarried group with their own dialect. As Portuguese influence waned so did Macau's importance, but it still possesses considerable old-world charm. It is worth a day trip by jetfoil from Hong Kong to spend a few hours wandering its cobbled streets lined with a colorful blend of European and Chinese architecture (for example the Largo do Senado and the Rua Central), sampling the excellent Sino-Portuguese restaurants, or to bet in the casinos (a forbidden activity in Hong Kong until 1999). It is also possible to enter China from here.

Macau's most famous landmark is the baroque facade of **Sao Paolo▶▶**, built by Japanese Jesuits in 1635 to a design by C. Spinola. Fire destroyed the wooden church in 1835, but many of its fine polychrome wooden figures are now in the Sao Jose Church. Nearby is the 17th-century **Monte Fortress▶** (*Open* Tue–Sat 10–6. *Admission: inexpensive*).

The impressive Ming-dynasty **A-ma Temple▶▶**, near the peninsula's southern tip, is dedicated to A-ma, Goddess of the Sea, who has given her name to Macau. Her feast day is on the 23rd day of the third lunar month.

On Estrada Adolfo Loureiro is the 19th-century classical Lou Lim Yeoc garden, but perhaps more interesting are the **Camoes Gardens▶**, where the great 16th-century Portuguese poet Luis Vaz de Camoes came to relax and the site of the Casa Villa, a charming colonial building housing a **museum▶▶**, which has some fine Ming bronzes and Chinese furniture. Nearby is the Protestant cemetery where the English painter George Chinnery is buried.

Every November the Macau Grand Prix takes place around the streets. **The Grand Prix Museum** (*Open* daily 10–6. *Admission: inexpensive*) celebrates the event.

Above: cobbles add to the old-world flavor of a backstreet in Macau

Ornate Jingdezhen ware

BUILDING BRIDGES

In December 1999, the Lotus Flower Bridge, which connects China with the Maccanese islands of Taipa and Coloane, was opened as part of the handover ceremonies. There is now a plan being mooted to build a massive bridge linking Macau with the Hong Kong island of Lantau.

Ceramics have a long history in China. During the neolithic period there were two principal types: a red earthenware, often decorated with black animal and geometric designs, from the Yangshao culture (as seen at Banpo in Xi'an), and black ware from the Longshan culture.

A TASTE FOR PORCELAIN
As foreign powers started to take an interest in China from the 16th century, so their desire increased for Chinese ceramics. It is recorded that at least 16 million Chinese porcelain dishes were exported by the Dutch East Indies Company between 1602 and 1682.

There is nothing more Chinese than porcelain or "china"
Top and below: the celebrated Shiwan porcelain from Foshan

Discoveries During the Bronze Age Chinese potters discovered that stoneware clays, when fired at high temperatures, fused to form a waterproof surface much tougher than that of earthenware. In the Han period green lead glazes began to appear on earthenware ceramics used as funerary ornaments.

Decorative porcelain, a finer item than earthenware or stoneware, appeared at about the time of the Sui dynasty (AD 581–618). The porcelain was made of a special feldspar clay, found with variations in many areas of China, and fired at a high temperature (the critical feature that distinguishes it from simple pottery) and simultaneously fused with a glaze. Always resonant, the porcelain is sometimes translucent. By the time of the Tang dynasty, porcelain was widely used and exported in enormous quantities, although its method of manufacture remained a mystery outside China until the 18th century. But it was during the Song dynasty that the production of porcelain achieved an artistic elegance that set a precedent not only for subsequent Chinese dynasties but also for the eventual production of porcelain in Europe.

Specialization During the Song, kilns of different types, both coal-fired and wood-fired, sprang up all over the country and produced both stoneware and porcelain. As production increased, areas began to specialize according to their strengths. In the north, cream-colored porcelain, often with molded designs, predominated, although olive-green or grayish-toned glaze ware, known as celadon, was also produced; in the south, where the best clays were found, a "bluish-white" ware was produced. Production overlapped to some extent, not least because Chinese political life was concentrated in the north until the 12th century, and although each kiln tended to specialize in one type of ware, there is evidence to suggest that they would have produced a quantity of the other types as well.

Throughout the Song Empire, however, all porcelain was distinctive for its simple elegance and monochrome glazes. The only exception was cream Cizhou ware from Hebei, which was decorated either with narrative painting or deep carving.

Technology During the Mongol (Yuan) dynasty the most important advance was the introduction of blue and white underglaze painting. This used cobalt, imported from the Near East, over a white undercoat of clay, a translucent glaze, and high-temperature firing (in excess of 2,335°F).

During the Ming dynasty, considered by many the zenith of Chinese porcelain production, the use of underglaze blue and white painting achieved an unsurpassed elegance. There was also a revival of the three-color glazes that were popular during the Tang and the beginnings of overglaze coloring. The latter allowed greater variation since overglazes were added to the finished product and did not have to endure firing at a high temperature. The new technique permitted a revival in monochromes at the beginning of the Qing, but using rich pastel colors. By the late 19th century, however, design had become heavy and ornate and, although porcelain is still produced in vast quantities today, the elegance of the great dynasties has yet to reassert itself.

Ceramics from the Ming dynasty, considered by many to have been the greatest period of Chinese porcelain production

EARLY EXPORTS

Porcelain began to be exported in earnest during the Tang dynasty. Chinese ceramics from this period have been discovered in places as far afield as Japan, Korea, Borneo, and Egypt. Much was taken by camel along the Silk Road. Al b'Isa, 9th-century governor of Khorosan in Persia (modern Iran), offered over 2,000 porcelain vessels as tribute to the Abbasid caliph, and hundreds of shards have been discovered near Cairo. In AD 851, an Arab merchant noted: "The Chinese make pottery clay vessels as translucent as glass. Wine poured into them can be seen from outside."

Monochromatic porcelain jar of the 18th-century Qing period with animal-head handles

Although Ningbo is fast losing its ancient streets, the Tianyige library is one of the finest examples of extant Chinese architecture

AN OVERSEAS VIP
One of Ningbo's most illustrious sons was Sir Y. K. Pao, the shipping magnate who made his fortune in Hong Kong. Among the many companies he owned was the Star Ferry Company, which provides the service across Hong Kong harbor. Like many Chinese-born entrepreneurs living overseas, he invested capital back in China and many of the harbor improvements at Ningbo are due to him. He died in 1991.

▶ Nanchang *200C4*

The capital of Jiangxi is well known as the temporary home of the 16th-century Jesuit missionary Matteo Ricci and as the site of a communist uprising in 1927. About 6 miles from Nanchang the **Blue Cloud Text** (**Qingyun Pu**) is the Taoist retreat of the innovative 17th-century painter Zhu Da (*Open* daily 8:15–5. *Admission: inexpensive*), a descendant of the imperial Ming family, whose paintings are displayed in the Shanghai Museum. The Buddhist **Youmin Temple▶** has a bronze bell cast in AD 967. Beside the river is the **Tengwang Pavilion** (*Open* daily 8–5:30. *Admission: moderate*) built in 1989 on the site of the original Tang construction, where traditional dances are performed throughout the day.

▶ Ningbo *201E5*

From the Song to the Ming dynasties Ningbo was one of China's most important ports, with a foreign trading presence starting in the 16th century. Under the Treaty of Nanjing in 1842 it became a treaty port, but its position was later eclipsed by Shanghai. Now it is being resurrected as a container port. It is famous for the 16th-century **Tianyige▶▶**, on Changchun Lu, the oldest surviving private library building in China. Fire has always been a threat (it is made of wood), as well as theft—in the past all the family members had to be present before the door could be opened. The library is tucked away among merchant houses dating back to the Ming and Qing dynasties, many of which are being torn down.

The area around the Xinjiang Bridge has an exhilarating port atmosphere. To its north is the old foreign concession, filled with crumbling Western-style houses. Ningbo's main thoroughfare is Zhongshan Lu; from there Kaiming Jie leads away to the Tang-dynasty **Tianfeng Pagoda**, currently under restoration. The **Drum Tower** is just north of Zhongshan Lu leading to Congyuan Lu and its old houses. Outside the town, 10 miles west, is **Baoguo Temple▶**, one of the oldest wooden temples in China dating back to AD 1013. **Yuwang Temple**, 15 miles southeast, is noteworthy for its miniature stupa containing a relic of Buddha.

Off the coast is **Putuoshan▶▶▶** (*Open* daily. *Admission: moderate*), one of the four sacred Buddhist mountains on a beautiful island. A four-hour boat trip from Ningbo, the island is an active center for pilgrims and has terrific walks.

▶ Qikou (Xikou) *201E5*

Qikou or Xikou, 40 miles south of Ningbo, was the family home of Chiang Kaishek. Several items linked to Kaishek's family have been restored and are open to the public.

▶▶ Quanzhou *201D3*

A build-up of silt in the harbor has contributed to a decline in the economic importance of Quanzhou, once one of the foremost ports in the world, but it remains one of the most fascinating, if neglected places to visit in Fujian province, a town of narrow stone-paved lanes and good seafood. Quanzhou's early importance as a trading city led to the presence here of a large Muslim population, who called the city Zaiton, from which is derived the English word "satin." The **Qingzhen Mosque▶▶** on Tumen Jie is one of the oldest in China, dating from AD 1009 and intriguing for its absence of Chinese influence.

Women of Xunbo village examine floral hair adornments in Quanzhou market

DELICIOUS DUMPLINGS
Ningbo is well known as the home of a delicious dish called *ningbo* or "pigeon-egg dumplings." Rather sweet, looking like small white marbles, they are stuffed with an osmanthous paste and are served in warm water. They are excellent in winter.

The **Kaiyuan Buddhist Temple▶▶▶** on Xi Lu dates back to the 7th century AD—its main hall, lined with 100 stone columns bearing delicately carved figures, is magnificent. A 13th-century 224-ton sailing vessel discovered in 1974 is housed in the grounds, home to the **Quanzhou Museum of Overseas Communication (Haiyun Bowuguan) History▶▶** (*Open* daily 9–4:30. *Admission: moderate*) which illustrates the religious diversity and cosmopolitan nature of Quanzhou during the Song dynasty. There are tombstones and inscriptions relating to Islam, the Franciscans, Nestorian Christianity, and Manichaeism.

Near Quanzhou is Chongwu, a town that retains its Ming-dynasty walls.

Awaiting the faithful, the main Hall of Kaiyuan Temple, Quanzhou

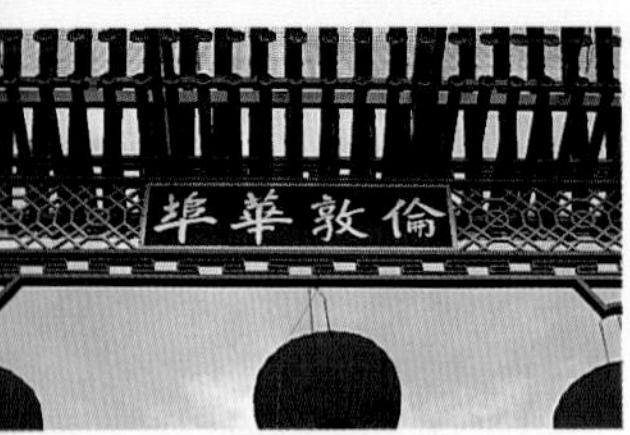

The Chinese restaurant is now a worldwide phenomenon, finding its way into even the smallest village. It is a convenient metaphor for the economic opportunities that have arisen for the Chinese since the expansion of the West into Asia, the Americas, and Oceania during the 19th century.

NATIONALS' PRODUCT
Such is the strength of overseas Chinese ties with the homeland that between 1929 and 1941 remittances home averaged $75—93 million per year, enough on occasion to offset China's balance of payments deficit.

CHINESE IN BRITAIN
Most Chinese people in Britain trace their origins back to Hong Kong's New Territories, where Cantonese is the local dialect. For 90 percent of the Chinese in Britain, Cantonese is likely to be the most common dialect in the community, although Hakka, Hokkien, and *putonghua* may also be spoken. Since 1979 many Hoa (Chinese) people have settled in Britain from Vietnam, speaking Vietnamese as their first language, rather than any Chinese dialect.

Early traders From the 15th to the 18th century, Chinese colonies grew up in the trading centers of Southeast Asia in the wake of the extraordinary voyages of the eunuch admiral, Zheng He, undertaken between 1405 and 1433. In the last years of the Ming, overseas trade was banned, and individual traders therefore found it expedient to settle overseas. This pattern continued under the Manchus, whose policy of evacuating coastal regions (to undermine Ming loyalists) forced coastal dwellers to seek a livelihood abroad. Eventually foreign trade restrictions were lifted, but attempts were made by the Qing rulers to control emigration. Emigrants were classed as criminals—an edict of 1712 declared that the Chinese government "shall request foreign governments to have those Chinese who have been abroad repatriated so that they may be executed." This measure was taken partly

Chinese immigrants have traditionally formed close communities
Right: Chinatown in San Francisco

Chinatown, London. All the ingredients for Chinese cooking are available here, including exotic tropical fruit

out of fear of sedition but it also stemmed from the traditional Confucian contempt for merchants.

Provenance The majority of immigrants came from the two southern maritime provinces of Guangdong and Fujian, which by 1500 had less cultivated land per head than anywhere in China. Few came from the Chinese heartlands of northern Mandarin China. Once settled, the immigrant sent for a young son or relation to join him, for the family was to be the mainstay of Chinese exiles' success. This can be seen partly as traditional Confucian filial piety and strong identification with ancestors and the native village, but also as simple practicality. With the help of the family, longer opening hours and lower wages are possible, although this attitude was later to become a source of friction with immigrants of other nationalities. Chinese communities abroad tended to clan together according to dialect or last name, but whoever they were, the desire eventually to return home a success was paramount, and almost the first thing that they did once abroad was to arrange for the return to China of their body in the event of death.

Nineteenth century Large-scale emigration only started in the late 19th century, when more than two million Chinese flooded into ports around the world. There were several reasons for this. One was a huge population explosion; another was the Taiping Rebellion that decimated the country; a third was the arrival of the Western powers who needed reliable manpower to work in their overseas colonies. While some immigrants arrived to seek their fortune, most were unskilled laborers. At first working in the Spanish, Dutch, British, and French colonies in the Far East, they soon found their way to African mines and South American sugar plantations or guano fields and then to the goldfields and railroads of the U.S.A. Theirs was indentured labor of the worst kind—meaningless contracts for years of badly paid, backbreaking work in appalling conditions. Respected companies organized the labor trade, while Chinese agents in treaty ports press-ganged men who did not volunteer. Many died overseas, some returned with pitiful savings, a very few made their fortunes. Thousands died on World War I battlefields. Ultimately, large numbers ended up creating sizeable communities in Britain, France, and the U.S.A.

In recent years there has been a new wave of emigration, backed by the Triads, while as many as two-thirds of Chinese students do not return home from overseas.

ORGANIZED CRIME

Most of the customs that immigrants brought with them from China have enriched the life of their adopted country. One that has not is the Chinese secret society, the Triad, founded originally by Hokkien immigrants to Taiwan. Very hierarchical, the Triad is structured in pyramid fashion, each level given a number or name. For example, the highest authority is Dragon Head or 489, while the lowest recruits are called 49 Boys. The origin of the numbers' symbolism is not certain, but they are accredited with mystical qualities.

Overseas Chinese money built the Jinling Hotel, Nanjing

PENNIES FOR HEAVEN
In China, towns become associated with a particular product or trade. Until 1949, Shaoxing produced the "joss-paper money," imitation lucre that mourners burned to keep the departing soul in comfort in the afterlife. Religious belief died after the revolution and the paper-money industry, died with it, but there are hopes of a revival now that many temples are functioning again.

Old China, alive and well in the old treaty port area around Anping Lu, Shantou

Plenty of fish to fry along South China's coast

► Shantou 201D3

Known as Swatow to the Westerners who once traded here, this lively major port on Guangdong province's east coast is now a Special Economic Zone. The British East India Company was present at Shantou from the 18th century, although formal trading rights were granted only after the 1860 Treaty of Tianjin. The place for a walk is the dock area around Anping Lu, while the main thoroughfares are Jinsha Lu, Shanzhang Lu, Zhongshan Lu, and Waima Lu. Boats leave regularly for **Mayu Island** carrying pilgrims who visit the two temples there.

► Shaoshan 200B4

Mao Zedong's birthplace is a village in lush countryside about 80 miles southwest of Changsha and was once a place of pilgrimage for millions. Many workaday items have been given the Mao treatment, but the main attraction is Mao's family house (*Open* daily. *Admission: inexpensive*); with family photographs and domestic chattels. There is a **Museum of Comrade Mao** (*Open* daily 9–4:30. *Admission: inexpensive*), devoted to Mao's life. The surrounding countryside is classic rural China, with well-worn paths leading through bamboo groves to the **Dripping Water Cave**—where Mao spent several days in 1966—and to Shaoshan Peak.

►►► Shaoxing 201E5

Famous for its yellow rice wine, Shaoxing, in Zhejiang province, was the capital of the State of Yue and important during the Song dynasty when the court moved to nearby Hangzhou. An unspoiled canal town of traditional houses, narrow alleys, and humpback bridges, among them is the **Lu Xun Museum►** (*Open* daily 8–5. *Admission: inexpensive*), the childhood home of Lu Xun, the revolutionary writer and philosopher. **Fushan Hill** offers good town views. From here you can walk east to Jiefang Lu, surrounded by charming streets, and head for the 13th-century **Bazi Bridge►**, across a canal lined with pretty houses. In the small alley of Dacheng, near Jiefang Nanlu, is the **Green Vine Study** (**Qingteng Shuwu**)►► (*Open* daily 8:30–4:30. *Admission: inexpensive*), the home of the notorious Ming artist Xu Wei and one of the prettiest examples of domestic architecture to survive in China. Outside Shaoxing is the **East Lake** (**Dong Hu**)►►, where boats can be rented to visit the Temple of Yu, dedicated to China's legendary founder.

▶ Tiantaishan *201E5*

Tiantaishan mountain, reaching 3,478 feet, is the home of the Taoist-influenced Tiantai Buddhist sect. A number of monasteries are scattered throughout the area, including the **Bajingtai** at the summit. A bus from the Tiantai Gouqing Monastery at the foot of the mountain goes up to Huadingfeng, a short walk from the monastery.

▶ Wenzhou *201E4*

A drab city on the coast of Zhejiang, Wenzhou was a key port servicing Sino-Japanese trade during the Song dynasty, and was famed for its scenery, hot springs, and porcelain. Unable to compete with Shanghai in the 19th century because it lacked a deep-water harbor, Wenzhou drifted into obscurity until 1984, when it was designated one of China's 14 Coastal Open Cities. Since then its development has been rapid. However, its attractions for the tourist are somewhat limited—the **city museum▶**, housed in an ancient monastery on an island in the Ou River, displays some fine examples of local porcelain from the 1st to the 14th centuries. In the nearby **Yandang mountains▶** there are Buddhist shrines, scenic cliffs, and a 358-foot waterfall.

▶▶ Wuyishan *200C4*

This is a mountain reserve in a magnificent setting in the north of Fujian. Raft trips to appreciate its outstanding scenery can be arranged through CITS offices on the spot or in Fuzhou or Xiamen.

COWED BY EAGLES
Wenzhou enjoys the distinction of possessing China's largest dairy. Dairy products are not widely eaten in China since there is little pasture for cows, but in 1926 a Mr. Wu Baiheng decided to compete against the only milk available at the time, "Flying Eagle" condensed milk. Having started the dairy, he called his own brand of condensed milk "Snatching Eagle."

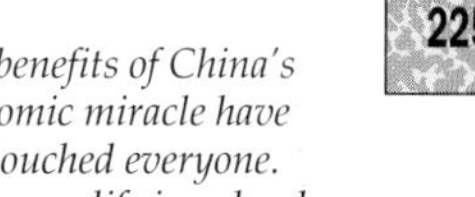

The benefits of China's economic miracle have not touched everyone. For some, life is as hard as ever it was

Xiamen University

XIAMEN AND ZHU XI
The philosopher Zhu Xi is supposed to have preached his Neo-Confucianist ideas in a cave here at the end of the 12th century. His interpretation of the teachings of Confucius became the principles on which the civil service examinations were based until early in the 20th century.

Colonial architecture on Gulangyu Island

▶▶ Xiamen *201D3*

Called "Amoy" by the foreign traders who settled here at the turn of the century, Xiamen consists of the island of the same name and the smaller island of Gulangyu. Xiamen Island is linked to the Fujian mainland by a causeway built in the early 1950s. The town was founded only in the Ming dynasty and was the stronghold of the Ming loyalist Zheng Chenggong (Koxinga). With the advent of Westerners in 1842, an international concession was allowed on Gulangyu, while a smaller concession grew up on Xiamen itself. Xiamen now prospers as a Special Economic Zone, despite the proximity of the nearby islands that still belong to Taiwan.

In Xiamen itself the **Wanshi Botanical Garden▶** on Huyuan Lu has an excellent collection of tropical and subtropical flora. On one side of its lake a large gray stone marks the spot where Koxinga killed his cousin. The **Nanputuo Temple▶** (*Open* daily. *Admission: moderate*), against a mountain backdrop, was originally built during the Tang dynasty and extensively restored in the 1980s. Gaudily impressive, its roofs are a colorful confusion of flowers, dragons, and mythical figures. Tablets in the pavilions on either side of the temple's main hall at the rear commemorate suppression by the Qing secret societies. Steps behind lead up to inscribed rocks, and in the summer, the lakes in front are covered with lotus flowers, symbols of purity.

Xiamen University, founded in the early 20th century, is on Daxue Lu, close to the temple. There is a small exhibition dedicated to Lu Xun, the eminent writer who taught here in 1926–1927. Nearby are some pleasant beaches. About 1.5 miles southeast along the coast road is the **Huli Cannon▶**, made in Germany by Krupp and placed here in 1891. The **Overseas Chinese Building** (**Huaqiao Bowuguan**)**▶▶** has displays showing the lives of Chinese immigrants, many of whom came from Fujian province (see page 222), as well as bronzes, ceramics, and paintings.

Downtown Xiamen centers on the waterfront and Zhongshan Lu. Just opposite where Zhongshan Lu meets the port is the ferry dock to Gulangyu: ferries make the 10-minute crossing regularly, at little cost.

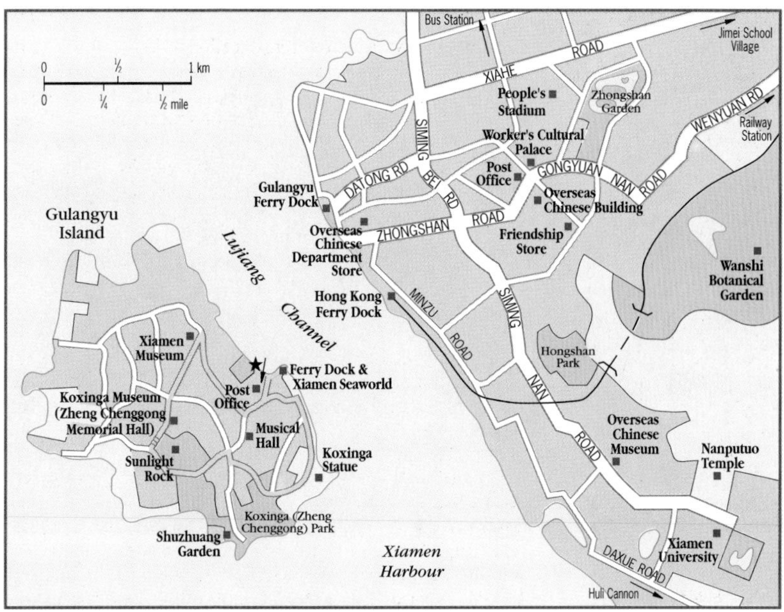

Walk

Xiamen: Gulangyu Island

This walk will give you a taste of old Xiamen—Sino-European architecture from the earlier part of the 20th century—and one or two key monuments. Disembark from the ferry, near which **Xiamen Seaworld** (*Open* daily 8:30–7. *Admission: expensive*) has been built, turn left and follow the waterfront with its extensive views across to Xiamen. Eventually you pass a **statue of Koxinga**, and the road, bearing right, begins to rise and then stretches of beach are visible before the road begins to descend amid the roofs of the **old colonial houses**. Keep on the same road, passing some **fine doorways** with interesting motifs. Emerge before a playing field, with an art gallery on the corner. Turn left here and continue past some stores selling antiques and shark's fin; the path will eventually bring you to the sea. Just before the beach turn right and then go up a flight of steps, coming out onto a small square. Here is the entrance to the **Sunlight Rock**, an array of inscribed rocks, terraces with excellent views across the city, and, about half-way up, the porticoed **Koxinga Museum**. Return to the entrance and bear left, which will bring you back to the playing field. Turn left at the corner, left again, and then right toward the **Risky Cave**. The next left brings you to a large building surmounted by a cross, the former **Protestant Church**. Then turn back and take the first right and then second left, then right and left up to the domed museum. Then return down to the market-square and, beyond it, the ferry dock.

The pastel shades of former European influence, Gulangyu Island, Xiamen

Timeless landscape in the Lesser Guilin: Seven Star Crags, Zhaoqing

► Zhaoqing 200B2

Noted for its scenery, Zhaoqing, 70 miles west of Canton, has as its focal point the **Seven Star Crags**►►, a group of limestone hills that emerge sharply out of the surrounding countryside. They stand in a park with artificial lakes, concrete walkways, and traditional pavilions, so sightseeing can be done either on foot or by boat.

Zhaoqing itself is an attractive town and can easily be explored on foot. The **Plum Monastery** and the **old quarter** lie to the west of the main street, Tianning Lu, which leads north to **Seven Star Crag Park** (*Open* daily. *Admission charge*) and south to the Xi River and Jiangbin Donglu. By turning left at the river you will come to the **Yuejiang Tower** (**Yuejianglou**) and on Tajiao Lu, amid interesting riverside houses, the **Chongxi** (**Flowery**) **Pagoda**. East of Zhaoqing is Dinghushan, a scenic area of some beauty.

▶ Zhongshan County and Dr. Sun Yatsen *200B2*

For those visiting China for a day from Macau, a popular destination is Zhongshan County and the village of Cuiheng, birthplace of the father of Chinese nationalism, Sun Yatsen (1866–1925). His residence was built in 1892 to his own design; a museum is devoted to the story of his life.

The cult of Mao all but obliterated the part played by Sun in the founding of a united China. He studied medicine in Honolulu and Hong Kong, where he developed his Three Principles: the Principle of Nationalism, which implied the expulsion of foreigners from the treaty ports and the dignity of sovereignty; the Principle of People's Democracy, meaning that the Chinese government must be responsible to the people, who must be educated and taught how to vote; and the Principle of People's Livelihood, which entailed the nationalization of basic industries and utilities and the peasants' right to own the land they worked.

Sun was forced to flee to Hong Kong in 1895 after seeking new recruits in Guangzhou, and later went to Japan where he formed the United League (*Tongmenghui*) dedicated to overthrowing the Qing. He was in the United States fundraising when the successful antidynastic uprising in Wuchang occurred in 1911. He became President but resigned in favor of Yuan Shikai, who had no intention of underwriting a republic. Sun died in Beijing in 1925.

POLITICAL AIDES
Sun Yatsen thought that he stood a better chance of achieving his aims if he could enlist the support of the Chinese secret societies. He therefore joined the Hung Men (Vast Gate) society in Honolulu; when he went to the U.S. in 1904 he went as a society official and was thus able more easily to gain immediate access to Chinese expatriate life.

Place of pilgrimage—Sun Yatsen's birthplace, Cuiheng, Zhongshan County

China's economy is one of the fastest growing in the world, although, as commentators are fond of pointing out, it could hardly be otherwise considering its lowly position before the era of reform.

CORRUPTING GOLF
One of the problems accompanying China's economic reforms is the proliferation of corruption. While socialism is still China's nominal guiding ethos, a get-rich-quick mentality is developing at all levels. Nothing could be less relevant to most Chinese than golf courses; but in 1993 it was discovered that the authorities had given the go-ahead for no less than ten of them, despite the fact that every scrap of land is vital for cultivation, and all the land is state-owned.

Growth In a comparatively short period miracles have been worked in the Chinese economy, and the China we see today is completely transformed from the China of only 15 or 20 years ago.

In 1992, while the rest of the world still searched for escape routes out of recession, China's economy allegedly grew by a staggering 12 percent. Industrial production increased by well over 20 percent. Throughout the 1980s there were hints of dramatic improvements to come, but the legacy of a state-run economy proved too much of a burden—reforms merely highlighted the deficiencies of a still largely "socialist" economy. Inflation began to rise as there was nothing to do with earnings except spend them (for example, one woman was reported to have spent all her savings on two tons of salt). Since then there have been many changes. China recently reported a record $195 billion in personal bank deposits, which can now be sunk into other forms of investment—stocks, bonds, and, incredibly, real estate.

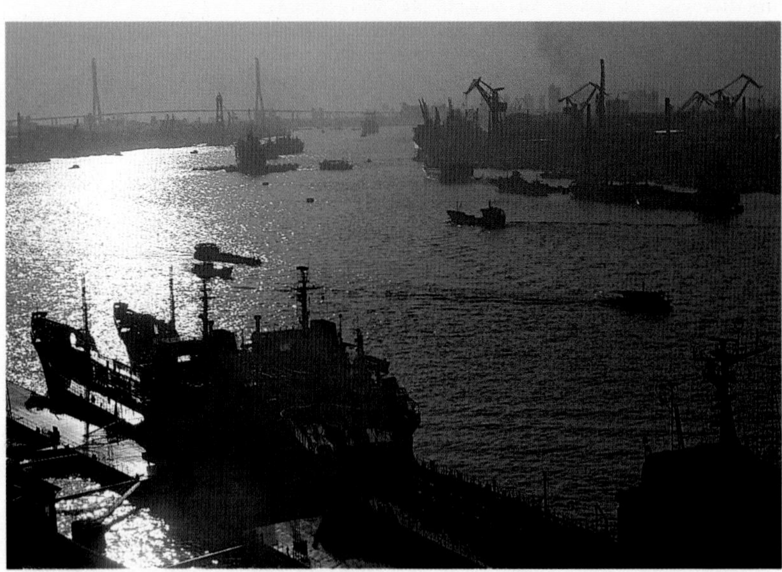

Top: Dalian harbor
Above: expanding docks on the Huangpu River, Shanghai

Contradictions The principle of state ownership of land was sacrosanct in China, with the figure of the landlord cast in the role of wicked villain. But in October 1992 the 14th Communist Party Congress gave its blessing to property speculation, an extraordinary about-face. Local governments have been quick to take advantage of this policy change, and it was reported that in Wangfujing, Beijing's commercial hub, for example, land was being sold for $5,200 per square yard. In theory the land deeds are valid for only 50 years on average, although this has not prevented spiralling prices. Even in Hainan Island (recently marketed, with official approval at least at the local level, as China's answer to Thailand's sex-industry) the price of a 1,000 square-foot apartment has reached $40,000; and yet the average annual per capita income in cities is a mere $450.

Optimism While most members of the government now support China's economic reforms to some degree, opinions differ on the speed and methods of implementation. Some who feel that the speed of change is too rapid want to stop reforms now, while others believe that the only way forward is to allow them to be as wide-ranging as possible. The root of the problem lies in the fact that many institutions are still effectively controlled by the government and so lack credibility to the outside world. At the same time, an element of state control is thought to be necessary to prevent exploitation and a slide toward poverty.

Extravagant property deals mean little to the peasant farmers in the poorer provinces, whose income has grown by a comparatively poor three percent, and among whom unemployment may have reached over 160 million. The gulf between rich and poor is growing, and fear of a reform "freeze" is almost tangible in prosperous regions. Talk of secession has begun to alarm the mandarins of Beijing.

The debate has been given new impetus by events in the former Soviet Union, and the Chinese government points to the chaos there as an example of what can happen when central control is weak. This view may find favor among the Chinese who crave stability, but it will not be long before state intervention is regarded as an unnecessary burden.

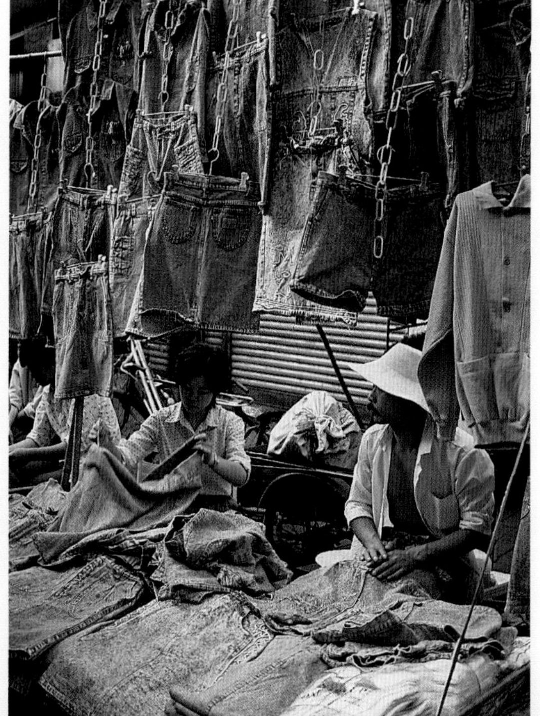

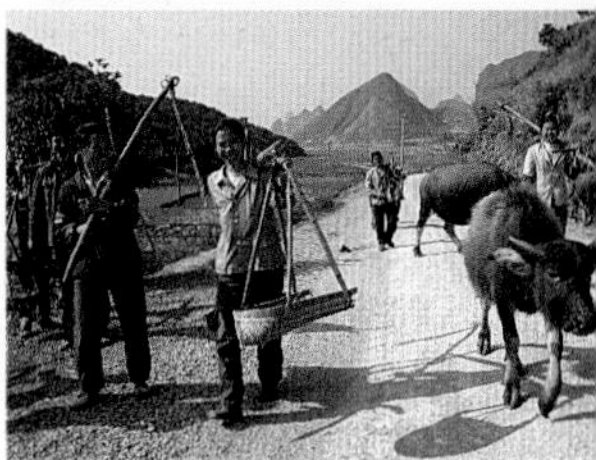

The great majority of China's population still works on the land

STOCK MARKET IN ALL BUT NAME
The currents and cross-currents of the Chinese economy are nowhere better illustrated than in central Chengdu, in Sichuan province, where in close proximity to a statue of Chairman Mao, several thousand people gather each day to trade the shares of Sichuan companies. The stock market is not recognized by the central government but the local authorities ignore this and simply charge an entrance fee to each trader.

Inexpensive, high-quality clothing, a mainstay of China's economy

"FLOATING WORKERS"
About 100 million peasants are believed to have moved from rural areas to the fast-growing cities and coastal regions, attracted by the Chinese economic boom. In Beijing, already struggling to meet the demands of its 10 million residents, the additional "floating population" may be as great as two million, overloading essential amenities, posing a serious security threat, and, according to government statistics, accounting for 43 percent of convicted criminals in the capital. Paradoxically, the population's new mobility is essential to the continuing success of China's economic boom.

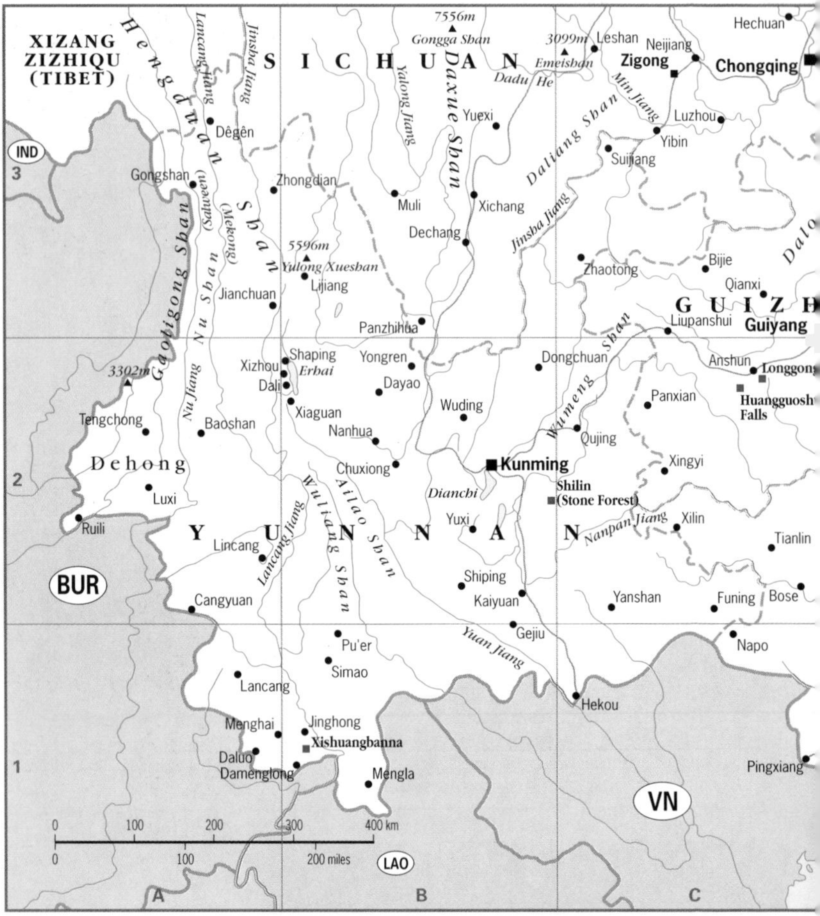

▶▶▶ REGION HIGHLIGHTS

Dali *page 236*
Guilin *pages 237–239*
Huangguoshu Falls *page 236*
Kunming *page 240–241*
Lijiang *pages 242–243*
Xishuangbanna *pages 246–247*

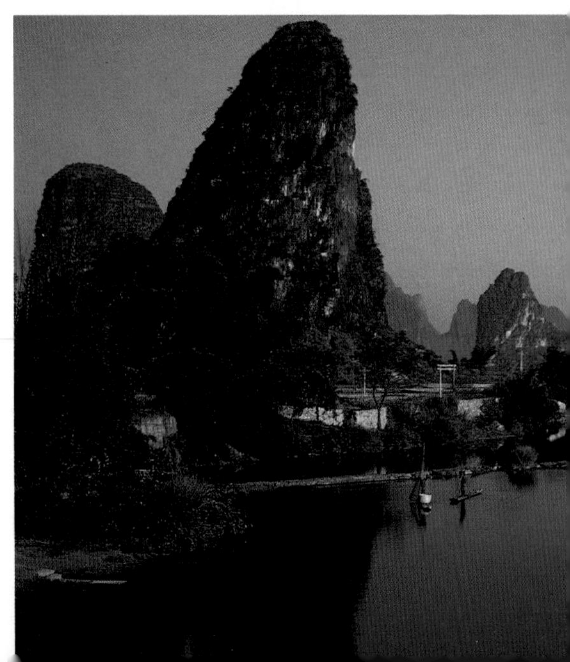

Quintessential China: karst scenery along the Li River

Far right: a Hani minority woman, Yunnan province

The Southwest

Fishermen on the Li River at Yangshuo, near Guilin, still use tame cormorants to catch fish

SOUTHWEST CHINA In this guide the Southwest is taken to mean Yunnan and Guizhou provinces along with the Guangxi Zhuang Autonomous Region. It is a region of minority peoples who were assimilated into China only centuries after the first Qin emperor conquered the rest of what was to become China. By the Han dynasty Chinese vanity was satisfied by bestowing imperial titles on the region's local rulers and more or less paying them to protect the southern borders of the Chinese Empire. It was not until the 13th century and the arrival of the Mongols that the region was finally and brutally subsumed within China, although it broke away each time a dynasty collapsed, ensuring that the new rulers would have to go to the trouble of reconquest.

Geographically much of the area is on the Yunnan–Guizhou plateau, which rises to an average altitude of 3,280 feet, reaching 6,560 feet in the northern part where it meets the border with Burma. The plateau is run through with river valleys (the Red River of Vietnam rises here, as do several major tributaries of the Yangtze) and broken by the occasional towering ridge. The altitude combined with the region's latitude means that the climate is the most pleasant in China: warm and mild, it is known as "spring at all seasons." There are areas of upland grazing as well as land devoted to the cultivation of rice, winter wheat, tea, beans, soya, hemp, and rape.

At the border with Vietnam and Laos the plateau falls away and the weather is hotter and wetter, ideal for rubber, bananas, and sugar; while Guangxi has a climate typical of southern China, ideal for the intensive farming of rice and tropical fruits and vegetables.

Southwest China, like everywhere else, is the sum of its parts. In some ways, considering its centuries-old resistance to rule from the center, it is surprising that the region is not more radically dissimilar to the rest of China. Although some of the minority peoples may have different facial features or physiques and, sometimes, different dress, there is no doubt that you are in China. This is the case in the more cosmopolitan parts of the

SOUTHERN RESISTANCE

The continuing resistance in the south to Chinese rule came to a head between 1857 and 1872, during the Muslim revolt, which was linked with the Taiping Rebellion. The ensuing slaughter severely reduced the Muslim population. Their leader, Du Wenxiu, declared himself Sultan of Yunnan, and pleaded with Great Britain's Queen Victoria to intervene, a request she declined.

region, and even in the remoter areas, where indigenous customs continue, life has a very Chinese flavor.

The greatest difference, other than peculiar attractions like the mountains of Guilin or Kunming's Stone Forest, is the pace of life, which is attractively languid, and the countryside, which is lush and colorful—Yunnan, in particular, is the home of many plants familiar to Westerners, like camellias and rhododendrons. The other distinctions are perhaps more modern—Kunming, for example, has a surprisingly carefree vitality considering its location. An area that was thought of as a place of exile for centuries, the Southwest has now become very attractive to northerners, who these days are less anxious to return to their staid homeland.

The minority peoples of the area are an important element of the region's strength. Half of China's 55 minorities live in Yunnan, while Guangxi is home to China's most numerous minority people, the Zhuang. Southeast Guizhou is also home to some minority peoples. As modernization hastens the disappearance of their traditional ways of life, interest from abroad has taught the Chinese to treat the minorities with more respect. Not only foreign visitors, but Chinese from other more austere parts of the country delight in the much more relaxed way of life that is the way of the indigenous people of the region.

Traditional architecture, Lijiang, Yunnan. The 1996 earthquake did much damage, but the town's old houses withstood it better than its modern buildings

SORGHUM SPIRIT
Guizhou province is the home of Maotai, China's most famous spirit wine. It is usually served at important banquets and, although for a time unobtainable, is now merely expensive. Its main ingredient is sorghum, which gives it a sharpness that is definitely an acquired taste.

SPIRITS AND GHOSTS
In China, spirits or gods (*shen*) were associated with Heaven (which controlled the natural and human world) and the *yang* (male) principle. In folk religion there were *shen* of trees, rivers, rain, thunder, lightning, the household kitchen, and the earth, the last particularly important in the agricultural society of ancient China. *Gui*, ghosts or devils, were associated with the Earth and the *yin* (female) principle, and were seen as evil beings. To Buddhists they were human beings who had committed evil acts in a previous life and so had been reborn as "hungry ghosts."

Opposite, lower right: Jiele Pagoda near Ruili, in the Dehong area

Below: two of the famous Three Pagodas, Dali

►► Anshun 232C2

In Guizhou province and once a center for the opium trade, Anshun is the best transit stop for the **Huangguoshu Falls►►►** (*Open* daily. *Admission: moderate*). In this pleasant town of old houses surrounded by pretty countryside, you can visit the Confucian temple or hunt for batik work, for which the area is famous. The falls are about 28 miles from town (they can also be reached via a five-hour bus ride from Guiyang). At 240 feet high and 260 feet wide they are the mightiest falls in China. The surrounding countryside is home to the Bouyei tribe, who are related to the Thais. The nearby **Gaotan Falls** are also spectacular, as are the **Longgong underground caves** at Longtan.

►►► Dali 232B2

Dali is a pretty town in Yunnan, 11 hours by bus from Kunming and picturesquely located on Erhai Lake beneath Cang mountain, which is famous for its marble. The main street is Fuxing Lu, at either end of which are the **Qing gates►**, part of the old city wall. The **Dali Museum** (*Open* daily 8:30–5. *Admission: inexpensive*) on Fuxing Lu has exhibits on Bai history and an art exhibition. Almost any road to the east off Fuxing Lu will lead you eventually to the **lake►►**, where fishermen still sometimes follow the traditional methods of fishing with tame cormorants. Dali's most famous landmarks are the **Three Pagodas►►** (*Open* daily 8–noon, 2–5. *Admission: inexpensive*), just to the north. The largest of them dates back to AD 824, is 210 feet high, and is decorated with Buddhas made from the local richly veined marble on each of its 16 stories. On the mountain behind Dali is the **Zhonghe Temple** (*Open* daily 8–12, 2–5. *Admission: inexpensive*). Reachable by chairlift it sits among gorgeous scenery. About 6 miles north is the **Butterfly Spring** (**Hudiequan**), a favorite spot surrounded by a marble balustrade and overhung by an ancient tree that produces butterflylike flowers. **Zhoucheng**, a nearby village, has an old Qing stage on the main square which was once used by itinerant opera troupes and is now the scene of a colorful market. From here it is possible to take a three-hour boat trip via a small island with a temple. **Shaping**, 20 miles north of Dali, is famous for its Monday market, but the daily morning market at the charming Bai town of **Xizhou►►** is also worth a visit.

►► Dehong 232A2

The Dehong Dai-Jinpo Autonomous Prefecture, home to the Dai and Jinpo peoples, is a remote area on the Burmese border that has been open to foreigners only since 1990. Although the Jinpo on the whole are friendly, visits to their villages are not welcome when there has been a recent death. There is also a significant drug problem in some parts.

Reed Flute Cave
DAQING ROAD
DAQING RD
Guanyin Hill
Mahuang Islet
Li
0 200 400 600 m
0 200 400 600 yards
Tiefeng Hill
Fiefeng Hill
Wugong Hill
HUANCHENG BEI YI ROAD
ZHONGSHAN BEI ROAD
Folded Brocade Hill
Fulong Islet
Old Man Hill
Treasured Hoard Hill
DIECAI RD
Whirlpool Hill
Western Hill
Huagaian Temple
YIWU ROAD
Solitary Beauty Peak
BINJIANG BEI ROAD
Xiaodong
Theatre
Cinema
LIJUN RD
JIEFANG ROAD
SAN DUO ROAD
Booking Office of Guilin Lijiang Navigation Co
LIBERATION BRIDGE
QIXIA ROAD
Tomb of Zhu Shouqian
FLOWER BRIDGE
XINYI ROAD
Banyan Lake
RONGHU ROAD
ZHONGSHAN ROAD
BINJIANG NAN ROAD
Putuo Hill
Seven Star Park
Fir Lake
Pier for Li River Boat Tours
Crescent Hill-Hidden Dragon Rock
Zoo
Camel Hill
MINZHU ROAD
Hospital
NANHUAN ROAD
Zhizhou Islet
HUAQIAO ROAD
Osmanthus Hotel
Bus Station
ZHONGSHAN NAN ROAD
Elephant Trunk Hill
HUANCHENG XI YI ROAD
Guilin Railway Station
CUIZHU RD
LIJIANG BRIDGE
SHANGHAI ROAD
LIJIANG ROAD
Nanxi Park
Chuanshan Park (Tunnel Hill)

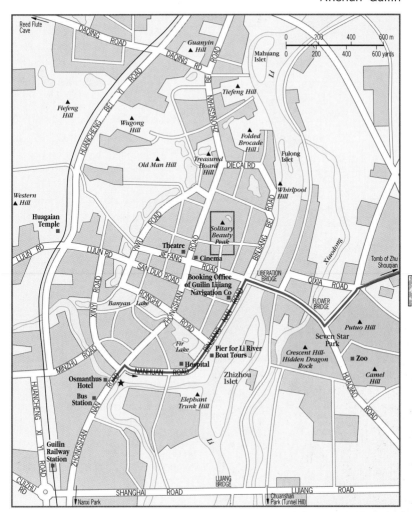

Map of Guilin

▶▶▶ Guilin *233D2*

Guilin has become one of the stars of Chinese—indeed, world—tourism. Its fame rests on its magical scenery: thousands of square miles of karst limestone outcrops that shoot up starkly from a flat plain of paddy fields and lush bamboo. The area around Guilin was covered by the sea 300 million years ago, and its unique landscape is the result of the movement of the earth's crust, which forced up layers of limestone into the round-topped mountains. Innumerable poems and paintings immortalize the bizarre landscape.

It is alleged that Guilin has been spoiled by "mass" tourism, but this is a little unfair. True, its attractions have been exploited to draw in large numbers of foreign tourists, hotels have sprung up to accommodate them, and petty crime and corruption are on the increase. In fact Guilin, which by Chinese standards is hardly more than a

Guilin
Map not to scale
Elephant Trunk Hill
Pagoda Hill
Tunnel Hill
Cockfighting Hill
Clean Vase Hill
Zhema
Aged Banyan in Longmen
Longmen
Guilin Airport
Lower River
Qifeng
Father-and-Son Cave
Daxu
Millstone Hill
Li
Liangfeng River
Zhujiang Dock
Happy Marriage at Biya Hill
Liangfeng
Nine Oxen Ridge and Three Islets
Yanshan
Helmet Crag
Londy Lady Rock
Caoping
Strange Half-Side Ferry
Crown Cave
Embroidery Hill
Bao'an
Yangdi
Miller-at-Work Hill
White Tiger Hill
Pen Peak
Langshi
Wave Crag
Nine Horse Fresco Hill
Putao
Yellow Cloth in the Water
Xingping
Luoshi Hill
Bijia Hill
Yulong River
Li
Baisha
Dragonhead Hill
Yangshuo
Green Lotus Peak
Fuli
Page Boy Hill
Tunnel Crag
Snow Lion Hill
Aged Banyan Tree at Chuanyan
Moon Hill
Gaotian

River cruise

Down the Li River from Guilin to Yangshuo

This worthwhile but extremely expensive boat trip begins either in Guilin itself, from the pier on Binjiang Nan Road, or—if the water level is too low, which it frequently is—at a point about 40 minutes' drive downstream. The cruise lasts between four and five hours and ends at the town of Yangshuo. From Yangshuo, passengers take a two-hour bus ride back to Guilin.

The river passes an endless procession of peaks, each of which has a descriptive sobriquet—Paint Brush Hill, Cock-fighting Hill, Oxen Gorge, Embroidery Hill, and so on. Even in the rain (and this is an all too regular occurrence) the scenery is breathtaking.

Purists will be dismayed at the level of organization demonstrated on the cruise—flotillas of double-decker boats crammed with tourists leave one after the other. However, all this is forgotten as soon as the journey begins, and the boats dwindle into insignificance as they are dwarfed by the grandeur of the surroundings.

The shallow river runs clear, past overhanging bamboo fronds and simple villages, and fishermen using trained cormorants to catch the fish (see panel, page 239) drift placidly by on bamboo rafts. Less expensive cruises can be arranged locally at Yangshuo.

Artist's view of Elephant Trunk Hill, Guilin

village, feels like a gold-rush town, such is the frenzy to make money, but the chief attraction, the scenery, has remained untainted.

The towering sugar-loaf mountains are apparent as you fly in. Guilin itself is attractive, but the highlight of a visit here is a trip on the **Li River**►►►, which threads its way through the heart of the mountains (see above).

Guilin started as a garrison town during the Qin dynasty and became a trading center when the Lingqu Canal linking the Pearl and Yangtze rivers was built. It was the capital of Guangxi from the Ming until 1914, when it was replaced by Nanning. During the Sino-Japanese War in the 1930s, its population swelled with refugees from the north and the town was heavily bombed, which explains the almost

Reed Flute Cave, Guilin, gaudy but entertaining

complete absence of ancient buildings. Guilin's name means "Forest of Cassia Trees" and in the last few years some million specimens have been planted in and around the town. The trees are in full bloom in fall, when they give off a lovely perfume, scenting the air all over the city.

Having seen so many peaks in the vicinity, you may also wish to climb some. There are, among others, **Duxiufeng** (**Solitary Beauty Peak**), **Fuboshan** (**Whirlpool Hill**) with caves containing ancient statues, and **Diecaishan** (**Folded Brocade Hill**), also with inscriptions and statues. All have superb views from their summits.

A short way outside the town is **Reed Flute Cave▶▶** (*Open* daily. *Admission: moderate*), an interesting cavern of exotic rock formations, its fantastical shapes lit by colored lights. A path will lead you along a circuit that takes approximately 45 minutes.

Since the land between the peaks is flat, Guilin is an ideal place for riding bicycles, which can be rented easily and inexpensively at many places throughout the town. See below for a suggested bicycle ride.

CORMORANT FISHING

Although a great draw for tourists, who like to be photographed with them, the cormorants of Guilin are not just a pretty sight. The Li River fishermen still use them to catch fish, controlling them by means of a leash tied around their throats that prevents them from swallowing the fish they catch but does not asphyxiate them. When fully trained the birds are valuable helpers.

Bike ride

From Guilin to Zhu Shouqian's tomb

See highlighted map, page 237.

This bicycle ride takes about 45 minutes one way, leaving from the Osmanthus Hotel. Cross the bridge (Zhongshan Nanlu) over a tributary and turn immediately right (Nanhuan Road) toward the Li River. Follow the road as it bears left by the river, with Elephant Trunk Hill on your right, until you come to Liberation Bridge. Turn right, cross the bridge, and take the first left on the other side. Follow the road as it curves right, staying with it for some time as it crosses a major road and gradually enters the countryside, passing fields and brick kilns. Out of the town, not long after passing the first peak, you will come to a track on the left that leads to a graveyard and the statues belonging to the sacred way of the tomb of **Zhu Shouqian▶▶**, nephew of the first Ming emperor, who established a principality here.

These guides at Stone Forest, near Kunming, are members of the Sani

TRANSPORTATION
Despite, or because of, their comparative remoteness, both Lijiang and Dali are soon to have airports that will make arrival easier but will also undoubtedly affect the area's charm. A railroad line is also being built from Kunming, which will provide an extremely scenic way of reaching these towns in some comfort.

Celestial temple guardian, Huatingsi, Kunming

▶ Guiyang *232C2*

The capital of Guizhou province, Guiyang is an industrial center with attractive scenery outside town. It is a possible departure point for the **Huangguoshu Falls▶▶▶** (see page 236); otherwise there is **Huaxi Park** (10 miles southwest), the **Hongfu Monastery** and **Kanzhu Pavilion**, the graceful **Jiaxiu Pavilion**, or scenic **Qianling Park**. The **Regional Museum** (*Open* daily Tue–Sun 9–5. *Admission: inexpensive*) on Beijing Lu, concentrates on the past and present ways of life of the minority peoples of the province.

▶▶▶ Kunming *232B2*

The capital of Yunnan province has as its main attraction the Stone Forest but, with its pleasant climate and bustling streets, it is of interest on its own account. It has played an important historical role since 100 BC when it became the capital of the Dian, a slave-owning society perhaps related to the peoples of Southeast Asia. In the early 20th century it became an important rail center when the French built the railroad linking Vietnam to China, and during World War II it was one end of the Burma Road built by the Allies as a supply route.

The **Yunnan Provincial Museum▶▶** (*Open* Tue–Sun 9–5. *Admission: moderate*), at the intersection of Dongfeng Lu and Wuyi Lu, has an important collection of bronze artefacts from the Dian kingdom that were excavated in the area. Made by the "lost wax method," and decorated with scenes of Dian life, the bronzes have a distinctive character rather unlike Chinese examples. There is also a display devoted to the province's minority peoples. The **Yuantong Buddhist Temple▶▶** (*Open* daily 8–5. *Admission: inexpensive*) (on Yuantong Jie), founded in the Tang dynasty, is one of the finest temples in China. A new mosque has been constructed on Zhengyi Lu.

A short distance west of Kunming lies Lake Dian. On its banks is **Daguan Park▶** with the early Qing-dynasty Grand View Tower (Daguanlou), famous for its inscriptions by the 18th-century poet Sun Ranweng.

*Three of the 500 clay figures (*luohans*) at the Bamboo Temple, Kunming*

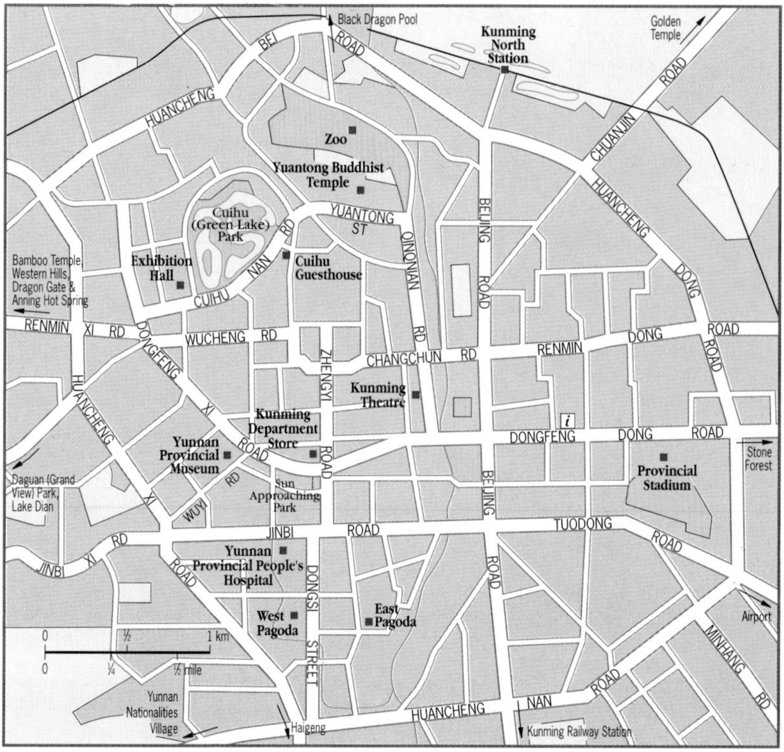

Black Dragon Pool
Golden Temple
Kunming North Station
BEI ROAD
HUANCHENG
Zoo
Yuantong Buddhist Temple
CHUANJIN ROAD
HUANCHENG DONG
YUANTONG ST
Cuihu (Green Lake) Park
Exhibition Hall
NAN RD
Cuihu Guesthouse
QINGNIAN RD
BEIJING ROAD
Bamboo Temple, Western Hills, Dragon Gate & Anning Hot Spring
CUIHU
RENMIN XI RD
WUCHENG RD
DONGFENG
ZHENGYI
CHANGCHUN RD
RENMIN DONG ROAD
ROAD
Kunming Theatre
HUANCHENG
XI
Kunming Department Store
ROAD
Yunnan Provincial Museum
DONGFENG DONG ROAD
Stone Forest
Provincial Stadium
BEIJING
Daguan (Grand View) Park, Lake Dian
RD
Sun Approaching Park
WUYI
XI
JINBI ROAD
TUODONG ROAD
JINBI XI RD
Yunnan Provincial People's Hospital
ROAD
DONGSI
ROAD
West Pagoda
East Pagoda
Airport
0 ½ 1 km
0 ¼ ½ mile
STREET
MINHANG RD
Yunnan Nationalities Village
Haigeng
HUANCHENG NAN ROAD
Kunming Railway Station

Kunming

In Haigeng Park on the northeast shore of the lake is the **Yunnan Nationalities Village** (*Open* daily. *Admission: moderate*), which illustrates the ways of life of Yunnan's minority peoples. Boat trips are available here, but there is a splendid view of the lake from the heights of the **Western Hills▶▶**, some 10 miles from Kunming, and the **Dragon Gate▶▶**, a series of winding steps, tunnels, and statue-filled grottoes leading to a lookout point also served by a chairlift. The Tang-dynasty **Bamboo Temple▶** (*Open* daily. *Admission: inexpensive*), 8 miles northwest of Kunming, thought to be the first Chan Buddhist temple in Yunnan, is known for its hall of 500 clay figures; while the **Golden Temple▶** (*Open* daily. *Admission charge*), 4 miles northeast, has an imitation-timber pavilion in bronze.

The **Stone Forest** (**Shilin**)**▶▶▶** (*Open* daily. *Admission: expensive*), a 270-million-year-old limestone karst formation of tightly bundled gray rocky outcrops, which from a distance resembles a petrified forest, is located 80 miles southeast of Kunming. The journey, through villages built in the traditional local style, lasts about three hours.

A walk (2 miles) through this landscape is recommended, for although the color of the rocks is monotonous, their sharp angles and delineations create strong shadowy contrasts, very good for photography. From the Shilin Hotel, turn left and follow the road until you pass **Lion Pond** on the left, then turn left to the **Lion Pavilion**. From here continue to a **stone screen**, inscribed with the name of the site. Then take the right-hand path to **Sword Peak Pond**; from here all paths lead back to the starting point.

Shilin, the Stone Forest near Kunming, Yunnan

The "Dongba" characters of the Naxi pictorial language, here depicting the Creation Myth and the Rite of Exorcism

Naxi women in traditional dress meet in a local market

►►► Lijiang 232B3

The seat of the Naxi minority peoples, Lijiang in the north of Yunnan province lies at 8,200 feet in a stupendous mountain setting on the border with Tibet, some 11 hours' drive from Kunming and now with its own airport. The route passes through hills covered in red earth and dotted with traditional-style villages, many still with their local temples. The Naxi peoples are a matriarchal society related to the Tibetans. Friendship takes the place of marriage, and any children of a union live with the mother, relying on financial support from the father. In Lijiang itself this social structure seems already to have broken down, although the traditional customs are still practiced farther north.

The earthquake in 1996 caused a lot of damage to Lijiang's **Old Town►►►**. However, a concerted effort is being made to rebuild in the old style. Despite this, the Old Town, now a UNESCO World Heritage Site, is utterly charming. It has a network of narrow streets lined with small restaurants, which are intersected by canals, and a lively market square—take any ascending path for marvellous views across the rooftops and to visit the Wanggu Lou Pagoda (*Open* daily. *Admission: inexpensive*). On the edge of the town to the north is the very pretty **Black Dragon Pool Park** with the Ming-dynasty **Wufenglou Temple**. In the evenings, there are concerts of Naxi music in the Old Town, including recitals of Taoist temple music lost elsewhere in China. The orchestra director, Xuan Ke,

has opened a museum about Naxi culture in his house at 11, Jishan Lane (*Open* daily. *Admission: inexpensive*).

Outside Lijiang you can visit the **Yufengsi Monastery**, perched on a slope overlooking a plain. The surrounding countryside beneath the 18,360-foot Yulong Xueshan (Jade Dragon Snow Mountain, or Mount Satseto) is excellent for bicycling and walking. The highest chairlift in Asia can be found here. Some 55 miles from Lijiang is **Tiger Leaping Gorge** (**Hutiaoxia**)▶▶▶ on the Jinsha Jiang (Yangtze), 10 miles long and between 8,000 and 9,850 feet deep. It is possible to walk its length along a path high above the river.

▶ Nanning *233D1*

The capital of Guangxi province since 1914, Nanning is a heavily industrialized city made important by the construction of the railroad line from Beijing to Vietnam. It is possible to obtain a visa for, and cross into, Vietnam from here. The railroad line links Nanning with Guilin and Kunming to the north. The **Guangxi Provincial Museum**▶▶ (*Open* daily 8:30–11:30AM, 2:30–5:30PM. *Admission: inexpensive*), houses a good collection of tribal and archeological items. Xinling Lu near the river or the exotic open market off the main street, Chaoyang Lu, are pleasant places to wander through. The **Nanning Arts Institute**▶▶ exhibits arts and crafts of the minority peoples. The **Dragon-boat races** are held on the fifth day of the fifth lunar month (around mid-June). An hour's drive away is the **Yiling Stalactite Cave**.

"BEYOND THE CLOUDS"
Lijiang has been the subject of a remarkable documentary called *Beyond the Clouds*, made by an independent British television company. The production team was given permission to live in this remote town and film every aspect of life there for a period of two years. The result was a frank, surprising, and often moving insight into the vicissitudes of small-town life in post-Mao China.

Naxi musicians, Lijiang, perhaps the last place where you can hear true Taoist music from the Tang dynasty

In China rice is the staple food. Although you are frequently told that rice is the staple of the south and wheat that of the north, in fact almost everyone in China eats rice, and anyone deprived of his or her daily portion feels uncomfortable and at a loss.

RICE RESEARCH
In the 11th and 12th centuries, Chinese farmers succeeded in producing strains of rice that matured in only 60 days, allowing a double, sometimes triple, harvest. Eventually, 30-day varieties were developed, reducing the risk of flood damage at a crucial moment in the crop's cycle and thus invaluable in obviating the worst effects of the chronic flooding that afflicts China to this day.

History Rice's distinguishing feature is its immersion in water for part of the year, a characteristic that conjures up for the foreigner an image that is almost inseparable from the picture of China as a land of straw-hatted farmers toiling under a torrid sky.

During the 1st century AD, the most densely populated part of China was the area around the Yellow River in the north, where rice cultivation was uncommon but where millet was grown, and pigs and sheep reared. Southern China was populated then by Thai-speaking peoples who practiced a primitive form of wet-rice farming, and the Chinese of the border regions of the Yangtze Valley also had a tradition of wet-rice cultivation. Organized irrigation techniques on any scale only began to be introduced in the 3rd and 4th centuries BC. The Chinese of the north were familiar with intensive farming methods, and the use of fertilizer, both animal and human, was known even if not yet widely practiced. In the 4th century AD, when many northerners were driven south as a result of political upheaval, they left their sheep but brought their pigs and their farming techniques. They applied these techniques to the wet-rice cultivation methods of the southerners, whose use of water buffalo and fondness for poultry they also adopted. By the 14th century, with the shift of Chinese civilization from the Yellow River to the Yangtze, advanced irrigated cultivation of rice was well established. Fast-growing rice was imported from India, making crop rotation possible. Strains were developed that required less water and could be grown on hillside terraces. Following the shift in population there was also a demand for a greater variety of foods, so sorghum, groundnuts, and later sweet potatoes (from the New World) were introduced.

Top: flooded rice fields in Guangxi province
Below: paddy terraces, Yunnan

To Chinese children, a bowl of rice is what a slice of bread is to a Western child

Cultivation Rice is not a particularly demanding cereal—it tolerates a wide range of soils and gives a high yield in a comparatively small area. Certain conditions must be met, however. Rice needs an average temperature of at least 68°F over a period of three to four months and at least 70 inches of rain during the growing season. Wet rice, as opposed to upland rice (which can be sustained on rain or spring water), must be submerged beneath water to an average depth of between 4 and 6 inches during three quarters of the growing period; the water has to be of equal depth to ensure even growth. For this reason cultivation takes place in small leveled fields (paddies, from the Malay word *padi* meaning "rice in the straw") surrounded by low earthen *bunds* (walls) that keep the water in and are quickly breached to let it out. Although hillside terracing is often associated with rice cultivation, most rice crops are grown in deltas or in the lower reaches of rivers where it is inexpensive to level fields. Here, water is near at hand, and the soil tends to be heavy and fine-grained, which prevents excessive drainage.

At the beginning of the season the dykes, bunds, and irrigation canals must be repaired and the soil plowed to reduce it to a muddy consistency. Ten percent of the fields are set aside as nurseries. After four or five weeks the seedlings are transplanted to the paddies and arranged in rows. As harvest approaches, the fields are drained and reaping begins. Finally the stalks are plowed back into the field, which is then fertilized for the next crop, which may be wheat or, in the deep south, another of rice. Paddy fields do not need to lie fallow, possibly because the water acts as a protection against damage by sun, wind, and rain, so the same fields are used year after year.

STAPLE FOODS

Although rice is the mainstay of agriculture in China, the Chinese have also imported foreign crops into their agriculture, several from the Americas. Corn and the sweet potato arrived through the Philippines via the Spanish in the 17th century, while the potato itself came via the Dutch from Indonesia, as did the snow pea, which is still called "Dutch bean" by the Chinese.

THE DAI
Linguistically and ethnologically the Dai people are closely related to the Thai peoples who are scattered over the very wide area that takes in Thailand, Burma, north Vietnam, and Laos, and who once lived in much of southern China. Although the Dai are subdivided into four, all speak Dai, which is broadly similar to Thai, although the Dai script differs considerably from Thai writing.

▶▶▶ Xishuangbanna *232B1*

Xishuangbanna Dai Autonomous Prefecture, in south Yunnan near the Burmese and Laotian borders, is the home of the Buddhist Dai people, who are related to the Thais. The Dai state was taken by the Mongols in the 13th century and subsequently by the Chinese, and although evidence of colonization remains, the area retains enough indigenous character from its many minority peoples to warrant a visit, particularly between mid-September and mid-May when the weather is warm but not stifling.

The capital and main port of entry is **Jinghong**, a pleasant town on the Mekong River and a useful base. Downtown is modern, but on the southern edge is a **village (Manjing)▶** where traditional Dai houses stand opposite more recent constructions. A pair of local Buddhist temples add to the ethnic flavor, and every evening performances of the famed Dai Peacock dance take place in several of the restaurants or hotels. There are good cafés, one of the best bearing the unlikely name of Natasha's Big Nose Café.

In the center of town is the **Tropical Plant Research Institute (Redai Zhiwu Yanjiusuo)▶** (*Open* daily. *Admission: inexpensive*), now open to the public, with a charming display of palms, fruit trees, and cascading flowers. But the main items of interest, **the minority villages▶▶▶**, lie outside the town.

Traveling west from Jinghong will soon bring you to the Dai villages of **Manjing Dai** and **Manluan Dian**, where the tradition of weaving bags, rugs, and richly colored cloth still thrives. Beyond is a succession of villages belonging either to the Dai or to the Aini. While most of the inhabitants of the villages near the road are well used to foreigners, their way of life continues much as it always has. Continuing west brings you to **Menghai**, a modern

Manfeilong White Pagoda—the Baita, Damenglong, Xishuangbanna

town known for its Sunday market, although the Sunday markets at Menghun and at Xiding, are just as interesting. After Menghai the road passes the **Qing-dynasty Octagonal Pavilion**, next to a Buddhist school, and continues to **Mengzhe** where the Tang-dynasty **Wat Gau Temple** was rebuilt in 1985. In the far west of the region you come to **Daluo**, where the Sunday market attracts Burmese traders.

South of the western road is **Nannuoshan**, famous for the King of Tea Trees, planted by the Hani 55 generations ago. Farther south from Jinghong is the **Manfeilong White Pagoda** at **Damenglong**, built in 1204 in honor of a footprint left behind by the Buddha. At the end of October or in early November the Pagoda is the focal point of the Tan Ta festival drawing hordes of local people who come to dance and set off amulet-filled rockets.

East of Jinghong, the Botanical Garden in the Dai village of **Menglun** is open to visitors. South of Menglun the road takes you to the Dai and Yao area of **Mengla**. Recently opened to foreigners, and now on the route to the open border with Laos, Mengla's rain forest as well as its villages have a fresh novelty and interest.

Menghan (**Ganlanba**), on the Mekong south of Jinghong, has a morning market. The nearby Dai village of **Manting** boasts a temple with the tallest Buddha in the area; just southwest of Menghan is the **Wat Ban Suan Men** (**Manchunman**), a fine example of Dai architecture.

There are some delightful forest walks among the hills outside Jinghong. The easier walks and a waterfall are at Mandian Jungle, while the Tropical Primitive Rain Forest Park has more demanding walks for the fit and energetic.

Xishuangbanna is famous for its Water Splashing Festival on April 13–15, over the Dai New Year, although accommodations are at a premium then.

NAME BORROWING

"Xishuangbanna" is the Chinese version of the Thai local name "Sip Sawng Panna," or "the twelve rice growing districts," the description given to this region when it was ruled by the Dai.

Dai people at Menghan Market, Xishuangbanna

"The very concept of completion is utterly alien to the Chinese way of thinking. The Chinese painter deliberately avoids a complete statement because he knows that we can never know everything." Michael Sullivan, A Short History of Chinese Art, *1967.*

PAINTING *QI*
As in so many other aspects of traditional life in China, the vital force known as *qi* plays an essential role in painting. For the Chinese painter, each living creature, every plant, and the oldest, stillest rock possesses *qi* that reacts with the *qi* of the painter. One must imagine therefore how it is to look and then put brush to paper at a moment that is both absolute concentration and absolute release.

Top: calligraphy brushes
Below: papier-mâché New Year's masks

Painting One of the delights of a visit to China is the opportunity to admire, and buy, Chinese art. A Chinese painting is a distinctive object, based, like so many things in China, on centuries-old traditions. Modern painters in China have found it difficult to escape age-old conventions (and of course political pressures have not encouraged experimentation), but the traditional styles, when executed with real skill, remain enormously attractive.

Traditional Chinese painting is carried out using a brush on paper or silk, often with black ink alone, resulting in a monochrome style derived, perhaps, from calligraphy. The ink is made from soot scented with musk or camphor and solidified with animal glue into the form of small inksticks, often decorated with intricate designs. Highly regarded as one of the "four treasures of the study" (*wenshusibao*, the others being brush, paper, and inkstone), the inksticks' colorful, faintly mysterious presence makes a visit to a traditional Chinese stationery store a delight.

Traditional brushes are made of animal hair glued into bamboo. The inkstone, usually black or gray, is a heavy ovoid block made of slate with a shallow bowl often surrounded by carved designs. A little water is placed in the bowl and the inkstick ground into it, with more water added until the correct consistency is reached. Intensely black in its original state, the ink can be diluted to the palest gray.

Painting styles The Song dynasty is considered to have been the greatest period of Chinese painting. Although few earlier examples survive, it is clear that painting in China was already a sophisticated art by the Han dynasty. Painters were either gentlemanly amateurs or professional craftsmen hired for particular occasions. Two styles of painting developed—academic painting, favoring a naturalistic approach to artistic excellence in which birds and flowers were reproduced in perfect detail; and a more scholarly style that specialized in grandiose representations of nature, concentrating on mountains in particular, where reality is stylized to expose its essence. The art of painting was to grasp reality, not merely the illusion of reality. Such paintings differ from their Western counterparts in that perspective is not from a fixed point, but instead moves between several different viewpoints. Man plays an insignificant role—a tiny figure diminished by mountains might help to direct the onlooker to the correct viewpoint, but it also shows how finite is man and how great and timeless is nature.

PAINTERS VILIFIED
During the Cultural Revolution painters, like writers, suffered terrible hardships and ridiculous indignities. The painter Huang Yongyu was sent to work in the countryside; then, after his return, he was accused by Mao Zedong's wife, a Gang of Four member, of insulting her by painting an owl with one eye closed. When his accuser was arrested, Huang celebrated by painting a similar owl every day.

Left: a Song-dynasty painting, Willows and Distant Mountains, *by Ma Yuan*
Below: the dramatic puppets of Fujian

Paintings were presented in two ways—the hand scroll or the hanging scroll. The former is read like a book, by unrolling one end as quickly or as slowly as one desires. The hanging scroll is designed to be appreciated all at once. Neither, however, was intended to be out on show all the time—mounted on silk with clasps of jade, scrolls were wrapped in damask and concealed in boxes to be opened and pored over on certain occasions.

Lacquerware Distinctively Chinese, lacquer is produced from the sap of the *Rhus verniciflua*, or lac tree, native to China; it was originally used as a timber preservative. By the Han dynasty lacquer dishes were used as food containers, and it was soon discovered that the addition of minerals produced fine colorings. The typical features of Chinese art—mountains, animals—began to appear on lacquer vessels with a wood or cloth base. Lacquer is carved by cutting through thick coatings of lacquer built up in layers on a wooden or metal base. It is still produced but only rarely with authentic materials.

Continued on page 250

CHINESE CARPETS
One of the crafts most often associated with China is that of carpet-making. Traditional Chinese carpets are now made in factories in Wuhan, Tianjin, and Shanghai, while other nationalities produce carpets on a smaller scale in Tibet and Xinjiang. Chinese carpets are distinguished by the fact that the pattern is in relief, usually produced by means of a combination of electric scissors and a sure eye.

Right: an example of the painting style of Huxian county, Shaanxi

At work in a cloisonné *factory*

Continued from page 249
Cloisonné A craft that excites disdain as much as admiration is *cloisonné* (from the French, meaning "cloistered"; *jingtailan* in Chinese).

The technique for this gaudily colored enamelware, made mainly in Beijing and Xi'an, was probably first introduced into China during the Yuan dynasty. The process of production is painstaking. First, a base is made of bronze or copper—a vase, for example—and then thin copper wires are glued over the surface to produce a network of tiny cells. Into each, by means of a dropper, different colored mineral paints are added. When dry, the article is fired in an oven, polished with a metal brush, topped up with more enamel, fired again, and burnished. The final touch is the gilding of the exposed wires. When the colors are carefully chosen the effect can be very pleasing, although all too often the result is somewhat tacky. Antique *cloisonné* is usually more satisfying because the colors are richer but less brash.

Crafts unlimited The range of Chinese crafts is almost limitless. Many are ingenious fun (paper cutouts, or dough-figurine modeling) but all demonstrate intricacy and dexterity. Some cities—Shanghai, for example—boast Arts and Crafts Research Institutes, which, are worth a visit.

Chinese dynasties and historical events

CHINA	REST OF THE WORLD
600,000 BC–400,000 BC	
First hominids (Lantian Man and Peking Man)	Homo sapiens *in Africa*
5000 BC	
Yangshao culture (red earthenware pots) and Longshan culture (black burnished wares)	*Egyptians invent the calendar of 12 months, each of 30 days*
Xia (2100–1600 BC)	
Earliest recorded dynasty *Earliest bronzeware and carved jade objects*	*Pyramids, the Great Sphinx, first great libraries in Egypt* *Minoan culture in Crete*
Shang (1600–1027 BC)	
Earliest Chinese characters—15,000 pictographs carved on oracle bones used in harvest rituals and medical diagnosis *Sophisticated bronze vessels*	*Trojan War (1193 BC)* *Moses leads the Israelites to Canaan* *Burial of Tutankhamen*
Western Zhou (1027–771 BC)	
Bronze working reaches its technical and artistic peak *Chinese script fully developed* *First mathematical textbooks*	*King David rules Israel (1000–960 BC)* *Carthage founded (814 BC)*
Eastern Zhou (770–256 BC) Spring and Autumn period (722–476 BC)	
Iron replaces bronze for tools and weapons *Confucius (ca551–479 BC)* *Laozi, founder of Taoism (ca570–490 BC)*	*Rome founded (753 BC)* *Homer (700 BC)* *Buddha in India (560–483 BC)* *Roman Republic founded (530 BC)*
Warring States period (475–221 BC)	
Metal coinage *The Legalists* *Invention of crossbow, calligraphy brushes, chopsticks*	*Socrates condemned to death (399 BC)* *Plato (428–347 BC)* *Alexander the Great (356–323 BC)* *Mexican sun temple at Teotihuacan (300 BC)*

Qin (221–206 BC)

Qin Shihuang: first emperor to rule all China
Great Wall completed
Standardization of weights, measures, and coinage
Suppression of Confucianism in favor of Legalist ideas
The Terra-cotta Army at Xi'an

Hannibal crosses the Alps to invade Italy (218 BC)
Cato, the Roman politician (234–149 BC)
Death of Archimedes, Greek mathematician (212 BC)

Han (206 BC–AD 220): Western Han (206 BC–AD 24)

Revival of Confucianism
First civil service examination
Silk Road opened

First clock (159 BC)
Venus de Milo carved (140 BC)
Virgil, Roman poet (70–19 BC)
Modern calendar introduced (46 BC)

Eastern Han (AD 24–220)

Buddhism brought to China via the Silk Road
Seismograph invented
Value of pi (π) *calculated to the first five decimal places*
First treatises on acupuncture and moxibustion

Christ crucified (AD 30)
First Christian church in Corinth (AD 40)
London founded (AD 43)
St. Paul's missionary travels begin (AD 45)
Gospels written (AD 85)
First Mayan monuments (AD 164)

Disunity and partition (220–581)

Three clans (Wu, Wei, and Shu) fighting for supremacy (221–265)
"Barbarians" (non-Chinese nomadic peoples) conquer parts of China and adopt Chinese customs
Chinese population shifts south to Yangtze Valley

Constantinople becomes capital of the Roman Empire (331)
The Roman Empire splits into Eastern and Western empires with two emperors (340)
Alaric the Goth sacks Athens (398) and Rome (410)
Death of British King Arthur (537)
Rats spread plague throughout Europe (542–547)

Sui (581–618)

The Grand Canal built from Beijing to Hangzhou

Petroleum ("burning water") first discovered in Japan (615)

Tang (618–907)

China's Golden Age: flourishing trade with central Asia
China's only empress (Wu Zetian, 690–705)
The poetry of Du Fu (712–770)
First printed books
Arabs defeat the Chinese in the Battle of the River Talas (751)

Mohammed (570–632)
Greek fire (sulfur, gasoline, resin, and salt) first used in warfare during the siege of Constantinople (678)
Charlemagne crowned first Holy Roman Emperor (800)
Doge's Palace, Venice (814) and St. Mark's (828)
Vikings discover Iceland (861)

Five Dynasties and Ten Kingdoms (907–960)

Paper money (910)
Gunpowder (919)

Fatamid dynasty in North Africa
Cordoba in Spain a flourishing center of Arabic learning and commerce

Song (960–1279): Northern Song (960–1127)

First movable type printing
Landscape painting reaches a peak of excellence
Neo-Confucianism

Arabic numerals first used in Europe (975)
Leif Ericson sails to America (1000)
First Crusade (1096)

Southern Song (1127–1279)

Mongols capture Beijing (1215)
Marco Polo's journeys in China (1271–1292)
Celadon porcelain

Earliest European windmills (1180)
First tea imports (1191)
Leprosy imported to Europe by Crusaders (1230)
Paris University founded (1250) followed by Oxford (1263)

Yuan (1279–1368)

Mongol rule in China
Kublai Khan (1214–1294)
Drama flourished

Dante (1265–1321)
Black Death in Europe (1347–1351)

Ming (1368–1644)

Admiral Zheng He (1371–1433) makes extensive voyages of exploration to Arabia
First Dalai Lama (1447)
First Portuguese explorers reach Guangdong (1514)
First British trade with Hangzhou (1637)

Gutenberg prints the first book in Europe (1450)
Columbus sails to the Americas (1492)
Vasco da Gama sails around the Cape of Good Hope to India (1497)
Luther's 59 Theses spark the Reformation (1517)
Cortes enters Mexico (1519)
Galileo's trial by the Inquisition (1633)

Protecting the Wall for posterity

保护文物 人人有责
严禁刻划 违者罚款
PROTECT THE GREAT
WALL DON'T CARVE ON IT

Qing (1644–1912)

Opium Wars (1839–1842) open ports to Western powers
Hong Kong ceded to Britain "in perpetuity" (1842)
Taiping Rebellion (1850–1864)
Boxer Rebellion (1900)
1st Sino-Japanese War (1904–1905)
Boy emperor Puyi abdicates (February 1912) ending 2,000 years of imperial rule in China

American Declaration of Independence (1776)
French Revolution (1789)
Marx (1818–1883)
Communist Manifesto issued by Marx and Engels (1848)
Industrial Revolution begins in Britain (late 18th century)

The Republic of China (1911–1949)

Sun Yatsen first president (1911)
Communist Party founded (1921)
With the death of Sun Yatsen (1925), Chiang Kaishek becomes nationalist leader
Massacre of communists in Shanghai (1927). Chiang Kaishek tries to drive communists from China by means of "Encirclement Campaigns" (1930)
Japan occupies Manchuria (1931)
Mao gathers the surviving communists to begin the Long March (1934–1935)
War with Japan (1937–1945)
Civil War (1946–1949)
Chiang Kaishek and nationalists flee to Taiwan (1949)

World War I (1914–1918)
Russian Revolution (1917)
Hitler becomes Chancellor of Germany (1933)
Wall Street Crash (1937)
Chamberlain's Munich Pact with Hitler (1938)
World War II (1939–1945)
Yalta Agreement (1945)
Atom bombs dropped on Hiroshima and Nagasaki; Japan surrenders (August 1945)
United Nations created out of the old League of Nations with New York as its permanent headquarters (1945)
Indian independence and creation of Pakistan (1947)

People's Republic of China (1949 to the present)

First Five-Year Plan (1953–1957)
Great Leap Forward (1958)
Tibetan uprising (1959)
Sino-Indian Border War (1962)
Cultural Revolution launched (1966)
Mao dies. Gang of Four arrested (1976)
Democracy movement (1978–1979)
Open-door policy launched (1982)
Sino-British agreement on the future of Hong Kong (1984)
Hu Yaobang forced to resign in aftermath of student demonstrations (1987)
Fourteenth Party Congress endorses concept of a socialist market economy
Tiananmen Square massacre (1989)
Death of Deng Xiaoping (1997)
Hong Kong reverts to China (1997)
President Jiang Zemin visits U.S.A. (1997)
Macau reverts to China (1999)
KMT loses power in Taiwan (2000)

Korean War (1950–1953)
Death of Stalin (1953)
Kennedy assassinated (1963)
Vietnam War (1964–1975)
Martin Luther King assassinated (1968)
Student riots in Paris, and Prague Spring ends in the invasion of Czechoslovakia by Russian tanks (1968)
First Moon landing (1969)
President Nixon visits China and establishes diplomatic relations (1972)
Mikhail Gorbachev becomes Soviet head of state (1988), introduces glasnost *(openness), and presides over the collapse of communism in Europe (1989–1991)*
Chinese embassy in Belgrade accidentally bombed by U.S. (1999)
Slobodon Milosovic toppled from power in Serbia (2000)

Travel Facts

Domestic air travel—modernized but still chaotic

Arriving and departing

By air Most visitors begin their trip to China in either Beijing or Hong Kong. There are direct flights from all over the world both on Air China (formerly CAAC) and other major national carriers to Beijing. All China's major cities are served by direct flights from Hong Kong either on Air China or via the Hong Kong carrier Dragonair. Some cities, for example Shanghai, Guangzhou, Kunming, Xiamen, Dalian, and Ürümqi, are served by direct flights from other countries.

By train You can also enter China by train either via Siberia and Mongolia, or through Hong Kong. The former is time-consuming (about six days from Moscow to Beijing) but fascinating (although there have been reports of theft on the Trans-Siberian Express); the journey from Hong Kong to Guangzhou takes under three hours. There is also a newly opened train link between Alma Ata (Kazakhstan) and Ürümqi, in Xinjiang. There is also service from Vietnam. A new service now links Hong Kong with Beijing.

By boat There is a comfortable ship service between Hong Kong and Shanghai (journey time is under three days), leaving at least every five days. There are also services to most of China's major ports, including Hainan, Jiangmen (near Macau), Shantou, Shenzhen, Wuzhou, Xiamen, Zhaoqing, and Zhongshan. Catamaran, ferry, and hovercraft services link Hong Kong and Guangzhou. Some cruise ship companies stop at China's coastal cities.

Customs

Two liters of liquor and 400 cigarettes are permitted, plus limitless cash or securities. Pornographic items are forbidden although there is no hard and fast rule about literature or magazines. Travelers are recommended to take no more than one Bible into China. You will be required to fill in a customs declaration form that must be retained until departure.

Departing

A departure tax is payable when you leave. X-ray machines are widespread but are advertised as film-safe.

An unusually quiet moment at Beijing Train station

Entry requirements
Entering the country is straightforward provided visas are obtained in advance. Upon arrival in China a simple health form and a landing card (unnecessary for people traveling on group visas) will have to be completed. Currency declaration forms are no longer required. In most ports of entry there will be a red and green customs channel, but usually only a few luggage carts. Taxis are freely available but there are few tourist information facilities except at Beijing airport.

Travel insurance
You are strongly advised to obtain travel insurance sufficiently comprehensive to cover repatriation in the event of serious illness and, ideally, to cover delays.

Visas
If you are traveling in a group, you will probably travel on a group visa organized on your behalf by the tour company and held by the group leader. An individual visa is easily obtained and usually valid for 30 days' travel in China, but easily extended at public security offices in China. To obtain a Chinese visa, contact the consular section of your nearest Chinese embassy; the procedure requires completion of a simple form, a full passport (which must have at least two blank pages and six months' validity) and one recent passport-size photograph. Three working days to process the visa are usually required, although visas can be rushed for an extra fee and on the presentation of airline tickets.

Hong Kong, though now part of China, does not require a Chinese visa. Visas for the mainland, including 90-day or 6-month visas, can be easily obtained either from **CITS** (6/F Tower 2, South Seas Centre, 75 Mody Road, Tsimshatsui, Kowloon) or directly from the visa office of the Foreign Ministry of the People's Republic of China, China Resources Building, Wanchai.

Visitors often ask if they can have their passports stamped upon entering or leaving China, but the immigration officers will exhibit a marked reluctance to do so unless the passport contains an individual visa.

Individual tourists wishing to visit Tibet must contact the **Tibet Tourism Office** (10 Renmin Beilu, Chengdu; fax: 028 333526) or **Tibet Tourism Office** (Room 3423 Poly Plaza, 14 Dongzhimennanjie, Beijing. Tel: 650 01188 ext 3423; fax: 659 18258).
A special permit is no longer required (just a valid visa for China). However, the government occasionally closes Tibet to individual visitors (because of political disturbances), usually only for a short time. Check with the embassy before setting off.

A typical hallway in an apartment building, Shanghai

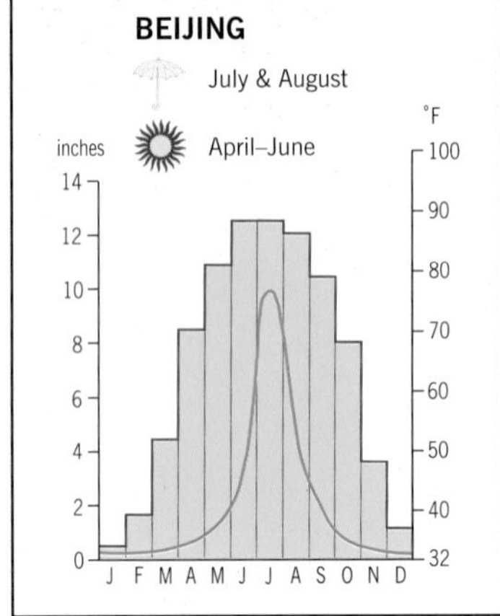

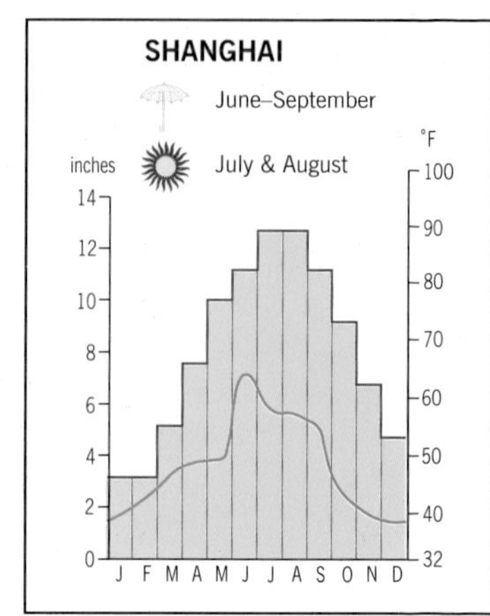

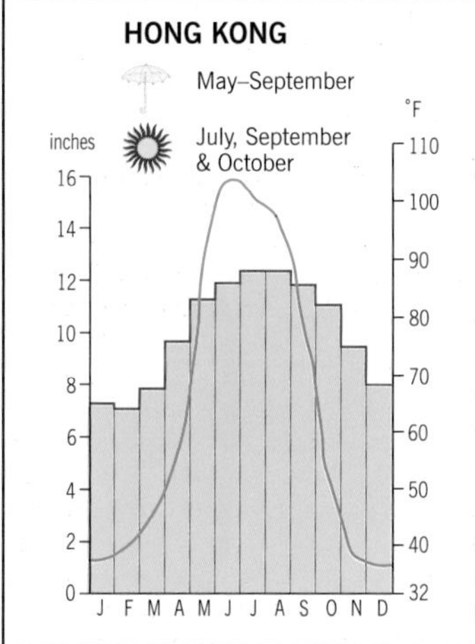

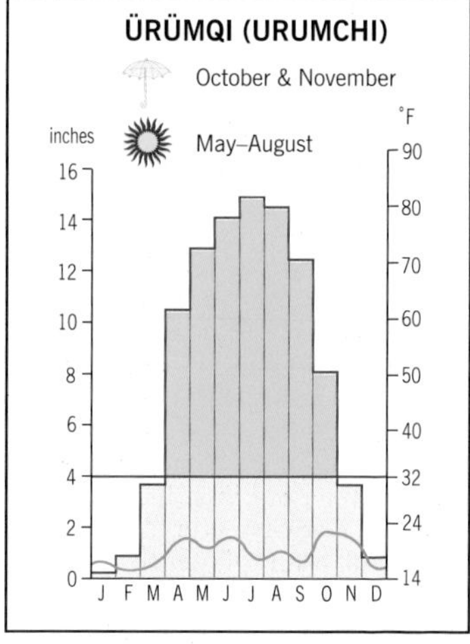

Essential facts

When to go

China is a vast country with wide-ranging climatic conditions, so decide about when to go based on the regions your trip will cover.

Standard tours usually take in a little of everywhere, so the most comfortable seasons are late spring (May) or early fall (September to early October). There are other considerations, however: blossom in the north appears in April, orchids in the south bloom in February.

Some national holidays (see opposite) may be attractions or deterrents. Bear in mind that accommodations at these times can be heavily booked.

Climate

Broadly speaking, summers (late May through August) are extremely hot everywhere (except at high altitude, as in Tibet) and very humid in the south. Winters vary from one part of China to another: central China, along the Yangtze, has a short, cold winter (late November through mid-March) while the regions to the north are very cold and, in Beijing and northward, well below freezing. South of the Yangtze temperatures rarely fall below freezing but vary from cool to warm; in the lowland southwest, winters are very warm. The rainy season runs from May through August. In April sandstorms sometimes occur in Beijing and Inner Mongolia.

Roads like this (in Beijing) remain an essentially urban phenomenon

National holidays

China has nine national holidays: New Year's Day (January 1); Chinese New Year or Spring Festival (the first day of the lunar calendar, usually February), which lasts between three days and a week, when everything closes (an added irritation is the popular pastime of exploding terrifyingly loud firecrackers, although this has been banned in major cities); International Working Women's Day (March 8); International Labor Day (May 1); Youth Day (May 4); Children's Day (June 1); Communist Party Anniversary Day (July 1); People's Liberation Army Day (August 1); National Day (October 1, usually with an additional day).

Other traditional festivals include the Lantern Festival on the 15th day of the 1st lunar month; the Dragon Boat Festival on the 5th day of the 5th lunar month; and the Mid-Fall Festival on the 15th day of the 8th lunar month.

Time differences

China is 13 hours ahead of New York, eight hours ahead of G.M.T., and two hours behind Melbourne. China adopts Summer Time (forward one hour) in mid-April and Winter Time (back one hour) in mid-September.

Clocks throughout China are set according to Beijing time, which means, given the size of the country, that sunrise and sunset can occur at peculiar hours.

Money matters

Until recently there were two types of money—one for locals, called Renminbi (RMB), and another for foreigners which came in the form of Foreign Exchange Certificates or FECs. Thankfully this system has been done away with and everybody now uses the national currency, the *yuan* or RMB, divided into 100 *fen*. Ten *fen* are called a *mao* or *jiao*. Exchange rates vary from day to day but little, if at all, from place to place. When you buy *yuan*, keep the receipts in case you need to reexchange when you leave China (although you are allowed to return no more than 50 percent of what you have bought). Travelers' checks and all major currencies are acceptable, and many larger stores are happy to accept U.S. dollars directly. Credit cards can be used in all major hotels and in some stores.

Foreigners usually pay more than locals on planes, trains, and some buses, for hospital care, accommodations, and museums.

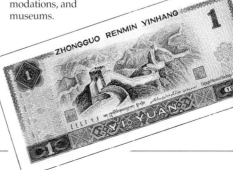

China's police, an ubiquitous presence

Emergencies

Crime and the police

Until recently China was one of the safest places in the world for foreign visitors. It remains very safe compared to almost everywhere else but you are advised to take sensible precautions:

- keep valuables in safe boxes where available;
- do not leave valuables in hotel rooms;
- conceal money and valuables when out on the streets;
- lock your suitcases.

Violent crime against foreigners is rare but recent reports of muggings may indicate that this is changing.

Unless the crime is serious enough to reflect badly on China, swift action is unlikely. Nonetheless, report cases of theft to the police or the nearest Foreign Affairs branch of the Public Security Bureau for insurance purposes.

If you feel a serious crime is being ignored, you should contact your embassy or consulate.

Emergency telephone numbers

The emergency travel assistance number of CITS is Beijing (010) 6603 1185 or 6513 0828.

Other emergency numbers are:
Police 110;
Fire 119;
Ambulance 120

Embassies and consulates

In Beijing

Australia: 21 Dongzhimenwai Dajie (tel: 010 6532 2331)
Canada: 19 Dongzhimenwai Dajie (tel: 010 6532 3536)
Ireland: 3 Ritan Donglu (fax: 010 6532 2168)
New Zealand: 1 Ritan Donger Jie (tel: 010 6532 2731)
United Kingdom: 11 Guanghua Lu, Jianguomenwai (tel: 010 6532 1961)
United States: 3 Xiushui Beijie, Jianguomenwai (tel: 010 6532 383)

In Guangzhou (Canton)

Australia: Main Building, Citic Plaza, 339 Huanshi Donglu (tel: 8335 0909)
Canada: Room 801, China Hotel (tel: 8666 0569)
France: China Hotel, Liuhua Lu (tel: 8667 7522)
Japan: Garden Hotel Tower, 368 Huanshi Donglu (tel: 8334 3090)
Thailand: White Swan Hotel, Shamian (tel: 8188 6968)
United States: White Swan Hotel, 1 Shamian Nanjie, Shamian Island (tel: 8188 8911)
Vietnam: 4th Floor, 92 Huashi Xilu (tel: 8647 7908)

In Shanghai

Australia: Rm 401, Shanghai Centre, 1376 Nanjing Xilu (tel: 6433 4604)
Canada: West Tower, Shanghai Centre, 1376 Nanjing Xilu (tel: 6279 8400)
France: 21–23 Floor, Qihua Tower,

1375 Huaihai Zhonglu (tel: 6437 7414)
United Kingdom: RM 301, Shanghai Centre, 1376 Nanjing Xilu (tel: 6279 7650)
United States: 1469 Huaihai Zhonglu (tel: 6433 6880)

Lost property (*shiwu zhaolingchu*)
If you lose anything, inform your hotel—there is every chance that it will have been handed in to Reception.

If credit cards or traveler's checks have been stolen, inform the issuer as soon as possible. If in doubt contact your embassy.

Health, vaccinations, and pharmacies
Health Considering its comparative poverty and its climatic extremes, China is a remarkably healthy country. In the main tourist areas the Chinese are punctilious about hygiene, particularly where food and drink are served.

Tap water is not safe, but any water you are offered to drink will almost certainly have been boiled; mineral water is widely available. Food ingredients are always fresh and cooked or cleaned thoroughly. But, stomach upsets are possible so take a proprietary medicine with you.

More common ailments are sore throats and chest colds. The summer heat can seriously affect your health, and a steady supply of liquids is essential to prevent dehydration.

Hospital care is, on the whole, reasonable, and in major cities foreigners receive special attention (for special prices). Usually payment is made afterward, but some hospitals may ask for payment in advance; check the cost beforehand.

Traditional Chinese medicine can be efficacious but requires patience.

For minor ailments, hotels often have their own clinics.

For information on Beijing, see page 79.

Vaccinations Currently no vaccinations are required, but you should check with your doctor for up-to-date information. Tetanus and typhoid injections are essential for travel anywhere, and it is advisable to consider vaccinations against rabies and hepatitis. There is a risk of malaria in south China in the remoter areas; check on the situation before you go.

Pharmacies Pharmacies in the big cities are well stocked with both Western and Chinese drugs. Without a prescription, however, it will be difficult to explain what you want, so if you are already taking a course of prescribed drugs, bring your own supply.

Women are advised to stock up on personal hygiene items if visiting remoter areas.

The British Embassy, Beijing. Most of the embassies are grouped together in an area close to the Friendship Store

Getting around

Car rental

It is not possible to rent a car in China as yet, with the exception of foreigners, who are resident for one reason or another. However, cars with drivers may be rented (at a price) on a daily or weekly basis in major cities—addresses of such companies can be obtained through CITS, or your hotel.

Traffic tips

Traditionally, roads and traffic regulations tend to favor pedestrians and bicycles, although this becomes less the case as the number of cars increases. Traffic in towns moves very slowly, and learning to negotiate it involves the acquisition of special skills. Patience is vital and so is the ability to feel your way through streams of bicycles, handcarts, and donkeys.

On the whole people are law-abiding road-users, although country-dwellers, who now visit cities like Beijing in considerable numbers, are quite unused to speeding cars and busy roads.

Old trams still running in Anshan, Liaoning province

Horns are honked all the time, which, while very annoying, is necessary since if there is no beep, the car in front takes this to mean that the coast is clear.

The use of headlights is curious, too: night drivers often dispense with them altogether, merely using full-beam from time to time to warn on-coming vehicles, a rather unnerving habit; drivers seem to think it is easier on the eyes.

Drive on the right-hand side of the road. In most cities it is permissible to turn right on red.

Public transportation

Domestic flights China's size and the virtual absence of a highway system means that the principal methods of getting from place to place are train and plane. Although it has improved over the last few years, Air China does not enjoy a favorable reputation, despite being broken up into a series of regional carriers, a process supposed to increase efficiency. The main fault is delay, made all the more frustrating because of the absence of explanation or apology. However, delays are much less frequent than in the past and the aircraft fleet is made up of modern planes from the U.S., Europe, and Russia, and airports in major cities have been modernized. Nonetheless, Air China does not have an enviable safety record.

Tickets for domestic flights are reasonably priced but prices are beginning to increase. Main routes are very busy and need to be reserved well in advance either through CITS or a similar agent, or direct from Air China offices. Airport tax, variable from place to place, is payable for domestic flights, usually at a special desk before you check in. All flights are nonsmoking. Hand baggage is limited to one item and check-in baggage must be locked. You will be expected to present your passport and visa, with boarding-pass, and to go through X-ray checks. Flights are usually announced in English as well as Chinese, but surrounding noise can render these incomprehensible.

Yibin buses, run on natural gas, Sichuan

Trains The train system, on the other hand, is very good. Tickets, obtainable through CITS and other agents, or directly from stations, are reasonably priced (though prices for foreigners are higher than for locals), and the trains generally dependable. There are two classes, so-called "soft" and "hard," both of which are manned by attendants. Pullman cars exist (crowded wooden benches in hard class, upholstered seats in soft) but, because of the distances involved, most rolling stock is made up of sleeping cars. A hard-class sleeping car (*yingwoche*) has a series of alcoves filled with triple-tiered wooden-slat bunks with thin mattresses and no bedding. There will be a basic bathroom at one end. A soft-class sleeping car (*ruanwoche*) is divided into compartments, each containing four bunks with bedding and thermoses filled with hot water. There will be a bathroom at each end of the car, one Western, one Eastern. Very few cars on certain routes are air-conditioned; most are cooled by fans in the summer. Long-distance trains have dining cars, often serving meals of surprisingly high quality.

Trains are graded according to speed: *tekuai* is very fast, *zhikuai* is fast, and *kuaike* reasonably fast.

Buses Buses are widely used within towns and cities and between towns. The least expensive form of travel, they are also the least comfortable. Urban buses, while offering a comprehensive service, are frequently impossibly crowded, and long-distance buses are rather old-fashioned, even though there are now nonstop services on some

A foreigner-priced train ticket

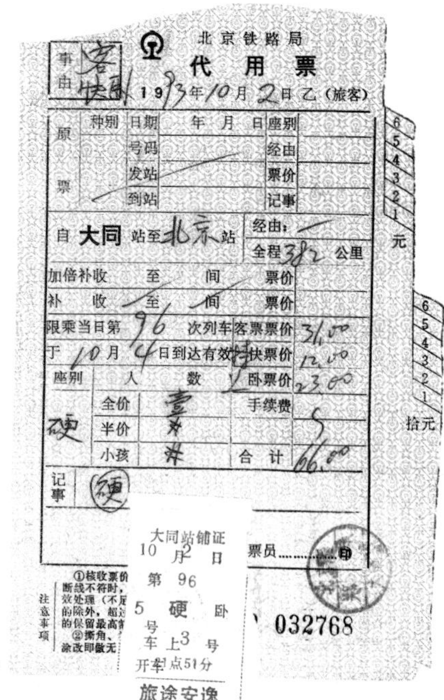

北京铁路局
代用票
事由 客快卧 1993年10月2日 乙（旅客）
原票 种别 日期 年 月 日 座别 号码 经由 发站 票价 到站 记事
自 大同 站至 北京 站 经由： 全程 382 公里
加倍补收 至 间 票价
补收 至 间 票价
限乘当日第 96 次列车 客票票价 31.00
于 10 月 4 日到达有效 特快票价 12.00
座别 人数 卧票价 23.00
硬 全价 壹 手续费
半价 ✕ 5
小孩 ✕ 合计 66.00
记事 硬
票员……印
注意事项 ①核收票价……断线不符时，……效处理（不足……的除外，超过……的保留最高……②撕角、……涂改即做无……
032768
大同站铺证
10 月 2 日
第 96
5 硬 卧
号
车 上3 号
开车 点51分
旅途安逸
红旗大酒家

longer routes. However, to travel by bus is to travel as most Chinese do. Buy tickets for urban buses on board; for long-distance buses, buy in advance from the bus station. Inside, there is little room for baggage—it will frequently go on the roof. Government-run bus services may be safer than the privateers.

Above: pedicab driver
Below: transportation, Chengdu-style

Taxis Taxis are easy to get in most cities and can generally be hailed on the street. Most drivers use the meter but sometimes a reminder to use it is greeted with disdain, in which case it is wise to agree to a price before you start. There are several categories of taxi, both state-owned and private. Basically, the smaller the taxi the cheaper the fare. (See also page 79).

Bicycles

Bicycles (*zixingche*) are widely used and can be rented at little cost in most cities from hotels or from specialist outlets. Check the condition of the bicycle and observe how the traffic functions—joining it unprepared can be an unnerving experience. Wayside repairs can often easily be effected by mechanics who ply their trade on the sidewalks.

Student and youth travel

The China Youth Travel Service (23-B Dongjiaominxiang, Beijing 100006; fax: 6513 4824) is the branch of CITS. that specializes in travel arrangements for students. Travel agencies that specialize in travel to China can often make arrangements for younger people according to need, especially for groups of children or students, and it is often possible to make arrangements in advance to visit institutions that may be of particular interest. Bear in mind that few concessions are made to youth, particularly when it comes to money.

Other information

Camping
There are no opportunities for camping in the casual way that is taken for granted in many other countries. Even if the authorities permitted it, bedding down at the side of the road with a small tent would prove difficult because there is precious little land that is not cultivated, except in the wide empty provinces in the fringe areas of China. Camping is possible only when organized through CITS or one of its branches, and there are no organized campgrounds.

There are no opportunities for renting a house or apartment, unless you happen to know a foreign resident who is vacating his house.

Visitors with disabilities
Despite a general improvement in many services and facilities, China's provision for dealing with visitors with disabilities is almost non-existent. In general public transportation, institutions, and Chinese towns lack facilities for visitors with disabilities, and although modern hotels are well equipped, most towns have crowded streets and steps to negotiate. Airlines and airports have made some efforts to improve their facilities, and wheelchairs can be found when necessary.

Opening times
Banks, offices, government departments, and public security bureaus Monday to Friday, usually 8–5. Most close for at least one hour at lunchtime, usually from noon. Banks open Saturdays, 8–11:30AM.

Stores Usually remain open seven days a week, generally 9–7.

Monuments and museums Aside from the larger ones like the Forbidden City, most often close for lunch and close finally at 5PM. Many are open seven days a week; those that are not usually close on a Monday.

Restaurants and bars These are beginning to stay open later at night, and although at one time it was impossible to eat after 8PM, now you can find a meal at most times of the day. Small open-air restaurant stalls often stay open until after midnight.

Places of worship
Buddhists will have no trouble finding places of worship since temples reopened all over China following the end of the Cultural Revolution. They are open all day, every day.

For Muslims there is usually at least one mosque in every major city.

There are not yet synagogues in China. In theory Christian worship, still subject to persecution, is feasible in most large cities (and in some smaller ones), but churches often open only for services, usually at difficult hours.

Restrooms (*cesuo*)
Where they exist, public restrooms in China are usually dreadful, even in large cities. You are advised to do your utmost to avoid them, but when desperate enter armed with

your own toilet paper at the very least. Be prepared for a hole in the ground, no privacy, and a lack of accuracy by other users. Do not expect any washing facilities (except in a few cases where there is an attendant, to whom you will be required to pay a small fee). In restaurants or places that cater for foreigners, the standard is higher, though toilet paper may be absent here, too.

Photography

In many ways China is a photographer's dream. Despite the general absence of brilliant color, the country is immensely photogenic because there is so much taking place on the streets or in the fields and because the countryside is uniquely beautiful. Furthermore, people are oblivious to cameras on the whole, although you should make sure that the privacy of those who do object is respected.

Photography is forbidden in most museums and archeological sites (notably the main pit of the Terracotta Warriors), but some institutions permit it on payment of a fee, in advance, with a stiff fine for those who do not comply.

Color print film is widely available, black and white or slide film much less so. Video film can be found but not always readily. All security X-ray machines on mainland China and at Hong Kong airport are film-safe.

As the atmosphere in China is often hazy, filters are advisable.

Electricity

Electricity is 220 volts, 50 cycles AC. Plugs are usually two-prong, set at an angle to each other, and adapters can come in handy.

Computing in the 21st century: the abacus is still widely used

Etiquette and local customs

Getting along with the Chinese One of the purposes of a visit to China is to see and try to understand a culture that is, at least superficially, contrary to everything taken for granted at home. The Chinese people are a vital, fascinating part of the experience. The word often used to describe the Chinese is "inscrutable," and while it is certainly true that the Chinese give few emotional messages, this is not to say that they are unfathomable or that foreigners cannot empathize with them.

The Chinese do not display emotion and feelings in public and find plain-speaking unnerving. Often, therefore, decisions that would be made instantly elsewhere are accompanied by long preambles and detailed, if futile, consultations. This demands patience and politeness from those on the outside, for anger is seen as weakness.

Many Chinese have an excellent sense of humor, but it usually avoids sexual or political subjects. Skimpy clothing, while sometimes worn by the more daring among the nation's youth, is frowned upon on the whole.

The lack of information or the omission of relevant facts that may be obvious to the Chinese host but not to his visitor can be particularly irritating to the foreigner. It is important, therefore, to check all arrangements as unobtrusively as possible.

Foreign visitors may attract attention, especially in the country, which can be unsettling but is nothing more than harmless curiosity. Privacy, it must be remembered, is an alien notion to the Chinese.

Tipping Despite official disapproval, tipping is no longer an offense; in fact it is now expected by tourist guides, who prefer money—preferably American dollars—to any well-intentioned gift. Hotel porters will usually happily accept a tip, and so will taxi drivers, although it is not necessarily expected. Tips are not usually expected in restaurants, except in some of the top establishments.

CONVERSION CHARTS

FROM	TO	MULTIPLY BY
Inches	Centimeters	2.54
Centimeters	Inches	0.3937
Feet	Meters	0.3048
Meters	Feet	3.2810
Yards	Meters	0.9144
Meters	Yards	1.0940
Miles	Kilometers	1.6090
Kilometers	Miles	0.6214
Acres	Hectares	0.4047
Hectares	Acres	2.4710
Gallons	Liters	4.5460
Liters	Gallons	0.2200
Ounces	Grams	28.35
Grams	Ounces	0.0353
Pounds	Grams	453.6
Grams	Pounds	0.0022
Pounds	Kilograms	0.4536
Kilograms	Pounds	2.205
Tons	Tonnes	1.0160
Tonnes	Tons	0.9842

MEN'S SUITS

U.K.	36	38	40	42	44	46	48
Rest of Europe	46	48	50	52	54	56	58
U.S.	36	38	40	42	44	46	48

DRESS SIZES

U.K.	8	10	12	14	16	18
France	36	38	40	42	44	46
Italy	38	40	42	44	46	48
Rest of Europe	34	36	38	40	42	44
U.S.	6	8	10	12	14	16

MEN'S SHIRTS

U.K.	14	14.5	15	15.5	16	16.5	17
Rest of Europe	36	37	38	39/40	41	42	43
U.S.	14	14.5	15	15.5	16	16.5	17

MEN'S SHOES

U.K.	7	7.5	8.5	9.5	10.5	11
Rest of Europe	41	42	43	44	45	46
U.S.	8	8.5	9.5	10.5	11.5	12

WOMEN'S SHOES

U.K.	4.5	5	5.5	6	6.5	7
Rest of Europe	38	38	39	39	40	41
U.S.	6	6.5	7	7.5	8	8.5

Tourism is now highly developed in some areas

Tourist Offices

China has very few tourist information offices. Most people travel in groups, so the main source of information will be local guides. The China International Travel Service (CITS, the state-run travel service) will often help even when you are not organizing your trip through them; otherwise, try an independent agent.

CITS main offices and other travel services

Beijing: China International Travel Service (CITS), 28 Jianguomenwai Dajie (tel: 010 6515 8562; fax: 010 6515 8603); China Travel Service (CTS), 2, Beisanhuan Dong Lu, Beijing 100028 (tel: 6462 2288; fax: 6461 2576)
Changchun: CITS, 10 Xinming Dajie (tel: 565 6313)
Changsha: 9 Wuyi Dong Lu (tel: 228 0439)
Chengdu:180 Renmin Nan Lu (tel: 667 5578)
Chongqing: 175 Renmin Lu (tel: 385 0589)
Dalian: Chantong Jie (tel: 368 7843)
Fuzhou: 73 Dongda Lu (tel: 337 0073)
Guangzhou (Canton): Guangdong CITS 179 Huanshi Lu, Guangzhou 510010 (tel: 020 8666 6279; fax: 020 8666 8048)
Guangdong CTS, 10 Qiaoguang Lu, Guangzhou 8510115, Guangdong (tel: 020 8333 6888; fax: 020 8333 6625)
Guilin: Binjiang Lu, Guilin 541002, Guangxi (tel: 282 7254)
Guiyang: 20 Yan'an Zhong Lu (tel: 582 5873)
Haikou: Rm 306, 3/f, HTSO Building, Sanjiaochi (tel: 675 6266)
Hangzhou: 1 Beishan Lu (tel: 515 2888)
Harbin: 95–1 Zhongshan Lu (tel: 230 2476)
Jinan: CITS, 9, Qianfoshan Dong Erlu (tel: 296 7401)
Kunming: 218 Huancheng Nan Lu (tel: 314 8308)
Lanzhou: Nongmin Xiang (tel: 881 3222)
Lhasa: 148 Beijing Xi Lu (tel: 22980)
Nanchang: Fuzhou Lu (tel: 626 3437)
Nanjing: 202–1 Zhongshan Beilu (tel: 342 8999)
Nanning: 40 Xinmin Lu (tel: 281 6197)
Shanghai: 2 Jinling Dong Lu, Shanghai 200002 (tel: 63 217 200; fax: 63 291 788)
Shanghai Jinjiang Tours Ltd, 27/F Union Building, 100 Yan'an Dong Lu East, Shanghai 200002 (tel: 6329 1025; fax: 63 200 595)
Tourist Information Offices:
Peoples Square (tel: 6438 1693)
Hongqiao Airport (tel: 6268 8899 ext 56750)

Shenyang: 113 Huanghe Nan Dajie (tel: 612 2445)
Suzhou: Suzhou Fandian (tel: 522 2223)
Taiyuan: International Travel Building, 282 Yingze Dajie (tel: 407 4209)
Tianjin: 22 Youyi Lu (tel: 2835 8499)
Ürümqi: 51 Xinhua Beilu (tel: 282 6719)
Wuhan: 26 Taibei Yi Lu (tel: 8578 4125)
Wuxi: 88 Huo Che Zhang Lu (tel: 230 1249)
Xiamen: Zhonghsan Lu (tel: 212 6917)
Xi'an: 32 North Chang'an Beiduan, Xi'an 710061 (tel: 524 1864; fax: 526 1558)
Xining: Qinghai Hotel (tel: 614 4888)
Yinchuan: 150 Jiefang Xijie (tel: 504 8006)
Zhengzhou: 15 Jinshui Lu (tel: 595 2072)

China has a selection of good information offices based in major cities around the world:
Fremdenverkehrsamt der VR China, Ilkenhansstrasse 6, 6000 **Frankfurt**/M50, Germany (tel: 069-520135; fax: 069-520137)
China National Tourist Office, 4 Glentworth Street, **London** NW1, England (tel: 020 7935 9787; fax: 020 7487 5842)
China National Tourist Office, **Los Angeles**, 333 W Broadway, Suite 201, Glendale, CA 91204, USA (tel: 818/545 7504; fax: 818/545 7506)
Oficina Nacional de Turismo de China, Gran Via, 88 Grupo 2, Planta 16, 28013 **Madrid**, Spain (tel: 34 1 5480011; fax: 34 1 5480597)
China National Tourist Office, Suite 6413, Empire State Building, 350 Fifth Avenue, **New York**, U.S.A. NY 10118 (tel: 212 760 9700; fax: 212 760 8809)
Office du Tourisme de Chine, 116 Avenue des Champs-Elysées, 75008 **Paris**, France (tel: 44 21 8282; fax: 44 21 8100)
China National Tourist Office, 1 Shenton Way, No 17-05 Robina House, **Singapore** 0106 (tel: 0065-2218681; fax: 2219267)
CNTO, 19th Fl, 44 Market Street, **Sydney**, NSW 2000, Australia (tel: 02 9299 4057; fax: 9290 1958)
CITS, New Mandarin Plaza, Tower A, 12th Fl, 14 Science Museum Road, Tsimshatsui East (tel: 2732 5888; fax: 2721 7154), **Hong Kong**
China National Tourist Office, 19 Frishman Street, POB, 3281, **Tel-Aviv** 61030, Israel (tel: 972 3 5226272; fax: 972 3 5226281)
China National Tourist Office, Hachidai Hamamatsu Cho Building, 6F, 1-27-13 Hamamatsu Cho, Minato-Ku, **Tokyo** 105, Japan (tel: 03 3433 1461; fax: 03 433 8653)

Chinese people travel around China in greater numbers today

This post and telecommunications office in Daju, Yunnan is typical of those found in the more remote areas of China

Communications

The media

Freedom of the press does not yet exist in China. Foreign observers trying to establish political trends, a notoriously difficult endeavor in China, have learned to read the newspapers for clues, since they tend to act as subtle mouthpieces for the government.

However, the English-language newspaper, the *China Daily*, available from most hotels, reads pretty well and is not overtly biased, and international magazines such as the *Economist* are easily available in the major cities, although there is still a tendency to cut out articles considered offensive to the Chinese Government.

Although national television is similarly restricted, the CNN world service or BBC is received uncensored in hotels across the country in all but the remotest corners of China. The same is true of radio services, although English-language services are sometimes also provided locally, for example in Beijing, on Beijing Radio.

The internet is accessible but can be slow and is subject to censorship.

Post offices

China's postal service is extremely efficient, and it is easiest to buy stamps for letters and postcards from your hotel. The airmail rate for postcards is slightly less than for letters.

For insured postage, express mail, and other services, you will usually have to go to public post offices, which are open from 8 to 7.

Telephone (*dianhua*) and fax (*chuanzhen*)

The international telephone system is surprisingly good, and the national service is improving as the system is gradually updated. Local calls are usually free, although some hotels levy a charge. Two 5-*fen* coins are needed for public telephones.

Check the rates for international calls before using the service—there is often a minimum charge and sometimes a small fee is made even when there is no answer. This is also the case if you wish to send a fax. Many of the more modern hotels now boast "business centers" which have fax machines and other office services.

If you need to receive incoming telephone calls, give the caller your room number in advance, since operators and receptionists frequently have difficulty understanding foreign names.

The Chinese language

The national language is Mandarin (*putonghua*), based on the Beijing dialect. Although there are a vast number of other dialects, most people understand *putonghua*, and all Chinese speakers share the same written language. A surprisingly large number of people know a smattering of English. However, knowledge of some basic spoken Chinese is useful as well as courteous.

Each Chinese character represents a single-syllable sound, which in turn is converted into the Latin alphabet by the process of "romanization". The official romanisation system is *pinyin*, used throughout China. In addition, syllables are given "tone" values in order to differentiate between several characters that have the same romanization but radically different meanings—thus the syllable *ma* can mean "mother", "horse", "hemp", or "scold" depending on which tone is used.

Putonghua has four tones, indicated by the following symbols:

¯ 1st tone: high, level
´ 2nd tone: starting lowish and rising
ˇ 3rd tone: starting low, falling then rising
` 4th tone: starting high and falling.

Pinyin pronunciation guide

a as in car
b as in back
c when an initial consonant is a "ts" sound as in bits
d as in doll
e as in her
f as in fat
g as in go
h as in house
i is an "ee" sound as in feet unless preceded by c, ch, r, s, sh, z, zh, when it becomes "e" as in her
j is like the g in gin
k as in kit
l as in lot
m as in man
n as in ran
o as in ford
p as in pin
q is "ch" as in chin
r as in rum
s as in simple; sh as in shut
t as in time
u is "oo" as in cool
w as in wade
x is like the "sh" in sheep but with more emphasis on the s
y as in yoyo
z is a "ds" sound as in lids; zh is a "j" sound as in jam.

Geographic legend

This list of geographical terms may be useful when reading maps

bandao	**peninsula**
bei	**north**
co	**lake**
da	**great, greater**
dajie	**road, street**
dao	**island**
ding	**mountain, peak**
dong	**east**
feng	**mount, peak**
gang	**harbor**
gaoyuan	**plateau**
guan	**pass**
hai	**lake, sea**
haixia	**strait, channel**
he	**river**
hu	**lake**
jiang	**river**
jiao	**cape**
jie	**road, street**
kou	**estuary, river mouth**
la	**pass**
liedao	**archipelago, islands**
ling	**mountain, range**
lu	**road, street**
nan	**south**
nur	**lake, salt lake**
pao	**lake**
pendi	**basin**
qu	**canal**
qundao	**archipelago, islands**
ringco	**lake**
shamo	**desert**
shan	**mountain, range**
shan kou	**pass**
shi	**municipality**
tag	**mountains**
wan	**gulf, bay**
xi	**west**
xiao	**lesser, little**
yanchi	**salt lake**
yumco	**lake**
yunhe	**canal**
zangbo	**river**

Numerals

English	Pinyin	Chinese
1	*yī*	一
2	*èr*	二
3	*sān*	三
4	*sì*	四
5	*wǔ*	五
6	*liù*	六
7	*qī*	七
8	*bā*	八
9	*jiǔ*	九
10	*shí*	十
11	*shí yī (10+1)*	十一
12	*shí èr*	十二
13	*shí sān*	十三
20	*èr shí*	二十
21	*èr shí yī (2x10+1)*	二十一
100	*(yī) bǎi*	一百
101	*yī bǎi líng yī*	一百一
1000	*(yī) qīan*	(一) 千
10,000	*(yī) wàn*	(一) 万

Useful words and phrases

English *Pinyin*	Chinese
hello/how are you? *ní hǎo/ní hǎo ma?*	你好?/你好吗?
goodbye *zài jiàn*	再见
thank you *xiè xiè*	谢谢
good/OK *hǎo*	好
very good *hén hǎo*	很好
not good/bad *bù hǎo*	不好
cheers/to your health *gān bēi*	干杯
please *qǐng*	请
yes/have/ there is/are *yǒu*	有
no/have not/ there isn't/aren't (any) *méi yǒu*	没有
I *wǒ*	我
you (you, plural) *nǐ/nǐmen*	你/你们
he/she *tā*	他
we *wǒmen*	我们
be/is/yes *ǐes*	是
when? *shěn me shí hòu?*	什么时候?
today *jīn tiān*	今天
tomorrow *míng tiān*	明天
yesterday *zuó tiān*	昨天
morning *shàng wǔ/* or *zǎo shàng*	上午/早上
evening *wǎn shàng*	晚上
afternoon *xià wǔ*	下午
where?/ where is? *zài ná lǐ / zài nǎ er*	在哪里/在哪儿?

Calligrapher at work

wait a minute 等一下
děng yī xià

please give/bring me..... 请给我
qǐng géi wǒ......

I would like..... 我想要 ......
wó xiǎng yào.....

is there anyone who speaks English? 有没有人会说英文?
yǒu méi yǒu rén huì shuō yīng wén?

may I take a photograph? 我可以照相吗?
wǒ ké yǐ zhào xiàng ma?

I understand 我懂
wǒ dǒng

I don't understand 我不懂
wǒ bù dǒng

please write (it down) 请写
qíng xiě

At the hotel

hotel/guest house 饭店/宾馆
fàndiàn/bīnguǎn

room 房间
fáng jiān

how much is it? 多少钱?
duō shǎo qián?

cheap/cheaper 便宜/便宜的
pián yí/pián yí de

expensive/too expensive 贵/太贵
guì/tài guì

At the post office/bank/stores

post office 邮局
yóu jú

stamps 邮票
yóu piào

postcards 明信片
míng xìn piàn

airmail 航空
háng kōng

phone call/telephone 电话
diàn huà

long-distance phone call 长途电话
cháng tú diàn huà

bank/Bank of China 银行/中国银行
yín háng/zhōng guó yín háng

money exchange 换钱处
huàn qián chù

Traveling around

CITS (China International Travel Service) 中国旅行社
zhōng guó lǚ xíng shè

can you take me to.....? 你可不可以带我去 ......?
nǐ ké bù ké yǐ dài wǒ qù.....?

(to) buy 买
mǎi

ticket 票
piào

taxi 出租汽车
chū zū qì chē

airport/CAAC 飞机场/中国民航
fēi jī chǎng/zhōng guó mín háng

train/train station 火车/火车站
huǒ chē/huǒ chē zhàn

bus: public bus 公共汽车
gōng gòng qì chē

long-distance bus 长途汽车
cháng tú qì chē

bus station 汽车站
qì chē zhàn

boat 船
chuán

bicycle 自行车
zì xíng chē

In a restaurant

restaurant:
fàn guǎn 饭馆

fàn diàn 饭店

cān tīng 餐厅

do you have an English menu? 有没有英文菜单?
yǒu méi yǒu yīng wén cài dān?

I am a vegetarian 我是素食者
wǒ shì sù shí zhě

May I have the bill? 请给我帐单
qǐng gěi wǒ zhàng dān

water/boiled water 水/开水
shuǐ/kāi shuǐ

coffee 咖啡
kā fēi

black tea 红茶
hóng chá

jasmine tea 茉莉花茶
mò lì huā chá

beer 啤酒
pí jiǔ

soft drink 汽水
qì shuǐ

rice 饭
fàn

glass/cup 玻璃杯/杯子
bō lí bēi/bēi zi

table knife 餐刀
cān dāo

fork 叉子
chā zi

spoon 勺子
sháo zi

Medical emergencies

I feel ill 我不舒服
wǒ bù shū fú

doctor 医生
yī shēng

pharmacy 药店
yào diàn

Signs you will see in public places

entrance 入口
rù kǒu

exit 出口
chū kǒu

restroom 厕所
cè suǒ

embassy 大使馆
dà shí guǎn

Countries

U.S.A. 美国
měi guó

Canada 加拿大
jiā ná dà

Australia 澳大利亚
ào dà lì yà

Great Britain 英国
yīng guó

France 法国
fǎ guó

Germany 德国
dé guó

Japan 日本
rì běn

China 中国
zhōng guó

Accommodations & Restaurants

ACCOMMODATIONS

Most significant tourist destinations in China have a wide range of accommodations, from budget to five-star, international standard hotels. You will be spoiled for choice in large cities such as Beijing, Shanghai, and Guangzhou, but more rural choices (such as Lijiang, Dali, and Yangshuo) have far more limited options. Service standards are reflected in the price, English skills vary enormously; restaurant options are generally good. Push for discounts in the low season.

It should be noted that the telephone system in China is undergoing constant modernization and this may result in changes in telephone and fax numbers.

Hotels have been graded as follows:
- Inexpensive hotels with private facilities ($)
- Good, comfortable hotels in medium range ($$)
- The best hotels available ($$$)

Beijing

Bamboo Garden Hotel ($$)
24 Xiaoshiqiao Hutong tel: 64032229 fax: 64012633
Attractively set midrange hotel to the northwest of the Drum and Bell Towers and within reach of Beijing's more historic lanes and alleys.

Beijing Hotel ($$$)
33 Dongchang'an Avenue tel: 65137766 fax: 65137307
Century-old historic hotel left somewhat behind by the recent explosion in five-star hotels. Excellent location, nonetheless, with additional wing.

Beijing Movenpick Hotel ($$/$$$)
Capital Airport, Xiaotianzhu Village, Shunyi County tel: 64565588 fax: 64565678
Four-star hotel at the airport with tennis courts, swimming pool and business facilities.

China World Hotel ($$$)
1 Jianguomenwai Dajie tel: 65052266 fax: 65054323
Large, modern business hotel in the China World Trade Centre with large choice of restaurants, located east of the city's central districts.

Fareast Hotel ($)
90 Tieshuxie Jie tel: 63018811 fax: 63018233
Nicely located budget hotel buried in Beijing's *hutongs* near the antique shopping district of Liulichang.

Friendship Hotel ($$)
3 Baishiqiao Lu tel: 68498888 fax: 68314661
Old, sprawling Mao-era hotel with a certain sense of history; decent value and an excellent outdoor pool.

Grand Hotel Beijing ($$$)
33 Dong Chang'an Avenue tel: 65130057 fax: 65130050
Superbly located, top-notch hotel just up the road from Tiananmen Square and the premier shopping district of Wangfujing, with rooms overlooking the Forbidden City.

Great Wall Sheraton ($$$)
10 Dongsanhuan Beilu tel: 65005566 fax: 65002580
One of Beijing's first luxury hotels, reasonably located near the diplomatic zone. There are restaurants, adjacent Hard Rock Café, nightclub, health club, pool, theater, and tennis courts.

Haoyuan Hotel ($)
53 Shijia Hutong tel: 65125557 fax: 65125557
Clean, restful hotel hidden away down a *hutong* (alley) to the east of Wangfujing. Very good value rooms for those on a budget.

Holiday Inn Crowne Plaza ($$)
48 Wangfujing Dajie tel: 65133388 fax: 65132513
A good value hotel in a very central location. The hotel has a pool and several restaurants. A baby-sitting service is also available.

Holiday Inn Lido ($$/$$$)
Jichang Lu, Jiangtai Lu tel: 64376688 fax: 64376237
Massive and excellently equipped Holiday Inn—absolutely first rate, although noncentral, but handy for the airport. Great value for money. Tennis courts, indoor pools, decent nightclub.

Jianguo Hotel ($$/$$$)
5 Jianguomenwai Dajie tel: 65002233 fax: 65002871
Good-value and popular four-star hotel—one of Beijing's first joint-venture efforts. Business center, pool and airport shuttle bus.

Jinghua Youth Hostel ($)
Yongdingmenwai Dajie, Fengtai tel: 67222211 fax: 67211455
Very popular but noncentral backpacker haunt, and an excellent place to plan a trip around China. Bicycle rental, travel info, internet, trips to the Great Wall.

Kempinski Hotel ($$$)
Lufthansa Centre, 50 Liangmaqiao Lu tel: 64653388 fax: 64653366
Luxury hotel. Shoppers will find the next-door Lufthansa shopping center a marvel, and it's near the wining and dining Sanlitun district.

Lihua Hotel ($)
71 Yangqiao, Yongdingmenwai, Fengtai tel: 67211144 fax: 67211367
Dependable backpacker hotel with reasonable service and decent rooms in south of town. Laundry service; no credit cards.

Lusongyuan Hotel ($)
22 Banchang Lane, Kuanjie tel: 64040436 fax: 64030418
Picturesque, albeit a bit tatty, traditional walled courtyard hotel in Beijing's historic *hutong* district. Inexpensive, centrally located; bicycle rental.

Minzu Hotel ($$/$$$)
51 Fuxingmennei Dajie tel: 66014466 fax: 66014849
East of Fuxingmen subway station, the Minzu has good prices and provides adequate comfort and a decent range of facilities.

The Palace Hotel ($$$)
8 Goldfish Lane (Jinyu Hutong), Wangfujing tel: 65128899 fax: 010 65129050
The Palace is a splendid hotel, centrally positioned just off Wangfujing and not far from the Forbidden City. Fine spread of restaurants, indoor pool, Rolls Royce limousine service.

Peace Hotel ($$)
3 Goldfish Lane (Jinyu Hutong), Wangfujing tel: 65128833 fax: 65126863
Excellently positioned and inexpensive four-star hotel just off the Wangfujing shopping district.

Qianmen Hotel ($/$$)
175 Yongan Lu tel: 63016688 fax: 63013883
Older, 1950s-style hotel within striking distance of

Liulichang and Tiananmen Square, with modernized and inexpensive rooms.

Qiaoyuan Hotel ($)
135 Youanmen Dongbinhe Lu, Fentai
tel: 63012244 fax: 63030119
Long-running budget option to the southeast of Tiantan (Temple of Heaven) Park. Garners mixed reviews.

Shangri-La Hotel ($$$)
29 Zizhuyuan Lu tel: 68412211 fax: 68418006
A superb link in the glittering chain of first rate Shangri-La hotels that cover China. Located in northwest Beijing, this hotel has a pool, delicatessen, and several fine restaurants.

Tiantan Haoyuan Hotel ($$)
9a Tiantan Donglu tel: 67012404/67012404
Picturesquely-located traditional courtyard hotel south of Tiantan (Temple of Heaven) Park. Well-looked after, with a charming sense of history that eludes most top-end options.

Trader's Hotel ($$/$$$)
1 Jianguomenwai Dajie tel: 65052277
fax: 65050818
Decent, four-star business hotel in the east of town with a large spread of restaurants.

Youhao Hotel ($)
7 Houyuansi, Jiaodaokou tel: 64031114
fax: 64014603
Pleasantly located courtyard (*siheyuan*) hotel in the engaging *hutong* district southeast of the Drum and Bell Towers. Former residence of Chiang Kaishek.

Canton: see Guangzhou

Changsha

Cygnet Hotel ($$)
178 Wuyi Zhonglu tel: (0731) 4410400
fax: 4423698
Three-star joint venture hotel, centrally located on Changsha's main thoroughfare and sporting a variety of restaurants.

Hua Tian ($$$)
380 Jiefang Donglu tel: 4442888 fax: 4442270
Five-star luxury hotel offering high standards at a reasonable price. Conveniently located and popular with the business class.

Chengdu

Holiday Inn Crowne Plaza Chengdu ($$$)
31 Zongfu Lu tel: (028) 6786666
fax: 6786599
Chengdu's premier hotel, this five-star extravaganza of a hotel is equipped with a dazzling lobby and a plethora of restaurants. Facilities include an indoor pool and health club.

Jinjiang Hotel ($$$)
180 Renmin Nanlu tel: 5582222 fax: 5581849
The Jinjiang (by the Jinjiang River) is still one of Chengdu's best hotels, although it is putting on the years. Bristling with first-rate facilities, including a medical clinic, an outdoor pool, tennis courts, and a bowling alley.

Traffic Hotel ($)
77 Jinjiang Lu tel: 5551017 fax: 5582777
Rather sloppy service (from dealing with too many backpackers), but the rooms are spacious and this is a great place to meet other travelers. The travel bureau is useful, as is the traveler's bulletin board. Bike rental, some credit cards, free breakfast.

Chongqing

Huixian Hotel ($)
186 Minzu Lu tel: (023) 63845101
fax: 63844234
Slap-bang in the center of town, a presentable budget option with decent ticketing service. Very good value for money, not far from the Luohan Temple.

Yangtze Chongqing Holiday Inn ($$$)
15 Nanping Beilu tel: 62803380
fax: 62800884
Competent four-star hotel with spacious rooms and decent restaurants. Not in an excellent location south of the Yangzi River, but equipped with the usual Holiday Inn reliability. Outdoor pool and health club.

Renmin Hotel ($$)
175 Renmin Lu tel: 63851421 fax: 63852076
Modeled on Beijing's Temple of Heaven, the Renmin is an old tourist hotel and a landmark feature of the city. More noted for its exterior than for its accommodations potential.

Dali

Jinhua Hotel ($)
Huguo Lu tel: (0872) 2673343/2673845
fax: 2673846
The hotel doesn't fit in with the overall character of Dali, but offers maybe marginally more in terms of comfort than most of the other outfits in town. Look around though.

Dalian

Shangri-La Hotel ($$/$$$)
66 Renmin Lu tel: (0411) 2525000
fax: 2525050
Well-located on Renmin Lu not far from picturesque Zhongshan Square, the Shangri-La is a sophisticated and reliably excellent hotel. Tennis courts.

Dunhuang

The Silk Road Dunhuang Hotel ($$/$$$)
Dunyue Lu tel: (0937) 8825388
fax: 8825211
South of town in the sand dunes and well-located for excursions to Crescent Moon Lake, the palatial exterior is attractive and the setting fabulous. Not cheap, but worth the outlay. Camel riding tours.

Fuzhou

Hot Spring Hotel ($$/$$$)
218 Wusi Lu tel: 7851818 fax: 7835150
Decent facilities, a pool and piped-in natural hot spring water in the bathrooms. Located in the north of town.

Guangzhou (Canton)

China Hotel ($$$)
Liuhua Lu tel: (020) 86666888
fax: 86677014
Magnificent hotel just west of Yuexiu Park. Built in the 1940s, modernized and well equipped. Outdoor pool, bowling alley, tennis courts. Restaurants options include a Hard Rock Café.

Garden Hotel ($$$)
368 Huanshi Donglu tel: 83338989
fax: 83310467
Well-located for the Friendship Store, airport, and train station. Magnificent five-star achievement, with first rate facilities. Revolving restaurant. Pool hall.

Shamian Hotel ($)
52 Shamian Nanjie, Shamian Island
tel: 81912288 fax: 81911628
This is a very affordable and good value budget option located on the south of Shamian Island. Quite rudimentary and no credit cards, but clean and dependable.

White Swan Hotel ($$$)
1 Shamian Nanjie, Shamian Island
tel: 81886968 fax: 81861188
Excellent amenities and service, the first floor swarming with stores. Sits resplendently on the attractive Shamian Island. Wide range of restaurants. Pearl River night cruises. Outdoor pools, tennis courts, squash courts.

Guilin

Guilin Fubo Hotel ($)
121 Binjiang Lu tel: 2829988 fax: 2822328
Clean, well-managed three-star hotel, excellently located just by one of Guilin's famous peaks and the Li River. Experienced at dealing with foreign travelers.

Holiday Inn Guilin ($$/$$$)
14 Ronghu Nanlu tel: 2823950 fax: 2822101
Comfortable, good value hotel, but very busy during the peak months. Discounts offered during quieter periods. Outdoor swimming pool, tennis courts.

Nanxi (South Stream) Hotel ($)
84 Zhongshan Nanlu tel: 3834943
Usefully located just by the train station, popular budget option albeit rather crowded. Bicycle rental (very useful).

Osmanthus Hotel ($$)
451 Zhongshan Nanlu tel: 3834300
fax: 3835316
Maybe the best location in the city, lying alongside a creek off the main street. Presentable and popular.

Sheraton Guilin ($$/$$$)
Binjiang Nanlu tel: 2825588 fax: 2805440
Superb location near the Li River, although the hotel has a worn feel to it. Outdoor swimming pool, health club, billiard room.

Hangzhou

Huagang Hotel ($)
4 Xishan Lu tel: (0571) 7998899 fax: 7962481
Located in attractive surroundings on the southwest of West Lake, the hotel is well-located for visits to Huagang Park. Good value rooms.

Shangri-La Hotel Hangzhou ($$$)
78 Beishan Lu tel: 7077951 fax: 7096637
Marvelously positioned above the north shore of West Lake, set in picturesque, forested grounds, this is Hanzhou's best hotel. Most of China's Shangri-La hotels are highly reliable. Indoor swimming pool, pool/billiards hall. Bicycle rental.

Wanghu Hotel ($$)
2 Huangcheng Xilu tel: 7071024 fax: 7071350
Large and affordable, with a wide range of rooms and decently located on the northeastern shore. Bicycle rental.

Hong Kong Island

Ma Wui Mount Davis Youth Hostel ($)
Mount Davis Path tel: 28175715
Not a central location at all (Kennedy Town area), but the most popular backpacker sight in Hong Kong. A midnight curfew is imposed. Phone ahead to check for vacancies.

Ritz-Carlton ($$$)
3 Connaught Rd, Central tel: 28776666
fax: 28776778
Hong Kong's smallest five-star establishment, but a real gem. This is an intimate hotel with an attentive, personable staff; small-scale, unrushed and welcoming. Excellent spread of restaurants, including the fine Toscana (Italian) as well as an outdoor pool.

Island Shangri-La ($$$)
Pacific Place, Supreme Court Road, Central
tel: 28773838 fax: 25218742
Set above the fantastic shopping mall of Pacific Place, in a stylishly designed building, staying at the Shangri-La is a splendid experience. Chinese, Japanese, and French restaurants. Outdoor swimming pool.

Mandarin Oriental ($$$)
5 Connaught Road, Central tel: 25220111
fax: 28106190
Famous hotel smack in the heart of Central. Great reputation, top grade service, rooms and amenities, but very expensive. Pool.

YWCA Garden View International ($$)
1 MacDonnell Road, Central tel: 28773737
fax: 28456263
Good location uphill off Garden Road for the excellent Zoological and Botanical Gardens, with Hong Kong Park farther downhill. Convenient for the Peak Tram.

Hong Kong Kowloon

The Peninsula ($$$)
Salisbury Road tel: 29202888 fax: 27224170
Splendid and remarkably styled hotel with spectacular nocturnal views over to Central—staying here is a memorable event. At hand, among all the marble, are some of Hong Kong's finest restaurants—Felix and Gaddi's. Indoor pool. Excellent shopping arcade.

Kowloon Hotel ($$)
19–21 Nathan Road tel: 29292888
fax: 27399811
Located on Nathan Road and owned by the Peninsula group, the Kowloon Hotel is a less expensive alternative to staying at the group's flagship hotel nearby. Modern facilities; very near Tsimshatsui subway.

Salisbury YMCA ($$)
41 Salisbury Road tel: 23692211
fax: 27399315
Again, excellently located in Tsimshatsui. Inexpensive rooms and certainly one of the most appealing mid-range hotels in Hong Kong. Indoor pool.

Sheraton Hotel ($$$)
20 Nathan Road tel: 23691111 fax: 23681999
Recently renovated and impressive luxury hotel at the foot of Nathan Road and a hop, skip, and a jump away from the Star Ferry. Near Tsimshatsui subway.

Jinghong

Tai Garden Hotel ($$)
8 Nonglin Nanlu tel: (0691) 2123888
fax: 2126060
Classy hotel set in peaceful surrounds in the south of town that makes an effort to be a cut above the rest.

Kunming

Camellia Hotel ($)
86 Dongfeng Donglu tel: (0871) 3163000
fax: 3147033
This is a reliable budget option. Very good value, with nicer upgraded rooms in the old block. Bicycle rental, laundry service, ticketing service, garden.

Kunming Hotel ($$/$$$)
52 Dongfeng Donglu tel: 3162063/3162172 fax: 3163784/3138220
Clean and classy four-star hotel; well-designed exterior, sparkling interior. Well-located and with good spread of amenities; excellent executive floors. Tennis courts, indoor pool, bicycle rental.

Lanzhou

Lanzhou Hotel ($)
434 Donggang Xilu tel: (0931) 8416321 fax: 8418608
Large, old but renovated hotel with clean rooms. Good range of differently priced accommodations. Travel service.
Lanzhou Legend Hotel ($$)
599 Tianshui Lu tel: 8882876 fax: 8887876
Lanzhou's most luxurious hotel. Four stars, good location and facilities. Breakfast included.

Lhasa

Lhasa Hotel ($$)
1 Minzu Lu tel: (0891) 6822221 fax: 6835796
Three-star former Holiday Inn. Needs improving. Five restaurants, business center, ticketing office. Swimming pool.
Snowlands Hotel ($)
4 Zangyiyuan Lu tel: 6323687 fax: 6327145
This accommodating budget outfit near the Jokhang Temple has good amenities. The Snowlands Restaurant next door is a must.

Lijiang

Grand Lijiang Hotel ($$)
Xinyi Jie tel: (0888) 5128888 fax: 5127878
Joint venture hotel on the edges of the Old Town, offering the best in terms of service and comfort.

Luoyang

Friendship Hotel ($/$$)
6 Xiyuan Lu tel: (0379) 4912780 fax: 4913808
Hotel catering largely to tour groups out in the west of Luoyang. Comfortable, old-fashioned, swimming pool.
Peony Hotel ($$)
15 Zhongzhou Xilu tel: (0379) 4013699 fax: 4013668
Favored by tour groups, the Peony is a centrally located and inexpensive joint venture hotel.

Macau

Bela Vista ($$$)
Rua Comendador Kou, Ho Neng 8 tel: (0853) 965333 fax: 965588
Macau's first colonial hotel—very elegant, with a long history, dating from 1870. Eight rooms, each very expensive. Run by the Mandarin Oriental Hotel Group. Reserve in advance.
East Asia Hotel ($)
1A Rua da Madeira tel: 922433
Despite being at the heart of Macau's prostitute industry, this hotel has its colonial charms in the crumbling western district, and is inexpensive.
Holiday Inn ($$)
82–86 Rua de Pequim tel: 783333 fax: 782321
Good standards as you would expect from a Holiday Inn hotel; indoor pool. Prices are far more favorable if you reserve through a Hong Kong travel agent or at the Jetfoil Pier. Shuttle bus from Jetfoil Pier.
Hyatt Regency ($$/$$$)
2 Estrada Almirante Marques Esparteiro, Taipa Island tel: 831234 fax: 830195
The best hotel on the lovely island of Taipa and conveniently located for the airport. First rate facilities and restaurants, including Flamingo. Casino, outdoor pool, tennis courts, squash courts, bicycle rental.

Nanjing

Jinling Hotel ($$$)
2 Hanzhong Lu, Xinjiekou tel: (025) 4455888 fax: 4704141
Well-located, top-end hotel in the city center; pool, shopping arcade and wide spread of restaurants.
Nanjing Holiday Inn ($$$)
45 Zhongshan Lu tel: 3308888 fax: 330 9898
Recently opened link in the Holiday Inn chain covering China. Reliable service and dependable choice of restaurants.

Qingdao

Shangri-La Hotel Qingdao ($$$)
9 Xianggang Zhonglu tel: (0532) 3883838 fax: 3886868
Plush and elegant hotel in the east of Qingdao, with superb facilities and restaurants. Indoor pool, tennis courts.

Qufu

Queli Hotel ($)
1 Queli Jie tel: (0531) 4411300 fax: 4412022
Traditional Chinese style hotel in a very good location near both the Confucius Temple and the Confucius Mansions.

Shanghai

Garden Hotel ($$$)
58 Maoming Lu tel: 64151111 fax: 64158866
Elegant, well-positioned hotel in the old French Concession on the site of the former "Cercle Sportif Francais."
Grand Hyatt Hotel ($$$)
177 Lujiazui Lu, Pudong tel: 58303338 fax: 58308838
A hotel in the clouds—the highest in the world, beginning on the 54th floor of the Jinmao Building in Pudong, one of Shanghai's most famous recent constructions. Magnificent views.
Jinjiang Hotel ($$/$$$)
59 Maoming Nanlu tel: 62582582 fax: 64725588
Carefully renovated and stylish hotel in the old French Concession, not to be confused with the modern Jinjiang Tower. Good restaurants and bars.
Park Hotel ($$)
170 Nanjing Xilu tel: 63275225 fax: 63276958
Historic hotel excellently located north of People's Square; dating from 1934, the Park has a marvellous art deco interior. Not the most up-to-date of hotels, but reeking of nostalgia.
Peace Hotel ($$)
20 Nanjing Donglu tel: 63216888 fax: 63290300
Probably Shanghai's most famous hotel and landmark, the Peace is rather frayed and sitting on its laurels. But the sense of history remains and the Bund is on your doorstep, despite the limited range of amenities.

The Portman Ritz-Carlton ($$$)
Shanghai Centre, 1376 Nanjing Xilu
tel: 62798888 fax: 62798800
One of Shanghai's finest hotels, the Portman had a massive facelift in 1999. Located in the prestigious Shanghai Centre, and with an impressive range of Oriental and Western restaurants. Pool, tennis courts.

Pudong Shangri-La ($$$)
Pudong Shangri-La Shanghai, 33 Fucheng Lu, Lujiazui tel: 68826888 fax: 68820160
From its waterfront perch in Pudong, you get magnificent views across the Huangpu River to the Bund. Excellent hotel in all departments. Indoor pool.

Pujiang Hotel ($)
15 Huangpu Lu tel: 63246388 fax: 63243179
Excellent value and superbly located 19th century hotel with a great sense of ages past. Period photos line the walls. Marvellous wooden floorboards and huge rooms, with the Bund just down the road.

Ruijin Guesthouse ($/$$)
118 Ruijin Erlu tel: 64725222 fax: 64732277
Splendid rooms in a historical building in the old French Concession; variety of room prices to suit your budget. Attractive gardens.

Sofitel Hyland Hotel ($$$)
505 Nanjing Donglu tel: 63205888
fax: 63204088
Excellent position on Nanjing Donglu, and very near the Bund. One of Shanghai's best hotels.

Shenyang

Liaoning Hotel ($)
Zhongshan Square tel: (024) 3839166
fax: 3839103
Looking out over the square with its bizarre Mao statue, the Liaoning is a historic and atmospheric hotel built in the early 20th century.

Trader's Hotel ($$$)
68 Zhonghua Lu tel: 23412288 fax: 23413838
A well-positioned Shangri-La hotel, full of amenities and next to the excellent Traders Shopping Centre. Shenyang's best hotel.

Suzhou

Bamboo Grove Hotel ($$)
168 Zhuhui Lu tel: (0512) 5205601
fax: 5208778
Well-located in the south of town, the Bamboo Grove is attractively set with a central rock pool. A bit frayed, but not overly expensive either.

Suzhou Hotel ($)
115 Shiquan Jie tel: 5204646 fax: 5204015
This hotel has good amenities and caters mainly to tour groups. Well-located, comfortable and with a branch of CITS next door.

Tianjin

Astor Hotel ($$)
33 Taierzhuang Lu tel: (022) 23311112
fax: 23316282
Famous and grand hotel built in the mid-19th century, still oozing history via period pieces. The Last Emperor stayed here.

Hyatt Hotel Tianjin ($$/$$$)
218 Jiefang Beilu tel: 23301234
fax: 23311234
Marvellous, grand four-star hotel, ideally located and boasting some first-rate restaurants. Top notch service. Much recommended.

Imperial Palace Hotel ($/$$)
177 Jiefang Beilu tel: 23790888
fax: 23790222
Attractively-set hotel in a renovated, historical building located near the Hai River in former foreign concession territory.

Ürümqi

Holiday Inn ($$/$$$)
168 Xinhua Beilu tel: (0991) 2818788
fax: 2817422
Ürümqi's best hotel (but there's not much competition). Decent western and Uighur restaurants and delicatessen. Limousine rental.

Wuhan

Shangri-La Hotel Wuhan ($$/$$$)
700 Jianshe Dadao tel: (027) 85806868
fax: 85776868
Expect the usual high standards of Shangri-La attentiveness and excellence. Entertaining sports bar (BATS) and decent restaurants.

Jianghan Hotel ($$)
245 Shengli Jie tel: 2811600 fax: 2814342
Classy early 19th-century French hotel with an impressive colonial feel in old concession quarter of Hankou. Post office, fine Chinese restaurant.

Wuxi

Holiday Inn Milido ($$)
2 Liangxi Lu tel: (0510) 5865665
fax: 5801668
A reasonably priced establishment on the edges of central Wuxi. Bicycle rental.

Sheraton Hotel ($$)
443 Zhongshan Lu tel: 2721888
fax: 2752781
Welcome addition to the Wuxi hotel scene, offering high standards of service and accommodations. Complimentary breakfast.

Xiamen

Gulangyu Guesthouse ($)
25 Huangyan Lu tel: (0592) 2066050
An atmospheric and characterful, colonial villa compound located near Sunlight Rock on picturesque Gulangyu Island.

Holiday Inn Crowne Plaza Harbour View ($$$)
12-8 Zhenhai Lu tel: 202333 fax: 203666
First-rate hotel with great range of facilities and some excellent restaurants. Views over to Gulangyu Island. Outdoor swimming pool.

Xi'an

Bell Tower Hotel ($$)
Southwest corner of Bell Tower
tel: (029) 7279000 fax: 7218767
Finest location of any hotel in Xi'an and very good value rooms; one of Xi'an's first hotels to be built since the explosion in tourism.

City Hotel ($)
70 Nan Dajie tel: 7219988
fax: 7216688
Comfortable hotel south of the Bell Tower in Central Xi'an. Clean rooms and efficient service.

Hyatt Regency Xi'an ($$$)
158 Dong Dajie tel: 7231234 fax: 7216799
Five-star hotel with fabulous location within Xi'an's

city walls. The hotel has a marvelous interior, high standards of service, and excellent facilities. Indoor pool, tennis court.

Shangri-La Golden Flower Xi'an ($$$)
8 Changl e Xilu tel: 3232981
fax: 3235477
Despite an imperfect location outside the city walls, the Shangri-La is a magnificent hotel, with some fine dining options. Indoor pool, shopping arcade.

Yangshuo

Yangshuo Resort Hotel ($$)
116 Xi Jie tel: (0773) 8822109 fax: 8822106
Most hotels in Yangshuo are the abundant budget choices; this hotel has a relaxed atmosphere in an attractive landscaped setting and offers a certain degree of luxury.

RESTAURANTS

It is invidious to give a list of recommended restaurants in China when the country is still in a state of flux—eateries come and go like the seasons—and little that is new seems to have much sense of permanence. As prices are very often governed more by what you eat than by the "standing" or standard of the restaurants, no price grading for restaurants is given in this section.

However, it is possible to make some generalizations about eating in China. First, you can be reasonably sure of eating well in the restaurants of major hotels, but you will pay a premium price for the privilege. Secondly, there are certain restaurants that at any given time are used by CITS for tourist groups, and in the smaller, poorer cities, where there appears to be less choice, this can be fairly reassuring. Thirdly, it is fair to say that you run little risk of eating really badly in a country where good food is so highly appreciated (but avoid seafood in budget restaurants in the very interior provinces). Fourthly, aside from the CITS-recommended establishments, there is no way of knowing what is exceptionally good and what is not. Sticking to expensive hotels and CITS-approved restaurants will ensure quality at a price. Otherwise, you must trust your instincts.

Price and hygiene are the two things you must scrutinize. Foreigners are sometimes seen as fair game for higher prices and, although, compared with most similar countries China is hygienic, in the simpler restaurants you may need to judge the cleanliness. The Chinese themselves will often check chopsticks and bowls, often rinsing them in tea.

It is easy to eat inexpensively in China. Most streets have stalls selling plates of noodles or bowls of dumplings for next to nothing, where the quality is often high and the food is generally safe to eat. Small restaurants, selling beer and soft drinks, have more variety and are a little more expensive. Restaurants of this type often have another, costlier section offering more sophisticated food and surroundings.

How to order Eating in China is a group activity. In most of the restaurants listed below, tables can be reserved in advance. Some restaurants may require prior warning for certain, more complicated dishes.

A Chinese meal is normally served in sequence according to local specialties. Different dishes are placed in the middle of the table, and diners are expected to serve themselves (except at banquets and in Cantonese restaurants, where it is customary to be served) either with chopsticks or with serving spoons if provided. Cold dishes are served first, then hot dishes, which will arrive singly or in clusters. Rice usually arrives late in the meal, and soup usually appears at the end.

Chopsticks Chopsticks (*kuaizi*) are provided as a matter of course, but forks (*chazi*) are usually available or can be requested.

Beijing

Donglaishun
44 Dongjiaomin Lane tel: (010) 65241042 or 5th floor, 138 Wangfujing Dajie tel: 65280931
Well-known restaurant serving up hot pot (*huoguo*)—a very fun and sociable way to eat. Slide the lamb sliver, vegetables, and *doufu* into the boiling soup, and try the local beer.

Fangshan
1 Wenjin Jie, Beihai Park
tel: 64011879/64011889
Imperial-style recipes from the regal kitchens of the Forbidden City, Maybe somewhat overpriced, but a chance to sample good quality cooking in an unusual atmosphere. Located in Beihai Park.

Gongdelin Vegetarian Restaurant
158 Qianmen Nandajie
tel: 67020867/65112542
Very inexpensive and wholesome Buddhist vegetarian delights at this famous eatery south of Qianmen. Magnificent food arranged artfully to resemble meat—sometimes tasting more like meat than the real thing. Highly recommended. English menu available.

Nengrenju
5 Taipingqiao Dajie tel: 66012560
Near the White Pagoda Temple, this is Beijing's most popular hot spot for Mongolian hot pot. Best consumed during winter, hot pots are fun, warming, and very tasty affairs.

Qianmen Quanjude Roast Duck Restaurant
32 Qianmen Dajie tel: 65112418
The best roast duck on the planet, at a highly affordable price and a very convenient location. Choose from the different sections according to your budget and then walk off your meal at adjacent Tiananmen Square, or the Forbidden City.

The Sichuan
14 Liuyin Jie tel: 66156924/6925
Ensconced in the historic residence of Prince Gong, this well-known hotel specializes in the spicy flavors of Sichuan cooking. The restaurant is attractively located in one of the few older sections of the city.

TGI Friday's
19 Dongsanhuan Beilu tel: 65975314/18
Beichen Donglu tel: 6494065
A shameless slice of home cooking peeking out amid the mounds of rice and noodles. Very American and with that rarity in China—a no-smoking section.

Canton: see Guangzhou

Chengdu

Baguobuyi
20 Renmin Nanlu Siduan
tel: (028) 5573839/5531688
Chengdu is the heartland of fiery Sichuan food, and this respectable restaurant serves the *ne plus ultra* of this cuisine. Sichuan food in the rest of China is a pale imitation of what is served here. This is not a tourist restaurant, so there's no English menu.

Fuzhou

Shanghai Restaurant
155 Bayiqi Lu tel: (0591) 7553620
This popular restaurant chain serves fine *dim sum* and *xiaolongbao*—Shanghai pastry dumplings stuffed with pork wheeled around on trolleys.
Bakery on premises.

Guangzhou (Canton)

Home to one of the four main schools of Chinese cooking; light sauces and the freshest ingredients are the main characteristics. *Dim sum* are the snacks sold at the tables from trays.

Banxi
151 Longjin Xilu
tel: (020) 81815718/81815955
Very famous restaurant noted for its Cantonese *dim sum* (including shark's fin dumplings and monkey brains) and other regional dishes.

Foyouyuan Vegetarian Restaurant
74 Shangjiu Lu tel: 81887157
As the saying goes, the Cantonese will eat anything on four legs unless it's a table. If you don't want to join them, come to this Buddhist vegetarian option.

Dongbeiren
2nd floor, 1 Taojin Beilu
tel: 83576277/83575276
Excellent chain of restaurants serving up a huge and tasty range of dumplings (*jiaozi*)—very popular and fun. Come here to snack or for a full-fledged meal. English menu. Also at 36 Garden Building, Tianhe Nanerlu tel: 87501711.

Guangzhou
2 Wenchang Lu tel: 81888388
Famous Cantonese restaurant, built around a central garden courtyard. Fairly expensive.

Taotaoju
20 Dishipu Lu tel: 81816111/81396111
Very popular, centrally located restaurant with a long history, noted for its *dim sum*.

Hangzhou

Louwailou
30 Gushan Lu tel: (0571) 7969023
Hanghzou's most famous restaurants serving local delicacies alongside sweeping views over West Lake.

Tianwaitian Restaurant
2 Tianzhu Lu tel: 7965450
Located by the Lingyin Temple, this is the place for excellent seafood dishes.

Hong Kong

Felix
The Peninsula, Tsimshatsui
tel: (0852) 23666251
Imaginatively designed restaurant in an unbeatable location on the 28th floor of the Peninsula. International/Pan-Asian cuisine. Pricey, but impressive, and there are some splendid views.

Hunan Garden
3rd Floor, The Forum, Exchange Square, Central
tel: 28682880
If you want dishes with more bite than Cantonese cuisine, come here for spicy, hot Hunan food. Fine menu, elegant environment and excellent wine list.

Jimmy's Kitchen
South China Building, 1 Wyndham Street, Central
tel: 25265293
and 1st floor, Kowloon Centre, 29 Ahsley Road, Kowloon tel: 23684027
Long-standing European restaurant that constantly garners enthusiastic reviews. Reasonably priced food in a relaxing environment.

Luk Yu Teahouse & Restaurant
24-26 Stanely Street tel: 25235464
Famous old Hong Kong teahouse, serving decent *dim sum* daily from 7AM to 6PM. Centrally located.

Sai Kung Town

Sampan Seafood Restaurant
16 Main Street, Yung Shue Wan, Lamma Island
tel: 29822388
Cantonese seafood restaurant with a fine view out to sea from Lamma Island's main community; not far from the ferry pier. Satisfyingly rounds off a trip to the island.

Toscana
Ritz-Carlton Hotel, 3 Connaught Rd, Central
tel: 25322062
Excellent, very civilized Italian restaurant ensconced in the fine Ritz-Carlton Hotel. Closed on Sundays.

Kunming

Wei's Pizzeria
400 Tuodong Lu tel: (0871) 3166189
Considering this is southwest China, these pizzas are excellent and a welcome diversion. Very popular with Kunming expats and those on the road. No credit cards.

Lhasa

Snowlands Restaurant
4 Zangyiyuan Lu tel (0891) 6337323
Very popular restaurant offering a range of dishes including Tibetan, Nepalese, and Indian. Near the Jokhang Temple.

Macau

A Lorcha
289 Rua do Almirante Sergio
tel: (0853) 313193
Famous Portuguese restaurant near the southern tip of the Macau Peninsula. Try the African chicken, pork knuckles, or the raw codfish. Closed Tue.

Fernando's
9 Hac Sa Beach, Coloane Island tel: 882531
Probably Macau's most celebrated restaurant, tucked away on Hac Sa Beach on Coloane Island. It's well worth the small adventure coming out here, for the Portuguese dishes are divine. Fine wine list; weekend reservations necessary.

Flamingo
Hyatt Regency, 2 Estrada Almirante Marques Esparteiro, Taipa Island tel: 831234
Authentic spread of Portuguese/Macau dishes (African chicken, curry crab) set in a fine hotel on Taipa Island. Outside lakeside seating available. Decent wine selection.

Mezzaluna
Mandarin Oriental Hotel, 956 Avenida de Amizade tel: 9561110
Refined Italian restaurant noted for its excellent pasta dishes and some fantastic pizza. Not cheap, but stylish.

Nanjing

Laozhengxing Restaurant
119 Gongyuan Jie
Located in the Confucian Temple district, this restaurant serves up local specialties.
Wuzhou Treehouse Restaurant
22 Xiaofenqiao tel: (025) 9066066
Good value, centrally located Chinese eatery used to dealing with foreigners.

Shanghai

Gongdelin Vegetarian Restaurant
445 Nanjing Xilu tel: 63270218
Like its Beijing counterpart, the Buddhist Gongdelin excels at preparing vegetarian food to look and taste like meat. And you don't have to be a veggie to enjoy these fantastic dishes.
Huxinting Teahouse
257 Yuyuan Lu tel: 63736950
Right in the center of the pond in the Old Chinese City, the Huxinting (lake heart pavilion) is a traditional Chinese teahouse with yesteryear atmosphere.
M on the Bund
20 Guangdong Lu tel: 63509988
A relative of a famous Hong Kong restaurant, serving fantastic international dishes by the historic Bund. Welcome symptom of a new international presence in Shanghai.
Nanxiang Steamed Bread Shop
85 Yuyuan Lu tel: 63554206
Excellent restaurant for sampling Shanghai's most famous snack—*xiaolongbao*—little steamed scalding dumplings of meat. Take-out also available.
Pasta Fresca Da Salvatore
4 Hengshan Lu tel: 64730772
(and other branches)
Good value, simple yet reliable Italian cooking.
Quanjude
786 Huaihai Zhonglu
tel: 64337286/64335799
Heaving with patrons at the weekends, this Shanghai sibling of the famous Beijing restaurant is the place for *kaoya* (Peking duck). Large restaurant located on one of Shanghai's premier shopping streets.
TGI Friday's
2nd floor, Pacific City, 900 Huaihai Zhonglu
tel: 64665848
Western cooking served in an unashamedly American atmosphere. Burgers, fries, deep fried onion rings, the works. No-smoking section.

Suzhou

Authentic Chinese Dumpling House
144 Shiquan Jie tel: (0512) 5192728
The place to come for delicious and inexpensive dumplings (*jiaozi*)—simple, but filling food.
Songhelou
18 Taijian Nong, 141 Guanqian Jie
tel: 7277006
Restaurant with a long history and Imperial connections (Emperor Qianlong apparently feasted here). Near the Xuanmiao Taoist Temple.

Tianjin

Tianfu Laoma
85 Liuwei Lu tel: (022) 2421-6666
Hot and searing hot pots and a plethora of Sichuan dishes. Gregarious place with good atmosphere and English menus available.
Xiang Wei Zhai
Hyatt Hotel Tianjin, 219 Jiefang Beilu
tel: 022 23301234/23318888
Traditionally-designed dumpling restaurant in this fabulous hotel. The emphasis is on pastoral flavors and the dumplings (*jiaozi*) are superb.
Very relaxing, with considerable charm.

Wuhan

BATS Bar
Shangri-La Hotel, 700 Jianshe Dadao, Hankou
tel: (027) 85806868
Fun and entertaining bar serving decent international food in a stylish environment. Frequent live music and an enthusiastic crowd.
Laotongcheng
1 Dazhi Lu, Hankou tel: 5211843
Busy Chinese restaurant specializing in dumplings and word has it a haunt of Mao Zedong during his sojourns in Wuhan.

Wuxi

Wuxi specializes in Wuxi spare ribs and whitebait from Lake Tai.
Jinxi Revolving Restaurant
218 Zhongshan Lu tel: (0510) 2751688
Chinese and Western food set to a revolving panorama. Good value and quality.
Zhongguo Hotel
90 Hanchang Lu tel: 2720041
Near the train station, the hotel has a very popular and inexpensive restaurant serving dumplings (*jiaozi*).

Ürümqi

Kashgari's
Holiday Inn, 168 Xinhua Beilu
tel: (0991) 2818788
Uighur cuisine in a comfortable setting. Emphasis on heavily seasoned lamb dishes set to occasional Uighur entertainment nights.

Xiamen

Ludao
230 Zhongshan Lu tel: (0592) 2022264
Good Xiamen food prepared in the Fujian/Cantonese tradition.
Seafood Restaurant
1 Fengchaoshan Lu tel 2025561
This modest restaurant seves excellent local seafood dishes.

Xi'an

Shang Palace Shangri-La Golden Flower
8 Changle Xilu tel: (029) 3232981
This civilized restaurant specializes in Cantonese dishes and can be found in one of the best hotels in town.
Xi'an Restaurant
298 Dong Dajie tel: 7216262
Simple but decent dishes in this popular restaurant that goes to town on dumplings, noodles, and other filling recipes.

Index

F

G

H

Publisher's Acknowledgments

The Automobile Association wishes to thank the following photographers and libraries for their assistance in the preparation of this book.

INGRID MOREJOHN/BILDBRUKET PICTURE WORKS was commissioned to take all the pictures in this book with the exception of:

AA PHOTO LIBRARY 222a (M. Trelawny), 222b (R. Holmes), 223a (R. Victor). **AXIOM/GORDON DR. CLEMENTS** 14. **BRIDGEMAN ART LIBRARY** 249a *Willows and Distant Mountains* by Ma Yuan (*fl* 1190–1225) Song Dynasty (ink and colours on silk) Zhang Shui Cheng/Bridgeman Art Library, London. **MARY EVANS PICTURE LIBRARY** 42b Sun Yatsen, 43b Shanghai, The Club 1926. **FEI CHONG XIAN** 188b Shanghai Peace Hotel. **RONALD GRANT ARCHIVES** 78a *Raise the Red Lantern*, 118/9 *The Last Emperor*. **HULTON DEUTSCH COLLECTION LTD** 119b Pu yi Henry. **A. KOUPRIANOFF** back cover Hong Kong, 3 Chongqing, 8 Daning River, 50 Beijing. **MAGNUM PHOTOS LTD.** 44a Chiang Kaishek, Madam Chiang & General Stilwell, 46/7 People's Army arriving at Yan'an (Rene Burri), 111b Mao on Long March (Rene Burri). **NATURE PHOTOGRAPHERS LTD.** 158a Père David's deer (E. A. Janes), 158b Giant panda (R. Tidman), 159 Tiger (B. Burbidge). **PICTURES COLOUR LIBRARY** Front cover (b) Chinese dragon, Spine actor. **POWERSTOCK/ZEFA** Front cover (c) sunset in Yangzhou. **THE MANSELL COLLECTION** 42/3 Port of Shanghai. **SPECTRUM COLOUR LIBRARY** 116/7. **TONY STONE IMAGES** Front cover (a) Dong woman, Guizhou province. **WORLD PICTURES** 11.

Contributors

Revision copy editor: Sheila Hawkins
Original copy editor: Susan Whimster
Revision verifier: Christopher Knowles